Flowering Plants

for your *Garden*

Flowering Plants
for your Garden

Select Editions, Vancouver

CONTENTS

GROWING BULBS

Bulbs are the easiest of plants to grow—probably no other plant group gives as much variety and pleasure to the gardener with so little effort. Even people without yards can enjoy bulbs as there are so many that make excellent container plants.

Most people think of bulbs as an essential part of spring, but spring is by no means their only season—there are bulbs that flower through the summer, fall, and even through the depths of the winter. They are usually very easy to look after, and many types will go on giving pleasure for years with the minimum of attention.

ABOVE: These parrot tulips just breaking from their buds already show the typical ruffled petals and color streaking.

LEFT: Deepest blue hyacinths make a wonderful foil for the bright yellow tulips in this landscape planting.

BULBS, CORMS, TUBERS, AND RHIZOMES

What most people know as bulbs covers a whole range of plants with some kind of underground storage organ that allows their survival over their dormant season, which may be winter or summer. They include true bulbs and plants with corms, tubers, and rhizomes.

• True bulbs are made up of a bud enclosed by modified leaves or fleshy scales from which roots and shoots emerge. The shoots grow out of the pointed top and the roots from the other end. Most, such as onions, daffodils, and hyacinths, have an outer papery cover or tunic: lilies, which are bulbs, too, have a bulb of swollen leaf bases but lack the protective tunic.

• Corms are bulb-like structures formed by the enlargement of an underground stem base. They do not have the "rings" of true bulbs, but stems grow out of the top and roots from the base in the same way. Freesias, gladioli, and crocuses all grow from corms.

• Tubers are swollen underground parts of roots or stems. Dahlias grow from buds at the ends of tubers.

• Rhizomes may grow underground or along the soil surface. They are fleshy, tuberous roots with new growth emerging from the end. Some irises grow from rhizomes (other irises are bulbs). Some bulbous plants described as having rhizomes or tubers appear to have little more than a small crown from which the roots emerge.

For convenience, all the above groups are discussed throughout this book as bulbs.

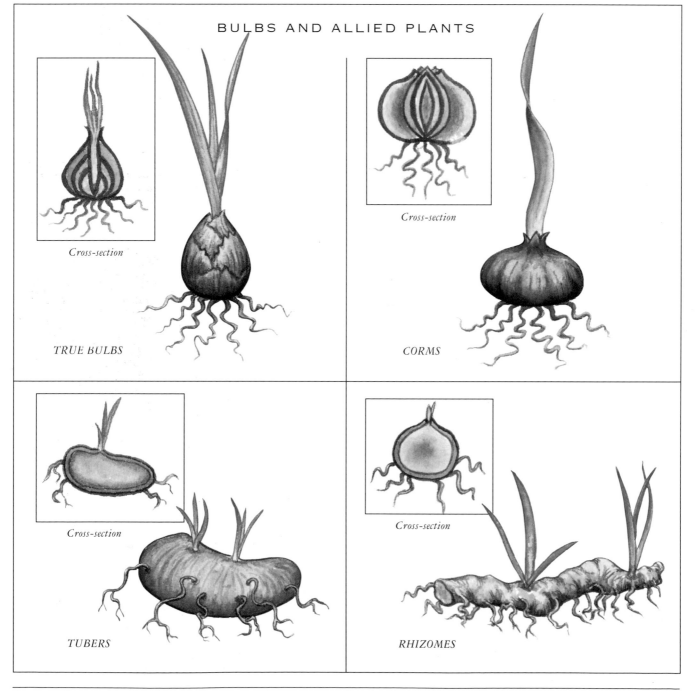

BULBS AND ALLIED PLANTS

Cross-section

TRUE BULBS

Cross-section

CORMS

Cross-section

TUBERS

Cross-section

RHIZOMES

TENDER BULBS

Indoors or out?

Some bulbs are not suitable for growing outdoors, and must be grown in a greenhouse or conservatory, or in the home, to produce good results. In many cases, bulbs can be started into growth under protection and brought outside later in the season when the weather has warmed up: when grown in containers, these look good on patios or even positioned amongst other flowering plants in borders so that the container is hidden. Other bulbs, however, need to be grown under protection throughout their lives, as their flowers would be spoiled outdoors.

Which bulbs must be considered tender enough for indoor cultivation often depends on the area in which you live, and the situation of your own garden. Species that can be grown successfully outside in mild areas would often fail in cold, exposed gardens, but even in mild regions a garden may be exposed to cold, windy weather that makes it unsuitable for the more tender plants.

Experience is often the only way to gain an accurate picture of which plants are hardy enough for your conditions, but when growing dubiously hardy bulbs, always play safe and overwinter one or two specimens under cover in case an unexpectedly cold winter destroys your outdoor stock. Protect slightly tender bulbs by heaping straw, dry leaves, or bracken over the planting site once the foliage has died down in the fall: this helps to prevent frost penetrating to the bulbs below ground. Deep planting is also recommended for extra protection.

The table below gives a guide to the plants that need indoor conditions, and those that are risky outdoors in all but the most favoured areas of the country. It is often adequate to bring tender bulbs under cover for the winter only. the information under each bulb entry gives further details.

THE TUBEROUS ROOTS of dahlias can be left in the ground in some areas, but are better lifted and stored in a frost-free place.

TENDER BULBS

BULBS FOR THE HOUSE, GREENHOUSE, OR CONSERVATORY ONLY

- Achimenes
- Clivia
- Gloriosa
- Hippeastrum
- Lachenalia
- Sinningia

BULBS NEEDING PROTECTION OR OVERWINTERING UNDER COVER IN COLD AREAS

- Agapanthus
- Amaryllis
- Canna
- Crinum
- Cyrtanthus
- Dierama
- Eremurus
- Eucomis
- Gladiolus callianthus
- Hedychium
- Hymenocallis
- Ixia
- Nerine
- Polianthes
- Romulea
- Schizostylis
- Sparaxis
- Sprekelia
- Tigridia
- Tritonia
- Zantedeschia
- Zephyranthes

AGAPANTHUS PLANTS are suitable for leaving outdoors over winter in warmer areas of the country only.

STRONGLY CONTRASTING white and rich crimson tulips are mass planted under a silver birch tree in this lovely garden. The tulip planting is brilliantly set off by the wide, sweeping border of purple Virginian stock.

CHOOSING BULBS

What do you want from your plants?

There are so many bulbs, in such a range of colors, sizes, and forms, that it is all too easy to get carried away when buying them. Their appeal is instantaneous: here they are, ready packaged, just needing to be popped into the soil—and within a short time, with no further effort, you can expect to be enjoying the brilliant flowers pictured on the display units at garden centres.

Perhaps one of their greatest virtues is that the bulk of bulbs appear for sale at just the time when summer is finally drawing to a close. The summer flowers are nearly over, trees will soon be shedding their leaves, and the days growing shorter and more gloomy; the cold, wet, miserable weeks of winter stretch out ahead. No wonder we are so pleased to see the arrival of bulbs, with their promise of the spring to come!

But in order to achieve the best possible results from your bulbs, you should plan for them more carefully. Consider the type of garden in which they are to be grown; whether it is mild and sheltered or cold and exposed. Where in the garden are the bulbs to grow? Is there space on a rock garden or in a border? Do you have an area of lawn where bulbs could be naturalized, and if so, are you prepared for the grass to be untidy while the bulb foliage is dying down? Do you want all your bulbs to flower in spring, or would a longer flowering season be more appropriate? Do you want bulbs in pots for growing on the patio, or varieties that will flower out of season to brighten up the home in the middle of winter? If you have a good idea of what you want from your bulbs *before* you go out to buy them, it could save you making some expensive mistakes.

Choose for color

Consider the color schemes of your bulb planting as you would any other item, either inside your home or outside it. Do you want strong contrasts in color, gradations of a single color, or colors that complement each other? Do you want to create a bright, warm, active look or do you want to give a cooler, calmer impression? Warm, active colors are red, yellow, orange, and bright pink, while blue, lavender, white, cream, pale pink, and pale yellow are cooler colors.

Blue and white spring-flowering bulbs include spring star flower, grape hyacinth, bluebell, and hyacinth, all of which would team well with white or cream daffodils. Some of the brightest bulbs in the "hot" color range are ranunculus and harlequin flowers (sparaxis). Both these are more commonly available in mixed colors but sometimes you can find a supplier who is able to sell them as single colors. Anemones also come in strong colors and these too can be purchased in single colors. Greater impact is generally achieved by planting blocks of single colors rather than mixtures. Try bulbs in blocks of red, orange, and yellow for a tremendous impact, or if you want a quieter look, plant groups of two shades of pink and white.

Many bulbous plants, such as daffodils, come in a wide range of varieties but a fairly limited color range: they also look their best if planted in groups of one variety. Corn lily is another good example. Although there is a wide color range available, and corn lilies can be purchased in mixtures, these flowers look best if planted in blocks of one color. They can, of course, be planted as mixtures, especially in an informal garden setting, but in nature they would be more likely to grow in blocks of one color.

Consider flowering time

Some gardeners prefer one huge display over three or four weeks in spring while others may find more interest in spreading the season over several months of the year. For instance, with crocus alone, different varieties provide blooms from late fall right through to mid-spring. There is some form of bulbous plant to give a display in every month of the year if that is what you require.

It can be hard to give precise information on exactly when different species will be in bloom, as the time can vary from one district to another and even from one garden to another because of variation in microclimates. However, if you spend some time noting the times when bulbs flower in your garden, in future seasons you will be able to plan to have a succession of bulbs in flower during many months of the year.

BUYING BULBS

There are several different ways in which you can buy bulbs. Most garden centres, and several other stores, sell bulbs in perforated plastic bags backed by a card giving planting details, along with a picture of the bulb in flower. Bulbs are also available in small netting sacks with attached pictures and growing instructions. Most garden centres and nurseries sell bulbs in bulk in the main planting season, and you can make your own selection from large bins. Another option is to send away for catalogs from bulb-growing nurseries and order bulbs by mail—these growers advertize in popular gardening magazines. The range of bulbs available from specialist nurseries is generally very much more extensive than what is on offer at your local garden centre. Mail order is a good option if you want some of the more unusual varieties, and if you want to order a lot of bulbs as it can be a good deal cheaper, though you need to take postal charges into account. When planning to buy by mail order, remember that you need to order well in advance of the planting date; if you leave it until bulbs are starting to appear in stores, the specialist suppliers are likely to have sold out of many of the less common varieties. Once you are on the mailing list of mail order suppliers, they will send you their catalogues in plenty of time in future years.

When buying bulbs at a garden centre, try to buy them as soon as possible after they have been delivered, as they tend to deteriorate in the warm conditions, and will soon become bruised as other buyers sort through them to make their choice. Select plump, firm, well-rounded bulbs and make sure there are no soft spots or patches of mould. Especially avoid buying any bulbs that are starting to shoot and showing signs

HYACINTH BULBS will be on sale from early fall. Select yours early to be sure of getting the best available.

GOLDEN DAFFODILS planted in sweeping drifts beneath a fine magnolia tree show to advantage against an old stone wall.

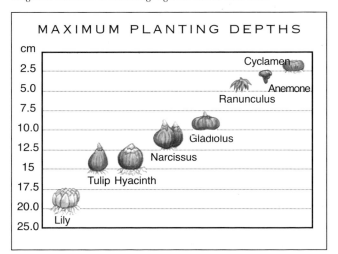

MAXIMUM PLANTING DEPTHS

cm

2.5 — Cyclamen

5.0 — Anemone
Ranunculus

7.5

10.0 — Gladiolus

12.5 — Narcissus

15 —

17.5 — Tulip Hyacinth

20.0

25.0 — Lily

GROUPS OF BRIGHT PINK, fall-flowering nerines provide showy splashes of color as summer flowers fade.

BLUEBELLS, TULIPS, and daffodils are here planted informally in a lovely woodland setting beside a tiny stream.

of growth. Unless there is just the tiniest shoot appearing and you know you can plant the bulbs at once, these bulbs will be a bad buy as they will not thrive. Some chain stores and supermarkets sell bulbs and continue to display them long after they should have been planted out or discarded. If you see long pale shoots emerging from bulbs definitely don't buy them. These bulbs have been stored for too long in poor conditions. They are badly stressed and have used up a great deal of their stored reserves of energy and growing capacity so that they may fail completely or do very poorly. Try to make your selection early in the season so that you have a choice of the best on offer.

Bulbs are best planted as soon as possible once you get them home, but if you are forced to delay planting for a short while, store the bulbs in paper bags or nets—not plastic bags—and keep them in a cool, dry, airy place. If the weather is very warm, the crisper drawer of a refrigerator can be a good place to keep bulbs in good condition, but do not put them in the main part of the refrigerator as this will dry them out.

PLANTING BULBS

Choosing a site

For the majority of bulbs, choose an open planting site where they will receive sun for at least half a day. There are a few bulbs that will grow well in shade but most like at least some sun. Even woodland species such as bluebell and wood anemone grow as understorey plants in deciduous woodlands and so receive some sun during their early growing and flowering period, before the trees are fully in leaf.

The vast majority of bulbs need well-drained soil or they will rot. If there is any doubt about the drainage, plant bulbs

in raised beds or mix sharp sand or grit with the soil in the planting area. Bulbs like a fairly rich, fertile soil. At least a month before planting, incorporate a generous amount of well-rotted manure or garden compost into the planting area.

Positioning the bulbs

Your bulbs will look more natural if you plant them in clumps or groups, not in straight lines. The depth depends on the size of the bulb but it is usually two or three times its diameter (see diagram on page 11). Details of planting depths are given in the individual entries for each bulb, and refer to the depth of soil above the tip of the bulb. Spacing between bulbs is also dependent on size. Larger bulbs are usually set out about 3in apart and smaller ones 1–2in apart, but they can be crowded together for effect.

Be sure to plant the bulbs the right way up. Usually the pointed part points upwards, but there are exceptions to this rule: ranunculus and anemone have the claws or points facing down into the soil and some lilies and crown imperials are sometimes planted on their sides to avoid moisture collecting between the scales, which can lead to rotting.

In dry conditions, bulbs may need to be watered in after planting, but it is usually not necessary to water again at least until leaf shoots have appeared.

Planting under trees

Mass planting of bulbs that flower through winter and early spring under deciduous trees can turn what might otherwise be a somewhat dull area of the garden into a lovely feature. Although it is sometimes difficult to dig and plant in these areas as the soil is hard and full of matted roots, the result can be well worth the effort. The leaves that fall from the trees in fall break down into leafmould which provides ideal growing conditions for the bulbs.

MAJESTIC WHITE LILIES grown in a large ceramic container make a stunning decoration for a courtyard.

INCREASING YOUR STOCK OF BULBS

Left to themselves, many bulbs will multiply of their own accord, but there are a number of ways in which you can help the process along.

Separation

Many bulbs produce offsets or bulblets that can be gently broken away from the mother bulb when the bulbs are lifted, and planted separately. Most first-year bulblets will reach flowering size in two or three years if they are planted separately, but some are slower to flower. When separating clumps of dahlia tubers, make sure each tuber has an "eye" attached or it will not sprout and flower.

PROPAGATING DAHLIAS

bud

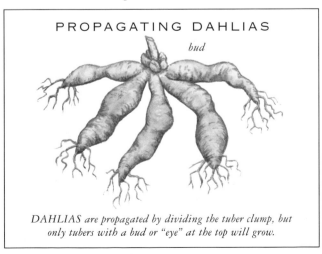

DAHLIAS are propagated by dividing the tuber clump, but only tubers with a bud or "eye" at the top will grow.

THREE WAYS TO PROPAGATE LILIES

1. DETACHING SCALES

THE LILY BULB consists of lots of scales. Remove the outer scales.

PUSH the individual scales, right way up, into a box of moist peat.

BULBLETS will appear at the base of each scale.

POT UP the scales when the new bulblets appear.

2. DETACHING AERIAL BULBILS

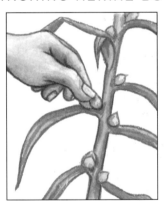

BULBILS grow in the leaf axis of some species. Collect them and pot them up.

3. DETACHING BULBLETS

OFFSETS on the base of some lilies can be detached and planted out.

LIFTING BULBS

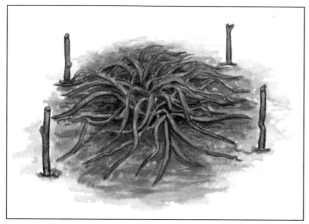

1. PUT A FEW STAKES around the edge of the clump so that you know where to dig when the leaves have died down.

2. AFTER THE LEAVES have died down, use a spade to outline the area of the clump.

3. LIFT THE CLUMP UP with a fork and shake off as much soil as possible.

4. SEPARATE THE BULBS from the clump, clean them and then store them in a dry, airy place or replant them.

Scoring and scooping

Cut a V-shape into the base plate of a mature bulb at planting time, taking care not to damage the growth bud of the bulb. This should result in many small offsets being produced by the end of the growing season. Or score through the basal plate of the bulb at right angles with a sharp knife to produce the same result. Depending on species these small offsets should produce bulbs of flowering size in two to four years.

With a sharp-sided teaspoon or curved knife, you can scoop out the entire basal plate and bulblets will form around the rim of the scooped out area. Wear gloves if you are treating hyacinths as the sap can sometimes irritate the skin.

Lilies

These techniques are not suitable for lilies, which are propagated by other methods (see page 13).
• A mature lily bulb is composed of numerous individual scales. The individual scales can be carefully removed and planted upright in a coarse, free-draining mixture such as three parts coarse washed sand and one part peatmoss or peat substitute. The scales should produce bulblets at their bases.

• Some lilies produce aerial bulbils in the axis of the leaf and these can be collected as they are about to fall. Potted into pots or trays they should produce leaves by the following spring and reach flowering size in two or three years.
• Other lilies produce bulblets just below the soil surface, around the base of the stem. If these are carefully dug out from among the roots they can be potted up and will form flowering plants in two or three years.

CARING FOR GROWING BULBS

Once planted, bulbs need little maintenance. Once the plants are actively growing, the soil should be kept moist, but never soggy. Bulbs do not usually need feeding before they flower. They are fed after blooming, when they are storing food for the following season's growth. Special instructions for feeding and watering are included in the entries for individual plants where appropriate.

AFTER FLOWERING

• After flowers have finished, cut off the spent flower stems but do not cut back the foliage. If you cut off the leaves before they have died down naturally, the bulb will not have the reserves to grow and flower the following season.

• After flowering, feed the plants with a liquid or granular balanced fertilizer and continue to water in dry conditions until the leaves begin to die off naturally. This may take about two or three months.

• If bulbs have been planted in clumps, you may be able to plant annuals between the clumps, using either seed or seedlings. Quick growers such as Virginian stock will provide a pretty distraction from the dying bulb foliage. You could also put in summer-flowering annuals or perennials that will be ready to take over the display once the bulbs have truly died down. Or you can, of course, purchase some "potted color"—annuals that are already in bloom.

• Bulbs do not usually need to be lifted every season. Most are left in the ground and lifted only every two or three years, or in a number of cases only every four or five years. Many bulbs flower well when they are crowded and then it is only necessary to lift and divide clumps when the flower numbers or quality drop off.

• Take care when you lift bulbs that you do not cut or

TALL WHITE RANUNCULUS dominate this white border, formed of plants with contrasting shapes, textures, and sizes.

A CARPET OF COLOR has been created in this garden bed by combining white tulips with violas and anemones in a range of colors. To achieve such a pleasing effect, careful planning before planting is necessary.

TALL BEARDED IRIS make an elegant border for this attractive garden path. Irises come in a rich array of colors.

ZEPHYR LILY, with its starry white flowers and deep green glossy foliage, makes an ideal edging plant. Here it grows with portulacas.

damage them—it is easy to slice into them with a spade or spear them with a fork. Discard damaged, soft, or rotted bulbs immediately. Place the sound bulbs to dry in a cool, airy spot, brush off excess soil and then store them in nets, old stockings, or in single layers in cardboard boxes. Ideally, bulbs should be stored so that they do not touch each other: they can be kept separate with shredded paper or something similar.

• Because lilies have no protective outer sheath on their bulbs, they must be lifted, the clumps divided if necessary, and the bulbs replanted at once. They can be stored for short periods in damp sphagnum moss but take care that they don't dry out.

• Some bulbous plants, such as freesias, produce quite a lot of seed if the spent flower stems are not cut off. You can collect these seeds when they are ripe or allow them to self-sow. Seedlings may take two to five years to reach flowering size, depending on the type of bulb, and they will probably not be true to type. The results can, however, be interesting as you never know quite what to expect. Particularly good seedlings should be marked at flowering time so that the bulbs can be propagated at the end of the season.

MAKING THE MOST OF BULBS IN THE GARDEN

You may wish to plant groups of bulbs under deciduous trees or in other permanent places in the garden but there are many other options. Bulbs mix well with many herbaceous perennials as the new growth of the perennials tends to camouflage the not-so-attractive foliage of the bulbs as it yellows and dies off. Bulbs in this situation can usually be left in the ground for several years before they need to be lifted and divided.

Many bulbs can be treated like annuals for a seasonal display, then lifted, and stored for use the following season. This, of course, creates more work but the results can be well worth the effort, allowing you to create different displays each year. You can have a delightful show of bulbs on their own but consider the possibility of planting bulbs and spring bedding plants together for a really stunning spring display. As well as forming an attractive association, the bedding plants help to mask the dying foliage of the bulbs, which must be left to die down naturally if the bulbs are to flower well next season. Hardy annuals sown in the fall will also serve the same purpose. Plant your bulbs and bedding plants at the same time, placing a bulb between each of the plants. For best effect, planting should be quite dense. You can experiment with color combinations or opt for tried and tested associations such as yellow lily-flowered tulips and blue forget-me-nots.

• An early-flowering bedding plant such as white primula could be interplanted with cream or yellow narcissi, or deep blue anemones for a vivid contrast.

• White, yellow-centred primulas would team well with blue *Anemone blanda* and the dwarf narcissus "Tête-à-Tête".

• Other spring-flowering plants to combine with bulbs include polyanthus, wallflowers, and forget-me-nots.

Dwarf bulbs are ideal for growing on a rockery, usually providing color and interest before the other alpine plants come into their own. Suitable bulbs include alliums, chionodoxa, crocus, cyclamen, iris, muscari, narcissus, oxalis, and rhodohypoxis, among others.

IF YOU WANT show quality tuberous begonias, grow them under cover. Here they grow in a conservatory, where they can also be placed on raised benches so the flowers are more easily admired.

NATURALIZING BULBS IN GRASS

Bulbs naturalized in grass make a very attractive feature in gardens. However, you need to remember that the bulb foliage must be allowed to die down naturally if the bulbs are to perform well in future years, and that means that the grass cannot be mown for several weeks after the bulbs have finished flowering. This can look rather untidy, so a position for naturalized bulbs needs to be chosen with some care. Popular sites are the perimeters of lawns or under deciduous trees. In a small garden with a limited area of lawn used for many purposes, naturalizing in turf may not be a practical idea.

Choose bulbs that will flower at an appropriate period; early spring is convenient because the grass can then be mown from late spring onwards. Some summer-flowering bulbs are good in a wildflower meadow, and autumn-flowering bulbs such as colchicum also grow well in grass. You can either lift a square of turf, plant a group of bulbs, and replace the cut turf, or you can plant larger bulbs individually, using a trowel or bulb-planting tool to cut a hole in the turf. Place the bulb in the bottom of the hole and replace the plug of soil and turf. Give a good watering after planting, both to settle the bulbs and to help the turf re-establish.

After the bulbs have bloomed, give the plants an application of balanced fertilizer and water the area regularly if conditions are dry. Once the bulb foliage has yellowed and died off mowing can be resumed—this usually takes some six weeks after flowering.

MINIATURE PINK NERINES and other small bulbous plants grow between paving stones where they benefit from the sharp drainage.

ACHIMENES
Hot water plant

HOT CERISE PINK *flowers decorate this pretty little plant throughout summer. Hot water plants come in a range of colors.*

THE LARGE, *delicate purple-blue flowers of* Achimenes *"Paul Arnold" help to make this one of the most popular varieties.*

FEATURES

Achimenes are easy to grow and undemanding; they are raised from small rhizomes that look a little like miniature fir cones. Leaves are toothed, elongated, and slightly furry in texture, and the colorful, trumpet-shaped flowers are carried in profusion on short stems above the foliage. The plants often assume a semi-trailing habit, making them good for growing in a basket, or in a raised pot where the stems can cascade.

Flowers are available in a wide range of shades including cream, pink, red, purple, and blue; some varieties have attractively veined throats. Although individual flowers are quite short lived, they are quickly replaced by a profusion of others throughout the season. The plants grow to about 10in.

ACHIMENES AT A GLANCE

A colorful house and greenhouse plant, flowering throughout the summer. Minimum temperature 50°F (zone 11).

JAN	/	
FEB	plant 🌱	RECOMMENDED VARIETIES
MAR	plant 🌱	"Little Beauty"
APR	/	"Paul Arnold"
MAY	/	"Peach Blossom"
JUN	flowering 🌸	"Queen of Sheba"
JULY	flowering 🌸	
AUG	flowering 🌸	
SEPT	flowering 🌸	
OCT	/	
NOV	/	
DEC	/	

CONDITIONS

Aspect   Bright light is necessary, but not direct sun, which may scorch the foliage and flowers.

Site   House plant, preferring cool to moderately warm conditions without marked temperature fluctuations. Use soil-less potting compost, based on peat or peat substitute.

GROWING METHOD

Planting   Bury the rhizomes shallowly—about ¾in deep—in a pot of moist compost, spacing them about ½in apart, in early spring. Keep the pot in a warm room.

Feeding   Feed with a high potash liquid fertilizer every 10 days or so from when the flower buds appear. Keep the compost just moist when the rhizomes start to grow, increasing the watering slightly as flowers start to form, but ensure the compost is never saturated. Tepid water is preferred, hence their common name. Stop watering when the flowers have faded.

Problems   No specific problems, though aphids may attack the new growth.

FLOWERING

Season   Flowers profusely throughout the summer.

Cutting   Flowers are not suitable for cutting.

AFTER FLOWERING

Requirements Stop watering once the flowers have faded and allow the plants to dry off. Remove the dead top growth and keep the rhizomes in the pot of dry compost over winter in a frost-free place. The following spring, tip them out, pot them up carefully in fresh compost, and water to start them into growth again.

AGAPANTHUS
African lily

THE BLUE AND WHITE flowering heads of agapanthus are each composed of numerous individual flowers.

THIS DENSE PLANTING of agapanthus needs little attention and yet rewards the gardener with its wonderful summer flowers.

FEATURES

Usually sold as perennials, agapanthus have showy heads of bright blue, trumpet-shaped flowers. Their foliage is deep green and strap shaped, forming a rosette; the stout flowering stems arise from the centre in mid-summer. Several species are available, but they all like a sheltered spot—in cold gardens, they can be grown under cover in a greenhouse, being moved outside in warm summer weather. "Headbourne Hybrids" are the most widely available; flowers may be several shades of blue, or white. They are deciduous, reasonably hardy, and grow from 2–4ft. *Agapanthus umbellatus (A. africanus)* is evergreen with purple-blue flowers, but most plants under this name are in reality *A. campanulatus*, a deciduous species with blue or white flowers to 3ft.

AGAPANTHUS AT A GLANCE

Stately plants with eye-catching, rounded heads of blue flowers. Best in warmer gardens.

		RECOMMENDED VARIETIES
JAN	/	
FEB	/	"Headbourne Hybrids"
MAR	/	"Bressingham Blue"
APR	plant 🌱	
MAY	plant 🌱	
JUN	/	
JULY	flowering 🌸	
AUG	flowering 🌸	
SEPT	flowering 🌸	
OCT	/	
NOV	/	
DEC	/	

CONDITIONS

Aspect A sheltered position in full sun is required.
Site Usually best grown in tubs or large pots on a sunny patio. Suitable for reasonably sheltered gardens only: can be grown in a conservatory or greenhouse in cold areas. Plants need free-draining soil with plenty of organic matter such as well-rotted garden compost. In containers, use loam-based potting compost with extra organic matter added.

GROWING METHOD

Planting Plant the fleshy roots 4–6in deep in late spring. Take care not to let the roots dry out before planting.
Feeding Apply a high potash liquid fertilizer occasionally during the growing season; container-grown plants should be fed every 14 days. Keep the soil moist but never waterlogged through the growing season; do not let plants in pots dry out at any time.
Problems Plants may fail to perform well in exposed gardens, otherwise they are generally trouble free.

FLOWERING

Season Flowers from mid to late summer.
Cutting Stems may be cut when the lowest flowers on the globe-shaped head are opened, but they are better enjoyed on the plant.

AFTER FLOWERING

Requirements Allow the leaves of deciduous varieties to die down and cover the crowns with a layer of straw to protect them during the winter months. In cold areas, move the plants under cover until spring.

ANOMATHECA
Syn. *Lapeirousia laxa*

THE OPEN-FACED, trumpet-shaped flowers resemble those of freesias, and are carried on slender spikes above the foliage.

THESE PLANTS may well be quite small, but the bright color of the flowers really stands out in the garden, even when seen from a distance.

FEATURES

Occasionally known as scarlet freesia, this pretty little plant is trouble-free and most rewarding in the garden. It multiplies readily from seed sown in spring. The trumpet-shaped flowers are pale scarlet with darker markings. They appear in mid-summer and are followed by seed pods which split open to expose red seeds. The slightly stiff, ribbed, sword-shaped leaves grow about 6–8in high while the flowers are held on spikes which extend well above the foliage. There is a pure white cultivar, "Alba", but this is not nearly as vigorous as the species. *Anomatheca viridis* has unusual green flowers and is normally grown as an indoor plant, flowering in early spring.

ANOMATHECA AT A GLANCE

A graceful, pretty bulb with sprays of trumpet-shaped flowers. Reasonably hardy in most areas.

		RECOMMENDED VARIETIES
JAN	/	
FEB	/	
MAR	/	
APR	plant ✎	*Anomatheca laxa:*
MAY	/	"Alba"
JUN	/	"Joan Evans"
JULY	flowering ❀	
AUG	flowering ❀	*Anomatheca viridis*
SEPT	flowering ❀	
OCT	/	
NOV	/	
DEC	/	

CONDITIONS

Aspect Grows happily in full sun or partial shade.
Site This bulb is very useful for the front of borders, or for growing in pots for the patio or in the house or conservatory. Ideally, soil should be well drained but it need not be rich.

GROWING METHOD

Planting Plant corms about 2in deep and 4in apart in spring.
Feeding Supplementary feeding is generally not needed, but on poor soils a balanced fertilizer can be applied after planting. Plants in containers should be given a liquid feed every 14 days throughout the growing season. In very dry springs, water occasionally once plants have started into growth.
Problems No specific pest or disease problems are known for this plant.

FLOWERING

Season Flowers generally appear in mid-summer.
Cutting This is not a good choice as a cut flower.

AFTER FLOWERING

Requirements Cut off faded flower stems immediately after flowering if you do not want seed to set. In warm gardens the corms can be left in the ground, but in cooler areas they are better lifted in the fall and stored for replanting next spring.

CANNA
Indian shot

THE APRICOT-ORANGE FLOWERS of these cannas will contribute a rich, flamboyant color to the garden for many months.

THE COLOR of these scarlet cannas is highlighted by the darker green, slightly bronzed foliage that surrounds them.

FEATURES

Canna is an exotic-looking plant with bold, brilliantly colored flowers carried on tall stems, up to 4ft, above large, paddle-shaped leaves. The large blooms form an impressive spike; colors available are mainly shades of yellow, orange, and red. Sometimes the flowers are bi-colored, or spotted, streaked, or splashed with a contrasting shade. The foliage is also attractive, and in some varieties is tinged with bronze or purple. There are a number of varieties with attractively variegated foliage, which has yellow or pink veins.

Cannas are not hardy and must be protected from frost. *Canna indica* is the best known species, but most varieties generally available are hybrids, often sold as *Canna hybrida*. A wide range of named varieties is available from specialist suppliers.

CANNA AT A GLANCE

An impressive, exotic-looking plant with tall stems of brightly colored flowers and lush, attractive foliage.

		RECOMMENDED VARIETIES
JAN	/	
FEB	/	"Durban"
MAR	plant (indoors)	"Lucifer"
APR	plant (indoors)	"Oiseau de Feu" ("Firebird")
MAY	plant (outdoors)	"Picasso"
JUN	plant (outdoors)	"Wyoming"
JULY	flowering	
AUG	flowering	
SEPT	flowering	
OCT	/	
NOV	/	
DEC	/	

CONDITIONS

Aspect These plants must have an open but sheltered position in full sun.

Site Cannas make an impressive focal point in a bedding display, in mixed or herbaceous borders, or grow well in tubs and large containers. Soil should be free draining but rich in organic matter. In cold areas, the plants are best grown in a greenhouse or conservatory.

GROWING METHOD

Planting Set the rhizomes about 3in deep in fertile soil in late spring, once the risk of frosts is over. Better plants will be obtained by starting the rhizomes off in pots in a frost-free greenhouse in April, and planting them outide in early summer, once all risk of frost is over and the weather is suitably warm.

Feeding Give an occasional high potash liquid feed as the flower buds develop. Keep the soil moist at all times but make sure that it is never waterlogged.

Problems No specific problems are generally experienced.

FLOWERING

Season Flowers in mid to late summer, until the first frosts.

Cutting Flowers are not suitable for cutting—they are best enjoyed on the plants.

AFTER FLOWERING

Requirements Lift and dry the rhizomes in early fall, before the first frosts. Store them in a cool, frost-free place in just-moist peat or sand through the winter. If kept bone dry, the rhizomes will shrivel.

OXALIS
Wood sorrel

THE SATINY WHITE FLOWERS on Oxalis purpurea *"Alba"* are a far cry from the weedy forms of oxalis that invade our yards.

THIS PRETTY PINK OXALIS makes a charming groundcover here on the edge of a paved area.

FEATURES

A number of species of oxalis are very invasive, but others are very decorative and well worth growing. Most have clover-like leaves and five-petalled, satiny flowers which are furled in bud. The usual color is pink or white; there are also purple, yellow, orange, or red varieties. Some species need greenhouse cultivation in this country. Height varies from 2–8in.
O. adenophylla is the most popular species, with greyish leaves and silvery flowers;
O. enneaphylla has white flowers and attractive, folded, silvery leaves. *O. laciniata* has narrow leaflets and purple, veined flowers. Once known as *O. deppei*, *O. tetraphylla* has brown-marked leaves and pink flowers.

OXALIS AT A GLANCE

A low-growing, clump-forming plant with clover-like leaves and attractive, satiny flowers. Can be invasive.

JAN	/	
FEB	/	
MAR	/	RECOMMENDED VARIETIES
APR	/	"Beatrice Anderson"
MAY	/	"Bowles' White"
JUN	flowering	"Ione Hecker"
JULY	flowering	"Royal Velvet"
AUG	/	
SEPT	planting	*O. enneaphylla:*
OCT	planting	"Alba"
NOV	/	"Minutifolia"
DEC	/	"Rosea"

O. tetraphylla:
"Iron Cross"

CONDITIONS

Aspect Grow in full sun for good flowering and compact leaf growth.

Site Grow on a rockery or near the front of a border, preferably in a confined bed where growth can be controlled. The more invasive varieties are best grown in pots. Free-draining soil is preferred.

GROWING METHOD

Planting Plant in early fall, 3in deep and 4in apart. It is usual to plant clumps in growth rather than the tiny tubers or rhizomes.

Feeding Supplementary fertilizer is rarely needed.

Problems Few problems are usually encountered although some oxalis do suffer from the fungal leaf disease rust. Pick off the worst affected leaves and avoid overhead watering.

FLOWERING

Season Most species flower through early and mid-summer.

Cutting Flowers are unsuitable for cutting.

AFTER FLOWERING

Requirements Plants can be divided after flowering in summer. Clear away dead foliage once the leaves have died down; beware of putting plant debris from invasive varieties on the compost heap.

RHODOHYPOXIS BAURII
Rose grass

TINY MAGENTA CENTRES emphasise the stark white of this pretty rose grass. The unusual flower form is clearly seen here.

DEEP ROSE-PINK in color, this form of rose grass is sometimes sold as "Rosy Posy". It gives a long flowering display.

FEATURES

This enchanting little plant, which comes from high altitude areas of South Africa, is ideally suited to growing in a rock garden, on the edge of a border or in pots. The slightly hairy leaves, similar to those of a broad-leaf grass, grow to around 4in high. The flowers, which are white or pink through to deep rosy crimson, are about the same height. As they have become better known several varieties with deeper color or larger flowers have become available. They have six petals with one set of three appearing to be set on top of the other, so the flower has no visible eye. The floral display is long lasting, from late spring through to late summer.

If grown in the garden the positions of these plants should be marked in some way as they are completely dormant during winter.

RHODOHYPOXIS AT A GLANCE

A tuberous alpine with mounds of attractive pink or white flowers carried for a very long season.

		RECOMMENDED VARIETIES
JAN	/	
FEB	/	"Alba"
MAR	plant	"Dulcie"
APR	plant	"Dawn"
MAY	flowering	"Douglas"
JUN	flowering	"Eva-Kate"
JULY	flowering	"Fred Broome"
AUG	flowering	"Garnett"
SEPT	flowering	"Harlequin"
OCT	/	"Picta"
NOV	/	"Ruth"
DEC	/	"Stella"

CONDITIONS

Aspect Grows best in full sun in a sheltered spot.

Site Suitable for rockeries, scree gardens, or containers. The soil must be well drained but enriched with decayed organic matter. It needs to be lime free, as rose grass is not tolerant of alkaline soils. Good quality potting compost mixed with a little extra sharp sand should be adequate for containers.

GROWING METHOD

Planting Tubers should be planted in late spring about 2in deep and 4in apart. Lift and divide offsets in the fall.

Feeding Mulch garden plants with decayed manure or compost in late winter or early spring. Potted plants that have not been repotted will benefit from slow-release fertilizer in early spring. Water regularly during the growing period in dry spells, but keep dry through winter.

Problems No specific problems are known.

FLOWERING

Season The long flowering period runs from late spring through to late summer.

Cutting Flowers are unsuitable for picking.

AFTER FLOWERING

Requirements Spent blooms can be snipped off or ignored. Protect plants from excess winter rainfall; a sheet of glass supported horizontally over the plants on four wooden stakes should prevent the crowns rotting off in wet weather.

ROMULEA
Romulea

THE CHARMING FLOWERS of little Romulea rosea *may be best appreciated when it is grown in a container.*

PALE LAVENDER PETALS and a recessed deep gold throat make Romulea bulbocodium *worth growing. It tolerates cool conditions.*

FEATURES

These small plants have grassy leaves and brightly colored, crocus-like flowers. There are 75 species native to parts of Africa, the Mediterranean and Europe, most in cultivation being South African.

Growing 3–6in high, depending on species, they are ideal for rock gardens and pots where their neat growth can be admired. The color range includes cream and yellow, many shades of blue and violet, and also pinks and reds: many flowers have a very attractive "eye" of contrasting color in the centre of the flower. The most popular type, *R. bulbocodium*, has pale lavender flowers with a yellow throat, and is hardier than some of the other species. Flowers remain closed in dull weather.

ROMULEA AT A GLANCE

A low-growing plant with crocus-like flowers which open wide in full sun. Needs a protected position.

JAN	/	
FEB	/	
MAR	flowering	
APR	flowering	
MAY	flowering	
JUN	/	
JULY	/	
AUG	/	
SEPT	plant	
OCT	plant	
NOV	/	
DEC	/	

RECOMMENDED SPECIES

Romulea bulbocodium clusiana
Romulea flava
Romulea sabulosa

CONDITIONS

Aspect Needs full sun all day. The flowers will not open in shady conditions.

Site Grows best when grown in a sharply draining, rather sandy soil. Good for scree beds, rockeries and containers.

GROWING METHOD

Planting The small corms should be planted some 2in deep and 2–3in apart in the fall.

Feeding Feeding is not normally necessary for this plant, but in poor soils some balanced fertilizer may be applied as growth begins. Water freely to keep the soil moist through the growing season but keep plants dry during the summer, when they die down.

Problems No specific pest or disease problems are known for romulea.

FLOWERING

Season Flowers are carried throughout the spring months.

Cutting None of the species has flowers that are suitable for cutting.

AFTER FLOWERING

Requirements Protect the crowns with a mulch of peat or similar material for the winter months. Overcrowded clumps can be lifted and divided when the flowers have faded.

TRILLIUM
Wake robin, wood lily

THE LATIN NAME Trillium *refers to "three" and wake robin has everything in threes: three petals, three sepals, and a ring of three leaves.*

THE LITTLE FLOWERS *of wake robin will make a delightful sight as they light up a shaded part of the garden.*

FEATURES

Trillium grandiflorum is a charming woodland plant which hails from North America. With its three pure white petals and dark foliage, it is a most arresting sight when naturalized in groups under trees to simulate its native habitat. It is not a difficult plant to grow and is well worth seeking out—it can be vigorous and long lived in the right conditions. The white flowers slowly age to pink and there is an attractive double form available called *T. grandiflorum flore pleno*. Plants grow to 15in or so high.

Other species worth growing include *T. sessile*, with dark red flowers springing from bronze blotched foliage; *T. erectum*, with maroon flowers and lighter green foliage, and *T. undulatum*, which has white or pinkish flowers streaked with red.

TRILLIUM AT A GLANCE

Attractive plants for lightly shaded or woodland conditions, with white, three-petalled flowers in early summer.

		RECOMMENDED VARIETIES
JAN	/	
FEB	/	*Trillium grandiflorum*
MAR	/	"Flore Pleno"
APR	flowering	
MAY	flowering	*Trillium erectum albiflorum*
JUN	flowering	
JULY	/	*Trillium erectum luteum*
AUG	plant	
SEPT	plant	*Trillium sessile luteum*
OCT	plant	
NOV	/	
DEC	/	

CONDITIONS

Aspect Needs light shade at all times or the dappled sunlight provided by overhead trees or shrubs.

Site An ideal plant for a woodland garden or a shady border. Does best in very rich, moist, but free-draining soil. Copious quantities of well-rotted cow manure or leafmould should be dug into the soil before planting. Mulch well in late winter, too.

GROWING METHOD

Planting Plant rhizomes 3in deep in late summer or early fall. Plant in groups at 12in or so intervals.

Feeding An annual dressing of leafmould or well-rotted manure should provide sufficient nutrients, but an application of general fertilizer can be given in spring. The soil must not dry out in spring and summer and so give careful attention to watering in dry weather.

Problems Slugs and snails may damage newly emerging leaves or flowers; otherwise it is generally trouble-free.

FLOWERING

Season Flowers will appear somewhere between mid-spring and early summer.

Cutting Flowers are not suitable for picking.

AFTER FLOWERING

Requirements No special attention is needed after flowering apart from tidying dead foliage. Crowded clumps can be divided and replanted immediately in the fall.

TULIPA
Tulip

THE POINTED PETALS of these goblet-shaped, bright lipstick-pink tulips will open to form a starry shape.

A NATIVE of Crete, pale pink Tulipa saxatilis *needs a sunny, warm position with perfectly drained soil in which to grow.*

FEATURES

There are over 100 species of tulips and many hundreds of hybrids. Most modern garden tulips are the result of extensive breeding programmes that began in the late sixteenth century in Europe and are continuing to this day. Tulips were all the rage at that time as more and more species were introduced to Europe from Turkey, Iran, and central Asia. Tulip species range in height from about 6–24in but the greatest number of hybrids are probably in the range of 12–16in. Tulips look their best in mass plantings of one color but they can, of course, be mixed. They make very good container plants and are delightful cut flowers. Some of the most charming are the dwarf types which do particularly well in rock gardens and are also very suitable for containers.

Tulip bulbs are widely available in garden centres in late summer and early fall, but to get a wider choice it is often best to obtain catalogues from specialist bulb growers who run mail-order businesses. Many of the species tulips are only available from specialist growers. With careful selection it is possible to have a tulip in flower from early to very late spring.

Like daffodils, tulips are split into a number of divisions according to their flower form and time of flowering.

Single early	Cup-shaped single flowers, up to 16in in early to mid-spring.
Double early	Fully double flowers up to 16in in early to mid-spring.
Triumph	Conical then rounded, single flowers up to 20in in mid to late spring.
Darwin hybrid	Large, single flowers of varying shape, up to 24in in mid to late spring.
Single late	Single, blocky or square shaped flowers up to 30in in late spring and early summer.
Lily-flowered	Single, waisted flowers with pointed petals, up to 24in in late spring.
Fringed	Single flowers with very finely cut petal edges, up to 24in in late spring.
Viridiflora	Single flowers with green bands or streaks on the outside, up to 20in in late spring.
Rembrandt	Single flowers with a broken pattern of feathering or streaking caused by a virus. Up to 30in in late spring.
Parrot	Single flowers with very strongly frilled and curled petals, up to 24in in late spring.
Double late	Large, fully double flowers up to 24in in late spring.
Kaufmanniana	Single, often bi-colored flowers of a waterlily shape, up to 10in in late spring. Leaves may be mottled.
Fosteriana	Large, single, wide-opening flowers up to 20in in early to mid-spring.
Greigii	Large, single flowers up to 14in in mid to late spring. Leaves streaked and mottled.
Miscellaneous	Any other species, varieties, and hybrids.

THE BIZARRE FORM of parrot tulips is exemplified by this dark crimson flower. People either love these forms or hate them.

THE BURGUNDY of these full-blown tulips will appeal to lovers of the unusual but they may be hard to incorporate into the garden scheme.

CONDITIONS

Aspect   Tulips need full sun for at least half the day, with some wind protection.

Site   Grow tulips in beds and borders, on rockeries or in containers. Soil should be well drained with a high organic content. Add lime to acid soils.

GROWING METHOD

Planting   Bulbs should be planted in late fall. Planting depth varies according to the size of the bulbs; usually 6–8in for the larger types and 4in for the smaller species. Space them 4–8in apart.

Feeding   Apply liquid fertilizer as soon as buds appear and again after flowers have faded. Water regularly in dry spells, especially once the buds have appeared.

Problems   Tulip breaking virus, causing streaking of the flowers, is carried by aphids. Remove affected plants and keep aphids under control. Tulip fire disease is a type of botrytis or gray mould. It causes small brown spots on flowers and leaves; stems may rot and gray furry growth may develop on the damaged areas. Destroy plants infected with this disease and avoid planting tulips in the same spot for a couple of years. Spraying with a general fungicide may control early infection.

FLOWERING

Season   Tulips flower somewhere between late winter and late spring, depending on variety.

Cutting   If cutting blooms for the house, choose those that are not fully open and cut them early in the morning. Change vase water frequently.

AFTER FLOWERING

Requirements   Remove spent flower stems and dead foliage. Tulips may be left in the ground for two or three years, or the bulbs can be lifted once the foliage has died down, cleaned and stored in a cool, dry, airy place. Dwarf tulips tend to be left in the ground, but other varieties usually perform better if they are lifted and replanted every year. If you do not want to lift them annually, make sure the bulbs are planted deeply.

TULIPA AT A GLANCE

Well-known flowers in a very wide range of colors, sizes, and forms, flowering between late winter and late spring.

		RECOMMENDED VARIETIES
JAN	/	
FEB	flowering	"Peach Blossom"
MAR	flowering	"Apeldoorn"
APR	flowering	"Clara Butt"
MAY	flowering	"China Pink"
JUN	/	"Burgundy Lace"
JULY	/	"Spring Green"
AUG	/	"Texas Gold"
SEPT	/	"Angelique"
OCT	/	"Ancilla"
NOV	plant	*Tulipa fosteriana*
DEC	plant	*Tulipa greigii*
		Tulipa tarda

1.

2.

3.

6.

7.

TULIPS
(*TULIPA*)

Tulips, with their wide range of forms and colors, are divided into fifteen horticultural groups.

1. From a crimson bud "Leen van der Mark" opens to reveal a crystalline white centre.

2. A fully opened "Bokassa Red" shows its deep scarlet petals tipped with gold.

3. "Judith Lyster", a single late tulip, is rich cream merging to watermelon pink.

4. Goblet-shaped "Bokassa Rose" is deep rose pink with a yellow centre.

5. "Kees Nelis" is a bright, two-tone tulip in primary red and yellow.

6. No two parrot tulip flowers are identical as this flamboyant "Flaming Parrot" proves.

7. "Princess Victoria" is a heavy-textured tulip that is more weather resistant than some other varieties.

8. "Angélique", a pale pink ruffled beauty, is best grown in pots so it can be protected from weather.

9. "Monte Carlo" is a bright gold, fully double tulip with a light scent.

GROWING ANNUALS

Annuals are perhaps the easiest plants you will ever grow. Yet their ease of growth in no way detracts from their ability to provide color in the garden, in some cases virtually all-year-round. Whether your yard is large, or small, or you work within the confines of just a small courtyard, annuals are plants for you.

Miracles are happening in our gardens every day, but perhaps the greatest "miracle" in which we can take part is growing plants from seeds. Nothing is quite as amazing, or as humbling, as seeing a fully-grown plant, which started life as a tiny seed, burst into flower and create a riot of color just a few months after it was sown. Some annuals need no more care than simply scattering the seeds over the surface of the ground and "raking" them in using your fingertips—others demand only that they are sown to the correct depth and then given room to grow as they develop. By their very nature, many annuals produce brilliant results even in the poorest of soils. So get some seed catalogs, visit the local garden centre, and start performing your own garden miracles with the easiest plants on earth!

LEFT: *Annuals like these purple violas and white-flowered lobularia (alyssum) can be sown directly into the soil where you want them to flower, in criss-crossing patterns as here.*

ABOVE: *Rudbeckia or coneflower is available in a wide range of sizes, and provides valuable color in late summer.*

MANY ANNUALS THRIVE in some of the most inhospitable parts of the yard. These portulacas or sun flowers are perfectly at home growing on a rockery with very little soil for their roots—they are just as suited to light, sandy soils and make good summer bedding plants.

WHAT ARE ANNUALS?

Virtually all annuals are raised by sowing seeds, either in early spring under cover (in a heated greenhouse, conservatory, or on the kitchen windowsill), or directly into prepared soil outdoors. Some annuals are so adaptable that you only need sow them once—from then on these so-called "self-seeders" regularly drop seeds into the soil which then "come up", or germinate, of their own accord. In many ways these "hardy annuals" do a better job at sowing than we do—finding just the right spot for perfect growth—often in places we might never dream of actually sowing seeds, such as between the cracks in paving stones and in the gravel of driveways.

At the other extreme are annuals which need to be started into growth long before the warmer days of spring arrive outdoors. The so-called "half-hardy" annuals are those plants which are damaged by frosts, but which perform brilliantly during the summer months. For these you must be able to provide suitable growing conditions, especially at sowing time, when temperature is all-important for actually getting the seeds to come up. In some cases, such as with ricinus, the castor oil plant, it is grown as a half-hardy annual, even though it is by nature a shrub, which in its native habitat would, like the shrubs in our gardens, eventually form a large plant. Petunias are another example of a half-hardy annual which is really a perennial plant, and quite capable of surviving the winter if potted-up and kept protected in a cold but "frost-free" place overwinter. It helps to understand what the terms mean when growing annuals as you will come across them all the time in catalogs and on the back of seed packets.

HARDY ANNUALS

The easiest of all annuals to grow, sow hardy annuals exactly where you want the plants to flower. Many hardy annuals do not like root disturbance, so bear this in mind.

They are given their ideal planting distances by gradually "thinning out" as the young plants grow—all this means is carefully removing a few plants every few weeks in spring, to give those left behind more room to develop. By early summer this thinning should be complete, and plants can be left to produce flowers. Hardy annuals are not affected by low temperatures, and many, like calendula, the pot marigold, are sown and germinate outdoors in September for strong plants with earlier flowers the following spring. Most self-seeders belong to this group.

HALF-HARDY ANNUALS

As already mentioned, these plants are not able to withstand frost or freezing temperatures and must be raised from seed every season, often starting in late winter and very early spring. Many half-hardy annuals are actually "perennials"—plants which keep growing year after year, but which are better-suited to our needs when grown as strong, young plants every season. Half-hardy annuals are only planted (or moved outdoors if grown in containers) when spring frosts are finished. The exact timing of this depends on the actual area you garden in, but this book gives sowing/planting times for the average temperate conditions that exist in zones 5,6, and 7 (see map at back). At the other end of the season, the first frosts of fall will flatten most half-hardy annuals, and they can be removed for composting.

HARDY BIENNIALS

A biennial is simply a plant which straddles two growing seasons before it produces its show of flowers or foliage. A good example is cheiranthus, or wallflower, which is sown outdoors in early summer. The young leafy plants are grown on, then lifted and planted in October where you want flowers the following spring. Think of hardy biennials as annuals with a "foot" in two seasons—instead of producing their flowers or leaves all within what we think of as "summer", they get going in one season, spend the winter building up speed, then go all out for flowering the next spring and summer. Biennials are especially useful for filling any "gaps" between late spring and early summer, and many such as sweet William are easy and worthwhile plants for cut flowers.

BUYING SEEDS

Growing from seed is addictive—once you have sampled one seed catalog you will certainly want more. You can buy annual seeds by sending for them by post or a home delivery service, by visiting garden centres or the gardening section of large stores, or, increasingly, by buying them with your other shopping at the supermarket.

The choice will always be greater in catalogs, but the more limited range that you might find in garden centres can actually be more helpful. The seed packets here are guaranteed to be colorful, giving encouragement to the beginner. Some mail order seed companies pack in plain, information-only packets for mail order—this is no reflection on the quality of the seeds, but they do lack inspiration! Bright, colorful packets are a great help when planning a color-themed display with annuals, so do not be afraid to play around with a handful of packets until you get a good balance or contrast of colors just to your liking. If you do buy seeds from garden centers and similar outlets, always avoid any packets that are faded, yellow, and have obviously been exposed to the sun, as the results are likely to be disappointing.

SEED PACKETS

Remember that seeds are alive, and need looking after to keep them in tip-top condition until sowing. Inside most seed packets you will find another, smaller packet made of foil. Seeds are sealed inside this inner packet in a kind of "suspended animation" which preserves them until the foil seal is broken. This is when the normal ageing processes of the seed begins. Where this type of storage is not vital for success, seeds are simply found sealed within the outer paper packet. Foil packets should not be opened until the time of sowing for best results. On most packets the inspiration on the front is backed-up by full growing instructions on the reverse. The better packets give sowing times, expected flowering period, and alternative sowing times in the fall. Keep seed packets after sowing—along with catalogs they build up into an invaluable reference library which you can refer to as and when necessary. Always keep seeds in a cool, dry, frost-free place.

YOUNG PLANTS

Many half-hardy annuals included in this book can also be bought in spring and summer as "young plants", and this is stated, where relevant, in the paragraph "features" for each of the 90 annuals covered. The term "young plant" covers anything from ready-germinated trays of small seedlings to a large plant, perhaps in flower, growing in a 3½in pot which you will find for sale in garden centers. Buying young plants simply means that a lot of the work in raising the plants from seed has been done for you by the grower—which has advantages and disadvantages. Young plants are a great help if you do not have facilities for raising seeds or enough space, and they are often delivered ready to go straight into containers. The range compared to the number of varieties available from seed is limited, although this is always improving. You pay for convenience—seed raising is usually cheaper than buying in young plants.

WHAT CAN GO WRONG?

Yellow leaves
● Seedlings are being grown too cold in the early stages or plants may have been planted outdoors too early.
● Plants may need feeding—water thoroughly with an all-purpose liquid or soluble plant food, wetting the leaves at the same time to act as a foliar feed.

Curled or distorted leaves
● Look for clusters of aphids attacking flower buds and the youngest leaves at the shoot tips. Rub them off with your fingers or use a spray containing permethrin.
● Drift from weedkillers can cause this problem, so take great care if you are treating a lawn for weeds using a hormone weedkiller—avoid days when there is any breeze, and keep well away from bedding displays.

Holes and silvery trails on/in leaves
● Slugs and snails will eat most annual plants and are a particular threat in late spring and early summer, especially after rain when the air is warm and moist. They leave silver slime-trails on the soil and on plants where they have been feeding. Chemical slug pellets can be scattered sparingly among plants or an unbroken ring of sharp grit 2in wide can be used as a physical deterrent on smaller areas. Another option is to check plants at night and pick off slugs and snails while they feed, dropping them into salty water.

White "powder" on leaves
● Powdery mildew affects many annuals but not usually until late summer. This disease is not a serious threat and treatment is not needed.

Seedlings indoors suddenly collapse and fall over
● "Damping off" disease can attack annual seedlings, and is a particular problem if the compost becomes too wet. Always use clean pots for sowing and fresh compost. If it does attack, water lightly with a copper-based fungicide and resow to play safe.

Leaf edges chewed
● Various caterpillars will attack annuals and can soon strip leaves bare. Pick them off by hand or use a spray containing permethrin, wetting both sides of the leaves with a strong jet from the sprayer.

Plants cut off at ground level
● Cutworms can sever newly planted bedding plants outdoors causing a sudden wilting and yellowing of plants under attack. Search around in the soil and the greenish-brown caterpillars are easily found and destroyed.

Creamy-white grubs eating roots
● Vine weevil grubs can cause severe damage to container plants. Never re-use old compost, and if you find grubs, treat all pots with biological control or a chemical based on phenols as a drench.

Orange marigolds, red and orange nasturtiums, and brown-coned rudbeckia intermingle forming a color co-ordinated annual border.

One of the wisest approaches is to decide carefully just what you feel you can achieve with your existing facilities. If your "propagator" (somewhere that plants are raised from seeds in the early stages) is just the kitchen windowsill, then buying half-hardy annuals in as young plants might be the best option. These small plug plants are delivered in mid-spring and can be potted up and grown on on the windowsill or even next to the glass in an unheated conservatory. This cuts out the often tricky job of germinating the seeds to begin with, but means you can still grow the plants you really want. And of course there is nothing to stop you sowing hardy annuals straight into the soil outdoors at the right time.

If you are more restricted, say to just a small patio or balcony, young plants might be the whole solution—larger plants are delivered (or can be bought) in late spring and early summer and these can be planted straight into containers and hanging baskets without growing on. Even then there is nothing to stop you scattering a few seeds of malcolmia, Virginian stock, in the top of your patio pots for some quick and scented flowers!

Most seed catalogs and specialist young plant suppliers carry extensive and informative sections on young plants, and they are well worth getting hold of. Pay particular attention to "last order dates"—these are the cut-off points for placing young plant orders and many start to appear even as early as January and February.

ANNUALS IN CONTAINERS

A container in the broadest gardening sense is anything capable of holding compost and supporting plant growth—this could be a 3½in diameter plastic plant pot to a large terracotta trough or tub. Whatever you use, it must have some form of drainage, and this is usually through holes in the base. Molded plastic containers often have no preformed holes and so you must drill these before planting up. Waterlogged compost kills plant roots and the whole plant will soon die.

For most purposes a good "multipurpose" compost serves all of an annual plant's needs—from sowing to growing on and finally being planted up. Most multipurpose composts are based on peat with plant nutrients and other materials such as water-storing granules and "wetters" (allowing dried-out compost to be re-wetted) already added. An increasing number of composts available are based on recycled materials, and the coir-based ones are improving constantly. A few specific plants do prefer a soil-based compost, such as the "John Innes" types, both for sowing and growing—details of these are given under "growing method" where relevant. Always buy fresh bags of compost in spring, avoiding any that are over-heavy and wet, or split with green algae growing in them, or faded and past their sell-by date!

There is no reason why hardy annuals cannot be used for container growing— the fact that many are usually sown direct into the soil is not a problem. Simply sow them in small pots or multi-cell trays (plastic trays where the area is divided into individual units or "cells") at the same times as recommended for outdoor sowing, and plant into your containers during spring. Where appropriate under each plant entry, varieties suited to containers are given—these are usually dwarfer versions of taller varieties, and the range is increasing all the time. Half-hardy annuals offer great scope for container growing, for the reasons already discussed.

SOWING ANNUALS

Annual seeds are either sown indoors or outdoors. Those sown outdoors are the easiest—they need no extra warmth or heat, just sow them in a patch of well-prepared ground and thin to give them space as they grow. Sowing depth will depend on the size of the seed, but it is essential to work the soil using a rake (or your fingers in a small area) so it is fine and crumbly to at least 1in deep.

Seed can then be simply scattered over the soil and raked in, or sown in seed drills—these are simply grooves made in the soil with the head of a rake, the edge of a piece of wood, a length of bamboo cane or even the side of your hand. Whichever you use, just press the edge into the soil to make a groove of the right depth. Then sprinkle the seeds thinly along the drill, by rubbing them between your finger and thumb. Once finished, soil is moved back over the seeds with a rake or by lightly brushing the flat of your hand over the sown area. Take care not to disturb the sown seeds, and label with the variety and date sown. If you are sowing a large area with a variety of hardy annuals, or planning a mixture of hardy and half-hardy varieties, mark the sown patches with boundaries of light-colored sand—a traditional but still effective way of seeing just where you have been! By sowing in short drills within these marked areas it is easy to tell the annuals from the weeds because they come up in rows.

Indoors, half-hardy annuals are sown ideally in a heated propagator with temperature control, and this piece of "kit" is virtually essential when raising plants like pelargoniums (bedding geraniums) and begonias—both of which need high, constant, temperatures. Otherwise a brightly lit windowsill in a warm kitchen will work wonders—many half-hardy annuals are very undemanding once they have come up, and if not kept over-wet will grow steadily even in quite cool conditions.

Narrow "windowsill propagators" are available which have a heated base and allow you to move pots on and off as seedlings appear—these are invaluable if you plan to do a lot of seed-raising. For all the plants in this book a 3½in diameter pot is sufficient for the germination of an average packet of half-hardy annual seeds. If you raise half-hardy annuals remember that they will not be able to go out until after the last spring frosts. You can sow many plants later than the "ideal" times—this book describes the optimum sowing times unless otherwise stated—and to plan for a later display of flowers with the advantage of them being easier to raise and look after a little later in the spring season.

SOIL PREPARATION

All that annuals need to grow well is soil that has had plenty of "organic matter" added before sowing or planting, and this is best done by digging it in thoroughly the previous fall or in early spring. Suppliers of manure take some tracking down these days, so using home-made compost (or leaf mould) is a better option. Whatever you use, it must be dark, well-rotted, and thoroughly broken down. Organic matter is vital for improving the soil's ability to hold onto moisture at the height of summer, and also supplies some plant foods. To take proper care of feeding, scatter pelleted poultry manure over the area 2–3 weeks before sowing/planting and rake it in. This should provide ample nutrients for the rest of the summer.

THINNING OUT

"Thinning out" or "thinning" means allowing enough room for plants to develop fully. This is most important with hardy annuals—as young seedlings grow larger some are gradually removed to leave room for those left behind. Make sure you put your fingers on the soil when pulling plants out or there is a risk the plants you leave behind will be uprooted. Water well after thinning to settle seedlings back in. Thinning can start when plants are just 1in tall and is usually finished by early summer. Fall-sown annuals should be thinned in spring, in case some plants are lost during the winter months.

GROWING ON

Once seedlings have been transplanted (moved) to either individual pots or cell trays, they are "grown on". This stage lasts until they are finally hardened off before planting out outdoors or in pots. During growing on, make sure plants do not dry out, space them out (if pot-grown) as they develop, and keep an eye out for pests and diseases. Some plants (like thunbergia, black-eyed-Susan) benefit from being potted on when their roots fill the pot.

HARDENING OFF

Toughening plants raised indoors ready for outdoor conditions is vital if they are not to suffer a growth "check" when you put them out. Few of us have (or have the room for) the traditional "coldframe" which was the classic way of hardening off. These days we can make use of garden fleece, which is much easier, and just as effective. From mid-May onwards plants can be stood outside on warm days, in a sunny spot. For the first week bring them in at night, then leave them out, but covered with fleece at night. Gradually, unless frost is forecast, the fleece can be left off even at night, but replaced during frosty spells. By early June, plants will be hardened off and ready to plant.

PLANTING

Whether you are planting in beds or containers, water the pots/trays the night before to soak the roots. Planting can be done with a trowel—or even by hand on light soils. Using your hands is certainly the best way of planting up containers and hanging baskets. Never plant the base of plants deeper than they were growing originally, firm well, and water. Keep labels with plants for future reference, and note the planting date on the label as well.

WATERING

Lack of water causes many hardy annuals to flower and then quickly die. When the soil feels dry, enough water should be given so that it really gets down to the roots—the soil should feel moist at least 6in down. Use a trowel and check that this is happening. Containers need much more care as they rely solely on you for their water. Choosing a compost containing water-storing crystals provides the best insurance. Do not overwater early on or roots may rot, but check them at least every other day and never allow them to dry out.

FEEDING

By mixing slow-release fertilizer granules with the compost before planting you can take care of feeding for the whole season—you just need to water. Outdoors, bedding displays will benefit from liquid feeding every 2–4 weeks. Many hardy annuals need no extra feeding and actually thrive on poor, hungry soils.

USING ANNUALS IN YOUR GARDEN

With annuals the sky really is the limit. You can choose to grow just hardy or half-hardy annuals, a mixture of both, or you can be more adventurous and put them to work for you in a wide range of garden situations. Or, of course, you could just leave them to do their own thing!

AS EDGING PLANTS these Begonia semperflorens *are a good choice—being of even height they are good for growing in lines.*

Once you have annuals in your yard you will never want to be without them. Self-seeding annuals like limnanthes and nigella will want to do their own thing and grow where they fall, while others such as lavatera and ricinus are put to much better use by carefully planning where they will grow. You can find a spot for annuals in every yard, and sometimes they can even help you out of a tight corner! What better plants could you ask for?

ABOVE: The delicately veined flower of agrostemma, the corncockle, an easily-grown hardy annual that is sown outdoors in spring where you want it to flower.

BEDDING SCHEMES

We see annuals used in bedding schemes almost every day of our lives, on traffic roundabouts, in public parks, and in each others yards. The "scheme" part of the phrase comes from the fact that many of these flashy, colorful displays are pre-planned and in many ways made-to-measure. If that is the effect you are after, then you must do your homework. The "structure" of a basic bedding scheme is quite simple—you have tall plants in the centre of the bed, and the shortest plants around the edge. In between are plants in a range of sizes and with varying growth habits, which fill the space between the tallest and the shortest. Bedding schemes can be as simple, or as elaborate, as you like. The key points to remember are to work out which plants are going where, how many you need, and of course, whether they are suited to being grown together.

HARDY ANNUAL SCHEMES

Creating a show using just hardy annuals is both very easy and tremendous fun. The sheer range of hardy annual varieties is enormous and it is easy to be spoilt for choice. You can go out and sow an entire bed with hardy annuals at one go, then sit back and wait for the seedlings to come up. All you need to do then is keep down annual weeds (all perennial weeds should be removed before sowing), thin out every few weeks until early summer, push in twiggy supports for taller, straggly plants and enjoy the show. The

THIS SUMMER BEDDING SCHEME features zinnias in the centre of the bed (with variegated tradescantia creeping through) then scarlet salvias, dropping down to the pink fluffy heads of ageratum, the floss flower, below.

best effect is from bold groups of color, so sow in patches at least 2ft across. Sow roughly circular areas as a fool-proof guide, although interweaving shapes can create some dramatic effects, with different plants merging as they grow into each other. Take a tip from the traditions of the past and mark out the sown areas with sand, just so you know what is where, and label each patch, or mark the varieties clearly on a sketch plan if you have one. Using just hardy annuals means there is no need for heating early in the season, and no crisis when growing space runs short. Many hardy annuals can also be sown in the fall, usually September, to grow through the winter and then give a early performance the following spring.

CARE-FREE HARDY ANNUALS

What could be better than a plant you only buy once, but will then always have many of? It sounds too good to be true but that is just what you get with a great many hardy annuals—the self-seeders that arrive in a packet and then spread to all their favourite spots. We have to thank the origins of many of these plants for their valuable qualities. Agrostemma, the corncockle, for example, was once a common weed of cornfields, and many other care-free annuals like it thrive on the poorest and hungriest of soils. These plants will tell you where they prefer growing by seeding themselves there, and they will need no more attention other than being pulled out when they get too dominant or invasive in areas set aside for more carefully planned activities. Calendula, centaurea, eschscholzia, papaver, and tropaeolum are all good examples of care-free annuals.

BORDER FILLERS

With the sudden loss of a favourite plant your dreams of a "perfect" border can soon evaporate, and this is where annuals can get you out of a tight spot. Any spare patch of ground can be sown, or planted, with annuals, which will grow quickly to fill any gaps. You might even scatter seeds in amongst perennial plants and let them get on with it. Lunaria, honesty, is quite at home growing amongst spring-flowering perennial euphorbias, the purple lunaria flowers making a good contrast with the pale yellow-green euphorbias. For a touch of the tropical, ricinus, the castor oil plant, is unbeatable, with its large, exotic-looking leaves in a range of colors. Sunflowers (helianthus) are always a good bet for some instant color when needed, and the newer dwarf varieties like "Pacino" are easy to grow in pots for planting out as and when their bright flowers are called for to perk up flagging borders.

AGROSTEMMA
Corncockle

SOFT PINK "Milas" is one of the best known of the corncockle varieties. Pink and white varieties are also available.

GROW AGROSTEMMA in bold clumps in borders where the tall lanky, swaying plants help to give each other support.

FEATURES

A very easily grown hardy annual for use in cottage gardens and borders where it self-seeds year after year. Plants are tall, growing 2–3ft tall, and carry pink, purple, or white trumpet-like blooms. The seeds are poisonous. Commonly known as corncockle.

CONDITIONS

Aspect   Grow in full sun.

AGROSTEMMA AT A GLANCE

A tall hardy annual grown for its pink, purple, or white flowers which are ideal for cottage borders. Frost hardy to 5°F (zone 7).

JAN	/	
FEB	/	
MAR	sow	
APR	thin out	
MAY	flowering	
JUN	flowering	
JULY	flowering	
AUG	flowering	
SEPT	flowering	
OCT	sow	
NOV	/	
DEC	/	

RECOMMENDED VARIETIES

Agrostemma githago:
  "Milas"
  "Ocean Pearl"
  "Purple Queen"
  "Rose of Heaven"

Site   Succeeds on well-drained and even light, sandy soils that are quite "hungry" (it used to grow as a weed in cornfields). Excessive feeding may actually reduce the number of flowers.

GROWING METHOD

Sowing   Sow outdoors from March onwards when the soil is warming up, in patches or drills ½in deep where you want the plants to flower. Thin seedlings so they are eventually 6–12in apart. Do not transplant. Can also be sown in pots in the fall, overwintered in a sheltered spot then potted up in spring for flowers in early summer.

Feeding   Extra feeding is unnecessary, but water occasionally but thoroughly in dry spells.

Problems   Agrostemma is a floppy plant and twiggy supports can be useful.

FLOWERING

Season   Summer onwards, but earlier flowers are produced by sowing in the fall.

Cutting   Short-lived as a cut flower, and rather floppy.

AFTER FLOWERING

General   Dead-heading throughout summer will keep flowers coming but always leave a few to ripen and set seeds. Plants will self-sow and germinate the following spring. Alternatively, collect seedheads in paper bags and store.

ALCEA

Hollyhock

FLOWERS OF ALCEA come in a wide range of colors and are carried along the entire length of the tall leafy stems.

THE TALL STEMS of hollyhocks tend to lean over as they mature, so support them at the base with short lengths of bamboo cane.

FEATURES

Alcea is also known as althaea, and is the familiar "hollyhock" found in cottage borders. Flowers are single or double in a range of colors, and carried on stems which can be up to 8ft tall depending on variety. Tall varieties are best at the back of borders. Alcea is grown as an annual sown in spring, or as a biennial sown in summer. Spring-sown plants suffer less with rust disease. Fully hardy.

CONDITIONS

Aspect Needs full sun.
Site   Plants can often be found growing in cracks between paving slabs and in walls but the tallest spikes are produced by adding generous amounts of rotted manure or compost to the soil before planting. Soil must have good drainage. In windy spots stake tall varieties.

ALCEA AT A GLANCE

A hardy biennial grown as an annual or biennial for its tall spikes of flowers suited to cottage gardens. Frost hardy to 5°F (zone 7).

JAN	/	RECOMMENDED VARIETIES
FEB	sow	*Alcea rosea:*
MAR	grow on	**Single flowered**
APR	sow outdoors	"Nigra"
MAY	plant	"Single Mixed"
JUN	flowers/sow	**Double flowered**
JULY	flowering	"Chater's Double Mixed"
AUG	flowering	"Majorette Mixed"
SEPT	flowers/plant	"Peaches 'n' Dreams"
OCT	/	"Powder Puffs Mixed"
NOV	/	"Summer Carnival
DEC	/	Mixed"

GROWING METHOD

Sowing   To grow as an annual sow seed in 3½in pots of multipurpose compost in February. Just cover the seeds and keep at 68°F. Seedlings appear in about two weeks and can be transplanted to individual 3½in pots of compost. Grow on and plant in May after hardening off. Seeds can also be sown outdoors in April. To grow as biennials, sow seed in midsummer but germinate outdoors in a shaded spot. Plant in September.

Feeding   A monthly liquid feed encourages growth.
Problems Rust disease spoils the look of and weakens growth and is worse in wet summers. Control is difficult but for a few plants pick off leaves and try a spray containing mancozeb.

FLOWERING

Season   Early spring-sown plants grow rapidly and flower from early summer. Those planted in fall will overwinter in the ground and flower in early summer the following season.
Cutting Striking as cut flowers—take them when there are plenty of flowerbuds still to open.

AFTER FLOWERING

General Leave a few spikes to set self-sown seeds, but remove dead plants to reduce rust problems.

ARCTOTIS
African daisy

AFRICAN DAISIES should be pinched out when they are 5in tall to encourage branching and masses of summer flowers.

WHEN PLANTED in groups of 3–6 plants, arctotis will form spreading clumps in sunny, south-facing borders and on banks.

FEATURES

African daisy is a perennial grown as a half-hardy annual for its flowers in shades of pink, red, yellow, gold, white, and even blue, often with darker centre. Plants reach 18in in height and have attractive silvery leaves. Use in bedding or as a container plant. Flowers are good for cutting.

CONDITIONS

Aspect   Must have full sun all day long for the flowers to stay open and give the best display, so

ARCTOTIS AT A GLANCE

A half-hardy annual grown for its flowers, used in bedding, containers and as a cut flower. Frost hardy to 32°F (zone 10) .

JAN	/	
FEB	sow	**RECOMMENDED VARIETIES**
MAR	sow	*Arctotis hybrida:*
APR	transplant	"Harlequin"
MAY	transplant	"Special Hybrids Mixed"
JUN	flowering	"Treasure Chest"
JULY	flowering	"T&M Hybrids"
AUG	flowering	
SEPT	flowering	*Arctotis hirsuta*
OCT	/	
NOV	/	*Arctotis venusta*
DEC	/	

Site   choose a south-facing border, patio or bank. Soil must be well-drained but moisture-retentive, so work in rotted compost before planting. In containers use multipurpose compost and ensure drainage by adding a 2in layer of gravel or polystyrene chunks.

GROWING METHOD

Sowing   Sow in February/March in small pots of multipurpose compost, just covering the seed, and keep at 64°F. Seedlings appear in 2–3 weeks and are transplanted individually into 3½in pots. Grow on, harden off at the end of May before planting after frosts, spacing plants 12–18in apart.

Feeding   Extra feeding is rarely necessary but container-grown plants benefit from liquid feed every two weeks. Avoid getting the compost too wet, especially in cooler, wet spells.

Problems   Grows poorly on heavy, badly drained soils. Plants in containers must receive full sun.

FLOWERING

Season   Flowers from early summer onwards.
Cutting   A useful but short-lived cut flower.

AFTER FLOWERING

General   Pot up before frosts and keep dry and frost-free over winter. Take and root cuttings in spring.

BEGONIA
Begonia

FOR BEDDING DISPLAYS *in partial shade few plants can equal the mixed varieties of* Begonia semperflorens, *seen here.*

IN CONTAINERS *begonias give a show from early summer, and you can choose dark-leaved types for specific color schemes.*

FEATURES

Excellent for bedding and containers, begonias have fleshy green or bronze leaves and flowers in many colors, and are grown as half-hardy annuals. "Fibrous" rooted varieties of *Begonia semperflorens* grow up to 8in, have many small flowers and do well in shaded spots. "Tuberous" rooted types reach 10in tall with fewer but larger flowers up to 4in across. Trailing varieties are also available for hanging baskets, reaching 1–2ft. Flowers are in mixed or single colors. A wide range of all types are available as young plants.

CONDITIONS

Aspect   Will succeed best in partial shade with at least

BEGONIA AT A GLANCE

A half-hardy annual grown for its flowers and green/bronze foliage, useful for bedding/containers. Frost hardy to 32°F (zone 10).

JAN	sow	
FEB	sow	
MAR	transplant	
APR	grow on	
MAY	harden off	
JUN	flowering	
JULY	flowering	
AUG	flowering	
SEPT	flowering	
OCT	/	
NOV	/	
DEC	/	

RECOMMENDED VARIETIES

Begonia semperflorens:
  "Ambassador Mixed"
  "Cocktail Mixed"
  "Pink Sundae"
Tuberous varieties
  "Non-Stop Mixed"
  "Non-Stop Appleblossom"
  "Pin-Up"
Trailing varieties
  "Illumination Mixed"
  "Show Angels Mixed"

Site   some protection from direct hot sun.
Soil should be very well prepared with plenty of rotted manure or compost mixed in. Begonias produce masses of fine feeding roots. Plants do not like very heavy clay soils that stay wet for long periods, so grow in containers if necessary, using multipurpose compost when potting up in spring.

GROWING METHOD

Sowing   Sow January/February. Seed is as fine as dust, so mix with a little dry silver sand and sow on the surface of 3½in pots of seed compost based on peat or coir. Stand the pot in tepid water until the compost looks moist. Keep at 70°F in a heated propagator in a light spot, and carefully transplant seedlings to cell trays when they have produced several tiny leaves. Seed raising is a challenge so consider growing from young plants. Plant outdoors after the last frosts in early June, 6–8in apart depending on variety.

Feeding   Water regularly in dry spells and liquid feed bedding displays every 2–3 weeks, or mix slow-release fertilizer with compost first.

Problems   Overwatering causes root rot and death. Remove faded flowers, especially in wet spells.

FLOWERING

Season   Flowers from early summer until frost.
Cutting   Not suitable as a cut flower.

AFTER FLOWERING

General   Varieties that form round tubers can be potted up in the fall, dried off and then grown again the following spring.

CALCEOLARIA
Slipper flower

THE HOT COLORS OF THE "SUNSET" strain of calceolaria excel outdoors and combine well with marigolds.

FEATURES

Only a few varieties of calceolaria are suitable for outdoors; these are different to the indoor pot type. By nature shrubs, they are grown from seed each year as hardy annuals and are useful for bedding and containers. None grow more than 16in tall and wide.

CONDITIONS

Aspect   Needs full sun or part shade.

CALCEOLARIA AT A GLANCE	
A half-hardy annual, calceolaria is used for bedding and containers, with bright flowers. Frost hardy to 32°F (zone 10).	
JAN	sow	RECOMMENDED VARIETIES
FEB	sow	**Calceolaria hybrids:**
MAR	transplant	"Little Sweeties Mixed"
APR	grow on	"Midas"
MAY	harden off	"Sunshine"
JUN	flowering	"Sunset Mixed"
JULY	flowering	
AUG	flowering	
SEPT	flowering	
OCT	/	
NOV	/	
DEC	/	

Site   Slipper flowers thrive in moist soil where their roots stay as cool as possible. Mix in well-rotted compost or manure before planting and use a peat- or coir-based multipurpose compost for filling containers.

GROWING METHOD

Sowing   The fine seed can be sown on the surface of peat- or coir-based multipurpose compost in a 3½in pot, January–March, at a temperature of 64°F. Keep in a bright place. Seedlings appear in 2–3 weeks and can be transplanted to cell trays, then hardened off and planted after frosts, 6–12in apart, or used with other plants in containers.

Feeding   Liquid feed every 3–4 weeks or mix slow-release fertiliser with compost before planting.

Problems   Slugs will eat the leaves of young plants in wet spells during early summer. Protect plants with a barrier of grit or eggshell or scatter slug pellets sparingly around plants.

FLOWERING

Season   Plants will flower from early summer until frosts. Take off dead flowers weekly.

Cutting   A few stems can be taken but avoid damaging the overall shape and appearance of the plant.

AFTER FLOWERING

General   Remove plants in fall when finished.

CELOSIA
Prince of Wales' feathers

THE FEATHERY FLOWERS of celosia are made up of masses of smaller flowers, and have a distinctive, plume-like shape.

THE BRILLIANT PLUMES of cockscomb always look best in patio pots and containers when planted together in groups of 4–6 plants.

FEATURES

Also known as Prince of Wales' feathers, celosia, or cockscomb has plume-like or crested flowers (shown left) ranging in colour from deep crimson to scarlet, orange, and yellow. Tall forms grow to 30in, the dwarf forms to 10–12in. Grow it as a half-hardy annual and use in bedding or as a striking plant for containers. Good for cutting.

CONDITIONS

Aspect Must have a sunny, warm spot to do well.

CELOSIA AT A GLANCE

A half-hardy annual grown for its feathery, plume-like flower-heads in a range of colors. Frost hardy to 32°F (zone 10).

JAN	/	**RECOMMENDED VARIETIES**
FEB	sow	**Plumed**
MAR	sow	*Celosia argentea:*
APR	pot on	"Kimono Mixed"
MAY	harden off/plant	"Dwarf Geisha"
JUN	flowering	"Century Mixed"
JULY	flowering	"New Look"
AUG	flowering	*Celosia spicata:*
SEPT	flowering	"Flamingo Feather"
OCT	/	**Crested**
NOV	/	*Celosia cristata:*
DEC	/	"Jewel Box Mixed"

Site Needs well-drained soil that has been enriched with well-rotted manure or compost. Good soil preparation is essential to ensure strong plants and large flowerheads. Plant up containers using multipurpose compost

GROWING METHOD

Sowing Celosias dislike having their roots disturbed so sow 2–3 seeds per cell in a multi-cell tray using multipurpose compost, in February/March. Keep at 64°F and when the seedlings appear after 2–3 weeks, remove all but the strongest. Carefully pot the young plants on into 3½in pots, then harden off for two weeks before planting after the last frosts. Plant without damaging the roots, 6–12in apart, and water.

Feeding Feed bedding monthly with liquid feed. Mix slow-release fertilizer with the compost before planting up containers.

Problems Wet, cold soil/compost can cause rotting of the roots, so avoid heavy soils and grow in pots.

FLOWERING

Season Flowers appear throughout summer.

Cutting May be used as a cut flower for unusual indoor decoration. Cut some plumes and hang them upside down in a dry, airy place for later use in dried flower arrangements.

AFTER FLOWERING

General Remove plants after the first frosts of fall.

DELPHINIUM
Annual delphinium

"PACIFIC GIANTS MIXED" is a popular variety of delphinium and comes in a range of colors as well as the blue seen here.

ANNUAL DELPHINIUMS can be used as "gap fillers" in mixed borders, and can be left to grow as a permanent feature if required.

FEATURES

Certain varieties of delphinium can be grown from seed and treated as half-hardy annuals, even though they are by nature perennials. The flower spikes of up to 5ft are perfect for giving height to summer bedding schemes and are attractive for cutting. Favorite plants can be moved to a permanent position in the fall. Seeds and plants are poisonous.

CONDITIONS

Aspect   Best in full sun.

DELPHINIUM AT A GLANCE

A perennial treated as a half-hardy annual and grown for its tall spikes of flowers in summer. Frost hardy to 5°F. (zone 7)

JAN	/	
FEB	/	
MAR	sow	
APR	transplant	
MAY	grow/plant	
JUN	flowering	
JULY	flowering	
AUG	flowering	
SEPT	flowering	
OCT	/	
NOV	/	
DEC	/	

RECOMMENDED VARIETIES

Delphinium hybrids:
  "Connecticut Yankees"
  "Dreaming Spires"
  "Dwarf Pacific Mixed"
  "Dwarf Magic Fountains Mixed"
  "Pacific Giants Mixed"

Delphinium grandiflorum:
  "Blue Butterfly"
  "Sky Blue"

Site   Delphiniums need shelter from strong winds, and well-drained, moist soil enriched with rotted organic matter before planting. Plants may need support with twiggy sticks or short canes when growing strongly.

GROWING METHOD

Sowing   Sow in pots of multipurpose compost in March at 60°F, just covering the seeds. Move seedlings into cell trays and grow on in a cold frame or sheltered spot outdoors before planting in May where you want flowers, which appear from midsummer onwards.

Feeding   Keep well-watered after planting and liquid feed every 2–3 weeks using a hand-held feeder.

Problems   Slugs can decimate young plants in spring so scatter slug pellets or protect with a 2in wide band of sharp grit.

FLOWERING

Season   Flowers appear from midsummer onwards.
Cutting   For best results cut when the lowest flowers on the spike are fully open and the top buds are starting to show color.

AFTER FLOWERING

General   If you want to keep certain plants, cut off the foliage as it browns, label them clearly, and then lift and replant when they are fully dormant in the late fall or very early the following spring.

DIGITALIS
Foxglove

FOXGLOVES *are perfect for cottage-style borders and make good companions for the red poppies and white lavatera.*

WHITE FOXGLOVES *are useful for a specific color scheme—this is a white-flowered plant of the "Excelsior Hybrids".*

FEATURES

Varieties of *Digitalis purpurea* grow up to 6ft tall with spikes of tubular pink, white, magenta, cream, or purple flowers, each with a spotted lip. Plant in groups in borders or in a partly-shaded spot under trees. All parts of the plant are poisonous, including the seeds. Grow as a hardy biennial, although the variety "Foxy" can be treated as an annual and sown in spring.

CONDITIONS

Aspect Succeeds in part or dappled shade, or in sun.

DIGITALIS AT A GLANCE

A hardy biennial grown for tall spikes of flowers appearing in early summer. Useful for shade. Frost hardy to 5°F. (zone 7)

		RECOMMENDED VARIETIES
JAN	/	
FEB	/	*Digitalis purpurea:*
MAR	/	"Alba"
APR	sow	"Excelsior Hybrids"
MAY	sow/transplant	"Foxy Mixed"
JUN	sow/flowers	"Giant Spotted Mixed"
JULY	flowering	"Glittering Prizes Mixed"
AUG	grow	"Selected Mixed"
SEPT	grow	"Suttons Apricot"
OCT	plant	
NOV	/	
DEC	/	

Site Soil needs to be free-draining and enriched with organic matter well ahead of planting—use rotted compost or manure in generous amounts. Staking is necessary when plants are grown in a position exposed to winds.

GROWING METHOD

Sowing Sow the very small seed in a 3½in pot and barely cover, from April–June. Keep outside in a coldframe or sheltered spot, and transplant seedlings individually to 3½in pots. Grow on through the summer, potting on into 5in pots when roots fill the smaller pots. Plant out in October where you want the plants to flower. The variety "Foxy" can be sown in February in warmth and planted in May for flowers the same summer. Treat as a half-hardy annual.

Feeding Feed fortnightly with liquid feed while plants are in pots and do not allow to dry out. Water in spring during dry spells as growth begins.

Problems No special problems affect foxgloves.

FLOWERING

Season Flowers appear in early summer.

Cutting Not particularly good as a cut flower.

AFTER FLOWERING

General Once stems have flowered, cut them off just above the leaves and plants may then produce several shorter flowering stems. Leave a few spikes to set seed pods which will self-seed.

HELIANTHUS
Sunflower

SUNFLOWERS *have a central "disc" which eventually becomes the fat seedhead in fall and makes useful food for the birds.*

"PACINO" is a modern variety of Helianthus annuus, *small enough to be used in patio pots, growing to only 18in tall.*

FEATURES

Sunflowers range in height from 18in up to 15ft depending on the variety grown. They can be used in bedding, in patio containers, as cut flowers, or can be grown as traditional "giants" to several feet tall. Plants produce single or multi-flowered heads and the color range is enormous. "Teddy Bear" has furry, double flowers. Annual sunflowers are fully hardy and flower from mid-summer onwards. Certain varieties such as "Prado Sun & Fire" have been bred to be pollen-free and these are ideal for use as indoor cut flowers. Seedheads left in the yard in the fall provide food for birds.

CONDITIONS

Aspect Must have an open position in full sun.

HELIANTHUS AT A GLANCE

A hardy annual grown for its large flowers on both dwarf and tall plants; some are ideal for cutting. Frost hardy to 5°F. (zone 7)

JAN	/	
FEB	/	
MAR	sow	
APR	thin out	
MAY	support	
JUN	flowering	
JULY	flowering	
AUG	flowering	
SEPT	flowering	
OCT	/	
NOV	/	
DEC	/	

RECOMMENDED VARIETIES

Helianthus annuus:
Tall varieties
 "Italian White"
 "Pastiche"
 "Velvet Queen"
For containers
 "Big Smile"
 "Pacino"
Double flowers
 "Orange Sun"
 "Sungold Double"
 "Teddy Bear"

Site Tolerates most soil conditions but soil enriched with plenty of manure or compost makes growth both rapid and vigorous, producing the largest flowerheads. Plants grown in groups in borders tend to support each other, but in exposed spots tie tall varieties to a cane. Use multipurpose compost mixed with slow-release fertilizer for planting up patio containers and windowboxes.

GROWING METHOD

Sowing Seeds are large and easy to handle—sow three seeds outdoors where plants are to grow in March, removing all but the strongest when 6in tall. Can also be sown three seeds to a 3½in pot of compost and treated in the same way. Pot-grown plants can be kept outdoors and planted when the roots fill the pot. Spacing depends on the variety grown.

Feeding Extra feeding is not usually needed but keep plants well watered in long dry spells.

Problems Slugs and snails can attack young plants cutting them off at ground level, so protect with slug pellets or a barrier of sharp grit.

FLOWERING

Season Throughout summer and early fall.

Cutting A very good cut flower but use a heavy vase or add some weight to the bottom of it to prevent it toppling over. Pollen-free varieties should be grown if allergies are a known problem.

AFTER FLOWERING

General Leave the seedheads as bird food during fall and winter, and then dig out the extensive roots. Sunflower roots can help break-up and loosen heavy, compacted soils.

HELICHRYSUM
Strawflower

FOR DRYING cut helichrysum before the flowers reach this stage, while the petals are still curved inwards (bottom right).

PAPER DAISIES ARE APT to be rather leggy, but the range of flower colors can be stunning, as shown here.

FEATURES

Varieties of strawflower come from *Helichrysum bracteatum*, with plants growing 6–24in tall. They are among the easiest annuals to grow for dried flowers, with double blooms in many colors, and petals that feel straw-like. Dwarf varieties make long-lasting container plants. A half-hardy annual.

CONDITIONS

Aspect   Must have a warm spot in full sun.

HELICHRYSUM AT A GLANCE

A half-hardy annual grown for its long-lasting dried flowers, and also used in bedding and containers. Frost hardy to 32°F (zone10).

JAN	/	**RECOMMENDED VARIETIES**
FEB	/	
MAR	sow	*Helichrysum bracteatum:*
APR	transplant/grow	**Tall varieties**
MAY	harden off/plant	"Drakkar Pastel Mixed"
JUN	flowering	"Monstrosum Double Mixed"
JULY	flowering	"Pastel Mixed"
AUG	flowering	"Swiss Giants"
SEPT	flowers/cutting	**Dwarf varieties**
OCT	flowers/cutting	"Bright Bikini"
NOV	/	"Chico Mixed"
DEC	/	"Hot Bikini"

Site   Needs very well-drained soil that has been enriched with rotted compost or manure. If growing in containers use multipurpose compost and add slow-release fertilizer. Tall varieties will need staking as they develop.

GROWING METHOD

Sowing   Sow seeds in March in 3½in pots of multipurpose compost and germinate at 64°F. Transplant seedlings to cell trays when large enough and grow on, then harden off at the end of May, and plant 6–24in apart depending on the variety. Seed can also be sown direct into short drills in the soil during May and the young plants gradually thinned to the planting distances above. In containers pack 2–3 plants together in groups to get a good block of flower color.

Feeding   Helichrysum grows well without extra feeding, but water container-grown plants regularly.

Problems By late summer the leaves are often attacked by mildew, but it is not worth treating.

FLOWERING

Season   Flowers appear from early to midsummer.

Cutting   Pick the flowers when the petals are still incurved. Hang the bunches upside down in a dry, airy place to dry out. Long-lasting.

AFTER FLOWERING

General   Cut what you want and then pull up.

VIOLA CORNUTA
Viola

DIMINUITIVE *"Bambini" violas are guaranteed to steal your heart with their inquisitive whiskery faces.*

FOR A TOUCH OF DRAMA *try combining the moody "Blackjack" with a clear yellow variety in a hanging basket.*

FEATURES

Violas are smaller than pansies but they are no less prolific, and what they lack in size they make up for in sheer character. Most are varieties of *Viola cornuta*, and all are quite hardy, being sown in spring or summer. Grow single colors, mixtures like "Bambini", or trailing yellow "Sunbeam" for hanging baskets. Violas grow to around 6in, making bushy little plants for bedding or containers. Try planting them in cottage style wicker baskets. Available as young plants.

VIOLA AT A GLANCE

A hardy annual grown for its pretty little pansy flowers which appear on branching plants. Frost hardy to 5°F. (zone 7)

Month	Activity			RECOMMENDED VARIETIES
JAN	/			**Viola hybrids:**
FEB	sow			"Bambini Mixed"
MAR	sow			"Blackjack"
APR	sow/flower			"Blue Moon"
MAY	sow/flower			"Cuty"
JUN	sow/flower			"Juliette Mixed"
JULY	sow/flower			"Midnight Runner"
AUG	grow on/flowers			"Princess Mixed"
SEPT	grow on/flowers			"Sorbet Yesterday, Today & Tomorrow"
OCT	plant			"Sunbeam"
NOV	/			
DEC	/			

CONDITIONS

Aspect — Grows well in sun or dappled, light shade.
Site — Soil does not need to be over prepared, but must be well-drained. For container growing use multipurpose compost.

GROWING METHOD

Sowing — Sow from February under cover for flowers the same summer, or outside May–July for flowers the following spring. Either way, sow in a 3½in pot of multipurpose compost and barely cover seeds. In early spring keep at 60°F and transplant seedlings when large enough to cell trays, grow, harden off, and plant in late May. When summer sowing, stand the pot outside in shade to germinate then treat seedlings the same, planting out in October where you want the plants to flower.

Feeding — Extra feeding is not usually necessary.
Problems — Use slug pellets if the leaves are attacked.

FLOWERING

Season — Spring-sown plants flower during summer, summer-sown the following spring/summer.
Cutting — The delicate cut stems of "Queen Charlotte" are sometimes used for making scented posies.

AFTER FLOWERING

General — Plants often carry on as short-lived perennials, and also self-seed freely.

VIOLA TRICOLOR
Wild pansy

EACH FLOWER of wild pansy is like a tiny whiskered "face" and individual plants all vary from each other very slightly.

ONE PLANT left in the ground to mature through the summer will shed hundreds of seeds which will germinate the next spring.

FEATURES

Viola tricolor is the wild pansy, also known commonly as heartsease or Johnny-jump-up. It is usually grown as a hardy annual but can also be treated as a biennial. Much daintier than its relatives the pansies, these plants are at home in cottage-style beds and as pot edging. A few single colored varieties are available, such as the unusual "Bowles' Black", having black flowers with a small central yellow "eye".

VIOLA AT A GLANCE

A hardy annual grown for its pretty little pansy flowers which appear on branching plants. Frost hardy to 5°F. (zone 7)

Jan	/	
Feb	sow 🌱	**RECOMMENDED VARIETIES**
Mar	sow 🌱	
Apr	sow/flower 🌱🌸	*Viola tricolor*
May	sow/flower 🌱🌸	**Single colors:**
Jun	sow/flower 🌱🌸	Blue
July	sow/flower 🌱🌸	"Prince Henry"
Aug	grow on/flowers 🌸	Yellow
Sept	grow on/flowers 🌸	"Prince John"
Oct	plant 🌱	
Nov	/	
Dec	/	

CONDITIONS

Aspect Grows well in sun or dappled, light shade.
Site Soil does not need to be over prepared, but must be well-drained. Multipurpose compost is best for growing *Viola tricolor* in containers.

GROWING METHOD

Sowing Sow from February under cover for flowers the same summer, or outside May–July for flowers the following spring. Either way, sow in a 3½in pot of multipurpose compost and barely cover seeds. In early spring keep at 60°F and transplant seedlings when large enough to cell trays, grow, harden off, and plant in late May. When summer sowing, stand the pot outside in shade to germinate, treat seedlings the same, and plant in October.

Feeding Extra feeding is not usually necessary.
Problems Use slug pellets if the leaves are attacked.

FLOWERING

Season Spring-sown plants flower during summer, summer-sown the following spring/summer.
Cutting Not suitable for cutting.

AFTER FLOWERING

General Pull plants up and compost, or leave a few to shed seeds. They will sometimes grow as perennials and last for several years.

GROWING PERENNIALS

Many of the loveliest and best-loved flowering plants are perennials. Like annuals, perennials provide a colorful display, but they have the advantage that they don't need to be changed at least twice a year. Perennials are easy-care plants which have a major place in low-maintenance gardens.

Perennials remain alive for a number of years, unlike annuals which usually last only one season, and biennials which grow and flower through a second season or year. Perennials form a variable group in terms of their size and foliage, flower shape, style, and color. In fact, there is a perennial to suit almost every climate, aspect, and soil, and some can even be grown in containers. Perennials can also be planted among shrubs, to form a background for bulbs or annuals, or in their own separate areas. Perennial borders make lively, exciting features.

ABOVE: The white form of the purple coneflower showing its attractive, recurved petals.

LEFT: A tender, bright pink argyranthemum, and scabious, in the foreground add perennial interest to this colorful, mixed border featuring soft hues offset by green.

PERENNIALS COMBINE with annuals to form a free-flowing, rich, colorful border, a highlight of mid-summer in this gorgeous cottage garden. A pink shrub rose is flanked by two varieties of aster, while deep blue delphiniums add scale and height at the back.

EVERGREEN OR HERBACEOUS?

Some perennials are evergreen but many are herbaceous. Most herbaceous perennials grow rapidly during spring and summer to flower during the summer and the fall. After flowering they gradually die back to the crown or fleshy roots, and they remain dormant during cold winters. Since most of the hardy herbaceous perennials come from climates with very severe, cold winters, they die down naturally in the fall. In warmer areas, where they do not become completely dormant and some growth continues year round, the plants do not live as long. However, it is simple to renew these perennials as division is easy, and most increase rapidly. In time, a few can even become invasive.

PLANTING PERENNIALS

Soil preparation

Because perennials are long-term plants and because they are close planted, good soil preparation is essential. Although some perennials, such as astilbes and hostas, enjoy damp soil, many prefer well-drained conditions. If you are planting any of the latter group, check your drainage before planting. Dig some holes in the bed, fill them with water and see how long

PERENNIALS FOR SUN AND SHADE

SUNNY BORDERS

- Agapanthus
- Delphinium
- Diascia
- Eryngium
- Gypsophila
- Helenium

- Hemerocallis
- Miscanthus
- Oenothera
- Papaver
- Sedum
- Stachys

SHADY BORDERS

- *Alchemilla mollis*
- Aquilegia *Columbine*
- Bergenia
- Candelabra primula
- Digitalis
- Epimedium

- *Gunnera manicata*
- Helleborus
- Hosta
- Polygonatum
- Primula
- Pulmonaria
- Rodgersia (dappled)

PURE WHITE shasta daisies light up the summer garden, putting on a strong display from early summer to early fall.

A HIGH STONE WALL marks the boundary of this meadow garden filled with golden fern-leaf yarrow, daisies, and purple loosestrife.

it takes to drain away. If there is still water in the holes 12 hours later, you will need to improve the drainage by installing a system of sub-soil drains.

If the soil is very heavy clay, which remains wet but not waterlogged for a long time, you should dig in some gypsum, about 10.5oz per sq yd. Digging in large quantities of decayed manure or compost a few weeks before planting will also improve clay soils, and it is a must in sandy soils that have poor moisture and nutrient retention.

Thorough weeding of the area is essential, too, as it is difficult to remove weeds in densely planted beds. Remove the weeds you can see, dig or fork over the area again, water, and wait for the next lot of weeds to emerge. You may need to repeat this step if the area has been neglected for any length of time. Hand weeding or spraying with glyphosate should eliminate most weeds, but you will need to be persistent to control oxalis, bindweed and ground elder. This sounds like a lot of work when you are eager to plant out your garden, but it will be worth the wait and the effort in the long run.

Planting perennials from containers

Garden centers and nurseries will stock some perennials, especially when they are in flower. These can be planted in your yard like any other container-grown plant. When the plant is removed from its pot, loosen the rootball a little so that the roots can extend into the surrounding soil. It is essential that the planting hole is about twice the width of the container and approximately the same depth. The soil level around the plant should be exactly the same as it was in the container. Give a thorough soaking after planting. Also apply a deep mulch to the soil around the plant.

Planting bare-rooted perennials

There are also nurseries that specialise in perennials. These nurseries usually advertise in popular gardening magazines, have detailed catalogs with thorough plant descriptions, and sell by mail-order. Plants are delivered during their dormant season, which for the majority is from late fall

THESE GOLDEN-YELLOW, green-tipped spikes of a red hot poker cultivar provide a strong focus in this pastel border.

THE TALL, VERTICAL CLUMP of pink dahlias and the midnight blue spires of delphinium provide a colorful mix. They form a bright imaginative backdrop for the rich mix of annuals and perennials edging this beautiful garden bed, clearly illustrating the versatility of perennials.

through the winter. Plants are mailed, bare-rooted, or in small pots, having been carefully packed and labelled. On arrival, they should be planted at once. However, if the ground is frozen, or you are not ready to plant them, either unpack and water them (if necessary), and store in a bright, cool, frost-free place, or "heel in" as a temporary measure. To do this, dig a trench large enough to contain the plant roots in a sheltered part of your yard. Finally, lay the plants on their sides, cover the roots with soil, and lightly water them.

When planting bare-rooted plants, again make sure the hole is at least twice the width of the rootball, and deep enough to take the roots without kinking them. If some roots are very long, trim them cleanly with pruning shears. Hold the plant in the hole in one hand and fill the hole, poking soil between the roots. Sometimes you can make a slight mound in the centre of the hole so that the roots can be spread out over it, keeping the crown high. Make sure the crown of the plant is not buried: if necessary, lift the plant and push more soil in around the roots.

Water thoroughly immediately after planting if the soil is dry, but until the plants have developed plenty of shoot growth they will not require too much watering. The area around the plants should be mulched. If the soil has been well prepared, feeding at this time is not necessary but you may give a very light sprinkling of general fertilizer if you wish.

CARE OF PERENNIALS

Perennial plantings in areas that have been well prepared need little maintenance. You must deadhead through the flowering season to prolong blooming, and cut back or tidy up after flowering. Established perennials will only need watering in prolonged dry spells, and feeding in spring as growth commences. When they become too crowded they are divided between fall and late winter, or early spring. This may be only necessary every three or four years. For details, see plant entries in the A–Z section.

Watering

Never give perennials a light watering because it will encourage surface rooting at the expense of a deep, root system. The plants need big, strong roots to sustain several years of growth, and benefit most from being given a deep, regular watering. On sandy soils choose such perennials as sedum, oenothera, and dianthus that tolerate dry conditions. A deep mulch around the plants will help conserve moisture, as will adding quantities of organic matter to the soil as the mulch breaks down.

Feeding

Perennials should not need a lot of feeding. Apply an all-purpose plant food as growth begins; if the soil has been well prepared this should be enough for the whole growing season. If your soil is very poor though, you may like to use a slow-release granular fertilizer to feed plants through the growing season, or to apply a second helping of plant food as the flower buds start to appear. A mulch of decayed manure or compost around the plants serves two functions. It improves the soil condition, and also supplies small amounts of nutrients to the plants.

Keep the entire area free of weeds until the plants cover the ground. This will ensure that any fertilizer you apply will feed your perennials and not any unwanted weeds. Avoid high nitrogen fertilizers as they tend to promote leaf growth at the expense of flowers. Rose food is ideal.

THE PENSTEMONS AND SALVIAS in the foreground make a gorgeous foil for the stiff, upright growth of Russell lupins.

Cutting flowers and deadheading

A number of perennials make very good cut flowers, and many are grown for the cut flower trade. The various daisies, chrysanthemums, Russell lupins, delphiniums, pinks, and Peruvian lilies are just a few of the perennials that are commercially grown. Regularly picking the flowers will help to ensure a long succession of bloom. If the flowers are not removed they will mature, most setting seed so that the flowering cycle will finish abruptly as the plant decides its reproductive work is over. If you do not want to take cut flowers, remember to deadhead regularly.

Exceptions to this rule are plants such as cardoon and globe thistle that have decorative seedheads. Some gardeners prefer to leave them on the plant. Many remain attractive even when dry, and they can add interest to the garden in late fall and winter, especially when covered in frost or snow.

AFTER FLOWERING

After the flowering season is over, perennials can be cut back almost to the ground. If you live in an area prone to heavy frosts, some of the more tender perennials will then need to have the crown of the plant covered. A thick layer of straw, or fall leaves, held in place by a few sticks in windy sites, will protect them from winter damage.

Alternatively, you could leave some stems sticking out of the ground to create extra, interesting shapes over winter. Grasses are especially invaluable. They are at their best when covered with frost or snow, or when helping to cast a web of shadows from the low winter sun. The birds also benefit from the seedheads.

THE BRIGHT, HOT COLORS of orange and yellow feature in this very effective planting, which shows up so impressively against the cool green of the lawn. The large clump of red hot pokers and a generous drift of deep apricot-orange geum are especially notable.

INCREASING YOUR STOCK OF PERENNIALS

Division

Clumps of perennials are divided either when they become congested, or when you want to plant sections elsewhere in the garden. In general, most perennials need dividing about every three or four years, possibly longer. Division is done after flowering or while the plants are dormant.

If you want some pieces to plant elsewhere you can sever a section with a knife, or put a spade through the clump, and lift away what you want. This might lose some of the peripheral pieces but the process is quick and simple. Otherwise, dig up the whole clump, shake off the excess soil, and pull the clump apart or cut it into sections. Replant the sections immediately, trimming off very long roots. Remember that the outer growths are the youngest to be saved, and that the centre of the plant may have died, in which case it can be discarded. You may need to divide very large, heavy clumps by pushing two garden forks, back to back, into the centre to prise it apart. A sharp spade may also be used but this needs a lot of force and will, of course, result in the loss of some sections of plant. This may not be of any consequence with vigorous perennials.

If you are unable to replant at once or have pieces to give away, wrap them in damp newspaper or hessian and keep in a shaded, sheltered spot, giving time to decide where to plant them. "Heeling in", as described on the previous page, is another way to store plants temporarily, and they are less likely to dry out. They can, of course, be potted up in a good quality potting mix.

Taking cuttings

Many perennial plants can be grown from cuttings and a number, including geraniums and diascias, are among the easiest plants to strike. Others that will grow readily from cuttings include penstemons and sedums,

Make a mix of two or three parts of coarse sand and one of peat, or peat substitute compost. Put the prepared mix in clean pots, preferably no larger than 4in across. A pot of this size will take a good number of cuttings. They should not be forced to sit in soil that remains wet when watered, which would rot the roots.

Take tip cuttings of unflowered shoots, no more than 2–4in long. Cut, do not tear, pieces from the parent plant. Take the cuttings early in the morning, placing the pieces in a clean plastic bag, and quickly put in a cool, shady place. Trim the cuttings by removing the lower leaves, allowing just a very few to remain on top. Cleanly cut the base of the cutting below a node (leaf junction). Another aid to rooting is to "wound" the cutting by carefully scraping about ³/₈in of the outer bark or stem cover at the base of the stem. Hormone rooting powders can also be used but are not usually necessary with most perennials.

Use a clean stick or pencil to make a hole in the compost. Put the cutting in the hole and carefully firm the surrounding mix. Once all your cuttings are in the pot you can water them thoroughly and put the pot in a warm, sheltered place out of direct sun. In warm months geraniums and daisies may be well rooted after three weeks, but many plants can take a considerable time. Check regularly to see if the cuttings need water but do not keep them wet or, as explained they will rot.

DIVIDING A CLUMP

Step 1: Use a garden fork to lift the whole perennial clump from the soil.

Step 2: Separate matted clumps by inserting two garden forks, back to back, firmly into the clump.

Step 3: First press the fork handles together, and then force them apart to split the clump in two. Repeat until the clumps are the size you want.

Step 4: Use pruning shears to cut off dead, rotten or damaged roots. The clumps are now ready for replanting.

STRIKING A CUTTING

Step 1: Take a cutting just below a leaf node or joint. Use a sharp knife or pruning shears so that the cutting is not bruised. Trim it if necessary.

Step 2: Make a hole in the compost with your finger and insert the cutting into it. Firm the soil gently around it. If you are placing more than one cutting in the pot, plant them around the edge, giving them plenty of space.

Step 3: Water the cuttings in well, but take care not to dislodge them. Make sure the water is draining away well as the cuttings will rot if the soil remains wet.

Step 4: To make a humid atmosphere and keep the soil and cuttings moist, make a frame of sticks or wire tall enough to cover the cuttings. Place a polythene bag over the frame, and stand the pot out of direct sunlight.

A ROMANTIC GARDEN PATH is bordered by old-fashioned favorites, including perennial daisies and scented pinks.

Taking root cuttings

A number of plants, including perennials such as sea <u>lavender</u>, romneya, and <u>perennial phlox,</u> can be grown from <u>root cuttings.</u> As the plant will be disturbed when the cuttings are taken, this task is best done in <u>winter</u>.
- Remove the soil from around the base of the plant until you reach the roots. Trace them back until they are $\frac{1}{8}-\frac{3}{16}$in thick, and cut off some cleanly with a sharp knife or pruning shears. Immediately place them in a plastic bag so they do not dry out.
- Wash the soil from the roots and cut them into 1–2in lengths. If you intend to plant them vertically you will need to know which way is up; cut all the tops straight across and the bottoms at an angle.
- Place the cuttings vertically in a container, or lay them in horizontally and cover with about $\frac{3}{16}$in of John Innes No.1. Water thoroughly and check regularly to see whether further watering is needed.
- Once good shoots have appeared, your new plants can be potted up individually into small pots or planted into the ground. It is important to keep the cuttings moist, but if you saturate the compost the roots will rot.

WHAT CAN GO WRONG?

Perennials can be attacked by a number of insect pests and diseases, and problems that occur on specific plants will be discussed in the individual plant entries. Slugs and snails are among the worst pests for herbaceous perennials since they can destroy newly emerging growth as it appears in spring. If each successive burst of leaves is destroyed, the plant will eventually give up. You must search for and destroy these pests, perhaps picking them off by hand, or using bait or beer traps.

Overwatering or poorly drained heavy soils can also damage or kill perennials, especially if they are too wet during their dormant period when there is no foliage to transpire moisture from the plant. Waterlogged soils also provide ideal conditions for the growth and spread of various soil-borne, root-rotting fungi. A few plants, such as astilbe and hosta, actually enjoy damp or boggy ground, but most enjoy conditions with good drainage.

Yellow leaves
- Plants may have been overwatered or they may be too dry. You are actually more likely to overwater a perennial in a pot than in a border. They may also need feeding if this has not been done for some time. Try a light application of fertilizer; in warm weather there should be an improvement within two to three weeks. Towards the end of the growing season you can expect to see some leaves yellowing as they finish their useful life. Do not worry if a few leaves, especially down towards the ground, become brown or yellow during the active spring period.

Curled or distorted leaves
- Keep a regular check against aphids. They can be a terrible problem. They are small, sap-sucking insects that may be black, brown, green, or clear. They cluster thickly on the new growth of plants, sucking out the sap. This may cause curling or distortion of leaves, and flowers may fail to open if the sap has been sucked from the buds or they, too,

A HEALTHY display of violets.

may be distorted. Close inspection usually reveals these tiny insects; they can be squashed and wiped off the stems, hosed off or sprayed with insecticidal soap or pyrethrum-based sprays. Aphids need to be controlled as they also transmit virus diseases from plant to plant.

Silvery mottling on foliage
- Silver markings or discoloration of foliage may be the first sign of thrip attack. These tiny insects attack plant tissue and suck the sap. Unlike most sap-sucking insects they attack the top, not the under leaf. There are several different types that cause plant damage. They are readily recognizable, usually having black bodies and wings edged with hairs. Apart from the physical damage, some thrips are also responsible for transmitting virus diseases from plant to plant. Since many thrips use weeds as hosts it is important to keep them out of your beds and borders. If thrips are causing damage, make sure that the plants are not stressed through lack of water. When spraying, use an appropriate contact or systemic insecticide.

Curled and browned flowers
- Check plants for thrips because they can attack pale-colored flowers. For their control, see "Silvery mottling on foliage".

TAKING ROOT CUTTINGS

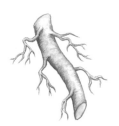

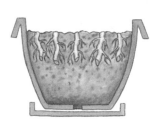

Step 1: To take root cuttings from most perennials, trace the roots back and cut out a section some ⅛–³⁄₁₆ in thick.

Step 2: Wash any soil from the roots and cut them into sections 1-2in long. Mark the top of each so you know which way up to plant them.

Step 3: Place the root cuttings vertically in a container, making sure that they are the right way up. Water them in thoroughly.

Alternatively, if plants have thin roots, take cuttings in the same way but lay them horizontally and cover with a thin layer of compost.

Holes in leaves or on leaf edges

• If your plants have chewed edges or large areas of leaf missing, check for snails. They are the most likely culprits. Pick the snails off and destroy them, or use a bait if you do not have a pet.

• If there is no sign of snails, start looking for caterpillars. Chewing insects such as caterpillars can do a great deal of damage in quite a short time because they can be such voracious feeders. They can be well camouflaged, lying along leaf margins or hiding under leaves. Try first to find and destroy them, but if the damage continues, dust the plants with derris.

Mottled leaves

• Leaf mottling may be the result of mite damage. Mites are not true insects, having eight legs like other members of the arachnid family. Mites are sap suckers, and foliage attacked by mites appears mottled and discolored. With the aid of a magnifying glass the tiny creatures and their clear circular eggs can sometimes be seen on the underside of leaves. If severe mite attacks go unnoticed initially, there may be fine webbing on the underside of foliage too. Sometimes with light attacks hosing under the leaves every two to three days is enough to reduce their population to an acceptable, non-damaging level. Mites are much worse in warm, dry weather or on plants that may be sheltered by the overhanging eaves of a house. Make sure that plants are well watered and well nourished. If mite numbers do reach unacceptable levels, clearly getting out of hand, you may need to spray with an appropriate insecticide. Many general, broad spectrum insecticides are useless against mites.

Gray/white powder on leaves

• This is probably caused by the common fungal disease, powdery mildew. In humid areas this disease is a constant problem. For plants that are very susceptible to powdery mildew, much work is being done to breed plant-resistant varieties. Meanwhile, it may be necessary to spray with a fungicide such as carbendazim or copper oxychloride or, alternatively, you can dust the plants with sulfur. If you have any kind of problem with powdery mildew, avoid watering the plants late in the day so that you do not increase the humidity around them overnight.

Black or dark spots on leaves

• There are many strains of fungal leaf spots that can attack a wide range of plants. If only a few leaves are affected, remove and destroy them. Avoid watering late in the day and, where possible, avoid splashing the foliage which will spread the fungal spores. Many fungal leaf spots respond well to simple fungicides such as copper oxychloride, but there are other effective fungicides available to the home gardener.

Yellow spots on top of leaves

• Yellow spots on the upper side of leaves that have blisters, or pustules on the underside, are likely to be some form of rust. There is an enormous number of rust strains, and they can attack a wide range of plants and perennials, including chrysanthemums. It is a good idea to remove the worst affected leaves immediately, and to avoid overhead watering which quickly splashes the spores around, increasing contamination. Copper oxychloride will control some rusts, though you may find you need to use a more specific fungicide.

A VIBRANT show of argyranthemums.

AQUILEGIA
Columbine

WIDELY CONTRASTING COLORS successfully combine in the flowers of this modern, long-spurred hybrid columbine.

AN OPEN WOODLAND SETTING is ideal for columbines, letting them freely self-seed forming, bold, distinctive groups.

FEATURES

SUMMER AUTUMN WINTER SPRING

HERBACEOUS

dappled shade

These old-fashioned favorites, also called granny's bonnets, give a fine display in the garden and make decorative cut flowers. The foliage is often blue-green, and the flowers come in single colors—white, pink, crimson, yellow, and blue—and combinations of pastel and brighter shades. There are also excellent black and whites ("Magpie"). The older forms have short-spurred flowers that resemble old-fashioned bonnets, especially "Nora Barlow", a good double which is a mix of red, pink, and green. Modern hybrids are long spurred, and available in many single colors and bicolors. Plants may be 16–28in high. Columbines are not long lived but are easily seed grown. Ideal for the dappled garden, grow them under deciduous trees and in borders.

AQUILEGIA AT A GLANCE

A clump-forming perennial, happy in semi-shade, perfect for the cottage garden where it freely self-seeds. Hardy to 5°F. (zone 7)

JAN	/	**RECOMMENDED VARIETIES**
FEB	/	
MAR	sow	*Aquilegia bertolonii*
APR	transplant	A. *canadensis*
MAY	flowering	A. *flabellata*
JUN	flowering	A. *f.* var. *pumila*
JULY	/	A. *f.* var. *f. alba*
AUG	/	"Henson Harebell"
SEPT	divide	"Magpie"
OCT	sow	Music series
NOV	/	A. *vulgaris* "Nora Barlow"
DEC	/	*dbl red pink green*

CONDITIONS

Aspect   Prefers semi-shade, and thrives in woodland gardens, but full sun is not a problem.

Site   Needs well-drained soil that contains plenty of organic matter.

GROWING METHOD

Propagation   Clumps are actually quite hard to divide, but it can be done, the fall being the best time. Columbine also grows from seed sown in early spring, or in the fall. Self-sown plants are hardy, but note that they may not always be true to type. Space plants about 12in apart. New young plants must not be allowed to dry out in prolonged dry spells in the spring and summer months. Keep a careful watch.

Feeding   Apply complete plant food in the spring as the new growth begins to emerge.

Problems   No particular pest or disease problems are known for this plant.

FLOWERING

Season   There is a long flowering period from mid-spring to mid-summer.

Cutting   Flower stems can be cut for the vase, and they make an attractive display, but the garden show lasts considerably longer.

AFTER FLOWERING

Requirements   Spent flower stems can either be removed or left on the plants enabling the seeds to mature. Cut back the old growth to ground level as it dies off.

ARMERIA MARITIMA
Sea thrift

EACH FLOWERHEAD resembles a tiny posy, which is why thrift makes a fine cut flower, alone or in a composition with other flowers.

POOR STONY GROUND, which resembles thrift's natural habitat, provides ideal conditions for growing this plant.

FEATURES

EVERGREEN

Also known as sea thrift, this evergreen perennial grows in little grassy mounds 2–5in high. It occurs naturally in northern Europe and around the Mediterranean, often in very exposed situations, including cliff tops. The rounded flowerheads are carried above the foliage on stems 6–12in high. Flowers vary in color in the species and may be white, pink, or almost red, and there are a number of named cultivars available. Thrift can be used as a groundcover or edging plant, or can be planted in rockeries, on dry walls, or in poor soil where few other plants will survive. It also makes a good container plant.

ARMERIA AT A GLANCE

A. maritima is an attractive evergreen, clump-forming perennial which colonizes inhospitable areas. Hardy to 0°F (zone 7).

Jan	/	
Feb	/	
Mar	division	**RECOMMENDED VARIETIES**
Apr	/	*Armeria maritima* "Alba"
May	transplant	*A. m.* "Corsica"
Jun	flowering	*A. m.* "Launcheana"
July	flowering	*A. m.* "Ruby Glow"
Aug	flowering	*A. m.* "Splendens"
Sept	/	*A. m.* "Vindictive"
Oct	/	
Nov	/	
Dec	/	

CONDITIONS

Aspect Needs full sun all day. Thrift tolerates dry, windy conditions and salt spray, and is an excellent choice for coastal gardens.

Site Grows in any kind of soil so long as it is very well drained. Adding sharp sand will improve the drainage.

GROWING METHOD

Propagation Divide established clumps in the spring and replant about 6–8in apart. The species can be grown from seed sown in the spring, or from semi-ripe cuttings taken in the summer

Feeding Give a light dressing of complete fertiliser in early spring.

Problems Thrift has a tendency to rot if soils are in any way too heavy, poorly drained, or overwatered. In humid weather and in sheltered positions it may also be susceptible to the fungal disease which is called rust. Use a fungicide to attack the problem.

FLOWERING

Season Thrift has a long flowering period through spring and summer, provided the plants are deadheaded regularly.

Cutting Makes a good cut flower.

AFTER FLOWERING

Requirements Regularly remove spent flower stems to give a prolonged flowering period.

CHRYSANTHEMUM HYBRIDS
Dendranthema

CASCADING OVER *the fence onto the massed erigeron below, this wonderful garden chrysanthemum gives a prolific display.*

THE QUILLED PETALS *are characteristic of this open "spider" style of chrysanthemum, as is the shading of color.*

HYBRID CHRYSANTHEMUMS *are justifiably highly popular in the cut flower trade, and are available for most of the year.*

FEATURES

HERBACEOUS

Chrysanthemums probably originated in China, but were introduced into Japan a very long time ago. A big favourite in garden and florists' displays, they are the highlight of the late summer and autumn border. They are also widely used as a long-lasting cut flower. Chrysanthemums have been renamed and moved to the genus *Dendranthema*, though the name has yet to catch on. Four kinds to look out for include: the Korean (e.g. "Yellow Starlet"), which give a long flowering performance but dislike excessive winter wet (store inside in severe conditions); the thigh-high, dwarf, bushy pompons ("Mei Kyo") with a sea of rounded flowers; the clump-forming rubellums (named hybrids of *C. rubellum*) which are hardiest, have a woody base, but again dislike extreme damp; and the sprays ("Pennine") which are grown both for the border and cutting.

Color The color range is wide, covering white, cream, yellow, many shades of pink and lilac, burgundy, pale apricot, and deep mahogany.

Types There are many forms of chrysanthemums, and they have been classified by specialist societies and nurseries according to floral type. Some of the types are decorative, anemone centered, spider, pompon, single, exhibition, and Korean spray. There is virtually a shape for every taste.

Staking Many of the taller varieties need staking, which needs to be carefully thought out if the display is to avoid looking too structured. One reliable, traditional method is to insert bamboo canes at intervals around and through the planting, and thread twine from cane to cane in a criss-cross fashion, perhaps 20–24in above the ground.

CONDITIONS

Aspect Grows best in full sun with protection from strong winds.

Site Needs well-drained soil that has been heavily enriched with organic matter before planting. Plants should also be mulched with decayed compost or manure.

THIS UNUSUAL chrysanthemum has the central petals incurved like those of the Korean spray, while the outer ones are widespread.

THE RUSSET COLORS of these flowers seem appropriate to their fall flowering season, when the leaves are turning.

GROWING METHOD

Propagation In spring lift and divide the new suckering growth so that each new plant has its own roots and shoots. Cuttings of the new growth can be taken. Space plants 16in apart.

Feeding Once the plants are well established you can fertilize them every four to six weeks with a soluble liquid fertilizer.

Problems • You can spot chrysanthemum leaf miners by the wavy white or brown lines in the foliage. Furthermore, hold up the leaf to the light and you might see the pupa or grub. Control by immediately removing the affected leaves and crushing the grubs, or better still by regular spraying with a systemic insecticide.

• Chrysanthemum eelworm is evident by browning, drying leaves. Immediately destroy all infected plants. There is no available remedy.

• A number of fungal diseases can attack these plants, including leaf spot, powdery mildew, rust, and white rust. Avoid overhead watering or watering late in the day, and ensure that residue from previous plantings is cleared away. You may need to spray with a registered fungicide. White rust is a particularly serious disease, and affected plants are probably best removed and destroyed.

• Watch for aphids clustering on new growth. Pick them off by hand, wash them off, or use an insecticidal spray.

FLOWERING

Season Flowering time is mid to late fall. The exciting new race of Yoder or cushion chrysanthemums from America are dwarf, hardy, free-flowering (starting in late summer), and perfect for the front of the border. Those to look out for include "Lynn", "Robin", and "Radiant Lynn".

Cutting Cut flowers will last two to three weeks with frequent water changes, as long as the foliage is removed from the parts of the stems that are under water.

AFTER FLOWERING

Requirements Once flowering has finished, cut off plants 5–6in above the ground.

CHRYSANTHEMUM AT A GLANCE

Chrysanthemums are the colorful mainstay of the the end-of-season border. The hardy forms will tolerate 5°F (zone 7).

		RECOMMENDED VARIETIES
JAN	/	
FEB	sow	"Anna Marie"
MAR	sow	"Bronze Elegance"
APR	divide	"Cappa"
MAY	transplant	"Faust"
JUN	/	"Lord Butler"
JULY	/	"Mrs Jessie Cooper"
AUG	flowering	"Poppet"
SEPT	flowering	"Salmon Fairie"
OCT	/	
NOV	/	
DEC	/	

COREOPSIS
Coreopsis

COREOPSIS ARE wonderful plants which can quickly colonize a space, say between shrubs, producing striking, bright yellow flowers.

THIS DOUBLE-FLOWERED FORM of golden coreopsis provides many weeks of marvellous color throughout the summer.

FEATURES

HERBACEOUS

Perennial coreopsis carries a profusion of bright yellow daisy-like flowers over a long period, generally through summer into the fall, though some do flower in spring. Regular deadheading will ensure a long display. *C. lanceolata*, known as calliopsis, has become naturalised in many parts of the world. The strong-growing *C. grandiflora* may grow 24–36in high, with *C.verticillata* about 8in shorter. There are several species worth trying, some with dwarf form or flowers displaying a dark eye. The foliage is variable too. The plants are easy to grow. Plant in bold clumps in a mixed border.

COREOPSIS AT A GLANCE

A genus with well over 100 species that make a big contribution to the summer and early fall display. Hardy to 5°F (zone 7).

JAN	/	**RECOMMENDED VARIETIES**
FEB	/	
MAR	/	*Coreopsis auriculata*
		"Schnittgold"
APR	sow	*C.* "Goldfink"
MAY	divide	*C. grandiflora* "Early Sunrise"
JUN	flowering	*C. g.* "Mayfield Giant"
JULY	flowering	"Sunray"
AUG	flowering	*C. verticillata*
SEPT	flowering	*C. v.* "Grandiflora"
OCT	/	*C. v.* "Zagreb"
NOV	/	
DEC	/	

CONDITIONS

Aspect Prefers an open, sunny position right through the day, with little shade.

Site Performs best in well-drained soil enriched with organic matter, but it will grow in poor soils too. Over-rich soil may produce a profusion of foliage with poor flowering.

GROWING METHOD

Propagation Grows most easily from divisions of existing clumps lifted in the spring. Space new plants at about 12in intervals. Species can be grown from seed sown in mid-spring. Since cultivars of *C. grandiflora* can be ephemeral, sow seed for continuity.

Feeding Apply complete plant food as growth begins in the spring. However, no further feeding should be needed.

Problems No pest or disease problems are known.

FLOWERING

Season The long flowering period extends through summer and the fall. *C.* "Early Sunrise", *C.lanceolata*, and "Sunray" flower in their first year from an early sowing.

Cutting Flowers can be cut for indoor decoration.

AFTER FLOWERING

Requirements Cut off spent flower stems and tidy up the foliage as it dies back. In mild, frost-free winters, coreopsis may not totally die back.

HELENIUM AUTUMNALE
Sneezeweed

STILL ONE OF THE BEST and most popular cultivars of sneeze-weed, "Moerheim Beauty" has been a favorite since the 1930s.

ORANGE AND TAWNY COLORS are a feature of sneezeweed, a reliable perennial that brightens the fall garden.

FEATURES

HERBACEOUS

As its Latin name suggests, this herbaceous perennial flowers from late summer to mid fall. The straight species has bright golden, daisy-like flowers with dark centres, but many of the most popular cultivars have flowers in rich tones of orange-red or copper-red. "Butterpat", "Moerheim Beauty", and "Waldtraut" are among the most popular varieties. Sneezeweed can grow 39–60in or more high, eventually forming large clumps over 20in across. Flowers cut well, but the plant is probably more valuable for its contribution to the autumn garden. Place at the back of a perennial border or among shrubs. Easy to grow.

HELENIUM AT A GLANCE

A group of annuals, biennials and perennials. Grown for their prolific, bright flowering display. Hardy to 5°F (zone 7).

JAN	/	
FEB	sow	**RECOMMENDED VARIETIES**
MAR	sow	
APR	transplant	"Butterpat"
MAY	transplant	"Chipperfield Orange"
JUN	/	"Crimson Beauty"
JULY	flowering	"Moerheim Beauty"
AUG	flowering	"Rotgold"
SEPT	flowering	"The Bishop"
OCT	/	
NOV	/	
DEC	/	

CONDITIONS

Aspect Needs to be grown in full sun right through the day. Avoid shade.

Site Needs a moisture-retentive soil heavily enriched with organic matter. It will not thrive in dry soil. Mulch around clumps to help keep soil moist.

GROWING METHOD

Propagation Established clumps can be lifted and divided about every three years. Discard the oldest central sections and replant the divisions about 12in apart in spring or fall. Give new young plants a regular watering right through the growing season.

Feeding Apply complete plant food as new growth commences in spring.

Problems Sneezeweed is generally free from problems, although slugs and snails can damage newly emerging growth in damp weather.

FLOWERING

Season The flowering season starts in mid-summer and continues into the fall.

Cutting Flowers cut well for indoor decoration.

AFTER FLOWERING

Requirements Spent flower stems should be removed. As the plant dies down, cut off and remove dead foliage. It can be chopped and left on the ground as a mulch. With flowers blooming into the fall, the foliage remains in good condition until attacked by frost.

HEMEROCALLIS
Daylily

MAHOGANY RED is one of the many strong colors available in the huge range of daylily cultivars now available from specialist growers.

THE MASS PLANTING of this creamy yellow daylily increases its impact. Blooms will appear one after the other for many weeks.

FEATURES

HERBACEOUS

EVERGREEN

Easily grown in a wide range of conditions, the daylily is a trouble-free plant with single or double flowers. As its name suggests, individual flowers last only one day, but they are produced over a long period. They come in a wide range of colors, the main ones being shades of yellow, orange, red, magenta, and purple. There is an enormous number of exciting, attractive hybrids available from specialist growers. The clumps of grassy foliage may be from 10–39in high; some are evergreen while others die down in winter. While straight species are not as readily available as the hybrids, they are important in hybridising new varieties and several species are worth seeking out. They include *H. altissima* from China, which has pale yellow fragrant flowers on stems 5ft or so high, and *H. lilio-asphodelus*, which has pale yellow fragrant flowers above leaves 22in high.

Categories Daylilies have been divided into five categories which list them according to flower type. The divisions are circular, double, spider-shaped, star-shaped, and triangular. Most are single; hot weather can produce extra petals and stamens.

Dwarf forms The number of dwarf forms available is steadily increasing and they may be better suited to today's smaller gardens. Those with a reliable reflowering habit can also be successfully grown in pots. Use a good quality potting mix and crowd three plants into a 8in pot for good effect. "Little Grapette", "Little Gypsy Vagabond", "Penny's Worth", and "Stella d'Oro" are good ones to try, all growing about 12 x 18in.

Uses Mass plantings of dwarf or tall forms create the best effect. Daylilies are not plants that should be dotted about in the garden. Use large numbers of either the one variety or use varieties of similar color; it is clearly preferable to planting a mixture of types or colors. In a mixed border they give a very pleasing effect as the foliage is very full.

"BURNING DAYLIGHT", one of the top daylilies, blooms prolifically in sun or semi-shade.

MANY OF the finest daylily cultivars are in creamy yellow or orange tones, not surprisingly as these are the colors of many of the species.

CONDITIONS

Aspect Grows best in full sun but tolerates semi-shade. Can be mass planted on banks or sloping ground as the roots are very efficient soil binders.

Site Grows in any type of soil, wet or dry, but to get maximum growth from the newer hybrids the soil should be enriched with manure or compost before planting.

HEMEROCALLIS AT A GLANCE

A genus of semi-, evergreen, and herbaceous perennials; 30,000 cultivars that give a long summer show. Hardy to 5°F (zone 7).

JAN	/	
FEB	sow	
MAR	sow	
APR	transplant	
MAY	transplant	
JUN	flowering	
JULY	flowering	
AUG	flowering	
SEPT	flowering	
OCT	divide	
NOV	/	
DEC	/	

RECOMMENDED VARIETIES

"Burning Daylight"
"Cartwheels"
"Golden Chimes"
"Neyron Rose"
"Pink Damask"
"Red Precious"
"Stafford"
"Whichford"
"Zara"

GROWING METHOD

Propagation Divide established clumps in spring or autumn. Cut back foliage before or straight after division. Spacing may be from 6–12in, depending on variety.
New plants need regular watering to establish. Once established, plants are very drought tolerant, but better sized blooms can be expected if deep waterings are given every week or two.

Feeding Grows without supplementary fertilizer, but an application of complete plant food in early spring encourages stronger, more vigorous growth.

Problems Daylilies growing in very soggy ground tend to survive quite well but produce few flowers. Otherwise no problems.

FLOWERING

Season Depending on variety, plants may be in bloom any time from late spring until the fall. Most flowers only last one day.

Cutting Single flowers can be cut for the vase. Attractive and well worth using.

AFTER FLOWERING

Requirements Cut off any spent flower stems. Herbaceous types that die down in the fall can have their foliage cut back too.

RANUNCULUS
Buttercup

A STRONG, vivid display of ranunculus showing how they can enliven a border. By mixing two or three different varieties you will certainly get extra impact. However, since some types of ranunculus can rapidly multiply and spread, you must take great care when selecting a particular variety.

FEATURES

EVERGREEN

HERBACEOUS

Buttercups basically divide into the invasive and the less-so. Take care which you chose for the border. The genus contains about 400 species of annuals, biennials, and perennials, with a wide range of demands, which vary from free-draining alpine slopes to ponds.

R. ficaria, lesser celandine, is a woodland type with early spring, yellow flowers that can become a weed. There are several cultivars; "Brazen Hussy" has dark brown foliage and yellow flowers, while "Salmon's White" is cream with a blue tint on the reverse.

R. aconitifolius "Flore Pleno", fair maids of France, likes full sun and has white, long-lasting flowers. And *R. flammula,* lesser spearwort, is a marginal aquatic for early summer with yellow flowers.

RANUNCULUS AT A GLANCE

A large genus of over 400 species with many annuals, biennials, and perennials, hardy to 5°F (zone 7) for all kinds of garden.

JAN	/	**RECOMMENDED VARIETIES**
FEB	/	
MAR	sow	*Ranunculus aconitifolius* "Flore Pleno"
APR	transplant	*R. calandrinioides*
MAY	flowering	*R. ficaria* "Brazen Hussy"
JUN	flowering	*R. f.* "Picton's Double"
JULY	flowering	*R. f.* "Salmon's White"
AUG	/	*R. flammula*
SEPT	/	*R. gramineus*
OCT	divide	*R. montanus* "Molten Gold"
NOV	/	
DEC	/	

CONDITIONS

Aspect It tolerates a wide range of conditions from medium to dappled shade, to full sun. When buying a ranunculus do carefully check its specific needs.

Site This too varies considerably from moist, rich soil, to fertile, free-draining ground, to gritty, fast-draining soil for the alpine types, to ponds and pond margins for the aquatics.

GROWING METHOD

Propagation Divide in the spring or fall, or sow fresh, ripe seed in the fall.

Feeding This depends entirely on the natural habitat and growing needs of the plant. Border perennials need reasonable applications of well-rotted manure in the spring, as new growth appears, while the woodland types need plenty of leafy compost dug in around the clumps.

Problems Slugs and snails are a particular nuisance; pick off or use chemical treatment.

FLOWERING

Season From late spring to mid-summer, depending on the chosen variety.

Cutting All ranunculus make excellent cut flowers, being especially useful in spring before the main flush of garden flowers.

AFTER FLOWERING

Requirements Cut back all spent stems.

RODGERSIA
Rodgersia

[handwritten: Partial Shade]

NO GARDEN IS COMPLETE without rodgersia. They can be grown apart from other plants, perhaps surrounded by gravel, highlighting the shapely, distinctive leaves, which on R. pinnata *grow 25cm (10in) long. Or grow them in a mixed border, where they add strength and structure.*

FEATURES

SUMMER AUTUMN WINTER SPRING

HERBACEOUS

A six-species genus with particularly interesting foliage, and flowers, ideal for the border or shady woodland garden. The three most commonly grown types are *R. aesculifolia, R. pinnata,* and *R. podophylla* (the last two having handsome, bronze new foliage). All form big, bold clumps in the right conditions. The first has crinkled leaves like those of a horse-chestnut, up to 10in long, with tall panicles of creamy white flowers; height 6½ft. *R. pinnata* "Superba", 4ft, has purple-bronze foliage and white, pink, or red flowers. And *R. podophylla,* 5ft, with creamy green flowers, also has horse-chestnut-type leaves, reddish in the fall.

RODGERSIA AT A GLANCE

These tall, clump-forming perennials add structure to any damp-ish garden. Whitish summer flowers; hardy to 0°F (zone 7).

JAN	/
FEB	/
MAR	sow
APR	dvide
MAY	transplant
JUN	/
JULY	flowering
AUG	flowering
SEPT	/
OCT	/
NOV	/
DEC	/

RECOMMENDED VARIETIES

Rodgersia aesculifolia *[handwritten: tall 8½ ft]*
R. pinnata *[handwritten: superba – purple bronze up to 4 ft wt pink or red flow]*
R. p. "Elegans"
R. p. "Superba"
R. podophylla *[handwritten: 5']*
R. sambucifolia

CONDITIONS

Aspect Rodgersia, from the mountaineous Far East, like full sun or partial shade. They thrive in both conditions.

Site Grow in rich, damp ground; they grow by streams in the wild, and also in woodland settings.

GROWING METHOD

Propagation Either divide, which is the easiest method, or grow from seed in the spring, raising the plants in a cold frame. Water the new young plants well, and do not let them dry out in prolonged, dry spells. They quickly wilt and lose energy, and their performance is badly affected.

Feeding Add plenty of well-rotted manure or compost to the soil. The shadier the conditions, the less rich the soil need be.

Problems Vine weevil grubs can demolish the roots of container-grown perennials. While slugs rarely attack the new emerging growth, when they do strike they can ruin a potentially impressive display with tall, astilbe-like flowers. Pick off any offenders or treat with a chemical.

FLOWERING

Season Flowers appear in mid- and late summer, and in early summer in the case of *R. sambucifolia.*

Cutting Rodgersia make good cut flowers, helping create an impressive display.

AFTER FLOWERING

Requirements Cut the spent stems to the ground, and promptly remove all debris.

GROWING FLOWERING SHRUBS

Beautiful borders can be created almost entirely from shrubs—the bones of a garden. They impart form and character and complement trees and herbaceous perennials. All shrubs flower—and many that have small, modest flowers produce bright berries that ornament the late summer, fall, and winter garden.

Shrubs are usually defined as perennial woody plants. They are frequently multi-stemmed, but not always, and the line between tall shrubs and small trees is rather vague. Indeed, gardeners and professional horticulturists do not always agree. Shrubs may be evergreen or deciduous, leaves are small or large, glossy or matt, and come in a huge range of shapes. Some shrubs, such as hibiscus, have showy flowers. Others, such as box, have tiny, insignificant ones. Cotton lavender (*santolina*) and rosemary, among others, have aromatic foliage. A few—such as syringa, mock orange, and choisya—are prized for their sweetly perfumed blooms.

Shrubs come in every shape and size. There is a species or variety to suit virtually every situation. When you are planning a garden, select kinds that favour a particular position. Will the shrub thrive in full sun, or does it prefer shade? Consider how high and wide it will grow. Some shrubs can take up to 5–10 years to mature, become well established, and assume their final shape. Never buy a large-growing shrub for a small space, thinking you can prune it to keep it small. Repeated cutting back will spoil its natural symmetry and you will eventually come to hate it and thus remove it.

ABOVE: Brilliant red "Royal William"—a bounteous Large Flowered rose.

LEFT: A sculpturally appealing symphony of golden pansies, box hedging, and green bottlebrush blooms of Euphorbia wulfenii.

PROPAGATION

Most shrubs are raised from stem cuttings. They may be grown from soft-tip cuttings (of, for example, hydrangea or fuchsia) taken in late spring and early summer; semi-ripe nodal cuttings of side shoots, or heel cuttings of shoots tugged from the main stem in midsummer—most shrubs being propagated this way; or from dormant hardwood cuttings of deciduous shrubs.

Soft-tip, semi-ripe nodal, and heel cuttings should be 2–4in long and taken from strong, healthy plants, preferably from stems that have not flowered. Hardwood cuttings of mature, dormant shoots, 10–12in long, are rooted in the fall, in a slit trench in the garden. Layering, that is, pegging down young, flexible stems close to the soil any time between spring and fall, is another easy way to multiply shrubs.

Soft-tip and semi-ripe nodal cuttings
Take these early in the day, when plump and dew-fresh. If you are not able to insert them into pots of compost immediately, enclose them in a plastic bag and keep them in a cool, shady place.

Use a very sharp knife or razor blade to remove all but the topmost two or three leaves. If the leaves are large, as in hydrangeas, it is best to shorten them by half their length. At the base of the cutting make a clean, horizontal cut, just below a node (joint) from which leaves appear. Encourage rapid rooting by dipping the cutting in hormone rooting compound. Prepare a rooting mix of three parts, by volume, of coarse, washed sand or Perlite and one part of peat or loam-based seed compost. Alternatively, use proprietary, peat-based cutting compost. Place the compost mix in a small, 4in pot and gently firm it. Make holes with a pencil where the cuttings are to go and insert them to a third of their length, about 2in apart.

Firm compost around the stems. You can place several cuttings in one pot. Water them in, allow compost to drain, then transfer them to a propagator or garden frame, or enclose them in an inflated plastic bag and place them on a windowsill. In warm conditions, soft-tip cuttings will root within 2–4 weeks. You can tell if a cutting has rooted if new leaves have formed and a gentle pull on the stem meets with resistance. A few weeks later, move the plant into a small pot of potting compost.

HARDWOOD CUTTINGS

They usually take many weeks or months to root. Leaves may form long before roots develop. They should be about 12in long and ¼–½in thick. Take them from the middle of well-ripened, current-year shoots. Prepare them by making a gently sloping cut just above the topmost bud and a horizontal cut immediately below the bottom node (joint). Next, in a sunny, well-drained area of deeply dug and friable soil, use a spade to take out a 6–8in deep trench with one vertical wall. Trickle a 1inch layer of sharp sand into it.

Insert cuttings to two-thirds their depth, 6in apart, pressing them into the sand. Tread soil firmly around them, hoe out footprints and water copiously.

Refirm cuttings in winter when hard frost lifts them. Roots will form in spring. By fall, plants will be ready for moving to where you wish to display them.

Some roses will grow quite readily from cuttings, but others will not grow vigorously on their own roots. Commercial nurseries "bud" rose varieties on to rootstocks of wild or species roses. (Budding is a form of grafting using dormant leaf buds.)

LAYERING

Take out a 6in hole next to the plant and remove any leaves that might be buried, from the selected shoot. Make a sloping, 1½in cut through a joint in the middle of the shoot and wedge open the cut with a matchstick. Half fill the hole with a mix of equal parts sharp sand and soil and then peg the cut part of the shoot into it. Cover the shoot with more of the same mix and tie the exposed end to a cane to keep it upright. Water the layer to settle the soil around it and place a large, flat stone over it to keep the soil damp.

About a year later, when roots have formed, sever the new shrub, or layer, from its parent by cutting the stem of the parent shrub where it enters the ground. Then leave your new shrub *in situ* or transplant it to a new position in the garden.

Some shrubs may be grown from seed, but only the species will produce plants that match their parent.

TYPES OF CUTTINGS

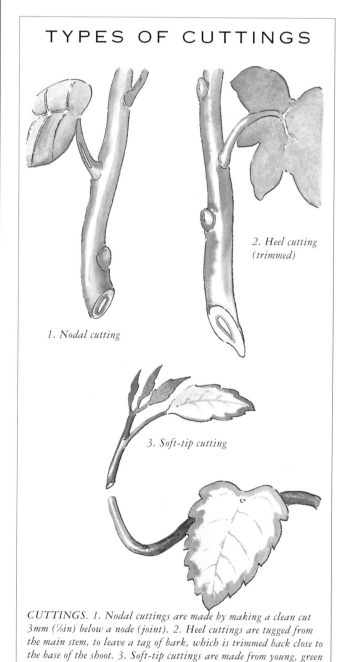

2. Heel cutting (trimmed)

1. Nodal cutting

3. Soft-tip cutting

CUTTINGS. *1. Nodal cuttings are made by making a clean cut 3mm (⅛in) below a node (joint). 2. Heel cuttings are tugged from the main stem, to leave a tag of bark, which is trimmed back close to the base of the shoot. 3. Soft-tip cuttings are made from young, green shoot tips. Remove lower leaves (as here) before inserting in compost.*

CHOOSING A PLANT

When choosing plants at a garden center, the biggest is not always the best. Look for those that are well shaped and have a good cover of healthy leaves. Avoid plants that have woody roots protruding from drainage holes, those that are excessively tall for the pot and those that have knobbly, thickened stem bases. All these features show that the plant is pot-bound and that it should have been moved into a larger container some time ago. All plants suffer from some degree of transplanting shock, but the smaller the plant the less traumatic the move. Ideally, select plants in bloom to ensure that you are getting the color and variety you want.

SOIL PREPARATION

Because most shrubs are fairly long-lived and form a garden's permanent framework, it is worth putting in a bit of time and effort into preparing a good home for them and thus protect your investment. Shrubs planted in suitable conditions will become established more quickly, and their healthy growth will be less vulnerable to attack by pests and disease than plants that are treated more hastily.

Few shrubs tolerate heavy, waterlogged soil. If drainage is poor, you may need to consider raising the planting area or installing subsoil drains. Heavy, clay soils can be improved by adding gypsum at the rate of 7–11oz per sq yd and by working in large quantities of well-rotted, organic material. Organic matter should be dug in several weeks ahead of planting. Sandy soils, in which water and nutrients are quickly lost, benefit greatly from the addition of large amounts of organic matter before planting. All plants and soils are better for being mulched with humus-forming, well-rotted animal manure, compost, leaf mould, straw, or decayed grass clippings, as these not only retain moisture in the soil but also keep the soil and plants well nourished. Mulches should only be laid on moist soil.

STRIKING SOFT-TIP CUTTINGS

1. TO TAKE A CUTTING, gather shoots when dew-fresh and place in a plastic bag. Prepare stems by trimming to length and cutting just below a node (joint). Keep cuttings cool and shaded. Remove lower leaves, which will rot if buried.

2. FILL A SMALL POT, which has plenty of drainage holes, with gritty cutting compost. Use a pencil to make holes for inserting cuttings to half their length. Firm compost around them.

3. WATER IN CUTTINGS well, but gently, taking care not to dislodge them. They should not need watering again until new growth indicates that roots have formed. If you are unsure of how dry the compost is, and the pot feels light, add just a little water.

4. MAKE A WIRE OR BAMBOO FRAME that fits inside the pot and is tall enough to clear cuttings. Place a plastic bag over the frame and secure it to the pot. The bag will keep air and soil moist. Root cuttings in good light but not direct sunlight.

Framed by statuesque conifers and a fiery, fall-hued tree, crimson-flowered Hebe *"Great Orme" makes a fine focal point beside this gravel path. Usefully, this evergreen shrub starts blooming in July but seldom finishes before late October.*

PLANTING

With good soil preparation and correct planting techniques your shrubs should flourish. Most container-grown shrubs are transplanted throughout the year, provided the soil is crumbly and workable and frost is not forecast. In winter, in gardens prone to hard frost, it is best to transplant only dormant, deciduous plants.

Bare-rooted shrubs, usually deciduous, are planted when leaves have fallen—from fall to early spring.

• Check that the position chosen for your shrub will allow it to develop full height and spread without your having to cut it back. You should also cater for its other needs: soil type—heavy or light, warm, and free-draining—and sun or shade.

• Dig a hole at least twice as wide as the plant's root system and about the same depth. Loosen soil in the bottom of the hole and around the sides. If it is clayey, work in grit or gravel to avoid creating a sump in which roots may drown.

• Do not put fresh manure into the hole. Instead, mix a balanced fertilizer, such as fish, blood, and bone meal, Growmore, or a slow-release brand, with soil you firm around the roots. Roots must not come into direct contact with fertilizer, which may burn them.

• If you are planting a container-grown shrub bought in a stiff plastic pot, thoroughly water the compost to loosen any roots clinging to the pot sides. Invert the plant and gently tap its pot rim on a hard surface so that the rootball slides out. Carefully tease out compacted, encircling roots from the rootball.

• Trim away any roots that are damaged.

• Place the plant in its hole, at the same depth that it was previously growing. Lay a cane over the hole, next to the plant, to check this. Backfill the hole with soil that you have dug out and tread the soil firmly around the rootball. Do not tread on the rootball itself.

• Water in thoroughly to remove any air pockets and settle the soil around the feeding root hairs.

• Mulch the root area, but keep mulch well clear of the stem, because its bark could rot. Organic mulches, such as manures and composts, help to condition soil and feed plants. They break down and disappear after a year or so, so replace them annually.

MAINTENANCE

Water newly planted shrubs regularly and copiously, specially in droughty weather until they are well established.

Re-feed autumn-planted shrubs in spring, and spring-planted in summer, by topdressing (sprinkling) the root area with a complete plant food. Fish, blood, and bone meal or pelleted poultry manure is ideal for most shrubs, but avoid using poultry manure on lime-hating rhododendrons and summer-flowering heathers, among others.

PRUNING

Many shrubs will never need shoots removing unless you wish to rejuvenate very old plants or take out wayward stems. If you wish to cut back a spring-flowering plant, prune it when its blooms fade. The only exception to this is plants, such as firethorn and cotoneaster, that are grown for their berries. Shrubs, such as *Buddleja davidii*, that flower from mid- to late summer are best pruned the following spring.

To train a single-stemmed standard, select a young shrub with a straight stem and shorten laterals (side shoots) to within 1in of the trunk. These leafy stumps help to conduct sap to the head of the standard. If the main stem is slender—it usually is—you may need to tie it to a cane. As the stem lengthens, shorten further side shoots to an inch or so until the stem is as high as required—normally 4–6ft. Then, when the head is developing well, trim it to a ball shape and cut off side shoots flush with the stem.

HARDINESS

All plants mentioned flourish outdoors, apart from frost-tender ardisia, echium, oleander, plumbago, pomegranate, and heliotrope, which are normally overwintered in a greenhouse or conservatory and moved to a sheltered, sunny place for summer. Of the relatively hardy kinds, some in very cold, windswept, or frost-pocket gardens may need tucking up for winter. The best way to protect them is to cover them with an open-topped wigwam of bubble plastic or several layers of fibre fleece. Make sure the material does not touch the leaves or stems, or, if moist, it might rot them.

WHAT CAN GO WRONG?

Yellow leaves
• Plants have been overwatered or are too dry.
• Plants may need feeding: fertilize the plant with a high-nitrogen tonic if this has not been done for two or three months and see if there is any improvement within the next two or three weeks.
• Older leaves may turn bright yellow before dropping. Do not worry; they have finished their useful life.
• When new leaves on azaleas are pale yellow yet the veins are green, they probably require a dose of iron chelates, which aids chlorophyll production. Apply this in spring and early summer, carefully following the manufacturer's directions on the label.

Curled or distorted leaves
• Look for aphids (greenfly)—tiny, sticky, reddish-brown, gray, or green, sap-sucking insects clustering on new growth. Control them with an insecticide containing pirimicarb, permethrin, biollethrin, horticultural soap, rotenone, or pyrethrins. Spray at dusk when bees and other beneficial insects have retired for the night. Avoid spraying when it is hot, too, because foliage may be scorched by high temperatures.
• Some viruses manifest themselves this way and there is no cure. Consult reference books or experts to see if your plant has succumbed to one of these diseases. If affected, dig it up and burn it.
• Check that there has been no drift of any herbicide from nearby spraying. Even small amounts of spray drift, especially from selective lawn weedkillers, can distort leaves of sensitive plants, such as tomatoes and roses.

Black spots on leaves
• These may be fungal leaf spots. On roses, they are probably caused by black spot, a common disease that badly blotches leaves. Control it by spraying with bupirimate with triforine, penconazole, or myclobutanil. Ideally, improve air circulation around plants and avoid wetting leaves when watering, which should not be done late in the day. Large, brownish-black spots on camellias probably resulted from sunburn.

Grayish-white powder on leaf surfaces
• This deposit is probably powdery mildew, which affects a wide range of plants. Roses, azaleas, hydrangeas, and many other shrubs are prone to this disease. Avoid watering late in the day and spray plants with bupirimate with triforine, myclobutanil, sulfur or penconazole. It is worse on wall shrubs in dry areas where air does not freely circulate.

Mottled leaves
• This is usually associated with sap-sucking insects such as scale, thrip, lace bug, and red spider mite, which is not a true insect. Stressed, rather than healthy, plants are more liable to be attacked by these insects. Plants may be stressed by drought or overwatering, or by simply growing them

away from their favoured aspect.
• Limpet-like scale insects come in various sizes and colors. Control small infestations by using a damp cloth to wipe them off leaves and stems. Eradicate severe infestations by spraying plants with malathion
• Thrips and lace bugs may be reduced by hosing the underside of leaves or by spraying with pyrethrins, malathion, pirimiphos-methyl, permethrin, or insecticidal soap.
• In hot, dry weather, red spider mite can be a problem on shrubs growing in rain-sheltered spots, such as under the house eaves. Hosing the foliage helps to keep them down and obviate the need for spraying. If you have to resort to insecticides, malathion, bifenthrin, and pirimiphos-methyl are effective.

Holes in leaves or on leaf margins
• This may be snail or slug damage. Snails often lurk high up on the foliage. Baiting is not effective in this instance, so pick off and kill pests. Eradicate the ground-hugging tribe by sprinkling blue-dyed molluscicide pellets containing metaldehyde or methiocarb, thinly around susceptible, soft-stemmed plants. Alternatively, ring them with grit.
• Caterpillars also chew leaves. Tackle them by hand

picking or biologically controlling them with *Bacillus thuringiensis*. Effective insecticides include permethrin, bifenthrin, and pirimiphos-methyl.

Stems and leaves webbed or matted together
• Webbing caterpillars, such as those of the lackey moth, can cover buds and new shoots and extensively defoliate trees and shrubs. Pull out the webbing with a gloved hand or cut out the damaged section. Spray with permethrin, bifenthrin or pirimiphos methyl, or control the pest biologically with *Bacillus thuringiensis*. Inspect shrubs several times a year to control this pest in its early stages.

Sooty mold (a dry, black coating on leaf surfaces)
• A fungus, sooty mould feeds on sticky honeydew secreted by sap-sucking insects, such as aphids and scales. Once the pest is controlled, the mold will gradually disappear. Hosing helps. Wipe large-leaved plants with a damp cloth.

Sudden death of plant
• If leaves turn brown but remain attached to the plant, the plant has probably died from root rot. Root systems may have been damaged by excessive watering—from rain or irrigation—quite some time before the plant expires, especially in cool weather. When plants are stressed by extreme heat or wind, damaged root systems cannot cope and death follows quickly.
• If a plant is suffering from drought, its leaves may be brown and rapidly drop when watered.

Pomegranate fruits may appear in a warm garden.

ABELIA
Abelia

Abelia's pretty pink flowers appear at the end of summer. Striking, red calyces prolong the display.

An informal abelia hedge adds a little magic to a sunny and sheltered garden. Trim it lightly in spring.

FEATURES

Semi-evergreen and vigorous in mild districts, *Abelia × grandiflora* makes a dashing statement and a fine flowering hedge. From July to September, its arching shoots, clad with small, oval, pointed leaves, 4–5ft long, are sleeved with showy heads of tubular, pale pink flowers with reddish calyces. The decorative calyx persists into late fall.

"Francis Mason" is a stunning variety with golden-variegated leaves that complement a wealth of pink blossom. Other prized kinds are lilac-pink *A. chinensis* "Edward Goucher" and rosy-lilac *A. schumannii*.

ABELIA AT A GLANCE

Sporting clusters of pink or lilac flowers from late summer to fall, it needs a sheltered position. Hardy to 14°F (zone 8).

		RECOMMENDED VARIETIES
JAN	/	
FEB	/	*A. chinensis* "Edward
MAR	prune	Goucher"
APR	plant, prune	*A. × grandiflora*
MAY	plant	*A. × grandiflora* "Francis
JUNE	plant	Mason"
JULY	plant, flower	*A. schumannii*
AUG	plant, flower	
SEPT	plant, flower	
OCT	/	
NOV	/	
DEC	/	

CONDITIONS

Aspect Thriving in full sun and tolerating very light shade, abelia is best planted against a sheltered, south- or west-facing wall.

Site Abelia prospers in a wide range of well-drained soils, from clay-loam to sand. Enrich rapid-draining, chalky, and sandy soils with well-rotted and moisture-conserving, bulky organic materials.

GROWING METHOD

Feeding Topdress the root area with bone meal in spring and fall to encourage sturdy growth and profuse blooms.
Water freely after planting and mulch thickly with old manure, bark, cocoa shell, or rotted garden compost to keep roots cool and active.

Propagation Take soft-tip cuttings in late spring and semi-ripe cuttings from mid- to late summer.

Problems Shoots are brittle and easily snapped, so be careful when pruning and planting.

PRUNING

Flowers form on current-year shoots. Once mature, keep it youthful by cutting out a third of its oldest branches in spring.

ABUTILON VITIFOLIUM

Abutilon

early

In a sheltered, sunny spot, Abutilon vitifolium becomes a glowing sentinel of saucer-shaped, pale to deep mauve blooms in early summer.

Plant award-winning "Canary Bird" in a fertile, sun-soaked spot and enjoy a summer-long succession of pendent blooms.

FEATURES

There are few more exhilarating, summer sights than a mature shrub of *Abutilon vitifolium* festooned with white to purple-blue, saucer-shaped blooms. Studding stems clothed with three- to five-lobed, soft, gray, hairy leaves are flowers that have you looking closely at them. Making an upright "obelisk" to around 15ft, this shrub is worth a little cosseting—as are its eye-catching varieties, mauve-flowered "Veronica Tennant" and "Tennant's White".

Closely related *A. x suntense*, a fast-growing hybrid to 12ft, rewards us with pendent, white to violet-blue "saucers".

Choice forms of this hybrid are purple-blue "Geoffrey Gorer", white "Gorer's White", deep mauve "Jermyns", and dark violet-blue "Violetta". Look out, too, for "Canary Bird", whose radiant lemon-yellow blooms illuminate a border.

ABUTILON AT A GLANCE

Loosely branched, deciduous shrub sleeved with saucer-shaped, white, blue, or purple blooms in summer. Hardy to 32°F (zone 10)

		RECOMMENDED VARIETIES
JAN	/	
FEB	/	*A. x suntense* — fast grower ☑ white–violet blue saucers
MAR	/	"Geoffrey Gorer" purple-blue
APR	plant, prune	"Gorer's White"
MAY	plant	"Jermyns" deep mauve
JUNE	flower, plant	"Ralph Gould"
JULY	flower, prune	"Violetta" dark violet-blue
AUG	plant	*A. vitifolium* "Tennant's mauve White"
SEPT	plant	*A. vitifolium* "Veronica Tennant" mauve
OCT	/	
NOV	/	
DEC	/	

CONDITIONS

Aspect Position all varieties in full sun where shoots grow stocky and are massed with bloom. Make sure abutilon is sheltered from shoot-killing, icy winds.

Site This shrub tolerates a wide range of well-drained soils, but for the best results enrich the planting area with plenty of crumbly organic matter.

GROWING METHOD

Feeding For the strongest shoots and bounteous blossom, topdress the root area with fish, blood, and bone meal or Growmore in spring and midsummer.

Water young plants regularly and mulch them with bulky organics to keep soil cool.

In long, dry spells, take out a moat around the plant and fill it repeatedly with water. When subsoil is soaked, replace excavated soil and cover with moisture-conserving mulch.

Propagation Increase favoured varieties from semi-ripe cuttings from mid- to late summer. *A. vitifolium* produces masses of fertile seed.

Problems Control aphids colonizing soft stems by spraying with pirmicarb, pyrethrins, or insecticidal soap. Leaves may be damaged by caterpillars and other chewing insects. If damage is slight, ignore it. If severe, control these pests biologically with *Bacillus thuringiensis*, or apply rotenone or pirimiphos-methyl.

PRUNING

Keep bushes compact and packed with flowering shoots by cutting back dead or dying stems to healthy growth in mid-spring. In early summer, shorten flowered stems to two-thirds their length.

ACACIA DEALBATA
Silver wattle

Silver wattle's ferny, silvery-green leaves are appealing all year round, specially if shoots are fan-trained against a warm wall.

There are few more riveting sights in a sheltered garden in early spring than Acacia dealbata *in full flower.*

FEATURES

There are around 900 species of wattle but only *Acacia dealbata* is sufficiently hardy for planting outdoors in mild districts. Rapidly growing to around 12ft, its soft shoots are richly and appealingly clothed with ferny and silvery-sheened, evergreen leaves.

In April, year-old shoots are thickly clustered with small, double pompoms of fragrant, bright yellow blossom.

Ideally, because several days of temperatures hovering around freezing point may kill shoots, it is best fan-trained against a warm, south-facing wall.

Only in relatively frost-free districts can you successfully grow it as a free-standing shrub in the open garden. Elsewhere, set it in a large pot or tub and grow it in a conservatory, moving it outdoors into the open garden only for summer.

SILVER WATTLE AT A GLANCE

An evergreen, tender tree with silvery, ferny leaves and bobbles of yellow flowers in spring. Hardy to 32°F (zone 10).

		RECOMMENDED VARIETIES
JAN	/	*A. dealbata*
FEB	flower	
MAR	flower	
APR	plant, flower	
MAY	prune, plant	
JUNE	plant	
JULY	plant	
AUG	plant	
SEPT	plant	
OCT	/	
NOV	/	
DEC	/	

CONDITIONS

Aspect Choose a warm, sunny site, ideally very sheltered and facing south or south-west, where it will not be exposed to leaf-blackening easterly or northerly winds.

Site Any well-drained, lime-free soil suits it. Fortify thin, sandy, or gravelly soils with bulky, humus-enriching manure, or well-rotted garden compost. Aerate heavy clay by working in plenty of grit or shingle. Alternatively, if puddles lie, dig a 18in drainage trench, leading to a soakaway, and fill it with gravel or rubble to within 8in of the soil surface.

GROWING METHOD

Feeding Encourage robust growth by annually sprinkling fish, blood, and bone meal, or Growmore over the rooting area in April and July. Water young plants regularly, especially in droughty spells, to help them develop a good, questing root system. Acacia appreciates occasional deep watering.

Propagation Increase acacia from semi-ripe cuttings in midsummer. Also grow from seed. Speed germination by soaking seeds overnight in hot water to soften the seed coat. Sow directly.

Problems Fortunately, it is seldom attacked by sap-sucking pests or caterpillars. If aphids cluster on shoots and cripple them, control them with pirimicarb, horticultural soap, or permethrin.

PRUNING

No regular pruning is necessary. In spring, shorten any stems killed by frost back to healthy side shoots. If acacia outgrows its situation, reduce wayward stems by up to two-thirds in late spring.

ARDISIA CRENATA
Coral berry

Fetching when enhancing a patio in summer, or conservatory in winter, ardisia is famed for its large clusters of scarlet berries.

A choice, compact evergreen, ardisia's panoply of white flowers in summer prelude a bounteous display of fruits.

FEATURES

Frost-sensitive, this evergreen shrub, clothed with attractive, rounded, toothed, and glossy, leathery leaves, has much to commend it. Coveted for its sprays of small, white, summer flowers, followed by a fetching and long-lasting display of bright red berries, it is easy to manage. Seldom more than 3ft high and across, it is normally grown in a large pot and confined to a frost-free conservatory in which temperatures are at least 20°F above freezing. In early summer when frosts finish, ardisia can be moved to highlight a lightly shaded patio.

CORAL BERRY AT A GLANCE

Sculptural evergreen with glossy leaves. White, summer flowers are followed by bright scarlet berries. Hardy to 50°F (zone 11).

JAN	/	RECOMMENDED VARIETIES
FEB	/	
MAR	/	*A. crenata*
APR	plant, prune	
MAY	plant	
JUN	plant	
JULY	flower	
AUG	flower	
SEPT	flower	
OCT	/	
NOV	/	
DEC	/	

CONDITIONS

Aspect   Outdoors, ardisia prefers a shaded to semi-shaded position sheltered from strong winds. Indoors, from early fall to late spring, display it in a lightly shaded conservatory.

Site   Help it excel by setting it in a large pot of John Innes potting compost No. 3. Based on moisture-retentive loam, it reduces the need for watering and encourages robust growth.

GROWING METHOD

Feeding   Encourage lustrous leaves and bounteous flowers and fruits by feeding weekly with a high-potash liquid fertilizer from spring to late summer. Alternatively, add a slow-release fertilizer to the compost in spring and replace it a year later. Water regularly from spring to fall to keep the compost nicely moist, but ease up from fall to winter when growth is slower. Cease feeding too.

Propagation   Take soft-tip cuttings in spring or summer.
Problems   Plants are occasionally attacked by sap-sucking scale insects, which cling like limpets to stems and leaves. Control them by spraying with malathion. Well-grown plants are seldom troubled by pests.

PRUNING

Ardisia is neat and symmetrical and cutting back is not normally necessary. If it grows too large, shorten stems to side shoots in spring.

BERBERIS THUNBERGII
Barberry

Berberis thunbergii *"Atropurpurea" glows with sunset hues in fall.*

Berberis stenophylla *brightens spring with a globe of yellow blossom. Keep it youthful by shearing off faded blooms in late spring.*

FEATURES

A huge, easy family of evergreen and deciduous species and varieties, berberis will grow almost anywhere. Small bushes enhance a rock garden; larger kinds light up a border or form a burglar-proof hedge. The most popular leaf-shedding kind is *Berberis thunbergii*. A dense, rounded shrub to about 5ft high and across, it is armed with long, sharp spines. Long-lived, with small, bright yellow flowers that sleeve slender, whippy stems and cheer spring, its leaves turn scarlet in fall. Bright red berries are a winter feature. Reddish-purple-leaved *B. thunbergii* "Atropurpurea"

becomes a firebrand in October. Other choice varieties of *B. thunbergii* ideal for small gardens are golden-leaved "Aurea", purple-blackish-leaved "Dart's Red Lady" and "Harlequin". Fetching, evergreen kinds are *B. × stenophylla* and *B. candidula*.

CONDITIONS

Aspect	Very hardy. Deciduous kinds especially resist icy winds. Berberis needs full sun to flower and fruit freely, but will tolerate light shade.
Site	Berberis prospers on a wide range of soils, from sand to heavy, often waterlogged clay.

GROWING METHOD

Feeding	Work bone meal into the root area in the fall. Water copiously and regularly in the first year after planting, to encourage good growth. Thereafter, little watering is necessary.
Propagation	Layer shoots from spring to fall, or take semi-ripe cuttings from early to mid-fall.
Problems	Control rust disease by spraying with a proprietary spray.

PRUNING

Bushes:	Apart from cutting back frost-damaged shoots in May, no regular pruning is needed. Renew old gaunt bushes by cutting back a third of the older stems to near ground level in April.
Hedges:	Trim when blooms fade in spring.

BARBERRY AT A GLANCE

Undemanding shrubs—many have fiery fall leaf tints—bearing yellow or orange spring flowers. Hardy to -13°F (zone 5).

Month	Activity	RECOMMENDED VARIETIES
JAN	/	
FEB	/	**Deciduous**
MAR	plant	*B. thunbergii*
APR	flower, prune	*B. thunbergii*
MAY	flower, plant	"Atropurpurea"
JUNE	plant	*B. thunbergii* "Dart's Red Lady"
JULY	plant	
AUG	plant	*B. thunbergii* "Aurea"
SEPT	plant	*B. thunbergii* "Harlequin"
OCT	plant	**Evergreen**
NOV	plant	*B. candidula*
DEC	/	*B. × stenophylla*

BUDDLEJA DAVIDII
Butterfly bush

Bone Meal

Irresistible to butterflies that cluster on its nectar-rich flowers, varieties of Buddleja davidii *make summer special.*

Spectacular blooms, large handsome leaves and an ability to grow almost anywhere sunny, buddleja is a good choice for beginners.

FEATURES

There are three distinctive, hardy species: deciduous *Buddleja davidii*, whose cone-shaped flowers are dark purple, purplish red, pink, white, or blue; *B. alternifolia*, yielding a waterfall of shoots sleeved with soft purple flowers; and evergreen *B. globosa*, with its clusters of small orange balls.

CONDITIONS

Aspect These plants perform best in full sun, but

tolerate slight shade; *B. davidii* resists chilly winds.

Site Thriving in most soils, they prefer a well-drained position enriched with organic matter.

GROWING METHOD

Feeding Boost growth by sprinkling bone meal around the shrub in April and October and hoeing it in. Take care not to damage roots. Water new plants regularly in spring and summer to encourage robust growth and bounteous blossom. Mulching helps to retain soil moisture in droughty spells.

Propagation All kinds are easily increased from soft-tip cuttings in early summer and hardwood cuttings in the fall.

Problems Control leaf-crippling aphids with pirimicarb, rotenone, permethrin, or pyrethrins. *B. alternifolia*, grown as a standard, needs staking throughout its life.

PRUNING

B. davidii: Cut back the previous year's flowering shoots to within 2in of the base in March.

B. alternifolia and globosa: Unlike *B. davidii*, which flowers on its current-year shoots, both *B. alternifolia* and *B. globosa* bloom on wood produced the previous year. Keep them youthful and flowering freely by shortening to the base a third of the oldest stems when the flowers fade.

BUTTERFLY BUSH AT A GLANCE

Hardy, deciduous, and evergreen or semi-evergreen shrubs. Cones or globes of blossom light up summer. Hardy to 14°F

		RECOMMENDED VARIETIES
JAN	/	
FEB	/	*B. alternifolia* – lite purple
MAR	plant, prune	*B. davidii* "Black Knight"
APR	plant	*B. davidii* "Dartmoor"
MAY	plant	*B. davidii* "Empire Blue"
JUNE	flower, plant	*B. davidii* "Peace"
JULY	flower, plant	*B. davidii* "Pink Delight"
AUG	flower, plant	*B. davidii* "Santana"
SEPT	plant	*B. fallowiana* "Alba"
OCT	plant	*B. globosa* – orange balls
NOV	plant	*B. × weyeriana*
DEC	/	

BUDDLEJA DAVIDII VARIETIES

LEFT: Buddleja globosa, also known as the orange ball tree, bears a wealth of blossom on new shoots in June.

RIGHT: Deep purple Buddleja *"Black Knight" associates strikingly with ferny and silvery-leaved* Artemisia *"Powis Castle".*

ABOVE: Plant "Peace", a large white-flowered form of Buddleja davidii, *to contrast with a deep green conifer.*

BELOW: "Pink Delight" is famed for its immense and long-lasting blooms, which complement large and grayish-green leaves.

ABOVE: Dramatic from spring to fall, "Harlequin's glowing red flowers tip elegant, wand-like shoots sleeved with cream or yellow-margined leaves.

ABOVE: "Nanho Purple" is a small variety in all its parts and is good for narrow borders or small yards.

CALLISTEMON
Bottlebrush

Bottlebrush flowers are most commonly bright red but they can also be mauve, cream, and gold. It is obvious how this evergreen shrub gained its name.

A handsome shrub, callistemon thrives in a sheltered, sunny spot.

FEATURES

Commonly called bottlebrush because its flower—principally stamens—reminds you of a bottle cleaner, the blooms enclasp slender stems clad with narrow, deep green leaves. There are several choice kinds. Hardiest is reckoned to be *Callistemon sieberi*, whose spikes of creamy-yellow flowers appear from late spring to summer. Also appealing are willow-leaved *C. salignus*, a species that glows with red, pink, or mauve flowers; *C. rigidus*, another hardyish, red-flowered kind for "borderline" gardens; and rich matt-red *C. linearis*, the narrow-leaved bottlebrush. Lemon-scented *C. citrinus* "Splendens" treats us to a memorable display of soft, pinkish-red, new shoots and vivid crimson flowers. All grow to around 7ft. Create a focus by underplanting a wall-trained shrub with white petunias.

BOTTLEBRUSH AT A GLANCE

An evergreen, frost-tender shrub with scarlet or creamy-yellow, bottlebrush flowers in June and July. Hardy to 23°F (zone 9).

		RECOMMENDED VARIETIES
JAN	/	
FEB	/	*C. citrinus* "Splendens"
MAR	/	*C. linearis*
APR	plant, prune	*C. rigidus* — very hardy – Red Pink or purp
MAY	plant	*C. salignus*
JUN	flower, plant	*C. sieberi* — hardiest – Y
JULY	flower, prune	
AUG	plant	
SEPT	plant	
OCT	/	
NOV	/	
DEC	/	

CONDITIONS

Aspect Callistemon flowers best if fan-trained against a sheltered, sunny wall that is never shaded. This showy Australian is not for chilly gardens whipped by icy winds. If in doubt, consign it to a conservatory.

Soil Preferring organically rich, light, loamy soil that drains freely, it thrives in clay if you add grit and bulky organics to improve aeration.

GROWING METHOD

Feeding Callistemon copes reasonably well without added fertilizer but performs better if fed with fish, blood, and bone meal in spring and midsummer.
Water new plantings regularly to encourage robust growth and rapid establishment. Mature plants tolerate long, dry periods but flower more profusely if the soil is moist.

Propagation The species are easily grown from seed, but named varieties must be raised from semi-ripe cuttings, ideally with a heel of wood, in late summer.

Problems Avoid alkaline soils in which leaves may turn pale yellow and die, and north- or east-facing sites, where cold winds may shrivel new shoots.

PRUNING

Trimming is not normally required, but occasional cutting back when blooms fade helps to keep growth compact and branches furnished with fresh green shoots.
Old shrubs can be rejuvenated if you prune them back quite hard in spring, but remove only a third of the bush in any one year. Keep stumps moist to encourage new growth.

CAMELLIA
Camellia

The exquisite beauty of delicately tinted camellia blooms—so effective in a vase—makes spring memorable.

Lime hating and thriving on deep, cool, leafy soil, flamboyant, and long-flowering camellias associate stunningly with azaleas.

FEATURES

Glossy-leaved and showered with blossom, evergreen camellias are a great asset. Some species and varieties flower successively from late fall through to spring. Blooms are white, pink, deep rose, or crimson, and suffusions of these colors. Ranging in size from 4–15ft, most varieties flower when 2–3 years old and mature within ten years. They grow to a great age. Plant them to form a statement in a lawn or mixed shrub border, or set them in a large pot or tub and clip them to form a loose obelisk, pyramid, or drumstick. They also make a dashing flowering hedge.

CAMELLIA AT A GLANCE

Evergreen, frost-tender, or hardy shrub with single, semi-double, or fully double blooms. Hardiness according to species.

JAN	flower	RECOMMENDED VARIETIES
FEB	flower	
MAR	flower	*C. japonica* "Adolphe Audusson"
APR	plant	
MAY	plant, prune	*C. japonica* "Berenice Boddy"
JUNE	plant, prune	*C. reticulata* "Captain Rawes"
JULY	plant	
AUG	plant	*C. sasanqua* "Fuji-No-Mine"
SEPT	plant	*C. sasanqua* "Nodami-Ushiro"
OCT	flower	*C. × williamsii*
NOV	flower	"Donation"
DEC	flower	"Jury's Yellow"

Selection   Most camellias species come from China and Japan; some from N. India and the Himalayas. They have now been extensively hybridized to yield a wide range of varieties. Specialist camellia nurseries and garden centers display flowering plants in spring. Choose a variety suited to the position you have in mind.

Types   There are four main types of camellia. *Camellia japonica*: Large and glossy leaved, hardier varieties will prosper in sheltered spots. Its varieties brighten fall to spring. *C. sasanqua*: Fall-flowered, from October to December, it thrives outdoors in the south. In cooler areas, varieties are better planted in pots, displayed outdoors for summer and transferred to a cool conservatory, porch or greenhouse for flowering in fall. *C. reticulata*: Flowering from February to April, varieties can be grown outside in warm, sheltered, gardens. Elsewhere, display them under glass. *C. × williamsii*: Producing tough, weather-resistant foliage, and flowering from November to April, its varieties bloom freely despite low light intensity. Each group is discussed in more detail on pages 86–87.

CONDITIONS

Aspect   Camellias grow best in sheltered, dappled shade. In cooler climates, set them in full sun or very light shade to ensure that blossom buds develop from July to October. Protect them from hot, drying, or frosty winds.

CAMELLIA

Some Camellia reticulata *varieties reward you with a breathtaking display of large, ruffled blooms from mid-winter to spring.*

Rare Camellia lutchuensis *treats you to a bounty of small and deliciously scented blooms from fall to spring.*

Site Ideally, position plants where early morning sunlight does not heat up frosted blossom buds and cause frozen tissues to rupture. Sasanqua varieties tolerate more sun than most other camellias and reticulatas need full sun for part of the day. Some varieties of *Camellia japonica*, such as "The Czar" and "Emperor of Russia", happily take full sun. They need very acid, well-drained soil rich in decomposed organic matter. Heavy, badly drained soils cause root rot and plants often die. Fortify thin, sandy soils with well-rotted leaf mold or bulky manure, before planting.

GROWING METHOD

Feeding Encourage lustrous leaves and a wealth of blossom by applying a balanced ericaceous fertilizer in April and July. It is vital that border soil or container compost is always moist, so water daily, if necessary, during prolonged hot spells. Mulch with crumbly, bulky organic manure to conserve moisture, but keep it well away from the stem, lest it causes bark to rot.

Propagation Increase plants from semi-ripe cuttings in late summer, removing a thin strip of bark from the base to reveal wood and stimulate rooting. Leaf-bud cuttings, 1inch or so long, again "wounding" the base of the shoot, are also taken then. Alternatively, layer low, flexible shoots from mid-spring to late summer. Some varieties, which are very hard to grow from cuttings, are grafted on to understocks of *C. sasanqua*.

Problems You may encounter the following:
*Bud drop: This can be caused by overwet or overdry soils, root rot, or root disturbance. Some very late-flowering varieties may have buds literally pushed off the stem by new spring growth.
*Brown petals and balled blooms: This usually occurs when buds or flowers are lit by early morning sunshine while still wet with dew. Petals may be scorched and some buds "ball" and fail to open. Some varieties with clusters of big buds are prone to this. Gently breaking off some of the buds when they first form helps to reduce balling.
*Oedema: If plants are overwet and conditions overcast, small, brown, corky swellings may develop on leaves. Reduce watering and try to improve air circulation.
*Scale insects: These may be found on the upper or lower leaf surface. Limpet-like scales suck sap and debilitate plants. Spraying with malathion controls them, but spray only in cool or cloudy weather so that it does not scorch leaves.
*Leaf gall: This causes abnormal thickening and discoloration of new growth. It occurs in spring and is caused by a fungus. Pick off and destroy affected leaves before spores disperse.
*Viruses: May be responsible for variable, bright yellow patterns on leaves, or ring spot. Rings develop on leaves. As the leaf ages it becomes yellowish; the center of the ring becomes bright green. There is no cure for viruses, but plants rarely lose much vigour or have their blooming affected. Pick off the worst-looking leaves if they are spoiling your plant's appearance.

PRUNING

Little pruning is needed. Cutting blooms for the vase is usually enough to keep plants compact. However, any thin, spindly, unproductive growth should be removed from the center of the shrub after flowering. Ageing, overgrown camellias can be rejuvenated by quite heavy pruning, provided cuts are made directly above a leaf bud. If severe pruning is necessary, do it in stages, over two years, to avoid stressing the plant.

CAMELLIA

RIGHT: Dense, upright, and slow growing, "Wilamina" is a small, double, incurved variety of Camellia japonica. Blooms last well when cut and hold for a long time on the bush.

BELOW: Prized for its deep pink, outer petals that shade into a creamy-white centre, "Buttons and Bows", is a medium-sized, formal, double hybrid of Camellia saluenensis. It flowers over a long period.

ABOVE: Vigorous and compact, Camellia japonica "Nuccio's Gem" is a formal, double variety with spirally arranged petals. Just a whiff of frost can result in brown-speckled petals.

BELOW: "Scentuous" is a small, informal, double hybrid of Camellia japonica "Tiffany" and the species C. lutchuensis. Its creamy-white flowers have pale pink outer petals and the perfume of C. lutchuensis. It blooms profusely.

RIGHT: "Wynne Rayner" is a saluenensis seedling. From early to mid-spring, a profusion of blooms is borne on freely branching stems clad with smallish, glossy green leaves

Camellia sasanqua
Sasanquas start the camellia season by producing flowers, depending on variety, from fall to mid-winter. They make a wonderful show in a sheltered border or cool conservatory.
The smaller, more compact varieties, such as single, rose-pink "Tanya" and double, bright rose-red "Shishigashira", make good container plants.
Others worth a little cosseting are fast-growing "Fuji-No-Mine", whose pure white, double blooms are borne on slender shoots; and bushy, upright

"Nodami-Ushiro", a sumptuous, semi-double, deep pink that pleases for weeks.

Camellia reticulata
This species presents us with the largest and most spectacular of all camellia blooms, but the shrubs themselves have a sparse, open-branching habit. Many of the more recently developed hybrids are crosses between C. japonica and C. reticulata. The result is a more leafy shrub that blooms longer with flowers that are more impressive.
To perform well, C. reticulata needs

lighter, more free-draining soil than other camellias. Choice varieties are rose-pink "Arbutus Gum" and carmine-rose "Captain Rawes".

Camellia japonica
This is the species that most people think of when camellias are mentioned. There is a wide range of varieties in white to pale or dark pink or red. There are picotee and bicolors. They are usually classified by flower type: that is, single, semi-double, and formal double. There are also peony and anemone forms.

VARIETIES

BELOW: "Betty Ridley", a rarely seen, sumptuous, and profusely blooming, formal, double variety of Camellia japonica, *is worth seeking from a specialist grower. Here it is compared with the tiny pink flower of the species,* C. rosiflora.

ABOVE: A rapturous but seldom seen white, flushed-pink, and semi-double variety of Camellia vernalis, *"Star Upon Star" is usually grouped with* C. sasanqua *because of similarities in habit and uses. Blooming late in spring, it is an upright grower and ideal for small gardens and patio pots.*

BELOW: "Desire", a large, formal, double variety of Camellia japonica, *bears arresting, mainly white petals, with rims delicately flushed with cerise pink.*

ABOVE: A collector's piece you may have to search for, "Lois Shinault" is a large-flowered variety of Camellia reticulata, *whose semi-double, orchid-pink flowers of fluted petals display a showy boss of golden stamens.*

Some varieties produce sports—flowers of a different color to the parent's. These "sports" are a source of new varieties. Varieties of *C. japonica*—they flower from late fall to spring—may be grown in patio tubs or planted as border specimens. They also provide a fabulous backcloth to smaller shrubs and herbaceous perennials. Varieties include: White—"Mary Costa": Unusual anemone form with incurving petals; upright growth. "Lily Pons": Single to semi-double with long, narrow petals around a barrel of stamens.

Pink—"Berenice Boddy": Semi-double; light pink with deeper pink under petals. Vigorous, spreading.
Red—"Adolphe Audusson": Semi-double; good glossy leaves, open upright growth. "C. M. Hovey": Formal double rose red; freely produced blooms.
Bicolor—"Lavinia Maggi": Formal double; carmine-red and pink stripes on a white background.
Picotee—"Margaret Davis" Informal double to loose peony; white petals rimmed with red; upright.

Camellia × williamsii

This is a very fine group of camellias bred by crossing *C. japonica* with *C. saluenensis*. The original crosses were made in Cornwall by J.C. Williams, who gave them their name. Available in the same color range as other camellias, most are semi-double. Eagerly sought are: semi-double, orchid-pink "Donation"; anemone-centred, creamy-white "Jury's Yellow"; deep rose-pink "Elegant Beauty", also with an anemone centre; and formal, vibrant, double, pink "Water Lily".

CEANOTHUS
Californian lilac

Evergreen ceanothus, such as "Puget Blue", are best fan-trained against a warm wall.

There are few more riveting, spring- and early summer-flowering shrubs—ideal for light soils that dry out quickly—than evergreen members of the Californian lilac family.

FEATURES

Prized for their massed clusters of principally pale blue to deep violet-blue, powderpuff blooms, there are evergreen and deciduous varieties. They range from carpeters to imposing bushes of around 15ft high. Most evergreens, such as "Blue Mound" and *Ceanothus thyrsiflorus* "Edinensis", bloom from May to June. Two exceptions, "Fallal Blue" and "Burkwoodii", perform from July to September. The best of the deciduous group—pink "Marie Simon" and blue "Gloire de Versailles"—flower from July to October.

CALIFORNIAN LILAC AT A GLANCE

Evergreen or deciduous shrubs with blue or pink blooms from spring to early fall. Hardy to 14°F (zone 8).

JAN	/	
FEB	/	RECOMMENDED VARIETIES
MAR	plant, prune	
APR	plant, prune	Evergreen
		"Blue Mound"
MAY	flower, plant	"Cascade"
JUN	flower, plant	"Concha"
JULY	flower, plant	"Puget Blue"
AUG	flower, plant	*C. thyrsiflorus* "Repens"
SEPT	flower, plant	"Zanzibar" (variegated)
		Deciduous
OCT	flower, plant	"Gloire de Versailles"
NOV	/	"Marie Simon"
DEC	/	"Perle Rose"

CONDITIONS

Aspect   All kinds, especially evergreen varieties which are best grown against a south-facing wall, need a sunny, sheltered spot where air circulates freely.

Site   Ceanothus prospers on well-drained clay loam, sandy or humus-rich, gravelly soils. It will not thrive on heavy clay that waterlogs in winter, where roots are liable to rot.

GROWING METHOD

Feeding   Keep plants lustrous and flowering freely by applying bone meal in spring and fall. Breaking down slowly, it is rich in phosphates, which encourage robust root growth. In its native habitat, this plant receives rain only in winter and has adapted to very dry summers.

Propagation   Most varieties are grown from semi-ripe cuttings taken from mid- to late summer.

Problems   Ceanothus is susceptible to root rot, caused by wet soil. It is seldom troubled by pests.

PRUNING

Evergreen varieties: Trim spring-flowering kinds when blooms fade in early summer, and cut late summer performers in April.

Deciduous varieties: In early spring, shorten the previous year's flowered shoots to within 2–3in of the older wood.

CEANOTHUS VARIETIES

ABOVE: "Concha" forms a dense, arching, evergreen bush to 5ft high and 6ft across and enriches spring with a profusion of red-budded, deep blue flowers. Find it a warm, sunny spot and it will handsomely reward you.

ABOVE: A sumptuous, evergreen variety, "Dark Star" is prized for its spicy perfumed, purplish-blue blossoms borne in showy bunches on shoot tips in late spring. Small, oval, toothed leaves clad an umbrella of branches.

ABOVE: Glorifying May and June, Ceanothus dentatus floribundus, as its name implies, is so massed with terminal or lateral clusters of glowing ultramarine-blue flowers that its small, evergreen leaves tend to "disappear".

ABOVE: From mid- to late spring, the rounded to oval, deeply veined, evergreen leaves of Santa Barbara ceanothus (Ceanothus impressus) complement a dashing display of clustered, dark blue flowers on shoot tips.

BELOW: A robust form of evergreen Ceanothus arboreus soaring to 20ft, "Trewithen Blue" drips with scented, mid-blue flowers in late spring and early summer. Plant it to make a spectacular focal point for a large, sunny, sheltered lawn.

BELOW: Plant evergreen "Puget Blue", a zestful variety of Ceanothus impressus, to clothe a sunny wall or fence. In spring, every shoot is thickly sleeved with rich indigo-blue flowers. Never prune it hard, for older growth seldom regenerates.

CHAENOMELES
Japonica

Eye-catching when grown as an espalier against a north- or east-facing wall, chaenomeles yields clusters of bloom from late winter to late spring.

Midwinter splendor: flowering quince is sleeved with blossom when many shrubs are resting.

FEATURES

Also known as japonica or flowering quince, this spiny, deciduous shrub makes a colorful bush to 7ft high or, if espalier-trained against a wall or fence, a striking drape to 9ft. Long-lived, it flowers early in life and reaches maturity in 3–5 years. It is valued for its thickly clustered blooms that transform bare branches from mid-winter to early spring. Flowers are followed by small, fragrant, quince-like fruits that ripen to bright yellow. Fruits are edible and make delicious jams and preserves. Showy varieties include apricot "Geisha Girl", pink "Moerloesii", white "Nivalis", and large, bright crimson "Rowallane". In borders, it makes a showy, rounded background plant for smaller shrubs, perennials, bulbs, and annuals.

JAPONICA AT A GLANCE

A hardy deciduous shrub, its clusters of white, pink, or red, saucer-shaped flowers brighten spring. Hardy to -13°F (zone 5).

		RECOMMENDED VARIETIES
JAN	/	
FEB	/	For walls
MAR	flower, plant	"Geisha Girl"
APR	flower, prune	"Moerloesii"
MAY	flower, prune	"Nivalis"
JUNE	plant	"Simonii"
JULY	prune	For bushes
AUG	plant	"Lemon and Lime"
SEPT	plant	"Pink Lady"
OCT	plant	"Knaphill Scarlet"
NOV	plant	"Rowallane"
DEC	/	

CONDITIONS

Aspect   Usefully adaptable, chaenomeles thrives in full sun or light shade, does not mind cold winds and colors cold, north- or east-facing walls.

Site   Though it prefers well-drained soil, it tolerates heavy, waterlogged clay. Help sandy soils stay cool and moist by working in plenty of bulky manure or well-rotted garden compost.

GROWING METHOD

Feeding   Unlike many other shrubs, chaenomeles thrives in poorish soil. For best results, build fertility by topdressing the root area with pelleted chicken manure, fish, blood, and bone meal, or Growmore in spring and midsummer. Water plants regularly in their first year.

Propagation   Take semi-ripe cuttings in late summer or detach and replant rooted suckers in fall.

Problems   If coral spot appears—shoots are pimpled with coral-pink or orange pustules—cut back to healthy, white wood and burn prunings. Paint stumps with fungicidal pruning compound.

PRUNING

Bushes: Apart from removing crowded shoots when flowers fade in spring, no regular cutting back is required.

Wall trained: Young plants: Tie espaliered shoots to a wire frame. In July, cut back to five leaves shoots growing away from the wall. Reduce to two buds further growth from shortened shoots. Established plants: Shorten the previous year's side shoots to two or three leaves when flowers fade in spring.

CHOISYA TERNATA
Mexican orange blossom

Wafting citrus scent on a warm breeze, starry-flowered, evergreen Mexican orange blooms in spring and fall.

Harmonizing beautifully with a pink-flowering Japanese cherry, Mexican orange blossom performs best in a sheltered, sunny spot.

FEATURES

A spring prince, evergreen *Choisya ternata*, to 6ft or more high, is regaled with orange-fragrant, starry, white flowers in April and May and again in October. Its glossy, trefoil leaves spill citrus scent when you brush against them.

"Sundance", a smaller, golden-leaved form, is particularly striking in winter when its foliage assumes orange-yellow tints. Intriguingly different—leaves are long and narrow—"Aztec Pearl" bears pink-budded, white blossoms.

CHOISYA AT A GLANCE

Hardy evergreen shrubs—"Sundance" has yellow leaves—with orange-scented, white flowers in spring. Hardy to 14°F (zone 8).

JAN	/	RECOMMENDED VARIETIES
FEB	/	
MAR	/	*C. ternata*
APR	flower, plant	*C. ternata* "Sundance"
MAY	flower, prune	*C. ternata* "Aztec Pearl"
JUNE	flower, prune	
JULY	plant	
AUG	plant	
SEPT	flower, plant	
OCT	/	
NOV	/	
DEC	/	

CONDITIONS

Aspect   Full sun or light shade, but "Sundance" needs more light than *C. ternata* or "Aztec Pearl", otherwise its leaves will pale to green and lose their appeal. In northern gardens, position all three kinds against a warm, sunny wall.

Site   Choisya thrives in fertile, acid, neutral, or alkaline soil. Enrich nutrient-starved, quick-draining, sandy loam, or stony patches with bulky organic manure.

GROWING METHOD

Feeding   Apply a complete plant food, such as Growmore or fish, blood, and bone meal in early spring and midsummer. Water regularly and copiously in long, dry periods.

Propagation   Increase choisya from semi-ripe cuttings from mid- to late summer, or layer stems from early to late summer.

Problems   No specific pests or diseases but flowering diminishes if shrubs are not pruned regularly and left to become woody.

PRUNING

In cold areas, cut back frost-damaged shoots to healthy, white wood in spring. Keep mature bushes—over five years old—flowering freely by removing from the base a third of the older branches when blooms fade in May or June.

CISTUS
Rock rose

A rapid succession of crumpled, silky, often-blotched blooms in white, pink and cerise are your reward for planting cistus.

A Mediterranean drought resister, free-flowering rock roses are also coveted for their aromatic leaves, which distil "honey" on a warm day.

FEATURES

A dandyish Mediterranean native, evergreen cistus delights us from June to August with a daily succession of saucer-shaped, crumpled, silky blooms. Bushes range in size from carpeting, white and maroon-blotched *Cistus lusitanicus* "Decumbens", to 2ft high, to white and yellow-centred *C. laurifolius*, an imposing sentinel that rises to 5ft. There are pink-, crimson- and lilac-flowered varieties, too. All varieties perform early in life and taller kinds make stunning, informal flowering hedges. Small, pot or tub-grown species and varieties, such as neat and bushy "Silver Pink" with its grayish-silvery leaves, illuminate a sun-baked patio.

ROCK ROSE AT A GLANCE

Drought-resisting evergreen for light soil, it is smothered with white, pink, or red blooms in summer. Hardy to 23°F (zone 9).

JAN	/	
FEB	/	
MAR	/	
APR	plant, prune	
MAY	flower, plant	
JUNE	flower, plant	
JULY	flower, plant	
AUG	plant, prune	
SEPT	plant	
OCT	/	
NOV	/	
DEC	/	

RECOMMENDED VARIETIES

Small—up to 3ft
C. × *corbariensis*
"Silver Pink"
C. × *skanbergii*
"Sunset"
Tall—over 3ft
"Alan Fradd"
C. laurifolius
C. × *purpureus*

CONDITIONS

Aspect

Rock roses must have full sun all day to make compact, free-flowering plants. They do not mind exposed sites or salt-laden breezes, but may be damaged by frosty winds. Avoid growing them in areas of high rainfall as blooms are spoilt by prolonged, wet weather.

Site

Plants make the strongest growth on humus-rich, sandy, or gravelly loam, which drains quickly; they are less spirited on heavy, badly drained soils. In nature, rock roses flourish on porous limestone. If your soil is acid, boost growth by adding lime before planting.

GROWING METHOD

Feeding

These plants need little or no fertilizer. Apply a light dressing of bone meal in spring and fall.
Once plants are growing strongly, water is seldom needed, even during weeks of drought.

Propagation

Take semi-ripe cuttings in summer. Species can be grown from seeds or cuttings. Varieties must be raised from cuttings.

Problems

No particular pest or disease afflicts cistus, but hard pruning into older wood can inhibit stumps from re-growing.

PRUNING

Encourage newly planted shrubs to branch freely and make dense bushes by pinching out shoot tips several times throughout the first two summers. Cut back frost-damaged stems to healthy growth in spring.

CONVOLVULUS CNEORUM
Shrubby bindweed

Canopied with dazzling white blossom from June to August, Convolvulus cneorum, *with red campion, flourishes in full sun.*

No garden? Plant silky-leaved, shrubby convolvulus to emblazon a patio pot or tub with a massed display of funnel-shaped flowers.

FEATURES

A coveted, silvery, silky-leaved evergreen whose pink buds open to flared, white and yellow-eyed, trumpet blooms from June to August, *Convolvulus cneorum* makes a low hummock to 18in high and 2.5ft across and has many uses.

Create a feature all will admire by associating it with *Ceanothus* "Zanzibar", prized for its powder-blue flowers and golden-variegated leaves.

Plant shrubby bindweed to highlight a rock garden or star in a patio pot or deep windowbox.

It is not fully hardy, so consign it to a very sheltered border and cover it in late fall with several layers of bubble plastic draped over an open-topped wigwam of canes. Make sure the plastic does not touch its foliage. If you plant it in a patio pot for summer, move it to a cold greenhouse for winter.

SHRUBBY BINDWEED AT A GLANCE

A borderline hardy evergreen with soft, silvery leaves; trumpet-shaped flowers appear from June to August. Hardy to 14°F (zone 8).

JAN	shield from frost	RECOMMENDED VARIETIES
FEB	shield from frost	
MAR	/	(only the species
APR	plant, prune	*C. cneorum* is grown)
MAY	plant	
JUNE	flower, plant	
JULY	flower, plant	
AUG	plant	
SEPT	plant	
OCT	/	
NOV	/	
DEC	/	

CONDITIONS

Aspect Find it a sheltered, sunny spot—it revels against a south- or west-facing wall—where it will not be damaged by chilly winds.

Site Not fussy, it thrives in well-drained, acid to neutral soil. If your garden has badly drained clay, work in plenty of grit or sharp sand or set the plant on a raised bed. It is vital that roots are not "treading" water.

GROWING METHOD

Feeding Boost growth by working fish, blood, and bone meal or Growmore into the root area in April and July. Add a slow-release fertilizer to patio tub compost. If planting coincides with a droughty spell, foliar feed weekly to help the plant absorb nutrients more quickly.
Water copiously after planting to settle soil around the roots. Follow by mulching with a 2in layer of well-rotted organic material to conserve moisture.

Propagation Increase shrubby bindweed from semi-ripe "heeled" cuttings of new side shoots from late summer to early fall.

Problems If hard frost causes shoot tips to die back, prune them to just above a healthy bud in late spring.

PRUNING

Pruning is unnecessary unless the plant is ageing. Then, in early spring, reduce gaunt and woody stems by half their length, cutting to just above a joint or to new shoots. Keep stumps moist to help them sprout. The best way to do this, apart from sprinkling them with water, is to coat them with a plastic-based anti-transpirant, normally used for helping Christmas trees retain their needles.

CORNUS
Flowering dogwood

In mid-spring, white or pink-tinted flowers (bracts) transform the Pacific dogwood (Cornus nuttallii) into a fascinating talking point.

Late winter sees the bare branches of Cornelian cherry (Cornus mas) studded with a multitude of tiny, primrose-yellow blossoms.

FEATURES

Suddenly, in late winter—from February to March—sulfur-yellow, powderpuff blooms light up bare, slender stems. *Cornus mas* has few rivals.

In spring, when flowers fade, oval, pointed, vivid green leaves unfold. Small, edible, cherry-shaped, red fruits, good for jam, form in fall when leaves assume reddish-purple tints before falling.

A coveted, leaf-shedding native of Europe and Western Asia, it slowly forms a handsome globe to around 15ft high and across. It can also be planted to create a stocky, dense flowering hedge.

Dramatically different, the Pacific dogwood (*C. nuttallii*) bears a plethora of saucer-shaped white, pink-tinged bracts (flowers), which light up late spring. When its flowers fade, they are fetchingly replaced by orbs of multi-seeded fruits.

FLOWERING DOGWOOD AT A GLANCE

Cornus mas has sulfur-yellow flowers in February; *C. nuttallii* bears whitish-pink blooms in June. Hardy to 4°F (zone 7).

JAN	/	
FEB	flower	RECOMMENDED VARIETIES
MAR	flower, prune	*C. mas* "Aurea"
APR	plant	*C. mas*
MAY	flower, plant	"Aureoelegantissima"
JUNE	flower, plant	*C. mas* "Hillier's Upright"
JULY	plant	*C. mas* "Variegata"
AUG	plant	*C. nuttallii* "Colrigo
SEPT	plant	Giant"
OCT	plant	
NOV	plant	
DEC	/	

CONDITIONS

Aspect Though performing better in full sun, both species are good contenders for lightly shaded spots. In deep shade, they form a looser, less symmetrical branching system. They are not harmed by cold winds.

Site *C. mas* thrives on virtually any soil, from light sand to heavy clay and chalk, provided it is not waterlogged. *C nuttallii* needs acid, fertile conditions. Enrich impoverished sand and chalk with bulky organic manure or well-rotted garden compost.

GROWING METHOD

Propagation *C. mas:* Take semi-ripe cuttings of maturing side shoots—ready when the bark at the base of the stem turns brown and firms up—in late summer.
C. nuttallii: Best increased from soft-tip cuttings from early to midsummer.

Feeding Boost growth by topdressing the root area with a granular form of complete plant food, or fish, blood, and bone meal in spring and midsummer. Water in if the soil is dry.
In droughty spells, keep shoots vigorous by soaking the root area or digging a moat around the shrub and repeatedly filling it with water. Follow by mulching thickly with moisture-retaining, well-rotted garden compost, bark, or cocoa shell.

Problems *C. mas* and *C. nuttallii* have a rugged constitution and are seldom troubled by pests and diseases.

PRUNING

Pruning is not needed, apart from removing awkwardly placed shoots after flowering. Use pruning shears and cut to just above a shoot.

COTINUS COGGYGRIA
Smoke Bush

In early summer, Cotinus "Notcutt's Variety" treats us to a fabulous display of amber, pink, and purple "smoke-like" inflorescences.

Prized for its richly hued leaves, Cotinus "Royal Purple" contrasts fetchingly with green-leaved berberis.

FEATURES

Remarkably drought-resistant shrub, *Cotinus coggygria*, from central and southern Europe, is appealing twice a year: in June and July when its plumy, 6–8in flowers are reminiscent of pink smoke; and in fall when leaves are suffused with vibrant, fiery, or sunset hues. Growing slowly to form an obelisk 9ft by 6ft, purple-leaved varieties associate beautifully with lemon-yellow-leaved mock orange (*Philadelphus coronarius* "Aureus"). Purple-leaved kinds also make a fetching host for scrambling *Lathyrus grandiflorus*, an exuberant, pink-flowered perennial pea.

If you do not have sufficient border space for a smoke bush, set it in a large tub of tree and shrub compost and position it to form a statement on your patio or at the end of a path. Plant a pair of shrubs to frame the entrance to a wide driveway.

SMOKE BUSH AT A GLANCE

Green or purple leaves assume sunset fall tints. "Smoky" flowering plumes make summer special. Hardy to 4°F (zone 7).

		RECOMMENDED VARIETIES
JAN	/	
FEB	/	"Atropurpurea"
MAR	plant, prune	"Grace"
APR	plant, prune	"Notcutt's Variety"
MAY	plant	"Royal Purple"
JUNE	flower, plant	
JULY	flower, plant	
AUG	plant	
SEPT	plant	
OCT	plant	
NOV	plant	
DEC	/	

CONDITIONS

Aspect Stalwarts both, green- and purple-leaved varieties are very hardy and unaffected by cold winds.

Site The green-leaved family excels in full sun or light shade, but purple-leaved varieties must have bright sunshine or their foliage will pale to insipid green. All prefer humus-rich soil enriched with bulky organic manure or well-rotted garden compost, but they will survive without stress on thin, sandy loam.

GROWING METHODS

Feeding Fortify the root area with fish, blood, and bone meal, or Growmore, twice a year: in spring and midsummer. Water it in if the soil is dry.

Propagation Increase plants from semi-ripe cuttings of new shoots from mid- to late summer. Root them in a lightly shaded garden frame or on a brightly lit windowsill.

Problems If shoot tips die after a very hard winter, shorten them to live buds in early spring. Should mildew attack purple-leaved varieties, control it by spraying with fungicide containing carbendazim.

PRUNING

Choose one of three methods:

For a mass of flowers on a large shrub, prune only to remove dead wood.

To achieve a balance of foliage and flowers, take out a third of the oldest shoots each spring.

For dashing foliage, spectacular fall color and no flowers—ideal for purple-leaved varieties—cut back all shoots to 6in from the base in early spring. Keep cuts moist to encourage regrowth.

COTONEASTER
Cotoneaster

Herringbone cotoneaster (Cotoneaster horizontalis) *is splendid for covering walls. Pinkish-white flowers are followed by scarlet berries.*

Cotoneaster conspicuus *"Decorus's froth of white summer blossom preludes a feast of bright red fall fruits.*

FEATURES

This versatile, evergreen, semi-evergreen, or deciduous family ranges in height from carpeters of 12in to towering bushes more than 10ft high.

Choice kinds are dense and weed-suppressing, evergreen "Coral Beauty", whose glowing orange berries light up fall; semi-evergreen *Cotoneaster horizontalis*, ideal for clothing a bank or wall beneath a ground floor window; and semi-evergreen "Cornubia", an imposing, arching bush to 10ft.

Evergreen *C. lacteus* and semi-evergreen *C. simonsii* make splendid, low, flowering, and berrying hedges.

Sprays of small, white spring flowers are followed by a glowing fall to winter display of red or yellow fruits. Cotoneasters take 5–10 years to mature, depending on species and conditions, and are long-lived. Fruits are nutritious food for garden birds and winter migrants.

COTONEASTER AT A GLANCE

Deciduous, semi- or fully evergreen shrub; white blossom heralds an fall display of vibrant fruits. Hardy to -13°F (zone 5).

JAN	/	RECOMMENDED VARIETIES
FEB	/	
MAR	plant	Ground covering to 30cm (12in)
APR	plant	"Coral Beauty"
MAY	flower, prune	"Oakwood"
JUNE	flower	"Skogholm"
JULY	plant	Small bushes (30–80cm/ 12–32in)
AUG	plant	*C. conspicuus* "Decorus"
SEPT	plant	*C. horizontalis*
OCT	plant, prune	Taller kinds
NOV	plant, prune	"Cornubia"
DEC	/	

CONDITIONS

Aspect All kinds grow best and flower and fruit more freely in full sun. They will tolerate partial shade, but shoots are looser and berries sparse.

Site Cotoneasters prefer well-drained, medium to heavyish loam, but any reasonably fertile soil encourages stocky growth. Improve thin, sandy, or gravelly areas by digging in bulky, humus-forming, well-rotted manure, decayed garden compost, or leaf mold.

GROWING METHOD

Feeding Not essential, but an application of Growmore or fish, blood, and bone meal, carefully pricked into the root area in spring and midsummer, encourages lustrous leaves. If you are growing a small-leafed, bushy variety such as *C. simonsii* as a close-planted hedge, apply fertilizer in spring and summer. Water newly planted cotoneasters regularly in spring and summer to help them grow away quickly. Once established, they will tolerate long periods without supplementary watering.

Propagation Take semi-ripe cuttings from mid- to late summer; layer shoots from spring to summer.

Problems Fireblight: Causing flowers to wilt and wither—they appear scorched—it is controlled by cutting back affected shoots to healthy, white wood. Burn prunings.

PRUNING

Keep plants flowering and fruiting well by removing one stem in three. Tackle evergreens in mid-spring and deciduous kinds in mid-fall.

CRATAEGUS
Hawthorn

Hawthorn's abundant, milky-scented, white flowers in early summer are followed by clusters of scarlet or orange berries in fall and winter.

A traditional English hedgerow shrub, hawthorn (Crataegus monogyna) also makes an elegant, small flowering tree.

FEATURES

Architectural, deciduous hawthorns—ideal for focal points or screening—can be shrubby or grow into small trees to 15ft. Clad with lobed or toothed leaves, suffused with fiery scarlet tints in fall, blossom mantles shoots in May and June. Bright orange or red berries—birds adore them—persist into winter. Stems are usually spiny and native may or quickthorn (*Crataegus monogyna*) makes a formidable barrier. Others, such as glossy-leaved *C. × lavallei*, whose large clusters of white blossom are followed by orange berries coupled with richly autumn-hued leaves, and deep red-flowered *C. laevigata* "Paul's Scarlet, make fetching sentinels.

HAWTHORN AT A GLANCE

Large, deciduous bushes or small trees, their summer blossom is followed by orange or scarlet fruits. Hardy to -13°F (zone 5).

		RECOMMENDED VARIETIES
JAN	/	
FEB	prune	"Crimson Cloud"
MAR	plant	*C. × grignonensis*
APR	plant	*C. × lavallei*
MAY	flower, plant	"Paul's Scarlet"
JUNE	flower	"Rosea Flore Pleno"
JULY	prune	
AUG	prune	
SEPT	/	
OCT	plant	
NOV	plant, prune	
DEC	prune	

CONDITIONS

Aspect
Stalwarts for exposed upland gardens raked by wind, or those fringing the sea, where leaves are powdered with salt, hawthorn flowers best in full sun. In light shade, bushes have a more open habit and fewer blooms.

Site
Though hawthorn prefers deep and heavyish but well-drained soils, it will tolerate light, sandy, or gravelly ground. Improve thin soils by working in plenty of bulky organic matter.

GROWING METHOD

Feeding
Work bone meal into the soil in spring and fall to ensure a continuous supply of root-promoting phosphates.
Water copiously in the first year after planting. Thereafter, when hawthorn is established, it is seldom stressed by drought.

Propagation
Raise species from seed, from berries mixed with damp sand and placed in a flower pot. Break dormancy by positioning the pot in the coldest part of the garden. In spring, remove seeds and sow them in an outdoor seed bed. Seedlings quickly appear.

Problems
Powdery mildew can whiten leaves. Control it by spraying with carbendazim, mancozeb, or triforine with bupirimate.

PRUNING

Bushes:
Encourage a profusion of blossom by shortening the previous year's shoots by two-thirds in late winter.

Hedges:
Clip in mid-July and in winter.

CYTISUS
Broom

From May to June, Cytisus scoparius *illuminates a sunny border with golden-yellow blossom. Contrast it with a purple-leaved cotinus.*

Bearing cone-shaped, richly pineapple-scented blooms in early summer, Cytisus battandieri *is best fan-trained against a sunny wall.*

FEATURES

Treating us to whippy stemmed and thickly clustered cascades of fragrant, pea flowers, deciduous and butter-yellow-flowered *Cytisus scoparius* and its kaleidoscope-hued hybrids make May and June special.

Plant them singly to punctuate a border, or group several of one color or in harmonizing shades to create an unforgettable statement. Its fetching, leaf-shedding relation Moroccan (pineapple) broom (*C. battandieri*) is famed for its June display of pineapple-scented cones of bright yellow blooms amid silvery, tri-lobed leaves. It has a lax, floppy habit so train it to embrace a sunny wall or frame a patio door. Alternatively, plant it to entwine a tall, metal obelisk in a border or at the end of a path. When in flower, a warm, breezy day wafts crushed pineapple scent around the garden.

BROOM AT A GLANCE

Massed, tiny, pea blooms or chunky, golden flower cones brighten borders from late spring to early summer. Hardy to 14°F (zone 8).

JAN	/	RECOMMENDED VARIETIES
FEB	/	
MAR	plant	*C. battandieri*
APR	plant	*C. scoparius* "Andreanus"
MAY	flower, plant	*C. scoparius* "Burkwoodii"
JUNE	flower, prune	*C. scoparius* "Goldfinch"
JULY	plant	*C. scoparius* "Killeney Red"
AUG	plant	*C. scoparius* "Killeney Salmon"
SEPT	plant	*C. scoparius* "Lena"
OCT	plant	*C. scoparius* "Zeelandia"
NOV	/	
DEC	/	

CONDITIONS

Aspect
C. scoparius and its varieties are hardier than *C. battandieri*, which needs to be sheltered from cold winds. Both flower at their best in full sun.

Site
Encourage robust growth by setting plants in free-draining and well-manured, neutral, or acid, sandy soil. Lime tends to cause weak, pale green leaves.

Feeding
After adding balanced fertilizer to planting holes, encourage sturdy growth by topdressing the root area with fish, blood, and bone meal in spring and again in midsummer. If your soil is chalky and hybrids are suffering from iron deficiency, help them recover by applying a soil-acidifying fertilizer.

Propagation
Increase *C. scoparius* and *C. battandieri* from semi-ripe cuttings taken from mid- to late summer.

Problems
When *C. scoparius* and its hybrids become woody and flower less—after ten or so years— they cannot be refurbished by hard pruning, so it is best to replace them with young, potted plants.

Occasionally, in summer, leaf buds develop into cauliflower-like growths covered with silvery hairs. Gall mites cause them. There is no chemical control, so remove affected plants and replace them with healthy stock.

PRUNING

Keep *C. scoparius* and its hybrids youthful and ablaze with flowers in spring by shearing flowered stems to just above older growth when pods form. *C. battandieri* isn't normally pruned, but cut out badly placed and weak stems after flowering If you are growing it against a wall, tie in new shoots then.

DAPHNE
Daphne

Sweetly scented Daphne odora *"Aureomarginata" rewards us with clusters of pinkish-white flowers in late winter.*

Lime-tolerant daphnes—this is Daphne odora*—have an unfounded reputation for being difficult. Find them a cool, moist, and sunny spot.*

FEATURES

Grown primarily for their sweetly fragrant blooms, daphnes are best planted close to a living room where, on a warm day with a window open, scent wafts indoors. Alternatively, set bushes in pots or tubs beside a garden seat. Herald spring with deciduous *Daphne mezereum*, to 3ft, with upright stems sleeved with starry, purplish-red flowers. Slightly taller but spreading and evergreen *D. odora* "Aureomarginata", with its cream-edged, green leaves that complement clusters of pinkish-white blooms, also flowers then. From May to June, evergreen *D. burkwoodii* "Somerset", wondrous when filling a large pedestal urn and forming a focal point, exudes vanilla perfume from pale pink blooms.

DAPHNE AT A GLANCE

Deciduous or evergreen shrubs with purple-red to pink flowers from late winter to early summer. Hardy to 19°F (zone 8).

JAN	/	
FEB	flower	RECOMMENDED VARIETIES
MAR	flower, plant	*D. bholua*
APR	flower, plant	*D. burkwoodii* "Somerset"
MAY	flower, prune	*D. cneorum*
JUNE	flower, prune	*D. mezereum*
JULY	plant	*D. odora*
AUG	plant	"Aureomarginata"
SEPT	plant	*D. retusa*
OCT	plant	
NOV	plant	
DEC	/	

CONDITIONS

Aspect Daphne prospers in full sun or very light shade. Shelter it from strong, drying winds.

Site It must have perfectly drained soil with a high organic content. Keep roots cool by mulching plants with well-decayed manure.

GROWING METHOD

Feeding Sustain strong flowering shoots by feeding with bone meal in spring and fall. Encourage newly planted shrubs by liquid feeding with a high-potash fertilizer at weekly intervals from spring to summer.
Deep, regular watering is necessary for young plants in long, dry spells. Make sure the soil does not become soggy, for roots may rot.

Propagation Multiply plants by layering shoots from mid-spring to late summer or by taking semi-ripe cuttings from mid- to late summer.

Problems Sudden death is usually caused by root rot triggered by bad drainage. Daphne may also be attacked by blackening, leaf-spot fungi that speckle foliage. Control leaf spot by spraying with carbendazim or mancozeb. Viruses are also liable to attack daphne. Characterized by twisted and puckered leaves, there is no control, so dig up and burn affected plants.

PRUNING

No regular cutting back needed, apart from shortening young, straggly stems in spring to keep bushes tidy. Do not prune into older, black-barked wood, for stumps may not regenerate.

DEUTZIA
Deutzia

Flowering from spring to early summer, single, white-flowered Deutzia gracilis *makes a charming background to these late yellow primroses.*

Soaring to around 7ft, Deutzia scabra *flaunts sprays of double, white, or pink-tinged blooms from July to August.*

FEATURES

Profusely blooming, deciduous, upright or rounded deutzias are easy to grow and best displayed in a mixed border. All, apart from late-flowering *Deutzia monbeigii* with its small leaves, appealingly white beneath and complementing dense clusters of starry, white flowers from July to August, perform from May to July. An elegant, upright shrub, deutzia varies in height from deep carmine-pink-flowered *D. × rosea*, 32in by 24in, to *D. scabra* "Pride of Rochester", a handsome leviathan that soars to 7ft. From June to July, its double, white blooms smother pleasingly, peeling-barked branches.

CONDITIONS

Aspect   Deutzia prefers full sun but will tolerate light shade. Plants should be sheltered from strong, northerly or easterly winds.

Site   This shrub flourishes on most well-drained soils, especially if fortified with organic matter.

GROWING METHOD

Feeding   Undemanding, deutzia does not need regular feeding. If growth is poor, topdress the root area with Growmore or fish, blood, and bone meal in spring and summer.

Propagation   Multiply deutzia from hardwood cuttings from mid-fall to early winter.

Problems   Late spring frosts may damage blossom buds of May-flowering varieties, so position plants carefully if you garden in a frost pocket.

PRUNING

Encourage a wealth of blossom by cutting back to near ground level a third of the older branches when flowers fade. If stems bearing flower buds are killed by frost, shorten them to healthy wood.

DEUTZIA AT A GLANCE

Deciduous shrub with shoots clothed in single or double, pink or white blooms in spring and summer. Hardy to -13°F (zone 5).

JAN	/	RECOMMENDED VARIETIES
FEB	/	
MAR	plant	*D. × elegantissima* "Rosealind"
APR	plant	*D. × hybrida* "Magician"
MAY	flower, plant	"Montrose"
JUNE	flower	*D. monbeigii*
JULY	flower, prune	*D. × rosea* "Campanulata"
AUG	plant, prune	*D. scabra* "Pride of Rochester"
SEPT	plant	
OCT	plant	
NOV	plant	
DEC	plant	

ECHIUM CANDICANS (FASTUOSUM)
Pride of Madeira

Tower of jewels is another evocative name for Echium candicans, *a remarkable, Canary Islands native.*

In a sheltered, frost-free garden, this amazing shrub will spread to 6ft across. Elsewhere, it should be grown in a container and overwintered under glass.

FEATURES

A somewhat sprawling shrub with gray-green leaves, Pride of Madeira is an exciting challenge. Growing to about 5ft high and spreading to 7ft or more, it produces long, fat spikes of sapphire to violet-blue flowers in late spring and early summer. Being frost tender, it is best grown in a pot and consigned to a high conservatory or large greenhouse. Move it to a sheltered, sunny patio or terrace in June and bring it indoors when nights turn chilly in September. It matures in 3–5 years and flowers early in life.

PRIDE OF MADEIRA AT A GLANCE

Frost tender, with blue flowers in summer. In chilly areas, it must be overwintered under glass. Hardy to 30°F (zone 9).

JAN	shield from frost	RECOMMENDED VARIETIES
FEB	shield from frost	
MAR	shield from frost	*E. candicans*
APR	plant	
MAY	plant	
JUNE	flower, plant	
JULY	flower, prune	
AUG	flower, prune	
SEPT	flower, plant	
OCT	/	
NOV	/	
DEC	/	

CONDITIONS

Aspect Echium needs full sun all day. Under glass, air must freely circulate.

Site Set this plant in a large pot of multipurpose compost augmented with a quarter part Perlite to ensure good drainage. Pot it on in early spring when roots fill the container and mat the compost as the need for watering increases.

GROWING METHOD

Feeding Boost growth by liquid feeding with a high-potash fertilizer, weekly from spring to late summer. Alternatively, insert aggregates of slow-release fertilizer granules into the compost in spring.

Watering: Echium tolerates very dry conditions and needs only an occasional soaking in prolonged droughty weather.

Propagation Echium is raised from seed in spring or early summer. Alternatively, take semi-ripe heeled cuttings tugged from older stems, in midsummer. Root cuttings in a propagator heated to around 70°F.

Problems No particular pest or disease troubles this plant. If aphids colonize shoot tips, tackle them with pirimicarb or natural pyrethrins.

PRUNING

Remove spent flower heads and shorten shoots outgrowing their allotted space.

ERICA
Heath

Plant a selection of lime-hating Erica cinerea *varieties and enjoy a succession of blossom from June to November.*

Performing from November to May, Erica carnea, *here complementing a golden-flowered berberis, is prized for its white, pink, red, lavender, or mauve display.*

FEATURES

A large, vibrant-flowered group of bushy and carpeting, evergreen shrubs, 9in–5ft high, their thickly clustered, tubular or bell-shaped blooms in white and a confection of pink, purple, coral, and crimson hues illuminate the year. Color winter with varieties of *Erica* x *darleyensis* and *E. carnea*; cheer spring by grouping *E. arborea,* and *E. erigena*; glorify summer and fall with *E. cinerea, E. tetralix,* and *E. vagans.*

Use them to brighten borders and rock gardens and suppress weeds. Ideally, associate them with dwarf conifers.

Create a tapestry of blossom by combining ericas with closely related varieties of ling (*Calluna vulgaris*), which flower from July to November, and Irish heath (*Daboecia cantabrica*). Some callunas, such as "Beoley Gold", yield radiant golden foliage.

CONDITIONS

Aspect Most are very hardy, tolerate chilly winds and are ideal for exposed, upland gardens. Heathers must have full sun and good air circulation. Do not crowd plants.

Site While all varieties prefer acid soil, winter-flowering *Erica carnea* tolerates slightly alkaline conditions. Good drainage is vital. Mulch plants annually, in spring, with leaf mould or well-rotted garden compost.

GROWING METHOD

Feeding Established plants need little or no fertilizer. If the soil is very poor, fortify the root area with a balanced, acidifying fertilizer in spring.

Propagation Take semi-ripe heeled cuttings from early to late summer; layer shoots in mid-spring.

Problems Heathers quickly succumb to root rot in heavy or overwet soils.

PRUNING

Lightly shear flowered shoots when blooms fade. Never cut back into older wood. Tackle fall- and winter-flowering varieties when new shoots appear in spring.

HEATH AT A GLANCE

Carpeting evergreens whose succession of blossom or foliage enchants us every month of the year. Hardy to 4°F (zone 7).

JAN	flower	RECOMMENDED VARIETIES
FEB	flower	
MAR	flower	Spring flowering
APR	plant, prune	"Albert's Gold"
		"Viking"
MAY	flower, plant	Summer flowering
JUNE	flower, prune	"C.D. Eason"
JULY	flower, prune	"Pink Ice"
AUG	flower, plant	Fall flowering
SEPT	flower, plant	"Andrew Proudley"
		"Stefanie"
OCT	flower	Winter flowering
NOV	flower	"Ann Sparkes"
DEC	flower	

ERICA VARIETIES

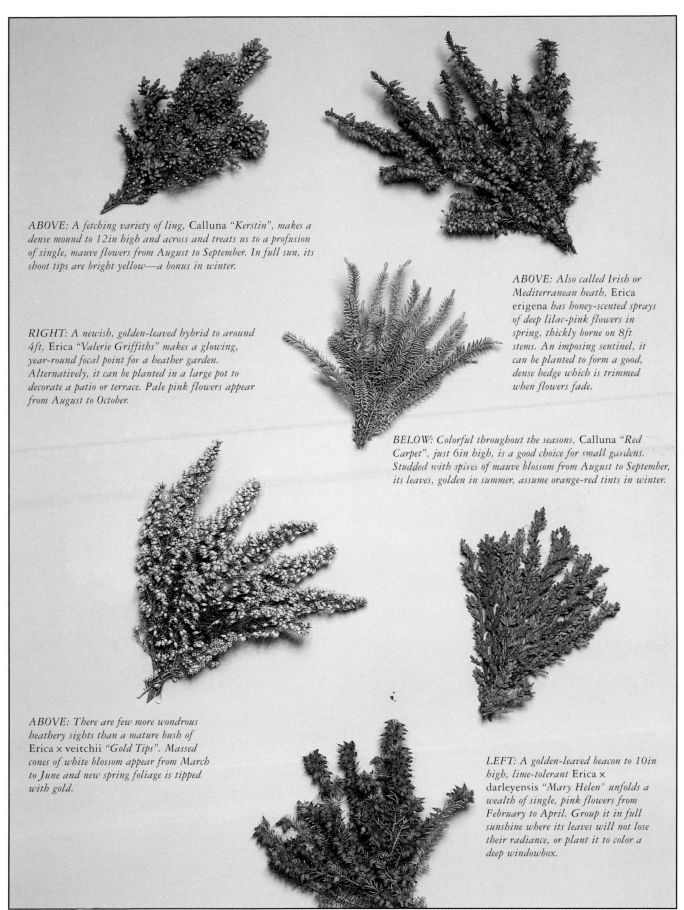

ABOVE: A fetching variety of ling, Calluna "Kerstin", makes a dense mound to 12in high and across and treats us to a profusion of single, mauve flowers from August to September. In full sun, its shoot tips are bright yellow—a bonus in winter.

RIGHT: A newish, golden-leaved hybrid to around 4ft, Erica "Valerie Griffiths" makes a glowing, year-round focal point for a heather garden. Alternatively, it can be planted in a large pot to decorate a patio or terrace. Pale pink flowers appear from August to October.

ABOVE: Also called Irish or Mediterranean heath, Erica erigena has honey-scented sprays of deep lilac-pink flowers in spring, thickly borne on 8ft stems. An imposing sentinel, it can be planted to form a good, dense hedge which is trimmed when flowers fade.

BELOW: Colorful throughout the seasons, Calluna "Red Carpet", just 6in high, is a good choice for small gardens. Studded with spires of mauve blossom from August to September, its leaves, golden in summer, assume orange-red tints in winter.

ABOVE: There are few more wondrous heathery sights than a mature bush of Erica × veitchii "Gold Tips". Massed cones of white blossom appear from March to June and new spring foliage is tipped with gold.

LEFT: A golden-leaved beacon to 10in high, lime-tolerant Erica × darleyensis "Mary Helen" unfolds a wealth of single, pink flowers from February to April. Group it in full sunshine where its leaves will not lose their radiance, or plant it to color a deep windowbox.

ESCALLONIA
Escallonia

A prized and colorful shrub, especially for windy gardens, Escallonia "Pride of Donard" rewards us with sprays of pink blossom.

Semi-evergreen and summer-blossoming escallonia can be trained to form a fetching, flowering hedge in mild districts.

FEATURES

Escallonia is evergreen in mild districts but semi-evergreen elsewhere. Its arching shoots, festooned with sprays of clustered, tubular, white, pink, or red flowers amid small, glossy leaves, highlight the summer months. Long-lived, it makes a stunning sentinel to around 6ft and as a flowering hedge.
The hardiest species—ideal for windswept, seaside gardens—*Escallonia rubra macrantha* delights us with many rose-crimson flowers. Other choice kinds are rich pink "Donard Radiance", rose-pink "Donard Star" and golden-leaved and rosy-red-flowered "Gold Brian".

ESCALLONIA AT A GLANCE

Evergreen or semi-evergreen, its arching shoots are sleeved with white, pink or red flowers in summer. Hardy to 14°F (zone 8).

		RECOMMENDED VARIETIES
JAN	/	
FEB	/	"Donard Radiance"
MAR	/	"Donard Seedling"
APR	plant, prune	"Glory of Donard"
MAY	plant, prune	"Gold Brian"
JUNE	flower, plant	"Iveyi"
JULY	flower, plant	*E. rubra macrantha*
AUG	flower, plant	"Slieve Donard"
SEPT	flower, plant	
OCT	/	
NOV	/	
DEC	/	

CONDITIONS

Aspect   Though escallonia needs full sun to flower best, it does not object to light shade. Most hybrids tolerate buffeting wind. In chilly or northern gardens, it should be planted against a sheltered, south-facing wall.

Site   This splendid shrub thrives in any well-drained soil. Aerate heavy clay by working in grit or gravel; fortify light and nutrient-starved, sandy soils by working in plenty of bulky, moisture-conserving organic materials.

GROWING METHOD

Feeding   Ensure a steady release of plant foods by applying bone meal in spring and fall. After planting, water freely and regularly in dry spells to encourage strong new growth. Keep roots cool and questing freely by mulching with shredded bark, cocoa shell, crumbly manure, or rotted garden compost.

Propagation   Multiply choice varieties from semi-ripe cuttings from the middle of summer to the middle of fall.

Problems   Cut darkly stained shoots infected with silver leaf back to healthy, white wood 6in beyond the point of infection.

PRUNING

Shorten a third of the oldest stems to near ground level when blooms fade. In cold gardens, cut back frost-damaged growth to strong, new shoots in late spring.

EUPHORBIA SPECIES
Spurge

The showiest part of a euphorbia "flower" is a pair of lime-green bracts (modified leaves). The true flower is a small, yellow "button".

Perfect for tempering hot orange and yellow flowers, Euphorbia characias wulfenii *performs best in full sun.*

FEATURES

Pleasing us with a spring to early summer display of yellowish-green, bottlebrush blooms on stems clad with whorls of evergreen leaves, *Euphorbia characias wulfenii* is architecturally magnificent. Forming a dense bush to 4ft, it is ideal for interplanting and tempering vibrant orange, yellow, and red-flowered border perennials. This euphorbia lives for around ten or more years and matures within 2–3 years. Use it in a shrub border or as a background for annuals and perennials.

A related sculptural gem, for sheltered gardens only, is Madeiran honey spurge (*E. mellifera*).

Seducing us with large and exotic, lance-shaped leaves, its honey-scented, brownish flower clusters form on shoot tips in spring.

CONDITIONS

Aspect   Hardy *E. characias* needs full sun; more tender *E. mellifera* requires a sheltered spot.

Site   These sub-shrubs thrive almost anywhere, even in heavy soils, provided drainage is good. Boost growth in light, sandy soil by incorporating bulky organic manure.

GROWING METHOD

Feeding   Feeding is not essential but apply fish, blood, and bone meal, Growmore, or pelleted chicken manure in spring.

Propagation   Take soft-tip cuttings from mid-spring to early summer.

Problems   When crowded, euphorbia may become infected with gray mold, a disease that coats leaves and stems with furry, brownish-gray mold. Control it by cutting infected shoots back to healthy tissue and spraying with carbendazim.

PRUNING

Wear gloves and safety glasses to cut back flowered stems to ground level in early summer. Strong, new shoots replace them and bloom the following year.

SPURGE AT A GLANCE

Evergreen shrub, *E. characias wulfenii* produces huge, bottlebrush blooms from spring to early summer. Hardy to 10°F (zone 7).

JAN	/	RECOMMENDED VARIETIES
FEB	/	
MAR	/	*E. characias* "John Tomlinson"
APR	flower, plant	*E. characias* "Lambrook Gold"
MAY	flower, plant	
JUNE	flower, prune	*E. characias* "Margery Fish Group"
JULY	prune, plant	*E. characias* "Purple and Gold"
AUG	plant	
SEPT	plant	*E. characias wulfenii*
OCT	/	*E. mellifera*
NOV	/	
DEC	/	

EUPHORBIA VARIETIES

RIGHT: Ideal for carpeting shady spots and improvised areas beneath trees, Euphorbia amygdaloides robbiae rarely needs watering. From April to June, it delights us with lime-green columns of blossom. Even when faded, they retain their charm.

ABOVE: Enchanting when draping a hot, sunny, rock-garden outcrop or spilling from a drystone retaining wall, drought-resisting and semi-prostrate Euphorbia myrsinites is easy to grow. In spring, terminal clusters of bright greenish-yellow blooms top shoots clothed with spiralling, blue-gray leaves.

RIGHT: Bearing distinctive, greenish, bottlebrush blooms from early spring to early summer, Euphorbia characias wulfenii *is sculpturally appealing. Plant it to form a focal point in a wide border or flank a path or drive.*

BELOW: No euphorbia collection is complete without Euphorbia polychroma, *a closely related herbaceous species. In spring, its captivating dome of glowing sulfur-yellow flowers lights up a border. The brighter the site the more intensely hued blooms are.*

LEFT: There are few more dramatic sights in spring than a bed of Euphorbia amygdaloides "Purpurea", *whose young, reddish-purple leaves contrast with heads of acid-yellow flowers. Group it with small, white daffodils.*

FATSIA JAPONICA
Fig-leaved palm

Exotic-fingered leaves are your reward for growing evergreen Fatsia japonica. *Plant it in a tub to light up a shady patio or terrace.*

Delighting us with its large heads of creamy, bobble-like blooms in fall, when most other shrubs are resting, fatsia tolerates dry soil.

FEATURES

Stunningly architectural, the large, glossy, palmate leaves of *Fatsia japonica* have an appealing leathery texture. In fall, it delights us with an exotic candelabrum of golf-ball-sized, white flower heads. Each comprises many tiny, five-petalled flowers. Large, handsome, black berries follow them. A native of South Korea and Japan, it has a spreading, suckering habit and makes a dome to 6ft high and 8ft across. Plant it to enhance a large patio tub. It tolerates air pollution, so is a good shrub for towns or cities. It resists salty sea breezes, too. Dramatize a sunny border by grouping it with golden-leaved yuccas.

If you plant fatsia in a border, create a striking feature by embracing it with tussock-forming and ground-covering *Liriope muscari*, whose spikes of bell-shaped, violet flowers complement the fatsia's white bobbles.

FIG-LEAVED PALM AT A GLANCE

Dashing focal point for a lightly shaded spot. Intriguing bobbles of white blossom appear in fall. Hardy to 4°F (zone 7).

JAN	/	RECOMMENDED VARIETIES
FEB	/	"Variegata"
MAR	/	
APR	prune, plant	
MAY	plant	
JUNE	plant	
JULY	plant	
AUG	plant	
SEPT	plant, flower	
OCT	flower	
NOV	flower	
DEC	/	

CONDITIONS

Aspect Ideal for brightening sheltered and lightly shaded spots, it objects to hot sunshine, which may scorch its leaves. Protect from icy winds, which also brown its foliage.

Site It is not fussy about soil but prefers deep, rich loam, which encourages the largest, most sculpturally appealing leaves. Add grit or gravel to soggy clay to improve drainage. Apply an acidifying fertilizer, such as sequestered iron, to chalky soil to reduce risk of chlorosis. When iron is "locked up" by calcium, roots cannot absorb it and leaves turn yellow and die.

GROWING METHOD

Feeding Boost lustrous foliage by topdressing the root area in spring, and again in summer, with fish, blood, and bone meal, which enriches the soil's humus content and encourages beneficial micro-organisms. Alternatively, use quick-acting but short-lived Growmore to accelerate shoot development.

Water freely after planting to settle soil around roots. Follow with a 2in mulch of old manure, bark, or cocoa shell.

Propagation Take semi-ripe cuttings in summer and strike them in a closed cold frame or on a sunny windowsill.

Problems Control aphids, which colonize and cripple shoot tips, by spraying with a systemic insecticide.

PRUNING

Apart from maintaining its symmetry by shortening long branches or frost-damaged shoots in spring, cutting to a joint or lower shoot, no regular attention is necessary.

FORSYTHIA
Golden bell bush

Forming a bushy shrub to around 6ft, generous flowering and sun-loving Forsythia "Lynwood" is draped with blossom in spring.

Create a vibrant March marriage of yellow blossom and scarlet bark by associating forsythia with a coppiced clumps of Cornus alba "Sibirica".

FEATURES

Heartening indeed is the spring sight of a bush thickly laden with starry, sulfur-yellow, or deep golden blooms. Flowers open naturally from March to April. Enjoy an earlier show by cutting fat-budded stems in February and forcing them into bloom in a warm room. There are two principal kinds: border forsythia (*Forsythia × intermedia*), which makes a rounded shrub to 8ft high and across, and *F. suspensa*, a snaking, weeping, or trailing form, enchanting when cascading over a wall or over the lower branches of pink, weeping cherry. Border forsythia can be also grown as a flowering hedge or trained to frame a window or doorway. Neat and compact "Golden Curls", just 2ft high and 3ft across, is ideal for a small yard.

GOLDEN BELL BUSH AT A GLANCE

Deciduous, bush, and trailing/weeping varieties have flowers clothing year-old shoots in spring. Hardy to -13°F (zone 5).

		RECOMMENDED VARIETIES
JAN	/	
FEB	/	"Fiesta"
MAR	flower, plant	"Gold Cluster"
APR	flower, plant	"Golden Curls"
MAY	plant, prune	"Gold Tide"
JUNE	plant	"Lynwood"
JULY	plant	"Spring Glory"
AUG	plant	"Suspensa"
SEPT	plant	"Weekend"
OCT	plant	
NOV	plant	
DEC	plant	

CONDITIONS

Aspect   A sunny position is vital. In shade a multitude of shoots form but many will refuse to flower. Growth also becomes loose and weak. Forsythia braves cold wind.

Site   This plant grows strongly in most well-drained soils, from heavy clay to light sand and chalk. Fortify impoverished borders, especially where roots from nearby trees invade, with humus-forming, old, crumbly, or proprietary composted manure, well-rotted garden compost, shredded bark, or leaf mold.

GROWING METHOD

Feeding   If the soil was initially enriched with plant foods, forsythia seldom needs further feeding. If growth is slow, boost it by topdressing with a balanced granular fertilizer. Alternatively, liquid feed weekly with a high-nitrogen fertilizer from spring to midsummer. Water newly planted shrubs copiously and frequently to help them recover quickly.

Propagation   Layer low flexible shoots from spring to late summer or take hardwood cuttings in the fall.

Problems   Occasionally—the cause is not known—warty galls distort stems. Overcome them by cutting back affected shoots to healthy wood and burning them.

PRUNING

Once established, keep plants youthful and flowering freely by removing from the base a third of the oldest shoots when flowers fade. Clip hedges at the same time of year, so that flower buds form for the following year.

GENISTA
Genista

Swagged with golden flowers in midsummer, the Mount Etna broom makes a striking shrubby tree and revels in a warm, dry spot.

Here Genista lydia, a hummock of blossom in June, looks good with silvery-leaved and yellow-flowered Brachyglottis *"Sunshine".*

FEATURES

Small or rushy leaved and wiry stemmed, this accommodating deciduous family, related to broom, embraces showy, prostrate carpeters and small or large bushes to several yards high. All sport pea-like flowers in various shades of yellow.

From May to June, cushion-like Spanish gorse (*Genista hispanica*), hummocky and cascading *G. lydia* and dazzling, carpeting *G. pilosa* "Vancouver Gold" treat us to a display so radiant that it deceives you into thinking it is sunny when it is not.

Come July and August, the spring brigade is eclipsed by bushy *G. tinctoria* "Royal Gold" and the imposing and fragrant Mount Etna broom (*G. aetnensis*), with its pendulous, rush-like shoots that shower from branches 9ft high.

CONDITIONS

Aspect Hardy and tolerating exposed positions, all genistas perform best in full sun. Drought resisting, they are ideal for hot spots that cannot easily be watered.

Site Happiest in humus-rich and light, free-draining sand and loam, they also prosper in clay if you work in gravel and crumbly organic materials to improve drainage.
Usefully, *G. tinctoria* excels in chalky soil.

GROWING METHOD

Feeding Encourage robust growth by topdressing the root area with a slow-release organic fertilizer, such as bone meal, in spring and fall. Water freely in droughty periods and keep roots cool and active by mulching with old manure, well-rotted garden compost, or bark.

Propagation Increase genista from semi-ripe cuttings of side shoots from mid- to late summer. Root them in pots on a bright windowsill or in a lightly shaded cold frame.

Problems Normally trouble free.

PRUNING

Avoid cutting back *G. aetnensis*, *G. lydia*, and *G. tinctoria*, whose stumps may not regrow. You can, however, rejuvenate ageing *G. hispanica* by shortening old woody stems by two-thirds their length in spring. Keep large stumps moist in dry, windy weather to help them regenerate.

GENISTA AT A GLANCE

Deciduous spring- or summer-flowering bushes, they need full sunshine to flower bounteously. Hardy to 14°F (zone 8).

Month	Activity	RECOMMENDED VARIETIES
JAN	/	
FEB	/	*G. aetnensis*
MAR	plant	*G. hispanica*
APR	plant, prune	*G. pilosa* "Vancouver Gold"
MAY	flower, prune	
JUNE	flower, plant	*G. tinctoria* "Flore Pleno"
JULY	flower, plant	*G. tinctoria* "Royal Gold"
AUG	flower, plant	
SEPT	plant	
OCT	plant	
NOV	plant	
DEC	/	

HEBE
Shrubby veronica

Salt-spray resistant, hebes are ideal for brightening coastal gardens in mild districts. They also tolerate air pollution.

Hebe "Great Orme", here contrasting effectively with an upright cypress, is studded with shapely spikes of blossom from July to October.

FEATURES

An immense and handsome family of small, rounded-leaved or larger, willow-leaved, evergreen New Zealanders, hebes' clustered or cone-shaped spikes of massed, tiny flowers illuminate May to late October. Resisting air pollution, these shrubs are ideal for seaside gardens in mild districts. There are three main, easy and reliable groups:

Carpeters: Forming a dense mat of weed-suppressing foliage to around 12in high, choice kinds include silvery gray-leaved and white-flowered *Hebe pinguifolia* "Pagei".

Bushes: Making bushy globes to 4ft, stunning varieties are "Fall Glory", whose violet-blue blossoms color June to November, and "Great Orme", smothered with bright pink flowers from July to October.

Taller kinds : Imposing sentinels to 6–10ft, lilac-white *H. salicifolia* is a prince among them.

CONDITIONS

Aspect Hebes need an open position in full sun to make robust and free-flowering growth.

Site Most well-drained soils suit these plants, but they perform best in humus-rich, sandy loam.

GROWING METHOD

Feeding Boost growth by sprinkling fish, blood, and bone meal, Growmore or pelleted chicken manure over the root area in April and July. Water copiously to establish new plants. Once growing strongly, little water is needed.

Propagation Take soft-tip cuttings in early summer and semi-ripe cuttings in midsummer.

Problems Control leaf spot disease by spraying with carbendazim or mancozeb.

PRUNING

Cut back late-flowering varieties to within 6in of the base, every two years in spring, to encourage bounteous blossom. Remove any reverted, green-leaved stems from variegated varieties as soon as they appear.

SHRUBBY VERONICA AT A GLANCE

Evergreen carpeters or bushes clothed with clustered, cone-shaped flowers in white and many other colors. Hardy to 23°F (zone 9).

		RECOMMENDED VARIETIES
JAN	/	
FEB	/	"Carl Teschner"
MAR	/	*H. × franciscana* "Blue Gem"
APR	plant, prune	"Great Orme"
MAY	flower, prune	*H. hulkeana*
JUNE	flower, plant	"Midsummer Beauty"
JULY	flower, plant	*H. pinguifolia* "Pagei"
AUG	flower, plant	*H. speciosa* "Gauntlettii"
SEPT	flower, plant	"Wiri Charm"
OCT	flower	
NOV	/	
DEC	/	

HELIANTHEMUM
Sun rose

Deep red and yellow-eyed blooms and silvery leaves make "Supreme" a prized variety.

Enjoy a tapestry of blossom by growing sun roses to cascade from a retaining wall. Here plants are camouflaging gaunt, leggy, rose stems.

FEATURES

Varieties of evergreen *Helianthemem nummularium*, commonly called rock or sun rose, make a spreading 4–12in mound to 36in across. From May to July, a network of wiry stems clothed with small, oval leaves are almost hidden beneath a daily succession of single or double flowers in glowing shades of yellow, pink, red, orange, white, or terracotta. Flowers tend to close up on dull days. Sun roses are perfect for draping rock garden pockets, cascading from retaining walls and aproning roses and other bushes flanking a path. They are not long-lived but easily raised from cuttings of maturing, current-year shoots.

CONDITIONS

Aspect
Sun rose performs best in an open, brightly lit and airy position where it has room to spread and is not crowded by other plants. Avoid even a hint of shade in which growth is looser, less comely and flowering is inhibited.

Site
This shrub needs well-drained and slightly alkaline conditions. Add garden lime to raise the pH of acid soil.

GROWING METHOD

Feeding
Boost lustrous foliage and a wealth of blossom by applying a high-potash rose fertilizer in spring and the middle of summer.
Water newly planted shrubs regularly and copiously to help them recover quickly and make good root growth in their first year. Thereafter, they will need watering only in droughty weather. Mulch plants generously with spent mushroom compost.

Propagation
Take semi-ripe heeled cuttings in midsummer. These should make flowering-sized plants by the following spring.

Problems
Poor drainage or overwatering may kill plants. Powdery mildew can be a problem in crowded borders where air circulates sluggishly. Control this disease by thinning growth and spraying with carbendazim or bupirimate with triforine.

PRUNING

From early to midsummer, when blooms fade, shear back shoots to two-thirds their length. This not only keeps bushes trim and flowering well in spring, but often results in a second, smaller, flush of blossom in fall.

SUN ROSE AT A GLANCE

A carpeting evergreen so thickly clothed with flowers from May to July that leaves are concealed by them. Hardy to 14°F (zone 8).

Month	Activity	RECOMMENDED VARIETIES
JAN	/	
FEB	/	"Golden Queen"
MAR	/	"Henfield Brilliant"
APR	plant	"Raspberry Ripple"
MAY	flower, plant	"Red Orient"
JUN	flower, plant	"Supreme"
JULY	flower, plant	"The Bride"
AUG	plant, prune	"Wisley Pink"
SEPT	plant	"Wisley Primrose"
OCT	/	
NOV	/	
DEC	/	

HELIOTROPIUM
Heliotrope

Old-fashioned heliotrope or cherry pie is festooned with spicy-perfumed blooms from early summer until the fall, when chilly nights halt the display.

"Marine" is captivating if planted to cascade its deep violet flowers from a patio or terrace tub.

FEATURES

Heliotropium arborescens, also known as cherry pie, is a half-hardy, soft-stemmed, evergreen Peruvian shrub. Growing to 4ft high and across, it is usually bedded out for summer and overwintered in a frost-free greenhouse. A succession of vanilla-fragrant, mauve to purple flowers are borne from summer to the middle of fall, or even longer under glass.

Plant it to spill from a border and on to paving, waterfall from a raised bed or beautify a patio tub. "Lord Roberts", with very dark purple-green leaves and deep violet flowers, is probably the most popular variety.

HELIOTROPIUM AT A GLANCE

Frost-sensitive evergreen with richly fragrant, pink, purple, violet, or white flowers, bedded out for summer. Hardy to 40°F (zone 10).

JAN	/	RECOMMENDED VARIETIES
FEB	/	
MAR	/	"Dame Alice de Hales"
		"Chatsworth"
APR	plant, prune	"Lord Roberts"
MAY	plant, prune	"White Lady"
JUNE	flower, plant	"Netherhall White"
JULY	flower	"Princess Marina"
AUG	flower	
SEPT	flower	
OCT	flower	
NOV	flower	
DEC	/	

CONDITIONS

Aspect　Outdoors: Heliotrope needs a warm position sheltered from chilly winds. It flowers best in full sunshine.

Under glass: Provide full sun but reduce risk of leaf scorch by shading plants when the temperature rises above 75°F.

Site　Outdoors: The soil should be crumbly and well drained. Enrich thin, sandy patches with humus-forming, well-decayed manure.

GROWING METHOD

Feeding　Outdoors and under glass: Liquid feed weekly with a high-potash fertilizer from spring to late summer.

In late summer or early fall, lift and pot up plants bedded out in borders and patio tub plants. Move them to a frost-free greenhouse or conservatory and keep the compost dry until late winter or early spring.

Propagation　Heliotrope is easily increased from soft-tip cuttings taken in spring, and semi-ripe cuttings struck in late summer.

Problems　Being half-hardy, this shrub must not be moved outdoors until frosts have finished in late May or early June.

PRUNING

Encourage new flowering stems by shortening a third of older, woody branches by half their length in early spring.

HIBISCUS
Hibiscus

A late-summer bonus of exotic, single, or double, saucer-shaped blooms are your reward for growing a hardy hibiscus.

Healthy and seldom attracting pests and diseases, hibiscus is best planted in a sunny position so shoots ripen and flower well.

FEATURES

Also known as shrubby mallow, this deciduous, late summer statement is festooned with saucer-shaped blooms from July to September. Flowers are single or double and range in color from white, pink and blue, to purple. Several are bicolored. Most popular varieties are violet-blue and white-eyed "Blue Bird", white and crimson-eyed "Hamabo" and rose-pink and dark-centred "Woodbridge". Long-lived, it makes an upright bush to 8ft high and across and flowers early in its life. It is very hardy.

CONDITIONS

Aspect Hibiscus grows best and flowers prolifically in full sun. Shield it from icy winds. Avoid even light shade, for shoots will not ripen well and so flowering is impaired.

Site This shrub thrives on well-drained, fertile, sandy loam but tolerates poorer soils. Enjoy good results by enriching the planting area with plenty of well-rotted organic matter.

GROWING METHOD

Feeding Apply all-purpose plant food, such as fish, blood, and bone meal, or Growmore, in spring and again in midsummer.
Water regularly in spring and summer to help newly planted hibiscus recover quickly.

Propagation Layer whippy shoots from mid-spring to late summer, and take semi-ripe heeled cuttings from late summer to early fall.

Problems Control aphids with pirimicarb, horticultural soap, or natural pyrethrins.

PRUNING

Rejuvenate ageing shrubs by shortening them to half their height in spring. This is also the best time to cut back frost-damaged shoots.

HIBISCUS AT A GLANCE

Deciduous and slow growing, large, saucer-shaped, pink, blue, or white blooms appear in late summer. Hardy to 4°F (zone 7).

		RECOMMENDED VARIETIES
JAN	/	
FEB	/	"Blue Bird"
MAR	plant	"Bredon Springs"
APR	plant, prune	"Hamabo"
MAY	plant	"Lady Stanley"
JUNE	plant	"Lenny"
JULY	flower, plant	"Meehanii"
AUG	flower, plant	✳ "Woodbridge"
SEPT	flower, plant	"William R. Smith"
OCT	plant	
NOV	plant	
DEC	/	

HYDRANGEA
Hydrangea

Ever popular hydrangea is a native of China and Japan. Ensure pink blossom by adding lime to the soil in spring. For ultramarine-blue flowers, feed with aluminium sulphate.

Position mophead and other hydrangeas in a sheltered spot in dappled shade.

FEATURES

Brightly studded with large, globular, mushroom-headed, or broadly conical flowers, hydrangeas richly color borders from July to September. Blooms come in white and shades of pink, blue, or red. Long-lived, this deciduous shrub grows 20in–8ft high and across.

Most widely grown are aptly named mophead and lacecap varieties of *Hydrangea macrophylla*. Yielding pink, mauve, or red blooms on alkaline soils and blue heads in acid conditions, they thrive in fertile ground. Characteristically, lacecaps have an outer ring of large, sterile flowers enclosing tiny, pink, or blue, fertile ones.

Other choice kinds are white, football-headed *H. arborescens* "Annabelle" and light pink, cone-flowered *H. paniculata* "Pink Diamond". *H. quercifolia* has oak-leaved foliage which complement trusses of rich creamy flowers and *H. villosa* is a gem with porcelain-blue mushrooms poised above stems clad with huge, velvety leaves.

A self-clinging climber, white, disc-flowered *H. petiolaris* beautifully transforms a cold, north-facing wall.

CONDITIONS

Aspect Dappled sunlight or morning sun and afternoon shade suit hydrangeas. Make sure they are sheltered from frosty winds, which will damage embryo blossoms. *H. macrophylla* varieties are reliable seaside plants for relatively frost-free areas.

Site These shrubs need damp soil high in organic matter, so improve poor areas by digging in plenty of well-decayed manure or compost a few months ahead of planting. Also mulch plants with well-rotted organic matter.

GROWING METHOD

Feeding Apply acidifying fertilizer like sulphate of ammonia in spring and midsummer to ensure a steady release of plant foods and encourage blue flowers.

Propagation Multiply favoured varieties by layering flexible shoots from mid-spring to late summer. Take soft-tip cuttings from late spring to early summer and semi-ripe cuttings from mid- to late summer.

Problems Excessive lime prevents chlorophyll from forming and causes leaves to yellow and die. Overcome it by applying iron chelates.

PRUNING

H. macrophylla: Cut off spent flowers in spring and remove crowding shoots.

H. paniculata: Prune stems to within two buds of the base in late March.

H. petiolaris: Cut out unwanted shoots when flowers fade.

H. villosa: Remove a third of older stems in spring.

HYDRANGEA AT A GLANCE

Deciduous shrubs bearing large heads of white, pink, red, or blue flowers from mid- to late summer. Hardy to 4°F (zone 7).

		RECOMMENDED VARIETIES
JAN	/	
FEB	/	Mopheads
MAR	plant, prune	"Hamburgh"
APR	plant, prune	"Madame E. Moullière"
MAY	plant	Lacecaps
JUNE	plant	"Blue Wave"
JULY	flower, plant	"White Wave"
AUG	flower, plant	*H. arborescens* "Annabelle"
SEPT	flower, plant	*H. paniculata* "Kyushu"
OCT	plant	*H. quercifolia*
NOV	plant	*H. villosa*
DEC	/	

HYDRANGEA VARIETIES

mopheads

RIGHT: *"Kyushu", a dashing paniculata variety, highlights late summer and fall with a shuttlecock of shoots topped with pyramidal sprays of starry blossom.*

ABOVE: *"Masja" luxuriates in damp soil and treats us to a memorable display of deep red to purplish-red "mopheads". Group it with white-flowering* Anemone *"Honorine Jobert".*

LEFT: *Unlike other hydrangeas, dramatically white-flowered* Hydrangea quercifolia *has large, oak-like leaves, which develop striking orange tints in October.*

ABOVE: *Impressive "Générale Vicomtesse de Vibraye" is an easy variety to "blue" in neutral to acid soils. Apart from using proprietary chemicals, you can transform blooms from pink to blue by working rusty metal into the root area.*

BELOW: *Exquisite lacecap varieties have a central dome of small fertile flowers embraced by a ring of large, handsome, sterile florets.*

RIGHT: *Seeking a deep red and free-flowering mophead? Opt for "Gerda Steiniger", whose clustered heads make August and Sepember special.*

JASMINUM
Jasmine

Illuminating a north or east-facing wall from November to March, Jasminum nudiflorum *flowers very freely on cascading shoots.*

Ideal for clothing a pergola or trellis work, twining Jasminum officinale affine *is swathed with scented flowers in summer.*

FEATURES

There are two forms of jasmine—climbing and bushy—both of which flower generously. Choice and reliable twining climbers—ideal for screening—are *Jasminum affine*, to 25ft, whose pink buds open to sweetly scented, white flowers from July to September; and *J. × stephanense*, to 15ft, which from early to midsummer pleases with a profusion of perfumed, pale pink blooms amid colorful, cream-flushed, green leaves.

Among bushy kinds, the popular, yellow-flowered winter jasmine (*J. nudiflorum*) is usually trained to transform a wall or fence from November to late February. After establishing a main framework, leave it to flower freely on cascading shoots. Aspiring to half that height, semi-evergreen *J. humile* "Revolutum" is dashingly clad with larger, fragrant, yellow blossoms from late spring to fall. Even smaller is yellow-flowered, mound

forming *J. parkeri*, which when planted on a rock garden brightens it in early summer.

CONDITIONS

Aspect
While climbing kinds need a sheltered spot and full sunshine for most of the day, the most popular bushy member—*G. nudiflorum*—thrives on a shaded, north wall lashed by frosty winds.

Site
Undemanding, all flourish on most well-drained soils. Enrich and improve the water retention of thin, sandy areas by digging in bulky organics several months before planting. Help clay drain better by forking in gravel.

GROWING METHOD

Feeding
Give young plants a good start by consigning them to generous planting holes fortified with bone meal or Growmore fertilizer. Soak the soil after planting to settle it around roots and remove air pockets. Encourage robust growth by working bone meal into the root area in spring and the fall.

Propagation
Layer whippy shoots from spring to late summer or take semi-ripe cuttings from mid-to late summer.

Problems
Gray mold, a fungus covering leaves with a grayish, furry patina, may occur if shoots are crowded. Control it by removing affected parts and spraying with carbendazim.

PRUNING

Climbing kinds are not normally cut back. If they outgrow their situation, shorten shoots after flowering. Keep *J. nudiflorum* youthful and massed with bloom by removing a third of the older flowered stems when flowers fade in early spring.

JASMINE AT A GLANCE

Semi-evergreen or deciduous, twining or bush forms color walls and fences in winter and summer. Hardy to 4°F (zone 7).

JAN	flower	RECOMMENDED VARIETIES
FEB	flower	
MAR	prune	*J. affine*
APR	plant	*J. humile* "Revolutum"
MAY	flower, plant	*J. nudiflorum*
JUN	flower, plant	*J. parkeri*
JULY	flower, plant	*J. × stephanense*
AUG	flower, prune	
SEPT	flower, plant	
OCT	plant	
NOV	plant	
DEC	/	

KERRIA JAPONICA
Kerria

A *charmingly tangled mass of bright yellow flowers in spring makes kerria an attractive screening plant, even at dusk.*

Kerria *has single or double flowers and leaves that develop radiant yellow tints in fall. This is the double "Pleniflora" version.*

FEATURES

Graceful and arching, deciduous *Kerria japonica* makes a fascinating focus to about 6ft high. From April to May, its radiant orange-yellow blooms clothe a profusion of suckering, cane-like, green stems.

Coveted forms are "Pleniflora", magnificent with its double, golden pompons; "Golden Guinea", with beautiful, single, buttercup-yellow flowers; and smaller "Picta"—just 3ft high—whose single, yellow blossoms complement cream-edged, green leaves. Very hardy and happy almost anywhere, taller kinds making dense and colorful hedges.

KERRIA AT A GLANCE

Deciduous shrub with green stems dotted with single or double, yellow blooms in spring. Hardy to -13°F (zone 5).

		RECOMMENDED VARIETIES
JAN	/	
FEB	/	"Albescens"
MAR	plant	"Golden Guinea"
APR	flower, plant	"Picta"
MAY	flower, plant	"Pleniflora"
JUNE	plant, prune	"Simplex"
JULY	plant	
AUG	plant	
SEPT	plant	
OCT	plant	
NOV	plant	
DEC	/	

CONDITIONS

Aspect   This shrub flowers best in full sun and performs passably well in shade.

Site   Kerria will thrive almost anywhere.

GROWING METHOD

Feeding   Keep growth vigorous and packed with blossom in spring by applying bone meal in March and October. Water new plants frequently to help them establish quickly.

Propagation   Probably the easiest shrub to multiply, it can be increased from semi-ripe cuttings in midsummer; layered shoots from mid-spring to late summer; hardwood cuttings in late fall; and suckers in early spring.

Problems   No particular pests or diseases.

PRUNING

Cut out from the base a third of older shoots when blooms fade in early summer. Remove green-leaved stems on variegated bushes.

LAVANDULA
Lavender

Blooming from July to September, evergreen lavender excels in free-draining "hot spots". Make sure you get the plant you want by buying it in flower.

Aromatic French lavender is a delightful cottage-garden plant. Brush against it and citrus scent fills the air.

FEATURES

Never out of fashion, hardy, evergreen lavender forms a rounded shrub 12–30in high. From July to September, its aromatic, gray-green foliage complements spikes of tightly clustered, pale blue, purple, pink, or white flowers. Interplant it with other shrubs or border perennials or set it to form a fetching divide between open-plan gardens.

Choice varieties are: dwarf, compact and rich purple-blue "Hidcote"; equally neat, lavender-blue "Munstead"; and taller French lavender (*Lavandula stoechas* "Papillon"), the dark purple flowers of which are borne in dense, lozenge-shaped heads. Flowers are used fresh in posies and dried for pot-pourri or cosmetics.

Lavender is an archetypal cottage-garden plant. Its common names of French, English, or Italian lavender apply to different species, but even experts find it hard to agree upon which is which.

LAVENDER AT A GLANCE

Aromatic, grayish-leaved evergreen with scented, lavender, purple, pink, or white flowers in summer. Hardy to 14°F (zone8).

JAN	/	
FEB	/	
MAR	/	RECOMMENDED VARIETIES
APR	plant, prune	
MAY	plant	"Hidcote"
		"Loddon Pink"
JUNE	plant	"Munstead"
JULY	flower, plant	"Nana Alba"
AUG	flower, plant	"Twickel Purple"
SEPT	flower, plant	*L. vera*
OCT	/	*L. stoechas* "Papillon"
NOV	/	
DEC	/	

CONDITIONS

Aspect Lavender needs an open situation in full sun with good air circulation. Do not crowd it with other plantings.

Site Thriving on most well-drained soils, it prefers coarse, sandy, or gravelly loam. Lime acid soils before planting.

GROWING METHOD

Feeding Boost growth of young plants by topdressing the root area with fish, blood, and bone meal in spring and midsummer. When established, after two years, no regular fertilizing is necessary.

Water new plantings copiously to help them recover quickly. When well established, lavender is seldom stressed by droughty spells.

Propagation Take semi-ripe cuttings from early to mid-fall. Alternatively, work sharp sand into the crown in spring, watering it well, so lower branches are buried. Detach rooted layers in fall and move them to their new positions.

Problems Lavender is seldom troubled by pests or diseases but may succumb to root rot in heavy or overwet soils. If crowded, in sheltered gardens, the foliage may die back. Remove dead growth and thin out stems to improve air circulation.

PRUNING

Use shears to trim dead blooms from bushes and hedges after flowering.

Rejuvenate older, "tired" plants and help them bloom freely by shortening the previous year's flowered stems to new shoots within 2–4in of the base. Do this from early to mid-spring. Never cut back into older wood, for it seldom regenerates and plants may die.

Lavandula varieties

RIGHT: *Create a feature by interplanting "Sawyers", a robust and deep purple-flowered variety, with* Perovskia *"Blue Spire", a Russian sage with grayish-white-stemmed spikes of rich blue flowers.*

ABOVE: *Thriving in a warm, sunny border, French lavender* (Lavandula stoechas) *forms an appealing globe to 2ft high and across. A wealth of lozenge-shaped flower heads in summer, and leaves, emit a strong citrus scent.*

LEFT: *Seeking a small, white variety for a patio pot? Opt for "Nana Alba". Just 8in high, it associates stunningly with a fringe of trailing, purple Surfinia petunias.*

BELOW: *An archetypal cottage-garden plant, old English lavender* (Lavandula angustifolia) *makes a handsome fountain of blossom to 3ft high.*

BELOW: *Keen to plant a low lavender hedge to flank a path or driveway? Plump for "Munstead", whose thickly clustered shoots are topped with dark lavender-blue flowers.*

LEPTOSPERMUM SCOPARIUM
New Zealand tea tree

Smothered with tiny, disc-like blooms from May to June, Leptospermum "Red Damask" is best fan-trained against a warm, sunny wall in all but very mild areas.

Keep tea tree youthful and glowing with blossom by removing a third of the older shoots when flowers fade.

FEATURES

Bejewelled from May to June with stalkless, disc-like blooms amid small, narrow leaves, twiggy and slender, purplish-stemmed *Leptospermum scoparium* is an evergreen worth caring for. Forming a rounded bush, 6–8ft high, it is usually grown against a sheltered wall. Alternatively, set it among other shrubs that shield it from biting winds.

Trained as a mini-standard, it makes a fetching feature for a sun-soaked patio.

Favoured varieties are double "Red Damask", single, clear pink "Huia", and double, white "Snow Flurry". Be warned: tea trees may be short-lived unless conditions are ideal.

TEA TREE AT A GLANCE

A slightly frost-tender evergreen, it is studded with tiny, red, pink, or white blooms from May to June. Hardy to 23°F (zone 9).

JAN	/	RECOMMENDED VARIETIES
FEB	/	
MAR	/	"Huia"
APR	plant	"Kiwi"
MAY	flower, plant	"Red Damask"
JUNE	flower, plant	"Snow Flurry"
JULY	plant, prune	
AUG	plant	
SEPT	plant	
OCT	/	
NOV	/	
DEC	/	

CONDITIONS

Aspect Leptospermum needs full sun and protection from cold, north or east winds. Ideally fan-train it against a south- or west-facing wall. Make sure air freely circulates to reduce risk of mildew felting and crippling leaves.

Site The planting area must be well drained. Improve light, sandy soils by digging in old manure or well-rotted garden compost.

GROWING METHOD

Feeding Encourage robust flowering growth by applying an acidifying fertilizer in spring and midsummer. Water young plants regularly in their first year after planting. Thereafter, soak the root area periodically in dry periods and mulch with shredded bark.

Propagation Multiply plants from soft-tip cuttings in June or semi-ripe cuttings in late summer.

Problems Plants are susceptible to root rot in clay soils. Avoid it by forking in grit or gravel before planting. Webbing caterpillars, such as lackey moth, can cause leaves to drop. Cut off and destroy egg bands or webbed shoots and spray with permethrin, bifenthrin, or fenitrothion.

PRUNING

If leptospermum outgrows its allotted space, remove one shoot in three from the base, when flowers fade in midsummer. Do not cut back into older wood as it seldom re-grows. Remove straggly shoots in spring.

LONICERA
Honeysuckle

Small and bushy Lonicera fragrantissima *treats us to a massed display of vanilla-perfumed, creamy flowers from mid- to late winter.*

Clothed with sweetly scented blooms from June to October, Lonicera japonica *"Halliana" makes a fetching screen for a sunny patio.*

FEATURES

A trio of sweetly scented, bushy honeysuckles worth cultivating are: *Lonicera fragrantissima*, with its vanilla-perfumed, creamy-white, bell-shaped blooms, which are freely borne on twiggy shoots to 6ft from January to March; slightly smaller *L. × purpusii,* which treats us to a similar display from November to March; and *L. syringantha*, with its profusion of clustered, lilac flowers on 3ft stems from late spring to early summer.

Twining varieties, trained to frame a door or clothe a wall, fence, arbour, pergola, or arch or to scramble through a tree, enhance a garden. Color spring by planting yellow and red *L. periclymenum* "Belgica" and continue the show—from June to October—with white and red *L.p.* "Serotina".

CONDITIONS

Aspect   Plant lonicera in full or lightly dappled shade to grow strongly and flower freely.

Site   These shrubs and climbers prefer well-drained and humus-rich, sandy loam, or clay loam but also tolerate chalky soil. Improve light soils, which dry out quickly, by working in bulky organic materials well before planting.

GROWING METHOD

Feeding   Speed robust growth and a panoply of blossom by enriching the root area with bone meal in spring and fall.

Water liberally to encourage young plants to establish quickly. Once growing strongly, all varieties are unstressed by droughty periods.

In spring, mulch thickly with humus-forming organics to keep roots cool and questing and encourage a fine display of blossom.

Propagation Shrubs: Take hardwood cuttings in late fall or early winter, or layer whippy stems from mid-spring to late summer.

Climbers: Take semi-ripe cuttings from early to midsummer.

Problems   Blackfly are attracted to new shoots, which they quickly smother. Control them with pirimicarb, natural pyrethrins, bifenthrin, or horticultural soap.

PRUNING

Keep winter-flowering *L. fragrantissima* and *L. × purpusii* shapely and full of young shoots, which flower freely, by removing one stem in three in mid-spring. Help spring- and early summer-blooming *L. syringantha* prosper by cutting back flowered shoots to new growth when blooms fade.

Prune *L. periclymenum* varieties and *L. japonica* "Halliana" by shortening flowered stems to new shoots when blooms fade.

HONEYSUCKLE AT A GLANCE

Semi-evergreen bushes and deciduous and evergreen climbers light up spring, summer and winter. Hardy to -13°F (zone 5).

		RECOMMENDED VARIETIES
JAN	flower	
FEB	flower	**Bushes**
MAR	plant	*L. fragrantissima*
APR	flower, prune	*L. × purpusii*
MAY	flower, prune	*L. syringantha*
		L. tartarica
JUNE	flower, prune	**Climbers**
JULY	flower, plant	"Belgica"
AUG	flower, prune	*L. heckrottii* "Goldflame"
SEPT	flower, prune	"Serotina"
OCT	plant	*L. japonica* "Halliana"
NOV	plant	*L. tragophylla*
DEC	/	

MAGNOLIA
Magnolia

Unfolding in March and April, before leaves appear, starry-flowered Magnolia stellata lights up dappled shade.

Planted to contrast with a dark green-leaved shrub, the star magnolia makes a statement. Underplant it with blue-flowered grape hyacinths.

FEATURES

Heralding spring, *Magnolia stellata*, a deciduous, bushy shrub to around 7ft, illuminates borders with a multitude of fragrant, strap-petalled, starry, white flowers from March to April. Also called star magnolia, it is ideal for small gardens. Fetching varieties are pink-budded, white-flowered "Royal Star", white-flowered "Centennial", whose blooms are 5½in across, and "Waterlily", another handsome, white variety with flared, double chalices that command close attention.

Most other magnolias, such as evergreen *M. grandiflora*, which flowers best if fan-trained on a sunny, sheltered wall, and varieties of *M. soulangeana*, soar to around 15ft.

CONDITIONS

Aspect No matter how large or small the variety, magnolias should be sheltered from strong winds. To flower well, they must receive at least half a day's sunshine.

Site *M. stellata* and *M. grandiflora* prosper in well-drained, acid, neutral, or alkaline soil. *M. soulangeana* abhors chalk. Dig in plenty of organic matter well ahead of planting.

GROWING METHOD

Feeding Encourage bountiful blooms by applying an acidifying fertilizer—brands for azaleas and camellias are ideal—in April and July.

Propagation Take soft-tip cuttings from late spring to early summer. Increase *M. grandiflora* from semi-ripe cuttings in midsummer.
Layering is more reliable but takes longer. Peg down shoots from spring to late summer and detach rooted stems a year later in fall.

Problems Soft, unfolding leaves can be scorched by hot, dry, or salty winds, so position plants carefully.

PRUNING

Seldom necessary. If a shrub requires shaping or crowded branches need removing, tackle it when flowers fade in mid-spring. Never prune in winter, as corky tissues are liable to rot.

MAGNOLIA AT A GLANCE

White or pink flowers are thickly borne on leafless branches in early spring. *M. stellata* is hardy to -13° (zone 5).

		RECOMMENDED VARIETIES
JAN	/	
FEB	/	*M. grandiflora**
MAR	flower, plant	*M. grandiflora* "Heaven Scent"*
APR	flower, plant	
MAY	flower, prune	*M. grandiflora* "Little Gem"*
JUN	plant, prune	
JULY	plant, flower*	*M. soulangeana* "Lennei"
AUG	plant, flower*	*M. soulangeana* "Picture"
SEPT	plant, flower*	*M. stellata*
OCT	/	*M. stellata* "Centennial"
NOV	/	*M. stellata* "Royal Star"
DEC	/	* summer flowering

MAGNOLIA VARIETIES

RIGHT: A glorious sight in May, a mature bush of Magnolia soulangeana "Alba Superba" is massed with upright, tulip-like, snow-white blossoms, purple at the base. Site it carefully—in a sheltered, sunny spot free from frost, which reduces blooms to soggy mops.

ABOVE: Showered in spring with goblet-shaped blooms, rosy purple outside, suffused cream and purple within, Magnolia soulangeana "Lennei" treats us to a further, smaller display in fall.

LEFT: A Japanese gem, Magnolia liliiflora "Nigra" rewards us with a multitude of long, slender, candle-like buds that open to deep purple blooms stained creamy white and purple within. When mature, petals reflex and become starry. As well as planting it in the garden, set it in a large, well-drained patio tub in which it will grow slowly and flower bounteously.

BELOW: A good choice for a small garden, Magnolia stellata makes a neat globe to around 5ft high after ten years or so. It is very accommodating, does not need pruning and is seldom attacked by pests or diseases.

RIGHT: A hybrid raised at the US National Arboretum, Washington, Magnolia liliiflora x stellata "Judy" is one of several hybrids superior to their parents in flower size, profusion of blossom, color, and scent.

MAHONIA
Mahonia

Tall, bushy mahonias display shuttlecocks of citrus-scented, pale lemon to golden flowers from early winter to early spring. Decorative, blue berries follow in the fall.

Mahonia × media "Charity" illuminates a dry, shady spot from mid- to late winter.

FEATURES

Ground-hugging, weed-suppressing, and good for stabilizing steep banks, tall and sculptural, evergreen mahonias have shiny, spiky, holly-like leaves that develop burnished coppery or reddish tints in winter. Flamboyant, citrus-scented heads of yellow or golden-clustered, slender, cone-like flowers appear from November to May. Blooms are followed by decorative, bluish-black berries. From 2ft to 8ft high, depending on the species, taller kinds make fetching focal points, dense screens, or dashing background plants.

Varieties of suckering, ground-covering *Mahonia aquifolium*, which thrives in light shade, effectively carpet rooty areas around trees and shrubs. Position orb-shaped and free-flowering *M. × media* "Charity" and more upright "Lionel Fortescue" to light up winter.

CONDITIONS

Aspect	Thriving in sun or dappled shade, mahonias resist cold winds.
Site	These shrubs flourish in all but very chalky conditions. Improve poor soils by adding bulky organic matter several weeks before planting.

GROWING METHOD

Feeding	Boost growth by working fish, blood, and bone meal or Growmore into the root area in mid-spring and midsummer. If they are growing where there is root competition, mulch thickly to help conserve moisture.
Propagation	Raise species from seeds in early to mid-spring, in a garden frame. Take leaf-bud cuttings in mid-fall or mid-spring and root in a heated propagator. Divide *M. aquifolium* into well-rooted portions in mid-spring.
Problems	Control mahonia rust by spraying with penconazole, mancozeb, or bupirimate with triforine. *M. aquifolium* and *M. bealei* have some resistance to this disease.

PRUNING

M. aquifolium:	Prevent plants from becoming leggy by removing one stem in three after flowering.
Tall, bushy hybrids:	Remove flower heads when blooms fade; rejuvenate old, gaunt plants by shortening stems by half their height in May.

MAHONIA AT A GLANCE

Carpeting or upright evergreens, with holly-like leaves, color borders from November to March. Hardy to -13°F (zone 5).

JAN	flower	RECOMMENDED VARIETIES
FEB	flower	
MAR	flower	*M. aquifolium* "Apollo"
APR	flower, plant	*M. aquifolium* "Atropurpurea"
MAY	prune, flower	*M. aquifolium* "Smaragd"
JUNE	plant	*M. japonica*
JULY	feed	*M. lomariifolia*
AUG	plant	*M. × media* "Charity"
SEPT	plant	"Lionel Fortescue"
OCT	plant	"Winter Sun"
NOV	flower	
DEC	flower	

NANDINA DOMESTICA

Sacred bamboo

Nandina's fall bounty of bright red berries follows a summer display of white flowers. Leaves are greenish but tinted cream, pink, orange, and red.

Unlike true bamboo, the sacred version is light, airy, and not invasive and is ideal for colonizing a restricted space.

FEATURES

Reminiscent of bamboo, nandina is a slender-stemmed evergreen that slowly spreads by suckers to make a fascinating focal point. Grown for its brightly hued, cream, orange, pink, and red leaves, its "airy" shoots create an impression of "lightness". Nandina, much prized for Japanese-style gardens, may also be sited elsewhere to contrast effectively with darker-toned and heavier-textured plants. Small, white flowers from June to July are followed by attractive, red berries, which linger into fall. Makes a handsome bush to 4ft high by 3ft across.

SACRED BAMBOO AT A GLANCE

Bamboo-like evergreen whose cream-, orange-, and pink-tinted leaves complement white flowers. Hardy to 14°F (zone 8).

		RECOMMENDED VARIETIES
JAN	/	
FEB	/	"Firepower"
MAR		"Nana Purpurea"
APR	plant	"Richmond"
MAY	prune	
JUNE	plant, flower	
JULY	plant, flower	
AUG	plant, flower	
SEPT	plant	
OCT	/	
NOV	/	
DEC	/	

CONDITIONS

Aspect
Thriving in full sun or semi-shade, it needs shielding from cold winds, which can blacken leaves. Ideally, plant it at the foot of a south- or west-facing wall.

Soil
Nandina prefers well-drained and humus rich, sandy loam. Augment chalk or heavy clay soils with bulky organic materials a month or two before planting.

GROWING METHOD

Feeding
Encourage luxuriant foliage and large clusters of fruit by working bone meal into the root area in spring and the fall.
Once established, nandina is fairly drought resistant. Mulch with well-rotted garden compost, manure, shredded bark, or cocoa shell in spring to insulate roots from moisture-extracting sunshine.

Propagation
In the fall, extract seeds from ripe berries, sow in pots and raise in a garden frame. Take semi-ripe cuttings from mid- to late summer. Use a spade to split up large clumps in mid-spring.

Problems
Severe winter weather may kill shoots to ground level and new growth from roots may be slow in appearing.

PRUNING

No regular cutting back is necessary. Rejuvenate old clumps in May by removing a third of the older stems at ground level.

NERIUM OLEANDER
Oleander

Delighting us with white, yellow, apricot, pink, or crimson blooms from spring to fall, evergreen but poisonous oleander is easy to grow.

Create a Mediterranean tapestry by grouping a pot-grown oleander next to a spiky-leaved yucca and scarlet pelargonium.

FEATURES

Frost-tender and principally a conservatory plant, evergreen oleander enjoys a summer airing on a sunny, sheltered patio or terrace. Depending on variety, it makes a handsome shrub, 4–6ft high. Sumptuous heads of white, yellow, pink, apricot, cerise, or scarlet, single or double blooms appear from June to November. Thrusting, upright stems are clad with slender, leathery leaves. Oleanders are long-lived and flower early in life. Choice varieties include: semi-double, light pink "Clare"; single, apricot "Madame Leon Blum"; double, white "Soeur Agnes"; and single, deep red "Hardy's Red". Double, pink-flowered "Variegatum", with cream or yellow-rimmed leaves, is very popular with flower arrangers. The plant is poisonous if eaten.

OLEANDER AT A GLANCE

Studded with showy blooms in many colors, frost-tender oleander is usually grown in a conservatory. Hardy to 45°F (zone 11).

JAN	/	RECOMMENDED VARIETIES
FEB	/	
MAR	plant	"Clare"
APR	plant, prune	"Emile"
MAY	flower, plant	"Géant des Batailles"
JUNE	flower, plant	"Luteum Plenum"
JULY	flower, plant	"Professor Granel"
AUG	flower, plant	"Soeur Agnes"
SEPT	flower, plant	"Soleil Levant"
OCT	flower	"Variegatum"
NOV	flower	
DEC	/	

CONDITIONS

Aspect Oleander needs full sun and shelter from cold winds to prosper and flower freely. Only in frost-free gardens can it be grown outdoors all year round. Elsewhere, grow it in a pot indoors—in a lounge or conservatory—and move it outside when frosts finish in late May.

Site This shrub thrives in most free-draining soil types but abhors heavy, waterlogged clay. If growing it in a large pot or tub, set it in proprietary tub or hanging basket compost.

GROWING METHOD

Feeding Border plants: Encourage large clusters of blossom by sprinkling bone meal over the root area in spring and fall and hoeing it in.
Tub grown (indoors in winter): Insert slow-release fertilizer granules into the compost in spring. Repot root-bound plants in spring. Though oleander tolerates long, dry periods, soak roots occasionally in hot, dry weather.

Propagation Raise plants from seeds sown in a heated propagator in spring or take semi-ripe cuttings in midsummer.

Problems If plants are attacked by limpet-like scale insects, control them by spraying two or three times, fortnightly, with malathion or horticultural soap.

PRUNING

Keep oleander youthful and blooming freely by shortening flowered shoots by half their length when blossoms fade. Ensure plants stay neat and bushy by shortening side shoots to 4in in spring.

OSMANTHUS
Osmanthus

Forming an umbrella of small, evergreen shoots, Osmanthus delavayi's *thickly clustered, tubular flowers sleeve shoots in spring.*

A beacon of bright, cream-rimmed, evergreen leaves from Osmanthus heterophyllus *"Variegatus" illuminates dull, winter days.*

FEATURES

An easy, enchanting, and small, glossy, leathery-leaved evergreen from western China and Japan, osmanthus forms an orb of shoots and colors spring and fall.

Light up April and May with *Osmanthus × burkwoodii.* Growing to around 6ft high by 4ft across, its toothed, pointed leaves foil slender stems massed with clusters of small, white, vanilla-fragrant, tubular blooms. Create a riveting feature by grouping it with orange or yellow deciduous azaleas. It also makes a dense, wind-proof hedge.

Closely related *O. delavayi* is another spring-flowering treasure. Arching to 5ft high, it too is smothered with bunches of small, white blooms that spill jasmine perfume on to the air. Small, black fruits follow them.

Later, from September to October, comes taller *O. heterophyllus,* to 10ft high and across, the soft leaves of which deceive you into thinking

it is a form of holly. It does a sterling job in coloring the closing year with a profusion of tiny, white blossoms.

Its colored-leaved varieties—purple "Purpureus" and creamy "Aureomarginatus"—are stunning throughout the year.

CONDITIONS

Aspect	All, apart from *O. delavayi* which is best grown again against a sheltering, warm wall in cold districts, thrive in the open.
Site	If possible, set plants in free-draining, humus-rich soil that does not dry out or become waterlogged. Fortify sandy or chalky soils with bulky organic manure.

GROWING METHOD

Feeding	Boost growth by sprinkling Growmore or some other balanced fertilizer over the root area in spring, repeating in midsummer. Water it in if the soil is dry. Foliar feed in droughty spells, when roots have difficulty absorbing plant foods, to speed uptake of nutrients. Water new plants copiously and follow with a mulch of bark, cocoa shell, or well-rotted garden compost.
Propagation	Increase varieties by layering flexible shoots from late spring to late summer or take semi-ripe cuttings from mid- to late summer.
Problems	Seldom attacked by pests or diseases.

PRUNING

No regular cutting back is necessary. If awkward shoots need removing, do it in spring when flowers have finished. Shorten stems to just above a joint or to new shoots. Trim a hedge of *O.* x *burkwoodii* when flowers fade in May.

OSMANTHUS AT A GLANCE

Spring- or fall-flowering evergreens for sun or light shade, *O.* × *burkwoodii* makes a stocky hedge. Hardy to 23°F (zone 9).

		RECOMMENDED VARIETIES
JAN	/	
FEB	/	*O.* × *burkwoodii*
MAR		*O. delavayi*
APR	flower, plant	*O. heterophyllus*
MAY	flower, plant	*O. heterophyllus* "Aureomarginatus"
JUNE	prune	
JULY	/	*O. heterophyllus* "Purpureus"
AUG	/	
SEPT	flower, plant	*O. heterophyllus* "Variegatus"
OCT	flower	
NOV	/	
DEC	/	

PHILADELPHUS
Mock orange

Semi-arching "Belle Etoile" is thickly clothed with richly vanilla-scented, single, large, white, and flushed-yellow blooms from June to July.

Plant soaring Philadelphus lemoinei "Erectus" to brighten a sunny spot with a myriad perfumed blooms sleeving upright shoots.

FEATURES

Often but erroneously called syringa—the correct name for lilac—its sumptuous, creamy white, single, or double and richly citrus-vanilla-scented blooms fill and brighten the high-summer gap, when the spring display of shrubs is fading and fall contenders have yet to form flower buds. Ranging in height from 2ft to over 10ft, there are candidates for most situations.

Coveted tall varieties, 6–10ft, are: large, single, and pink-centred "Beauclerk"; semi-double and yellowish-white *Philadelphus coronarius*; and double or semi-double, pure white "Virginal". Couple flowers with striking foliage by planting semi-double, creamy white *P. coronarius* "Aureus", the leaves of which open lemon-yellow and mature to greenish yellow. This plant is perfect for lighting up a sunny or dappled shady border.

Set the smallest member, "Manteau

d'Hermine", just 2–3ft high, on a rock garden and enjoy its massed, double, creamy white blossoms. Taller kinds are good for hedging.

CONDITIONS

Aspect   Ideal for windswept, hillside gardens and for tolerating salty breezes, mock orange thrives almost anywhere. All flower best in full sun and lemon-leaved *P. coronarius* "Aureus" keeps its radiant leaf color in light shade.

Site   Thriving in most soils—acid sand, chalk, or heavy clay—it is best to enrich poor patches with bulky organic matter dug in several months before planting.

GROWING METHOD

Feeding   Encourage bounteous blossom on sandy soil by applying annually sulfate of potash in late winter and late summer. Regardless of soil, topdress the root area with a balanced fertilizer in April and July.

In a dry spring, water regularly to encourage strong, new shoots, which will flower the following year.

Propagation   Strike cuttings of semi-ripe shoots from mid- to late summer. Root them in a cold frame or on a sunny windowsill.

Problems   Blackfly can colonize and cripple soft shoot tips. Control them by spraying with pirimicarb, which does not harm beneficial insects.

PRUNING

When blooms fade, cut back flowered shoots to current-year stems, which will perform the following year.

MOCK ORANGE AT A GLANCE

A deciduous shrub whose single or fully double, creamy white flowers appear from June to July. Hardy to -13°F (zone 5).

		RECOMMENDED VARIETIES
JAN	/	
FEB	/	Under 1.8m (6ft)
MAR	plant	"Belle Etoile"
APR	plant	*Coronarius* "Aureus"
MAY	plant	"Manteau d'Hermine"
JUNE	flower	"Sybille"
JULY	flower	Over 1.8m (6ft)
AUG	prune	"Beauclerk"
SEPT	/	*Coronarius*
OCT	plant	"Virginal"
NOV	plant	
DEC	/	

PHOTINIA
Photinia

The awakening year sees Photinia fraseri *draped with clusters of tiny, white flowers, occasionally followed by red berries.*

In spring and early summer, Photinia "Red Robin" *is a beacon of shining maroon-scarlet leaves. Here it is contrasting with an apple-green hebe.*

FEATURES

A valued New Zealand evergreen to around 6ft high by 5ft across, *Photinia* × *fraseri* "Red Robin" is a visual delight. From mid- to late spring, a foam of fluffy, white flowers, sometimes followed by scarlet berries, complements brilliant red, shiny leaves that mature to green. Riveting in a winter-color border, it is also appealing when fan-trained against a sunny, sheltered wall or fence. Alternatively, plant it in a large pot or tub and train it as a globe, pyramid, or drumstick. Clip trained forms in spring and summer. Photinia also makes a dense, low hedge.

PHOTINIA AT A GLANCE

The most popular kind, *P.* × *fraseri* "Red Robin", enchants us with a wealth of scarlet, new leaves. Hardy to 4°F (zone 7).

JAN	/	RECOMMENDED VARIETIES
FEB	/	
MAR	/	"Birmingham"
APR	flower, plant	"Red Robin"
MAY	flower, prune	"Robusta"
JUNE	flower, plant	"Rubens"
JULY	plant	
AUG	plant	
SEPT	plant	
OCT	/	
NOV	/	
DEC	/	

CONDITIONS

Aspect   Not the hardiest of shrubs, photinia prefers a sheltered, sunny situation in which its foliage colors magnificently. It tolerates light shade.

Site   This shrub thrives on most well-drained soils but hates heavy clay and chalk. Improve sandy patches by incorporating bulky organic manures several weeks before planting.

GROWING METHOD

Feeding   Encourage stocky shoots and lustrous leaves by topdressing the root area with fish, blood, and bone meal, or some other balanced fertilizer, in spring and midsummer.
Water young plants copiously in dry spells in their first year to initiate strong, new shoots.

Propagation   Layer young stems from spring to late summer; take semi-ripe cuttings in late summer.

Problems   Photinia is susceptible to apple scab, a fungus that causes leaves to develop grayish-green spots and fall early. Control it by raking up diseased leaves, pruning out and burning scabby shoots and spraying with carbendazim, mancozeb, or bupirimate with triforine.

PRUNING

Rejuvenate old, leggy bushes by shortening stems by a third of their length in mid-spring. Remove shoot tips periodically throughout spring and summer, to encourage flushes of new, red leaves.

PIERIS
Pieris

Young pieris leaves open a vivid shade of pink or scarlet before turning yellow and ultimately green.

Some varieties, such as "Wakehurst", not only produce scarlet, flower-bright leaves but also combine them with an unstinting display of lily-of-the-valley-like blossom.

FEATURES

A captivating, evergreen shrub, 16in–9ft high and across, its bell-shaped, white, pink, or red flowers glorify spring. Its other, equally prized asset is its glowing pink or reddish shuttlecocks of new leaves.

There are many varieties. Aptly named "Flaming Silver"—2ft high, ideal for a narrow border—has fiery, new leaves which when mature are suffused with silver.

PIERIS AT A GLANCE

New, red, evergreen leaves complement sprays of white, pink, or red, bell-shaped flowers in spring. Hardy to 14°F (zone 8).

JAN	/	
FEB	/	
MAR	flower	RECOMMENDED VARIETIES
APR	flower, plant	"Debutante"
MAY	flower, prune	"Firecrest"
JUNE	plant, prune	"Flaming Silver"
JULY	plant	"Forest Flame"
AUG	plant	"Mountain Fire"
SEPT	plant	"Pink Delight"
OCT	/	"Valley Valentine"
NOV	/	
DEC	/	

CONDITIONS

Aspect   Not a candidate for exposed gardens, pieris needs shielding from strong, cold winds and hot, leaf-scorching sunshine.

Site   Abhorring any degree of lime, this shrub needs deep, rich, well-drained soil. Create a good home for it by digging in generous amounts of organic material well ahead of planting time.

GROWING METHOD

Feeding   Boost robust growth by applying an acidifying fertilizer in spring and midsummer. Help young plants recover quickly from transplanting by watering regularly in droughty spells and mulching with moisture-conserving organics.

Propagation   Multiply plants by pegging down low shoots from mid-spring to late summer or take semi-ripe cuttings from mid- to late summer.

Problems   New leaves may be damaged by wind frost.

PRUNING

Cut off faded blooms and dead or damaged shoots in early summer. Rejuvenate old bushes by shortening gaunt shoots to half their height in mid-spring. Keep cuts moist in dry spells to encourage rapid regrowth.

POTENTILLA FRUTICOSA
Shrubby cinquefoil

Forming a spreading clump, "Red Ace"—riveting when interplanted with Artemisia "Powis Castle"—fires a border from May to October.

Prized for its display of butter-yellow flowers, "Dart's Golddigger" contrasts stunningly with rosy-pink bedding geraniums.

FEATURES

Potentilla fruticosa flowers continuously from late May to September, its small, saucer-shaped blossoms clustering on dense, wiry stems.

Carpeting or bushy, to 5ft—taller kinds making colorful hedges—it is hardy and a good choice for cold gardens.

Easy, eye-catching varieties are: grayish-green-leaved and white-flowered "Abbotswood"; creamy-yellow "Tilford Cream"; ground-covering "Dart's Golddigger"; chrome-yellow "Goldstar"; salmon-pink "Pretty Polly"; vermilion-flame "Red Ace"; and deep orange to brick-red "Sunset".

All are good contenders for patio and terrace tubs and pots or deep, generous windowboxes. Arrange a potted group in several harmonizing colors to flank a doorway or form a focal point at the end of a path. Shrubby cinquefoil can also be grown to embrace pergola posts.

SHRUBBY CINQUEFOIL AT A GLANCE

Deciduous, bushy plants, which also make good hedges, they flower from May to September. Hardy to -13°F (zone 5).

		RECOMMENDED VARIETIES
JAN	/	
FEB	/	
MAR	plant	**Carpeting**
APR	plant, prune	"Dart's Golddigger"
MAY	plant, flower	"Pretty Polly"
JUNE	plant, flower	"Red Ace"
JULY	plant, flower	"Sunset"
AUG	plant, flower	**Bushy**
SEPT	plant, flower	"Goldfinger"
OCT	plant, flower	"Goldstar"
NOV	plant	"Red Robin"
DEC	/	"Tilford Cream"

CONDITIONS

Aspect A good choice for borders exposed to cold winds, shrubby cinquefoil flowers profusely in an open, sunny position or very light shade. If possible, plant it facing south or west where trees will not overshadow it.

Site A very adaptable plant, it thrives in most soils, from heavy, often waterlogged clay to light, sandy areas that become parched in summer. It does not mind a little lime but on very chalky soils it is liable to become stressed and suffer from chlorosis, when leaves turn creamy or yellowish and die.

GROWING METHOD

Feeding Encourage robust flowering shoots by working fish, blood, and bone meal or some other balanced fertilizer into the root area in spring and midsummer. Apply bone meal in the fall to release plant foods in spring. If, in sandy soil, leaf margins turn brown, indicating potash deficiency, rectify by applying sulfate of potash in February and watering it in.

Once the plant is established, watering is seldom needed, but soak newly planted shrubs to settle the soil around the roots.

Propagation Increase plants from cuttings of semi-ripe shoots in midsummer. Root them in a garden frame or on a sunny windowsill.

Problems Shoots produce their leaves very late in spring, deceiving us into thinking them dead.

PRUNING

Keep bushes youthful and flowering freely year after year by removing a third of the older shoots in spring. Rejuvenate very old, woody plants at the same time by cutting them back to within 4in of the base. Trim hedges in spring.

PLUMBAGO
Cape leadwort

Commonly called Cape leadwort, plumbago rewards us with a succession of silvery-blue flowers from mid- to late summer.

Encourage plumbago to flower bounteously every year by shortening the previous year's flowered stems in February.

FEATURES

Usually grown to color a conservatory, greenhouse, or windowsill with a mist of starry, sky-blue flowers from midsummer to fall, *Plumbago auriculata* is a rambling, evergreen climber. Ideally, grow it in a large pot or tub to allow you to move it on to a patio when frosts finish in late May or early June. Growing to 15ft or so, in cultivation it is best pruned regularly to keep it neat, compact, and floriferous. In very sheltered, frost-free gardens, create a sensation in summer by training it over an arch, arbour, obelisk, or trellis.

CAPE LEADWORT AT A GLANCE

Scrambling, frost-tender climber studded with pale blue flowers from midsummer to early fall. Hardy to 46°F (zone 11).

JAN	/	
FEB	prune	RECOMMENDED VARIETIES
MAR	/	*P. auriculata*
APR	plant	*P. auriculata alba*
MAY	plant	"Royal Cape"
JUNE	plant	
JULY	flower	
AUG	flower	
SEPT	flower	
OCT	flower	
NOV	/	
DEC	/	

CONDITIONS

Aspect   Though plumbago flowers best in full sun, it tolerates very light shade.

Site   Set this shrub in a large, well-drained pot or small tub of multi-purpose compost.

GROWING METHOD

Feeding   Insert clusters of slow-release fertilizer granules into the compost in spring. From late spring to summer, apply a high-potash tomato feed.
When potting plants, add moisture-storage granules to help keep the compost damp during long, dry spells.
In late summer, when nights turn cold, return plumbago to a frost-free spot in good light. Keep the compost dryish from fall to spring.

Propagation   Take semi-ripe cuttings from early to midsummer.

Problems   Under glass, fluffy, waxy, white mealy bugs may colonize leaf joints and cripple growth. Control them biologically with *Aphidius colemani*, a parasitic wasp, or spray with horticultural soap.

PRUNING

Shorten the previous year's flowering shoots to within 2in of the older wood in February.

PRUNUS
Ornamental cherry

From early to mid-spring, a wealth of disc-shaped, double pink blooms transform Prunus x blireana's *bare, twiggy branches.*

Heralding spring and suitable for all sizes of garden, white-, pink-, or red-flowering cherries associate beautifully with magnolias.

FEATURES

Deciduous or evergreen shrubs or trees 4–14ft tall, the prunus family embraces a wide range of forms. Flowers are single or double, in white, pink, and red shades. Neat dwarf Russian almond (*Prunus tenella* "Firehill") has semi-double, rosy-crimson flowers, which sleeve 4ft stems in April. Also useful for small gardens is
P. × cistena "Crimson Dwarf", whose white flowers appear just before coppery-red leaves.
White-flowering and low-growing evergreen kinds—*P.* "Otto Luyken" among them—are

excellent for carpeting shady spots. Taller laurel (*P. laurocerasus* "Rotundifolia") makes a dense evergreen hedge to 6ft.

CONDITIONS

Aspect   Deciduous flowering cherries, needing full sun to perform well, should be sheltered from strong winds. Evergreens thrive in light shade.

Site   All prunus prosper on any well-drained soil enriched with organic matter. Evergreen varieties also thrive on thin, sandy soils.

GROWING METHOD

Feeding   Work bone meal into the root area in spring and fall. Water freely in dry spells, especially when flower buds are forming.

Propagation   Increase evergreen, carpeting and hedging varieties from semi-ripe cuttings from mid- to late summer. Flowering cherry trees, however, are normally grafted on to *P. avium* rootstock.

Problems   Control silver leaf disease by cutting back and burning affected shoots to 6in beyond infected, purple-stained tissue, in midsummer.

PRUNING

Evergreens: Shear laurel hedges in spring and late summer.

Deciduous varieties: No regular pruning is necessary. Cut out crowding shoots from mid- to late summer.

ORNAMENTAL CHERRY AT A GLANCE

A huge family of deciduous, spring-flowering cherries and carpeting or hedging evergreens. Hardiness rating, according to species.

Month	Activity	Recommended Varieties
JAN	/	
FEB	/	**Evergreen**
MAR	plant, flower	"Otto Luyken"
APR	prune, flower	*P. laurocerasus*
MAY	flower, plant	"Rotundifolia"
JUNE	plant, flower	"Zabeliana"
JULY	plant, prune	**Deciduous**
AUG	plant, prune	"Amanogawa"
SEPT	plant	*P. × blireana*
OCT	plant	"Cheal's Weeping"
NOV	plant	*P. mume*
DEC	/	*P. tenella* "Firehill"

PRUNUS VARIETIES

ABOVE: *Pale pink blooms that open white and contrast with dark reddish-purple leaves make Pissard's purple plum (*Prunus cerasifera *"Pissardii") a desirable garden tree. Red fruits follow in summer.*

ABOVE: *Prunus and malus flowers are very similar. This* Malus *"John Downie" could be mistaken for a flowering cherry.*

LEFT: *Enchanting in a small border,* Prunus triloba *treats us to massed rosettes of pale pink blooms that cluster on year-old shoots in April. Keep it youthful and blooming freely by pruning out one stem in three in early summer.*

BELOW: *A snowfall of single, white blooms smothers* Prunus *"Taihaku" in May. Position it in full sun, in a large lawn, where it can develop fully without having to be cut back. Alternatively, set it near a contrasting, deep green hedge to accentuate the whiteness of its flowers.*

ABOVE: *Famed for its profusion of white, candle-like blooms in spring and again in fall,* Prunus *"Otto Luyken" is also prized for its ground-hugging, evergreen, and weed-suppressing leaves. It flourishes in sun or shade.*

PUNICA
Pomegranate

Showy, bell-shaped, orange-scarlet flowers are your reward for growing a pomegranate in a warm garden or conservatory.

Delicious fruits appear on outdoor or patio pot plants after a long, warm summer. Under glass, in a higher temperature, fruits swell to a greater size.

FEATURES

Deciduous and bearing carnation-like, single or double, brilliant orange-red flowers for most of the summer, *Punica granatum* makes a bushy shrub to 7ft high and across. Only single-flowered varieties bear fruits. Grow them as specimen plants in very sheltered borders in frost-free gardens. Elsewhere, treat this shrub as a pot plant and confine it to a conservatory from fall to late spring. Move it on to a sunny patio or terrace when frosts finish in late May or early June.

POMEGRANATE AT A GLANCE

Deciduous and bearing orange flowers in summer, it can be grown outside only in very sheltered areas. Hardy to 39°F (zone 10).

JAN	/	
FEB	/	
MAR	/	
APR	plant, prune	
MAY	plant, prune	
JUNE	flower, plant	
JULY	flower, plant	
AUG	flower, plant	
SEPT	plant	
OCT	/	
NOV	/	
DEC	/	

RECOMMENDED VARIETIES

"Flore Pleno Luteo"
"Flore Pleno Rubro"
P. granatum nana
"Striata"

CONDITIONS

Aspect If you are growing pomegranate outdoors, it must be in full sunshine and protected from cold winds.

Site To excel, this shrub needs well-drained loam or clay-loam soil enriched with humus-forming organics.

GROWING METHOD

Feeding Boost growth and stimulate plenty of blossom-bearing shoots by applying bone meal in spring and the fall.
Encourage young plants to establish quickly by watering liberally in the first spring and summer after planting.
In September, return potted plants that have decorated a patio for summer to a frost-free conservatory or greenhouse.

Propagation Increase this plant from semi-ripe cuttings taken from mid- to late summer.

Problems New shoots on outdoor plants can be damaged by late spring frosts, so site the shrubs carefully.

PRUNING

Remove badly placed shoots from late spring to early summer. Keep wall-trained specimens shapely by shortening flowered shoots to within four leaves of the main framework when blooms fade.

PYRACANTHA
Firethorn

A spectacular autumn display of orange, red, or yellow berries, following a foam of creamy blossom, makes firethorn popular for transforming cold walls.

Planted to screen out ugly objects, firethorn's late-season bonanza of berries is a welcome winter feast for garden birds.

FEATURES

Planted mainly for screening, hedging, and training as an espalier, evergreen and hardy firethorn's spiky stems are clad with small, glossy green leaves. In early summer, showy clusters of white flowers, appearing early in the plant's life, are followed by a dramatic cloak of bright orange, yellow, or red berries from fall to winter. Garden birds feast on them. There are many long-lived varieties. Choice kinds include a trio of recently bred fireblight-resistant forms: orange-berried "Saphyr Orange"; red-berried "Saphyr Red"; and yellow-berried "Saphyr Yellow". These shrubs grow 6–10ft high, which they reach after 5–10 years.

FIRETHORN AT A GLANCE

An evergreen shrub coveted for its white flowers and display of red, orange, or yellow berries. Hardy to -13°F (zone 5).

		RECOMMENDED VARIETIES
JAN	/	
FEB	/	"Alexander Pendula"
MAR	/	"Dart's Red"
APR	plant, prune	"Golden Charmer"
MAY	plant	*P. rogersiana*
JUNE	flower, plant	"Saphyr Orange"
JULY	plant	"Saphyr Red"
AUG	plant	"Saphyr Yellow"
SEPT	plant	
OCT	/	
NOV	/	
DEC	/	

CONDITIONS

Aspect　Needing full sun for healthy, compact growth, firethorn flowers less and is more loosely branched in light shade. It tolerates strong gusts and is often grown as a windbreak.

Site　Tolerating a wide range of soil types including chalk, it prefers well-drained loam or clay-loam enriched with organic matter. It also prospers on humus-rich, gravelly patches.

GROWING METHOD

Feeding　Keep firethorn lustrous and flowering and berrying freely by working bone meal into the root area in spring and fall.
Help newly planted shrubs establish quickly by watering copiously in dry spells during their first spring and summer. Mulch thickly.

Propagation　Take semi-ripe cuttings from mid- to late summer.

Problems　Disfiguring leaves and berries with patches, pyracantha scab is a debilitating disease. Control it by pruning out and burning infected shoots and spraying fortnightly with carbendazim from March to July. Grow orange-red berried "Mohave", which is resistant to it.

PRUNING

Free-standing shrubs:　Cut back overgrown plants in April to keep them flowering and berrying profusely.

Wall-trained espaliers:　In spring, shorten non-blossoming side shoots to 4in from the base. In midsummer, reduce current-year shoots to three leaves.

RHODODENDRON
Rhododendron

Few shrubs can equal rhododendrons for a spectacular display of blossom from late winter to summer. This skillfully planned garden features a bold planting of white and rosy-red hardy hybrids framed by dark foliage that enhances rather than competes with the flowers.

FEATURES

Enriching gardens with spectacular trusses of vibrant or delicate pastel-hued blooms from December to August, there is an enormous range of evergreen and deciduous varieties. Without doubt, they are the key to creating fetching features on acid soil.

Yielding thickly or sparsely clustered, bell- or trumpet-shaped blooms, rhododendrons are long-lived and mature within 5–10 years. Plant them to enhance woodland glades, borders, rock gardens, patio pots, and conservatories. Associate them with other lime-hating plants, such as azaleas, Japanese maples, lilies, camellias, conifers, eucryphia, pieris, and embothrium.

TYPES

Hardy hybrids: Valued for their resistance to severe weather and ability to prosper in windy gardens, hardy hybrids flower from April to June. Most grow 5–8ft high and across.
They are easy to manage and the blooms, in white and shades of red, pink, lavender, purple, and yellow, are borne in large, showy trusses amid broad, pointed leaves.

Red hues: Outstanding are: ruby red "Bagshot Ruby"; bright brick-red "Vulcan"; bright red, black-speckled "Windlesham Scarlet"; dark red "Doncaster", black-veined within; and medium-red "Cynthia".

Pink hues: A trio no garden should be without is: dark green-leaved and rose-pink "Alice"; "Pink Pearl", whose rosy buds open to flesh-pink blooms; and "Furnivall's Daughter", a gem with rose-pink and dark-spotted flowers.

Purple, blue and mauve hues: Stunning among these are: violet-blue "Blue Boy"; semi-double and bluish-mauve "Fastuosum Flore Pleno"; and rosy-purple "Variegatum", whose white-rimmed leaves illuminate shady places.

White hues: White and pale yellow-eyed "Cunningham's White" and lavender-budded and white-flowered "Loder's White" light up mid-spring.

RHODODENDRON AT A GLANCE

Evergreen shrubs mantled with blooms from late winter to midsummer. All need acid soil. Hardiness ratings vary.

Month		RECOMMENDED VARIETIES
JAN	/	
FEB	flower	Hardy hybrids
MAR	flower	"Doncaster" – Red
APR	flower, plant	"Furnivall's Daughter"
MAY	flower, prune	"Pink Pearl"
JUN	flower, prune	"Fastuosum Flore-Pleno"
JULY	plant	"Cunningham's White"
AUG	plant	"Praecox"
SEPT	/	Yakushimanum hybrids
OCT	/	"Astrid" Pink
NOV	/	"Chelsea Seventy"
DEC	/	"Grumpy"

TOP: *Sun-loving, hardy hybrid "Blue Peter".*
ABOVE: *An exquisite-flowered Vireya rhododendron.*

A 19th-century Malaysian variety used for breeding, "Pink Delight" is spectacular for a shaded conservatory or very mild, frost-free garden, but it needs cosseting.

Low-growing varieties: Equally hardy, low-growing varieties make dense bushes 18–48in high.
Heralding spring, "Praecox" opens its rosy-lilac-to-mauve blooms in February and March; "Snow Lady" bears lovely, white flowers from March to April; and "Princess Anne" is smothered with clear yellow blooms from April to May.
Stunning, too, are drought-resisting hybrids of *Rhododendron yakushimanum*. Making dense bushes to 3ft, alluring varieties are: cerise-pink "Astrid"; salmon and carmine-rose "Chelsea Seventy"; and yellowish-white and shell-pink "Grumpy".
The sumptuous and very colorful Malaysian (Vireya) rhododendrons make exciting focal points for a frost-free greenhouse or lightly shaded and very sheltered patio or terrace in summer.

CONDITIONS

Aspect Hardy hybrids and species grow and flower best in a dappled, shady spot shielded from strong wind.

Site Soil must be acid and well-drained, cool and moist throughout the year and fortified with moisture-conserving organic matter. Dig in plenty of well-rotted manure, garden compost, or leaf mould before planting. Set greenhouse varieties in large pots of orchid-bark, mixed with ericaceous compost.

GROWING METHOD

Feeding Nourish plants with an acidifying fertilizer in spring and midsummer and mulch thickly with bulky organic materials to keep roots active and leaves lustrous in long, dry spells.

Use lime-free rain water to moisten dry soil or compost.

Propagation Take softwood cuttings from mid-spring to early summer and semi-ripe cuttings in early fall; layer stems from mid-spring to late summer.

Problems *Bud blast: This fungus turns flower buds brown and is characterized by bristly black outgrowths, is spread by rhododendron leaf hopper. This is also a pest, which lays its eggs in the bud scales. Control bud blast by picking off and burning affected buds and spraying with pirimiphos-methyl to eradicate hoppers.
*Leaf spot disease: Speckling leaves with brownish-purple spots containing raised, black, fungal fruiting bodies, it is best eradicated by spraying with mancozeb when symptoms appear.
If aphids colonize soft shoot tips, control them with pirimicarb, which is selective to this pest and does not harm beneficial insects.
*Lime-induced chlorosis: Caused by a deficiency of iron and manganese in alkaline soils, which inhibits chlorophyll production, leaves develop brown rims and yellow patches between bright green veins. Rectify it by applying a chelated compound based on iron, manganese, and other trace elements.

PRUNING

Snap off spent blooms when petals fall, to channel energy away from seed production and into strong new growth. Take care not to damage new leaves.
Keep mature bushes youthful and packed with blossom in spring by removing one in three of older, black-barked stems when flowers fade. Dwarf and low-growing varieties and species are best left unpruned.

RHODODENDRON
Azalea

Planted to light up a woodland glade, evergreen Kurume azalea "Kirin" treats us to a massed display of small blooms in May.

Leaf-shedding Mollis azaleas yield an unforgettable display of large clusters of vibrantly hued, trumpet blooms before leaves fully unfold.

FEATURES

Enchanting us from April to June, deciduous and evergreen azaleas come in a kaleidoscope of colors and range in height, 2–8ft. They are derived from various species of rhododendron and are among the world's most widely hybridized plants. Long-lived, azaleas mature within 3–5 years and flower from the first year of planting. Grouped in mixed shrub borders, taller varieties make a stunning backcloth for annuals or small perennials. It is best to buy plants in flower so that you can be sure of getting exactly what you want. Azaleas are often planted with acid-soil-loving camellias and purple- and green-leaved Japanese maples, where the foliage tempers the more vibrant-hued varieties.

Deciduous groups: Cherished for their May to June performance of clustered, trumpet blooms in glowing pastel and strident hues and vivid fall leaf tints, there are four deciduous types:

Mollis hybrids: Making stocky bushes to about 6ft high, their large heads of scentless, bright yellow, orange, red, cream, and salmon blooms open before leaves appear. Choice among them are orange-scarlet "Spek's Brilliant" and "Koster's Brilliant Red".

Knaphill and Exbury hybrids: Also unperfumed, their May blooms can be as large as a hardy hybrid rhododendron's. Dramatic varieties are: light yellow "April Showers"; salmon-pink "Coronation Lady"; and deep carmine "Homebush".

Ghent hybrids: Making neat, twiggy bushes clothed in long-tubed, sweet-smelling, honeysuckle-like flowers with showy stamens, blossoms peak in late May and June. Fine forms are soft yellow "Narcissiflorum" and rose-pink "Norma".

Occidentalis hybrids: Flowering from mid- to late May, they reward us with trusses of sumptuous, fragrant, pastel-hued blooms. Pure white and yellow-eyed "Bridesmaid" is a good example.

Evergreen and semi-evergreen groups: There are four widely grown divisions. Largest flowering are the prolific Vuyk and Glendale hybrids, whose blooms can be 3in in diameter. The Kaempferi hybrids, such as violet "Blue Danube", have slightly smaller flowers.
Smallest of all are the very popular and bounteous-performing Kurume hybrids. These have slightly greater tolerance to low temperatures than other evergreen varieties and blooms are single or hose-in-hose—when one flower appears inside another.

CONDITIONS

Aspect Most azaleas prefer semi-shade and shelter from strong winds and hot afternoon sunshine. A new race of "sun-loving" varieties is being

AZALEA AT A GLANCE

A form of deciduous or evergreen rhododendron bearing trumpet blooms, it colors lightly shaded spots. Hardy to 4°F (zone 7).

JAN	/	RECOMMENDED VARIETIES
FEB	/	
MAR	plant, prune	Deciduous
APR	flower, prune	"Bridesmaid"
MAY	flower, prune	"Coronation Lady"
JUN	flower, prune	"Firefly"
JULY	plant	"Gibraltar"
AUG	plant	"Koster's Brilliant Red"
SEPT	plant	Evergreen
OCT	plant	"Addy Wery"
NOV	plant	"Blue Danube"
DEC	/	"Driven Snow"
		"Hinode-giri"

RIGHT: Too tender for planting in the garden, though they benefit from spending June to September in a cool, shaded spot outdoors, Indica azaleas are massed with blossom from December to February.

BELOW: Complementing the hardy varieties' spring display, this glowing, half-hardy Indica azalea is unusual in that it has a clearly defined, white centre.

RIGHT: Deciduous Mollis azaleas come in vivid shades of orange yellow. This beautiful variety, flowering from early to mid-May, associates dramatically with pieris while it is displaying its scarlet, new leaves.

VARIETIES

LEFT: Few azaleas can surpass the brilliance of "Happy Days", a prized but rare Nuccio hybrid, the double flowers of which illuminate spring. Shield young plants from frost.

BELOW: Lighting up May and June, deciduous azaleas—this is a Mollis variety—reward us with clusters of flared-petal blooms and elegant thrusting stamens.

LEFT: This free-flowering Glenn Dale hybrid is one of many varieties bred to improve the frost-hardiness and color range of evergreen azaleas.

A riot of spring blossom in yellow, orange, and other sunny shades makes it worthwhile finding a choice site for a Mollis azalea.

Site

bred for more open situations.
The soil should be acid, well-drained, and humus-rich and fortified with plenty of well-decayed organic matter several weeks before planting. In even slightly alkaline conditions, when the pH hovers just above 7.0, azaleas will suffer from iron deficiency and creamy-green, chlorophyll-deficient leaves will die. Keep plants perky in hot spells by mulching with a thick layer of organic material, such as well-rotted manure, leaf mould, compost, or decayed grass clippings.

GROWING METHOD

Feeding

Nourish plants by applying an acidifying fertilizer in spring and summer and watering it in if the soil is dry.
Water new plants regularly in droughty periods to help them establish quickly. In prolonged dry weather, gently dig a moat around a bush and fill it with water. Refill it several times when the water has soaked away. Finish by replacing the soil.

Propagation

Azaleas are easily increased from soft-tip cuttings taken from mid-spring to early summer; semi-ripe cuttings from mid- to late summer; and layers pegged down from mid-spring to late summer.

Problems

Unfortunately azaleas suffer from a number of pests and diseases.
*Powdery mildew: Causing yellow patches to blemish upper leaf surfaces it can, occasionally, trouble heavily shaded plants in areas of high rainfall. It can also be aggravated by sluggish air flow, so remove crowded plants and set them elsewhere. Pick off and burn badly affected leaves and avoid wetting the foliage. Do not grow *Rhododendron cinnabarinum* or its hybrids, which are prone to this fungus. Control the disease chemically by spraying

with bupirimate with triforine or mancozeb the moment symptoms appear.
*Azalea gall: Blame the fungus *Exobasidium vaccinii*, which causes leaves to become swollen, fleshy, and pinkish red. Later, ripe, white spores powder the surface. In the fall, galls wither and turn brown. Fortunately, the plant does not appear to suffer from its presence. Some varieties are more susceptible than others to azalea gall. Remove and destroy affected leaves. There are no chemical controls.
*Rhododendron lace bug damages azalea and rhododendron leaves in spring, summer, and into the fall in mild seasons. Affected foliage is heavily mottled grayish white. Black or brown, shiny spots, the insect's excreta, are seen on the underside of leaves. When damage first appears, it may be possible to reduce the outbreak by hosing up under the foliage; otherwise, spray with horticultural soap, pyrethrins, pirimiphos-methyl, or permethrin as soon as the symptoms are seen.
*Thrips—brownish black and ⅛in long—suck sap from the leaves. The damage is similar to that of lace bug but the leaves may have a more silvery appearance. Control these pests by spraying with pirimiphos-methyl, malathion, or dimethoate. If the infestation is severe, in dry, warm weather when thrips multiply rapidly, you may need to repeat the dosage every three weeks.
*Two-spotted mite, commonly known as red spider mite, also sucks sap from the underside of leaves. Using a magnifying glass, it is possible to see the mites. Almost colorless, with two black spots on their backs, they are usually carrying clear, round eggs.
An attack is first noticed when leaves turn bronzy, tiny webs can be seen and minute creatures, with the aid of a hand lens, can be seen on the backs of leaves. Mites are more prevalent in hot, dry weather and more inclined to infest plants in sheltered spots, such as under eaves, than in open, airy situations. If the plants are not in flower when red spider mite invades, direct a hose up into the bush every couple of days to help reduce their numbers. Alternatively, spray with bifenthrin or horticultural soap.

PRUNING

Cutting flowers for a vase is usually all the pruning these plants need. But deadhead, too, to channel energy into new growth, by nipping out faded blooms when petals fall. Rejuvenate overgrown deciduous varieties by cutting back branches to within 2ft of the ground in March, before buds burst. Try and keep cuts moist to keep alive invisible buds around the stump edge. An easy way to achieve this, apart from splashing them with water, is to coat them with Christmas tree needle spray, which covers them with a plastic film that seals in moisture. If the bush is very old, prune back half the branches in the first year and the remainder the following year. Wayward stems may be cut back at any time.

RIBES
Flowering currant

Blooming generously from April to May, sun-loving Ribes *"Pulborough Scarlet", a flowering currant, also performs in light shade.*

*Trained against a warm wall and almost evergreen, the fuchsia-flowered currant (*Ribes speciosum*) makes a fascinating feature.*

FEATURES

A deciduous family that heralds spring, the most popular kind—*Ribes sanguineum* "Pulborough Scarlet"—is very hardy. Growing to around 8ft high and 6ft across, its upright shoots are thickly sleeved with pendent clusters of deep red, tubular flowers. "White Icicle", another choice form of *R. sanguineum*, has drooping, creamy-white candelabra blooms, dramatic when embraced with purple-red *Bergenia* "Evening Glow". *Ribes sanguineum* "Brocklebankii", to 4ft, is illuminatingly different, rewarding us with a heartening display of golden leaves and pink flowers. All varieties of *R. sanguineum* can be planted to form a stocky, flowering boundary hedge.
Starry, yellow-flowered *R. odoratum*, to 6ft, has leaves that assume purple tints in fall, and less hardy *R. speciosum*, prized for its scarlet, fuchsia-like flowers on upright spiny shoots and best grown against a warm wall, are also generous performers.

CONDITIONS

Aspect
Ribes is ideal for brightening a lightly shaded spot, but *R.* "Brocklebankii" must be shielded from hot sunlight otherwise its leaves will scorch. All, apart from slightly tender *R. speciosum*, prosper in exposed gardens. Make a statement by espalier training *R. speciosum* against a warm, sunny wall or set it to cascade from a pedestal pot.

Site
Undemanding ribes thrives almost anywhere. Fortify sandy spots, which parch in summer, with bulky, moisture-conserving organics. If you plant this shrub on heavy clay, add gravel to improve drainage. Chalky soils can cause leaves to become chlorotic (yellowish green). Avoid this by adding acidifying ferrilizer to lower the pH level.

GROWING METHOD

Feeding
Provided the soil is reasonably fertile, a single application of bone meal in the fall is all that is necessary. After planting, no matter how damp the ground, water well to settle soil around the roots.

Propagation
Take hardwood cuttings in late fall.

Problems
This genus is prone to coral spot fungus. Causing a rash of coral-pink or orange pustules that kills shoots, it should be controlled by cutting out and burning infected plant tissue. Remove crowded shoots to improve air flow.

PRUNING

Keep ribes youthful, shapely and flowering freely by shortening a third of older shoots to new growth or near ground level when blooms fade. Remove crowding branches and cut back diseased stems to healthy wood in spring.

FLOWERING CURRANT AT A GLANCE

Deciduous bush festooned with clusters of flowers from late March to mid-May. Hardiness rating according to species.

Month	Activity	Recommended Varieties
Jan	/	
Feb	/	*R. odoratum*
Mar	flower, plant	*R. sanguineum* "Brocklebankii"
Apr	flower, plant	
May	flower, plant	*R. sanguineum* "Icicle"
Jun	plant, prune	*R. sanguineum* "Porky Pink"
July	plant	
Aug	plant	*R. sanguineum* "Pulborough Scarlet"
Sept	plant	*R. speciosum*
Oct	/	
Nov	/	
Dec	/	

ROSA
Rose

A sport of the famous "Peace" rose, "Chicago Peace" is a vibrant Large Flowered variety that forms a stocky bush to 4ft high.

For sheltered, frost-free gardens, there are few more wonderful sights than the Cherokee rose (Rosa laevigata) draping a sunny wall.

FEATURES

For over two millennia, roses have played an important role in garden design. However, it was not until the 19th century, from an amalgam of new developments—Hybrid Musk, Hybrid Perpetual, and Large Flowered (Hybrid Tea) roses—that modern varieties evolved. Since the late 1960s, there has been great interest in what are known as "English" roses. Bred by David Austin, they are varieties that combine the many-petalled form, lovely fragrance and full vigor of an old-fashioned rose with the wide color range and repeat-flowering qualities of a modern rose.

Roses are cherished for their form and colorful blooms, and many are very fragrant. They can be evergreen or deciduous, and most varieties have prickles.

The Old Roses—varieties of *Rosa gallica*, beloved by the Greeks and Romans; Damasks, alleged to have been introduced from the Middle East by the Crusaders; Albas, grown by gardeners in the Middle Ages; and Centifolias, first seen in Britain around 1550, which flower just once, in early summer.

Modern roses—Cluster Flowered (Floribunda), Large Flowered (Hybrid Tea) produce successive flushes of bloom. Flowers may be single, semi-double, or fully double, in a wide range of colors: white, cream, yellow, apricot, orange, every shade of pink, and red. There are bicolors, too, but a true blue rose has yet to be borne. Weed-suppressing and ideal for covering banks too steep to mow, the County Series of ground-hugging roses, such as blush-pink "Avon", gold, cerise, pink, and scarlet "Cambridgeshire" and pure white "Kent", color summer with repeat pulses of bloom. Ramblers, including coppery pink and richly scented "Albertine" flower only in midsummer. Climbers particularly modern varieties, such as "Golden Showers", salmon-pink "Compassion"

and honey-champagne "Penny Lane", have Hybrid Tea-like flowers and bloom repeatedly from June to October.

Some species, such as *R. moyesii*, produce brilliant red hips in fall and are planted specially for these, although the flowers are good too!

Uses Roses may be mass-planted in beds and borders or planted singly as sentinels. Large Flowered, Cluster Flowered and some other bush varieties are also grown as round-headed or weeping standards to flank a path or add height to a bed of roses. Thrusting through an obelisk strategically positioned in a shrub border, "Handel", a short, creamy-white and rose-pink climber, makes a riveting focal point.

Climbers and ramblers also associate strikingly with pink, red, blue, and white varieties of *Clematis viticella*, which are pruned to within 12in of the base in spring. Create a sensation by planting violet-blue C. "Etoile Violette" to entwine the climbing rose "Compassion", whose fragrant, double, light salmon-shaded, orange blooms stud strong, healthy shoots all summer.

Miniature and patio roses are ideal for planting in pots or tubs to decorate a patio or terrace. Very hardy varieties of *Rosa rugosa* are often used as hedges. Set a Large Flowered or Cluster Flowered variety *en masse* to illuminate a bed or border, or embrace a single bush with annuals, perennials, or bulbs.

CONDITIONS

Aspect The hardiness of roses is variable. Many tolerate extreme cold while others can be singed by frost.

To form stocky shoots and flower bounteously, roses need full sun all day. Good air circulation is important, too, but some shelter from strong wind is desirable to avoid flower damage.

Site These shrubs prefer heavy but well-drained,

Flowering profusely in early summer and sporadically thereafter, leggy "Felicia", a Hybrid Musk, is ideal for screening eyesores.

humus-rich loam. Improve light, sandy, gravelly, or chalky soils by adding large amounts of well-rotted manure or decomposed garden compost several few weeks before planting. Add garden lime to very acid soil.

GROWING METHOD

Feeding
Encourage lustrous leaves and fine, large blooms by feeding with a proprietary rose fertilizer, containing magnesium, in mid-April and early July.

Propagation
Vigorous Cluster Flowered varieties, most shrub roses and ramblers and climbers are easily increased from hardwood cuttings in September. The only way to multiply Large Flowered varieties is to implant a bud of the variety, in July, on to a rootstock.

Problems
*Aphids, which are sap suckers, may cover new growth quite thickly. Spray with pirimicarb, horticultural soap, permethrin, pirimiphos-methyl, or derris.
*Leaf-rolling sawfly damages roses from late spring to early summer. When females lay eggs on leaves, they inject a chemical into the leaf, which causes it to roll up and protect the eggs. Affected leaflets hang down. When caterpillars emerge, they feed on the leaves. Control with heptenophos with permethrin or pirimiphos-methyl.
*Black spot causes large black blotches to disfigure leaves. Collect and burn fallen leaves and avoid overhead watering. Some roses are less prone to this disease than others.
Resistant Large Flowered varieties: "Alec"s Red", "Alexander", "Blessings", "Champs Elysees", "Chicago Peace", "Honey Favourite".
Resistant Cluster Flowered varieties: "Allgold", "Arthur Bell", "City of Belfast", "City of Leeds", "Manx Queen", "The Queen Elizabeth", "Tip Top".
*Powdery mildew, worse in dry spots and where air circulates sluggishly, distorts leaves, stems, and flower buds and felts them with grayish-white patches.
Control it by opening up crowded areas, watering and liquid feeding every ten days, from spring to late summer, with a high-potash fertilizer to encourage robust growth. Also guard against infection by spraying fortnightly from spring to late summer, with triforine with bupirimate, penconazole, mancozeb, or copper with ammonium hydroxide.
*Rust is another fungus that is worse in areas of high rainfall. In early summer, bright orange spots appear on the upper leaf surface and corresponding, orange spore clusters disfigure the lower surface. In late summer, dark brown winter spore masses replace summer pustules. Badly infected leaves are shed prematurely. Control rust by pruning out and burning affected stems and spraying regularly with myclobutanil, penconazole, bupirimate with triforine or mancozeb.

PRUNING

Tackle pruning in early spring before buds burst. In fall, shorten extra long stems on bush roses to avoid them catching the wind and loosening the stem. Always cut to just above a bud.

After planting:
Large Flowered and Cluster Flowered bush varieties: Shorten stems to within 6in of the base.
Shrub roses: No pruning necessary.
Ramblers: Cut back shoots to 12in from the ground.
Climbers: Shorten withered tips to healthy buds.

When established:
Large Flowered and Cluster Flowered: Shorten main stems by half their length; side shoots to two buds.
Shrub roses: Cut back dead and dying shoots to healthy buds.
Ramblers: Most varieties are pruned in fall; cut out flowered stems and replace with current-year shoots.
Climbers: Shorten flowered side shoots to two or three buds.
Deadhead all roses weekly to channel energy into new shoots and more flowers.

ROSE AT A GLANCE		
Bushes, standards, weepers, carpeters, and climbers flower from spring to fall. Most roses are hardy to 3ºF (zone 7).		
JAN	/	RECOMMENDED VARIETIES
FEB	/	
MAR	plant, prune	Large Flowered
APR	plant, prune	"Alec's Red"
MAY	flower, plant	"Elizabeth Harkness"
JUN	flower, plant	English roses
JULY	flower, plant	"Graham Thomas"
AUG	flower, plant	Cluster Flowered
SEPT	flower, plant	"English Miss"
OCT	flower, plant	Patio roses
NOV	plant	"Sweet Dream"
DEC	/	Climbers
		"Breath of life"

LEFT: A Large Flowered and upright grower to 4ft, richly scented "Double Delight" was introduced from America around 20 years ago. Its popularity has never waned.

RIGHT: Associating roses with other plants is an exciting challenge. Here this sumptuous Cluster Flowered variety is harmonizing with Crambe cordifolia *blossom.*

BELOW: Because they absorb light, it is vital to plant scarlet and other deeply hued roses in a bright, sunny spot. In even, light shade, blooms tend to disappear on dull days.

RIGHT: Vigorous and healthy bush to 3ft, "Sunblest" is a profuse Large Flowered variety, the strong stems of which are topped with tightly formed buds that open to reveal unfading, bright yellow blooms.

VARIETIES

LEFT: Though lacking the impact of semi- and fully double Large Flowered roses, single-flowered Polyantha varieties have innate charm and flower for months.

ABOVE: "Bernina", a Cluster Flowered rose yet to come to Britain, was developed for and named after the Swiss sewing machine company. It bears a multitude of scented and perfectly formed flowers.

LEFT: Appealing to flower arrangers, Cluster Flowered "Purple Tiger" is an extraordinary variety best grouped with silver-leaved Artemisia "Powis Castle".

RIGHT: Bicolored roses have special appeal. When cutting these and other varieties, plunge them to their necks in a bucket of water for a day, before arranging them.

ROSMARINUS
Rosemary

An aromatic shrub and herb, rosemary embellishes a bed, border or patio tub with spires of blue, pink, or white flowers in mid-spring.

Exploit the beauty of prostrate varieties by planting them to soften a hard corner or spill over a retaining wall.

FEATURES

Grown for its aromatic, evergreen foliage, *Rosmarinus officinalis*—there is only one species—embraces varieties with hooded, blue, pale violet, pink, or white flowers in April and May. There are upright kinds to 6ft and compact, ground-covering forms to 2ft across. Rosemary also makes a fetching, informal hedge. Plant it to enhance a mixed shrub and perennial border, or in patio pots. If possible, position it where you will brush against it and detect its pleasing aroma. It is long-lived, matures within 3–5 years and flowers early in life. Rosemary, also a culinary herb, symbolizes remembrance, love, and fidelity.

CONDITIONS

Aspect Rosemary, which must have full sun to develop stocky, free-flowering shoots, prospers in exposed inland and coastal gardens.

Site Preferring well-drained, poor, sandy, or gravelly soils, it abhors heavy clay.

GROWING METHOD

Feeding Apart from working bone meal into the planting hole, no further fertilizer is usually necessary to ensure that rosemary flourishes.

Propagation This shrub is easily increased from semi-ripe cuttings taken from mid- to late summer.

Problems It is seldom attacked by pests and diseases, but its roots are liable to rot in soggy clay.

PRUNING

Upright varieties and hedges: Keep plants compact and full of young growth by trimming them fairly hard with shears when flowers fade in late spring.

Carpeters: Prune unwanted shoots in spring.

ROSEMARY AT A GLANCE

A hardy, small-leaved, aromatic, upright, or carpeting evergreen, with usually blue, spring flowers. Hardy to 14°F (zone 8).

JAN	/	
FEB	/	RECOMMENDED VARIETIES
MAR	/	"Aureus"
APR	flower, plant	"Benenden Blue"
MAY	flower, plant	"Corsicus Prostratus"
JUN	prune, plant	"Miss Jessopp's Upright"
JULY	plant	Prostratus Group
AUG	plant	"Tuscan Blue"
SEPT	plant	
OCT	/	
NOV	/	
DEC	/	

SANTOLINA
Cotton lavender

Effectively mantling and silvering this border edge, the dwarf form of cotton lavender, Santolina chamaecyparissus nana, *is a hardy evergreen.*

An arresting succession of lemon-yellow flowers clothe Santolina rosmarinifolia's *feathery, deep green stems from June to August.*

FEATURES

Mound forming, evergreen, and ideal for making a low hedge to divide a lawn from a path or to segregate open-plan gardens, cotton lavender is prized for its aromatic, feathery, silvery-white, or gray foliage. There is also a green-leaved form.

If cotton lavender is left to mature, a wealth of button-like, yellow flowers appear from June to August. Flowers, however, tend to spoil its symmetry and give it a ragged look. If you prefer foliage to blooms, prune bushes hard each year.

It is a tough shrub and unaffected by salty winds, so makes a good seaside plant. It also has few enemies.

Widely planted *Santolina chamecyparissus,* grows to around 18in high and 30in across and is favoured for hedging or punctuating a border. Its dwarf form, *nana,* just 12in high, is fetching for edging a border or highlighting a rock garden.

Even whiter and more feathery is *S. pinnata neopolitana,* to 32in high.

Equally decorative but with thread-like, green leaves, *S. rosmarinifolia* (*virens*) is massed with long-stemmed, yellow flowers in summer.

CONDITIONS

Aspect   Santolina is very hardy and braves low temperatures. Provided you set plants in full sun, where silvery-white-leaved varieties develop full radiance, they will excel for you. The green-leaved species tolerates light shade.

Site   This shrub performs zestfully on sandy loam but abhors heavy clay, which becomes soggy and airless in winter. If you are stuck with heavy clay, drain it by working in grit and channelling a gravel-lined drainage trench to a soakaway.

GROWING METHOD

Feeding   There is little need to be diligent with feeding, for cotton lavender prospers on thin and nutrient-sparse soils. However, lush growth will please you if in spring and fall you work a dressing of bone meal into the root area.

Propagation   Increase your favorites from semi-ripe cuttings taken from early to mid-fall and rooted in a garden frame or multiply plants from hardwood cuttings in late fall.

Problems   Normally trouble free.

PRUNING

Shear off faded blooms in late August. Periodically—every 3 years or so when lower shoots are becoming woody—shorten stems to 6in from the base to stimulate new basal growth.

COTTON LAVENDER AT A GLANCE

Evergreen bush with ferny or thread-like leaves and yellow, "button" flowers from June to August. Hardy to 14°F (zone 8).

Month		RECOMMENDED VARIETIES
JAN	/	
FEB	/	*S. chamaecyparissus*
MAR	/	*S. chamaecyparissus nana*
APR	plant, prune	*S. pinnata neopolitana*
MAY	plant, prune	*S. virens*
JUN	flower, plant	
JULY	flower, plant	
AUG	flower, plant	
SEPT	flower, plant	
OCT	/	
NOV	/	
DEC	/	

SARCOCOCCA
Christmas box

Vanilla scent from the tiny flowers of Sarcococca hookeriana *"Digyna", a suckering evergreen to 6ft, can waft for yards.*

Glossy leaved and smothered with scented, white blooms in winter, undemanding Sarcococca confusa *thrives in light shade.*

FEATURES

An easy, suckering, lance- or oval-leaved evergreen, sarcococca is a delight in February when tufted flowers of white or creamy male petals and smaller female blooms sleeve stems and release rich vanilla fragrance.

On a warm, breezy day, scent is detectable many yards from the bush. If you plant a group of it beneath a living-room window, the perfume will waft indoors. Cut blooms will scent a room.

Carpeting thickly and suppressing weeds, *Sarcococca hookeriana* forms a 12in high thicket, 3ft across. *Digyna*, a form of *S. hookeriana*, has purple-tinged leaves and thrusts to 4ft. Its flowers are followed by black berries. Resembling privet, *S. confusa* is a neater version, to 2.5ft. Appealingly different, *S. ruscifolia* forms a rugged bush of broader leaves, to 3ft high and across, and blooms are followed by red berries.

CONDITIONS

Aspect   Ideal for clothing dappled shady areas beneath trees or borders on the north side of a wall or fence and between houses, it prospers in full sun, too. Avoid deeply shaded sites where growth is less compact and flowering inhibited.

Site   Sarcococca favours deep, humus- and nutrient-rich, acid or alkaline soils that drain freely. Improve poor, sandy patches by working in bulky organic manure. Lighten and aerate heavy clay by digging in some grit or pea shingle.
Plant it in a large tub or pot to perfume a patio or terrace in mild spells during winter. Alternatively, set it to flank a path or driveway where you will brush against it and enjoy its "clean", rich scent.

GROWING METHOD

Feeding   Encourage robust growth by working bone meal into the planting hole and pricking it into the root area in spring and fall. Help young plants establish quickly by watering copiously after planting and in dry spells in their first year.

Propagation   Increase your stock by using a spade to slice off rooted suckers in spring or take semi-ripe cuttings of new shoots in midsummer.

Problems   Small, young plants may take several months to settle down and grow enthusiastically. Encourage them to develop quickly by liquid feeding fortnightly with a high-nitrogen fertilizer in spring and summer.

PRUNING

No regular cutting back is necessary. Remove dead or damaged shoots in spring.

CHRISTMAS BOX AT A GLANCE

White-flowered and sweetly scented, bushy or carpeting ever-green for sunny or lightly shaded places. Hardy to 4°F (zone 7).

		RECOMMENDED VARIETIES
JAN	/	
FEB	flower	*S. confusa*
MAR	plant	*S. hookeriana digyna*
APR	plant, prune	*S. hookeriana humilis*
MAY	plant	*S. ruscifolia*
JUN	/	
JULY	/	
AUG	plant	
SEPT	plant	
OCT	/	
NOV	/	
DEC	/	

SPIRAEA
Spiraea

Transforming mid-spring with a fountain of snowy blossom on arching stems to 6ft, bridal wreath (Spiraea arguta) is magnificent.

Unusually, late summer-flowering Spiraea "Shirobana" yields a mix of mushroom-headed, white and rose-purple flowers.

FEATURES

An easy and floriferous family of deciduous shrubs, 18in–8ft high, spiraea rewards us with cone- or dome-shaped blooms on upright shoots or on pendulous or arching stems. There are two groups: spring flowering and summer flowering.

The finest early performers, from March to May, are epitomized by the aptly named bridal wreath (*Spiraea arguta*). Its arching stems, to 6ft, are so thickly enveloped with snowy blossom that its leaves are concealed.

Most popular summer-flowering members are forms of *S. japonica*: "Anthony Waterer", aglow with domes of carmine-pink flowers amid pink or cream-tinged leaves; and "Goldflame", prized for its dark pink flowers and radiant golden-orange leaves in spring. Another kind, *S. billiardii* "Triumphans", is ablaze with rose-purple flower cones in July and August. Plant spiraea to punctuate a border, carpet a rock garden pocket, adorn a patio tub, or screen out an ugly view.

CONDITIONS

Aspect   Very hardy, these shrubs prefer full sun in which stocky shoots flower well and colored-leaved varieties develop vivid hues.

Site   They also thrive in a wide range of well-drained soils but dislike dry or very alkaline conditions. Improve sandy patches by digging in plenty of rotted organic matter.

GROWING METHOD

Feeding   Encourage robust growth by gently working bone meal into the root area in spring and fall. Help new plants recover quickly from transplanting by watering liberally and mulching in dry spells in spring and summer.

Propagation   Take soft-tip cuttings in early summer; semi-ripe cuttings from mid- to late summer; or hardwood cuttings in fall. Some varieties can be divided or increased from suckers in early spring.

Problems   Control sap-sucking aphids, which colonize soft shoot tips, by spraying with pirimicarb, derris, or horticultural soap.

PRUNING

Spring- and summer-flowering kinds that flower on older shoots: Cut out from the base one older stem in three when blooms fade. Summer-flowering varieties that bloom on the current-year shoots: Shorten all stems to 4in from the base from early to mid-spring. Rejuvenate tall, old, woody varieties making little new growth by cutting all shoots to within 12in of the base in early spring.

SPIRAEA AT A GLANCE

Spring- or summer-flowering shrubs with white, pink, or purple-rose blooms. Some have orange foliage. Hardy to -13°F (zone 8).

Month	Activity	RECOMMENDED VARIETIES
JAN	/	
FEB	/	Spring flowering
MAR	plant, flower	*S. arguta*
APR	plant, flower	*S. thunbergii*
MAY	flower, prune	"Snowmound"
JUN	flower, prune	Summer flowering
JULY	flower, prune	"Anthony Waterer"
AUG	flower, prune	*S. × billiardii*
SEPT	flower, prune	"Gold Mound"
OCT	plant	"Little Princess"
NOV	plant	"Triumphans"
DEC	/	

SYRINGA
Lilac

Fragrant trusses of lilac blossom are a spring highlight. Syringa vulgaris *varieties bloom best in an open, sunny position.*

Cottage-garden pleasure: this white "Mme Lemoine" lilac has been skillfully pruned to form a globe of blossom in mid-May.

FEATURES

A vast and fragrant, deciduous family from S.E. Europe to E. Asia, its cone or plume-like flowers light up May and June. Most popular are varieties of *Syringa vulgaris*. Enchanting, double-flowered forms are mauve-pink "Belle de Nancy", dark purple "Charles Joly", and violet-red "Paul Hariot". Captivating singles include white "Maud Notcutt" and creamy-yellow "Primrose". All make upright focal points to 8–10ft.

The Canadian Hybrids—rose-hued "Bellicent" and pale lilac "Elinor"—tolerate shade better than *S. vulgaris* and bear plumy blossom. Accommodating dwarf varieties, to 4ft, for small gardens or rockeries, are lilac-pink *S. meyeri* "Palibin" and *S. pubescens* "Superba".

LILAC AT A GLANCE

Perfumed, cone- or plume-shaped blooms in many shades appear in spring. Hardiness rating according to species.

		RECOMMENDED VARIETIES
JAN	/	
FEB	/	*S. pubescens* "Miss Kim"
MAR	plant	*S. pubescens* "Superba"
APR	plant	*S. vulgaris* "Belle de Nancy"
MAY	flower, plant	*S. vulgaris* "Charles Joly"
JUN	flower, plant	
JULY	plant	*S. vulgaris* "Mme Lemoine"
AUG	plant	*S. vulgaris* "Mrs Edward Harding"
SEPT	plant	
OCT	plant	*S. vulgaris* "Primrose"
NOV	plant, prune	*S. × prestoniae* "Elinor"
DEC	prune	

CONDITIONS

Aspect Lilac flowers best in full sun but tolerates light shade. Choose an open site, protected from strong, drying winds, where air circulates freely, to reduce risk of leaves becoming mildewed.

Site These shrubs need well-drained, organically rich soil. Avoid chalky spots, which may cause lime-induced chlorosis, when leaves turn creamy yellow and die.

GROWING METHOD

Feeding Apply a complete plant food, such as Growmore or fish, blood, and bone meal in spring and midsummer.

Propagation Commercially, varieties are usually budded or grafted on to privet rootstock. Alternatively, take soft-tip cuttings in early summer or semi-ripe cuttings from mid- to late summer.

Problems Lilac blight, characterized by angular, brown spots, destroys leaves and buds. There are no chemical controls, so cut back affected shoots to healthy, white tissue and burn prunings. When mildew strikes, leaves are felted with powdery-white mold. Improve air flow by thinning crowded shoots and spraying with carbendazim, mancozeb, or sulfur when symptoms appear.

PRUNING

Cut out spent flowers when petals fade. Keep bushes youthful and blooming freely by pruning out a quarter of the older shoots each year in winter. Remove basal suckers.

VIBURNUM
Viburnum

Horizontally-tiered Viburnum plicatum *"Mariesii" displays its large, lacy, sterile blossoms embracing small, fertile flowers in spring.*

A spring star is Viburnum x burkwoodii, *whose multitude of orb-shaped, pinkish-white blooms spill rich vanilla scent into the air.*

FEATURES

Coveted for their blossom, berries, foliage and architectural habit, deciduous and evergreen viburnums have year-round appeal. Flowers—clusters, globes, and sprays—in pink or white, thickly clothe shoots. Most varieties are sweetly perfumed. Growing 30in–10ft or more, most species and varieties bloom within three years of planting. All make fetching statements: such as evergreen *Viburnum tinu*s, which also makes a dense, winter-flowering hedge; carpeting *V. davidii*, whose female plants are studded with turquoise-blue berries; *V carlesii*, studded with vanilla-scented, whitish-pink orbs in spring; and *V. x bodnantense* "Dawn", clustered with rose-pink flowers from October to March.

VIBURNUM AT A GLANCE

Light up winter to summer with showy flowers and fall with spectacular, scarlet berries. Hardiness according to species.

JAN	flower	RECOMMENDED VARIETIES
FEB	flower	
MAR	plant, flower	Winter flowering
APR	flower, prune	"Dawn"
MAY	flower, plant	"Deben"
JUN	flower, plant	*V. x bodnantense*
JULY	plant, prune	Spring flowering
AUG	plant	*V. carlesii* "Aurora"
SEPT	plant	*V. x carlcephalum*
OCT	plant	*V. x opulus* "Roseum"
NOV	plant	Fall berrying
DEC	/	*V. betulifolium*
		V. davidii

CONDITIONS

Aspect   Viburnums need at least half a day's full sunshine to prosper. Shield large-flowering varieties from cold wind.

Site   These shrubs prefer well-drained soil enriched with well-rotted organic matter several weeks before planting.
In light soils that parch quickly, mulch in spring with moisture-conserving, bulky organics to keep roots cool and active.

GROWING METHOD

Feeding   Nourish growth by applying a balanced fertilizer, such as Growmore, chicken pellets, or fish, blood, and bone meal, in spring and midsummer. In a cold spring, boost growth of young plants by foliar feeding fortnightly with a high-potash fertilizer.
Water frequently newly planted viburnums in warm, dry weather.

Propagation   Take soft-tip cuttings in spring; semi-ripe cuttings from mid- to late summer; and hardwood cuttings in late fall. Layer shoots from mid-spring to late summer.

Problems   Tackle viburnum beetle, which shreds leaves in summer, by spraying in late spring with permethrin, bifenthrin, or pyrethrum.

PRUNING

V. tinus: Trim shoots lightly in early spring. Deciduous, winter-flowering species: Remove one stem in three every 2–3 years in spring. Evergreens: Cut out one stem in three, in midsummer, every four years.

WEIGELA
Weigela

Weigela florida *"Variegata" brightens late spring with a generous confection of pinkish blossom on year-old shoots.*

Compact and low growing, so ideal for small gardens, Weigela 'Rumba's shoots are thickly sleeved with radiant blooms.

FEATURES

Flowering unstintingly from May to June, weigela is a reliable, hardy, deciduous shrub. Growing 4–6ft high and across, there are two main divisions: varieties of *Weigela florida* and a range of hybrids.

Two of the showiest forms of *W. florida* are dark purple-leaved and rose-pink-flowered "Foliis Purpureis" and widely grown "Variegata", whose green-and-yellow foliage complements pale pink blooms.

Appealing hybrids include "Briant Rubidor", where golden-yellow to green leaves combine pleasingly with a wealth of vibrant, ruby-red flowers. Very different is *W.* "Looymansii Aurea", which must be grown in light shade or its leaves, bright gold in spring, will scorch.

CONDITIONS

Aspect   Most varieties flower best if planted in full sun. Shield them from strong wind, too, which can damage flowers and "burn" soft, new leaves.

Site   Encourage vigorous growth by setting plants in well-drained soil, including chalk, enriched with plenty of well-decayed manure.

GROWING METHOD

Feeding   Boost sturdy shoots sleeved with blossom by topdressing the root area with bone meal in spring and fall and mulching in spring.

Propagation   Take soft-tip cuttings in early summer; semi-ripe cuttings from mid- to late summer; and hardwood cuttings in the fall.

Problems   Pale green capsid bugs, about $\frac{1}{4}$in long, suck sap from shoot tips and secrete a toxin that kills cells. When leaves unfold, damaged areas become ragged holes. Control by spraying with pirimiphos-methyl or fenitrothion when symptoms seen.

PRUNING

Keep bushes young and packed with blossom by removing from the base one in three of the oldest flowering stems when blooms turn fade.

WEIGELA AT A GLANCE

Bushy shrubs bearing trumpet-shaped, white, pink, red, or purple-red blooms from May to June. Hardy to -13ºF (zone 5).

JAN	/	RECOMMENDED VARIETIES
FEB	/	
MAR	plant	"Abel Carriere"
APR	plant	"Briant Rubidor"
MAY	flower, plant	"Carnival"
JUN	flower, plant	"Foliis Purpureis"
JULY	prune, plant	*W. middendorffiana*
AUG	plant	"Newport Red"
SEPT	plant	"Rumba"
OCT	plant	"Variegata"
NOV	plant	
DEC	/	

WISTERIA
Wisteria

Trained to cover a warm, sunny wall, Chinese wisteria (Wisteria sinensis) yields fragrant, lilac-blue to white flowers in May and June.

Festooned with chunky blooms in late spring, Wisteria brachybotrys is also called silky wisteria because of its softly hairy leaves.

FEATURES

Wisteria takes the accolade for cloaking beautifully in May and June a wall, fence, pergola, arch, or tree. Taking 3–4 years to establish and flowering freely, its long chains of pea-like blooms cascade from woody spurs. Blossoms on some varieties are followed by attractive, runner bean-like seed pods.

Buy only grafted plants—look for a bulge where scion and stock unite—because seedlings can take many years to flower and often they do not do so at all.

If space is limited, this handsome, twining, deciduous climber can be planted in a large patio tub and trained as a standard, to around 8ft high.

Choice kinds are sweetly scented Chinese wisteria (*Wisteria sinensis*), which displays lilac-blue to white flowers. Its varieties—white "Alba" and deep violet-blue "Caroline"—are spectacular. The silky wisteria (*W. brachybotrys*) has softly hairy, pinnate leaves, which complement shortish, yellow-blotched, violet to white blooms. The stunning Japanese wisteria (*W. floribunda* "Alba") treats us to clusters of white blossom, which extend impressively to 2ft long.

CONDITIONS

Aspect A sheltered, sunny, or very lightly shaded, south- or west-facing position is essential for flowering. For unless new shoots are exposed daily to many hours of sunlight or to bright incidental light, they may not ripen sufficiently for flowers to form.

Site Virtually any well-drained soil—the more fertile the better—suits this rampant climber. Chalky, alkaline soil may inhibit the uptake of iron vital for chlorophyll formation and cause leaves to become weak and creamy green.

GROWING METHOD

Feeding A spring and fall application of bone meal encourages robust growth. Mulch with bulky organic materials to conserve moisture. If, despite regular pruning, flowers fail to form, topdress the root area with 1oz per sq yd of shoot-ripening sulfate of potash in February.

Propagation Layer shoots from mid-spring to late summer or root soft-tip cuttings in a mist propagation unit in midsummer.

Problems Reluctance to flower can be due to planting a seedling, insufficient light or not pruning.

PRUNING

In July, shorten to five compound leaves new shoots springing from the main branches. In November, reduce shortened shoots to two buds to encourage flowering spurs to form.

WISTERIA AT A GLANCE

Spring-flowering climber laden with chains of pea flowers, for warm, sunny walls, fences, and trees. Hardy to 4°F (zone 7).

		RECOMMENDED VARIETIES
JAN	/	
FEB	/	*W. brachybotrys*
MAR	plant	*W. floribunda* "Alba"
APR	plant	*W. sinensis*
MAY	plant, flower	*W. sinensis* "Alba"
JUN	plant, flower	*W. sinensis* "Caroline"
JULY	prune	
AUG	plant	
SEPT	plant	
OCT	/	
NOV	prune	
DEC	/	

GROWING FOLIAGE PLANTS

Foliage plants have a lot to offer in both form and color. These plants include the ornamental grasses which add a soft, natural look to the garden and supply movement as they sway and bend with the breeze. In complete contrast, some foliage plants are grown for their striking, architectural shapes and sword-like leaves. As features in the garden, foliage plants always stand out.

Foliage plants can be used to complement a variety of planting styles, perhaps enhancing or contrasting a textural theme. The great advantage of using foliage plants and grasses is that these plants do not always rely on the seasons to produce their best. Mostly, foliage plants and grasses are attractive all year round, adding shape to the winter garden.

KEY TO AT A GLANCE TABLES

PLANTING

FLOWERING

At a glance charts are your quick guide.
For full information, consult the accompanying text.

LEFT: Variegated liriope makes a pretty edging plant. These plants multiply and the clump will thicken up over a couple of seasons.

THE FOUNTAIN-LIKE GRASSY SEDGE, Carex buchananii, *from New Zealand makes an excellent shapely contrast to nearby perennials. The copper colored foliage is also a good foil for green-leaved plants. This sedge is also grown on pond margins, making good reflections in the water.*

FOLIAGE PLANTS IN GARDEN DESIGN

A garden of plants grown mainly for their shape, texture, and foliage color can be just as interesting as a garden filled with flowers. Many foliage plants are grown as accents or features. They have sculptural or architectural qualities that add a special dimension to the garden—big, striking plants such as the *Paulownia tomentosa* are good examples.

An all-green garden can be an inviting, restful haven; consider the range of tones of green that are available as well as the foliage types that can be found. Contrast ferns with large-leaved *Fatsia japonica*, or plant the splayed leaves of the Chusan palm through the vertical growth of *Phormium tenax*. In fact, tall-growing species of *Phormium tenax* make excellent screens or windbreaks and are perfect as a backdrop for smaller shrubs or perennials. The many colored forms of flax now available can make a garden feature by themselves. These and many other foliage plants also make excellent container plants.

ORNAMENTAL GRASSES

The grass family contains a huge number and range of plants, from those used as lawn grasses through to small tufty ornamentals such as blue fescue and, at the other extreme, the towering giant bamboos. The impetus for including ornamental grasses in home gardens and larger landscapes came from Germany and the United States, and even though the last 20 years has seen an enormous increase in the use of grasses in

the garden, many people still feel uncertain about them. General nurseries do not often carry more than eight types, but more and more specialist nurseries are stocking an increasing range of interesting possibilities. Grasses have a lot to offer, both in form and color, adding a soft natural look. They can be used as features, fillers, groundcovers, edging plants, and screens. And by not cutting them back at the end of the fall, they contribute additional forms to the winter garden, especially when covered in frost.

Designers tend to use grasses in one of two ways. Either they make punctuation marks in the border, or a kind of division, where once box topiary might have been used. Big clumpy plants like *Stipa gigantea* are an obvious choice. And such repeat planting down a border helps draw the eye on to the end. Or they are being increasingly used in continuous, loose flowing sequences, much as they grow in the wild, emphasizing a natural, unfussy look. A block of *Molinia caerulea arundinacea* looks sensational when it turns amber in the fall.

Grasses add upright, simple shapes to the landscape, and as they bend with every breeze they also add movement. The many colors of grasses go beyond the numerous shades of green to include blue or blue-green, red, russet, purple, yellow, and silver, and the big range of variegated forms with cream or yellow stripes and margins. The plumes of the flowering spikes of grasses stand high above the clumps, adding another decorative feature.

Many of the ornamental grasses are herbaceous, dying back in winter, ensuring that each season's new growth is fresh and lovely. Most are very easy to maintain as they require only to be slashed back to the ground in winter or early spring to allow the new growth to be seen at its best.

GROWING NEEDS

Apart from sedges, the vast majority of grasses and plants used for their foliage prefer to be grown in a moderately rich soil that is also well drained. Plants grown in containers will need a good-quality potting mix that is also fast draining. Many of these foliage plants and grasses are long lived, so attention to soil preparation before planting will pay dividends in the future. Whatever type of soil you have, it will be greatly improved by digging in large quantities of decayed manure or compost a couple of weeks before planting. If you are planting in winter, do this at least a month ahead.

It is impossible to give general directions about such a diverse range of plants but with most members of this group, you should water the plants immediately after planting and continue to water regularly until you can see that they are putting on new growth. Many plants tolerate long, dry periods well, while others will always need water through dry summer months. Some may benefit from the use of fertilizer through their first growing season, and potted plants will in the main need feeding throughout their lives. Other plants dislike any supplementary feeding at all.

Maintenance

Most ornamental grasses and foliage plants will need little continuous maintenance, but it is important to keep plants looking their best as you are relying on their form and foliage for effect. Spend a little time grooming your plants to make them look as good as possible. Pulling off or pruning out dead foliage makes a big difference, as does the removal of flowering stems that are past their peak. In hot summers, the flowering spikes of grasses can start to look very tatty by the fall, but more usually they keep their form longer and can be left for "frosting", which gives a marvellous effect. Some grasses can be cut back easily with pruning shears, but if you have tough plants or a lot of them you may need to use a strimmer.

PROPAGATION

A great many of the plants covered in the this book are propagated by division of existing clumps. Colored or variegated forms of the species must be grown by separation of divisions, as the seed may be sterile and most likely will not grow true to type. Some plants can only be grown from seed, while others will not set seed at all unless they happen to be cultivated in their native habitat. If you want a labor-saving garden with just the occasional tidy up, pulling dead leaves out of clumps of leaves, and a spring cut back in order to let new growth shoot up and emerge, then a grass-based garden is just what you need. Colorful, shapely, stylish, vigorous, and whispy, it can be amazingly beautiful and varied.

WHAT CAN GO WRONG?

Grasses are remarkably free of pest and disease problems. Some of the foliage plants described in the following pages may have a few specific problems, but generally, these are a trouble-free group of plants. Any specific problems will be covered in individual entries.

THE DECORATIVE COLUMNS of small, shiny seed capsules on mat rush are punctuated with small spines.

THE SHAPELY SILVER FOLIAGE of cardoon makes a good foil for more sombre greens in the garden.

CANNA
Indian shot plant

THE BEST WAY TO ADD *starting height, shape, and color to the summer garden is by planting out a group of tropical Cannas. The best have flamboyant, paddle-shaped leaves, and gorgeous colored flowers that are just like a Sladidi's. The more you can plant the better.*

FEATURES

Sun

Cannas give an excellent exotic twist to the garden. They are half-hardy, rhizomatous perennials which need cutting down in the fall before the frosts, and storing over winter. They have large, colorful leaves up to 6ft high and relatively small flowers which range from quiet pink to shrieking red and orange. *Canna* "Striata" has eye-catching orange flowers and green and yellow striped leaves. "Black Knight" has rich purple foliage with crimson flowers, and others like "Endeavour" have fresh green foliage. Breeders are currently trying to produce a white flowering canna. The plants are best used as the focal point in a bedding scheme in gardens featuring other large-leaved or colorful plants like bananas, coleus, and dahlias.

CANNA AT A GLANCE

Dramatic, eye-catching bedding plants with big leaves topped by small, often startling bright flowers. Hardy to 32°F (zone 10).

		RECOMMENDED VARIETIES
JAN	/	*Canna* "Black Knight"
FEB	/	"Durban"
MAR	sow	"En Avant"
APR	dividing	*C. iridiflora*
MAY	transplant	"Lucifer"
JUN	/	"Praetoria"
JULY	flowering	"Striata"
AUG	flowering	"Wyoming"
SEPT	flowering	
OCT	/	
NOV	/	
DEC	/	

CONDITIONS

Aspect   Cannas prefer a sunny position, well away from the shade. It is important to avoid a windy site, however, or the leaves will get badly flayed.

Site   The plants are quite hungry and the soil needs to be fairly rich. During hot dry spells you will need to water well to counter any moisture loss from the large leaves.

GROWING METHOD

Propagation   The best way to increase stock is by dividing the rhizomes in the spring, making sure each section has the "eye" of a new shoot. These can be planted up, with gentle watering at first, and gradually hardened off before they are planted out.

Feeding   Add well-rotted compost before planting, or an all-purpose fertilizer in the spring and again in the summer.

Problems   The two potential summer pests are caterpillars and slugs. Keep an eye out for both. When grown under glass, cannas can suffer badly from red spider mite. The tell-tale sign is a speckling on the leaves, and in bad cases mini spiders' webs.

FLOWERING

Season   The gladiolus-like flowers appear from mid-summer until the early fall. Cultivars like "En Avant" have yellow flowers spotted with orange. The quieter tones of species varieties are also very beautiful. *Canna iridiflora*, for example, is a subtle lipstick pink.

CLEMATIS ARMANDII
Clematis

A CREAMY WHITE mass of flowers in mid-spring on Clematis armandii shows up well against its evergreen foliage.

FEATURES

Sun

Partial Shade

A highly distinctive and eye-catching evergreen clematis introduced in 1900 by the plant hunter Ernest Wilson from China. It has dark green, glossy leaves 5in long and 2in wide and can grow about 15ft high. It clambers up and over frames or shrubs using tendrils which tightly wrap around any available structure or stem. Do not attempt to constrain it. In late winter in sheltered areas clusters of flower buds begin to swell, and on opening in the spring they release a sweet scent. "Apple Blossom" has leaves with a marked bronze tint. There is another form called "Snowdrift" which is said to be a slight improvement on the species. The flowers are shaped like five-pointed stars.

CLEMATIS AT A GLANCE

C. armandii is famed for its shapely evergreen leaves, and scented spring flowers. Hardy to 23°C (zone 9).

		RECOMMENDED VARIETIES
JAN	/	
FEB	/	*Clematis alpina*
MAR	/	*C. cirrhosa* var. *balearica*
APR	flowering	"Doctor Ruppel"
MAY	mulch	"Etoile Violette"
JUN	tie in	*C. flammula*
JULY	tie in	"Jackmanii"
AUG	/	*C. montana*
SEPT	/	*C. tangutica*
OCT	/	
NOV	/	
DEC	/	

CONDITIONS

Aspect The key to success is a warm, sheltered position. Do not grow it where it is exposed to raw, cold winds because they will flay and ruin the leaves, its chief attraction.

Site Like all clematis it likes its roots in the shade and its head in the sun.

GROWING METHOD

Propagation This is notoriously hard which explains why the plant costs about twice as much as any other clematis. Though cuttings root easily they do not always shoot. The result is a pot full of roots with very little above. Grafting onto a stock plant is very successful but is best left to professional nurserymen.

Feeding Provide a rich soil that has had plenty of well-rotted compost dug into it before planting. Keep the compost away from the climber's roots. In following years a general purpose spring feed is fine. Water well in hot dry summers.

Problems Once this clematis takes off there is no stopping it. Try to make sure that you train it up towards the light, spreading it well out, stopping new growth from disappearing into nearby hedges.

FLOWERING

Season Mature plants in early spring are liberally covered in a mass of white flowers releasing a pervasive, soft perfume. Sheltered spots which are not struck by fierce spring frosts give the best results.

FARFUGIUM JAPONICUM
Leopard Plant

THE GOLD-SPLASHED LEAVES of Farfugium japonicum *light up the garden even when grown under trees.*

FARFUGIUM GROWS behind a standard azalea. It is teamed here with winter rose and groundcovering campanula.

FEATURES

Partial Shade

Although there are several variegated cultivars of this plant, the most widely planted and the one sometimes known as leopard plant is *Farfugium japonicum* "Aureomaculatum". This is an excellent plant to use as a tall groundcover or as a feature to light up shady corners of the garden. A single specimen has little effect; it is most striking when several plants are grouped together. It also lends itself well to container growing. Growing 16–24in high, the large kidney-shaped leaves are a rich, glossy green, heavily spotted or splashed gold. In good conditions, leaves can be up to 10in across, but they are more often about 6in. Growing from an underground rhizome, the leaves are held high on soft, thick stems that are covered in powdery bloom.

FARFUGIUM AT A GLANCE

F. japonicum is a rarely grown, terrific Japanese foliage plant with strongly variegated forms. Hardy to 23°F (zone 9).

		COMPANION PLANTS
JAN	/	Crocosmia
FEB	/	Geranium
MAR	sow 🖐	Grasses
APR	divide 🖐	Hedera
MAY	transplant 🖐	Iris
JUN	/	Narcissus
JULY	/	Penstemon
AUG	/	Pulmonaria
SEPT	divide 🖐	
OCT	flowering ❀	
NOV	flowering ❀	
DEC	/	

CONDITIONS

Aspect Grows best in dappled sunlight or light shade. It requires some shelter from strong wind.

Site The soil should be well drained and heavily enriched with manure or compost. Mulch plants well with organic matter.

GROWING METHOD

Propagation The best way to increase your stock of plants is to divide them in the fall, when the soil is still warm and new plants can start to grow, or in the spring. Set the new young plants out at gaps of 10in. You can also propagate by seed, sowing in a cold frame in the fall or in mid spring.

Feeding Apply pelleted poultry manure or complete plant food in spring. Provided the soil was well enriched with rotted manure before planting though, it is unlikely that the ground will need too many extra nutrients.

Problems Snails find the foliage of this plant very attractive, so take precautions. No other problems are commonly found.

FLOWERING

Season The yellow, daisy-like flowers that appear above the large leaves seem "out of place" and do not enhance the decorative effect of this foliage plant. This is certainly true of the excellent "Argenteum" and "Aureomaculatum" with their large, kidney-shaped variegated leaves. You can cut off the flowers as they appear, but it is a personal choice. The flowers appear from summer onwards, depending on climate.

FATSIA JAPONICA
Japanese aralia

IF YOU NEED A TALL SHRUB with big evergreen leaves for a slightly shady corner, try Fatsia Japonica. *It always catches the eye, and flowers in the fall. To thrive, all it needs is protection from fierce winds.*

FEATURES

Sun

Partial Shade

An essential ingredient for the exotic garden, Japanese aralia, as it is sometimes called, is an extremely well known, underrated evergreen shrub. It produces hand-like leaves divided into fingers, 1ft long, and grows about 10ft high. The display is enhanced in the fall when creamy white flowers open. If the plant becomes too tangled and big, it is easily cut down to about 1½ft, and quickly regrows. If growing it as an architectural plant, you can prune it cutting away unwanted branches to give a particular shape. It is a particularly useful plant because it tolerates city pollution, and shady corners. There are three forms, "Aurea", "Marginata", and "Variegata" which are variegated, but note they are all half-hardy. "Moseri" is slightly smaller with larger leaves.

FATSIA AT A GLANCE

F. japonica is a big-leaved evergreen with fall flowers which is ideal for slightly shady corners. Hardy to 23°F (zone 9).

		COMPANION PLANTS
JAN	/	Ceanothus
FEB	/	Euphorbia
MAR	sow 👈	Ficus
APR	/	Hedera
MAY	transplant 👈	*Paulownia tomentosa*
JUN	/	*Pseudopanax crassifolius*
JULY	/	Rosmarinus
AUG	/	Vitis
SEPT	flowering ✿	
OCT	flowering ✿	
NOV	/	
DEC	/	

CONDITIONS

Aspect It likes both full sun and light shade, but the variegated kind needs a much higher proportion of shade than sun. Protection against cold, ripping winds is essential. This is particularly important for varieties with variegated foliage.

Site It will thrive in any typical garden which avoids extreme soil conditions. Water well in hot dry summers to counter evaporation from the leaves. Give the soil a mulch of well-rotted manure in the spring. This will help it to retain moisture during dry periods later on in the year.

GROWING METHOD

Propagation Cuttings of new growth in the first part of summer yield the best results. They should quickly root. Alternatively, sow seed in the spring or fall.

Feeding A light summer feed is all that this plant requires. If it is fed too abundantly, fatsia becomes congested with elongated, soft new growth and leaves.

Problems Pests and diseases pose few problems, otherwise the main setbacks only occur when the plant is flayed by cold winds which ruin the leaves and cause die-back. Growing it against a wall is the best solution.

FLOWERING

Season The flowers only appear in the fall. They are decorative not beautiful, but are perfectly good for cut flower displays.

GROWING HERBS

No garden is complete without a few herbs, which are mainly used to add flavor and delight to food, but which have many other uses too: in cosmetics, craft arrangements, herbal remedies, and as good companions and edging plants in the garden. You can buy them, of course, but you will feel extra pride when using herbs you have grown yourself. And herbs are almost all very easy to grow.

To a botanist a herb is a plant that does not have a permanent woody stem; that is, one that is not a tree or shrub. Its edibility is irrelevant. Gardeners have a different definition. To them, a herb is a plant that can be added to food or used for medicinal purposes, even if the plant in question is actually a shrub, such as rosemary, or even a tree, such as the bay tree. Herbs are (or may be) used fresh, unlike spices, which are almost always dried or prepared in some other way first. (Spices, such as pepper or nutmeg, are the seeds, flowers, bark, or roots of tropical trees or shrubs.)

LEFT: A pink and gray border of pinks, lavender, and thyme harmonizes in this herb garden with old-fashioned roses, although they are not yet in bloom.

THE RICH GREEN COLOR and the soft texture of parsley makes as elegant a garnish for flowers as it does for a dinner plate. In this stunning garden it is used as contrast with miniature blue violas and white sweet alyssum.

USING HERBS

Today we use herbs most often when preparing food. Any cook knows how useful it is to have some herbs on hand. Even a pinch of dried herbs from a supermarket packet can make a great difference to a mediocre dish, but the same herbs fresh from the garden can add the savor and scent that makes the dish something special. Restraint, however, should be the order of the day. The recipe will be your guide, but remember that dried herbs are often sharper in flavour than fresh ones and fresh herbs vary in strength with the season. Add a little at a time, tasting as you go: you don't want to taste the herb before you taste the food. Go easy, too, in planning the menu. One herbed item on the plate is usually sufficient.

Herbs are used extensively in flower arrangements and crafts, where they add fragrance and different textures. Herbal pot-pourris and wall hangings are especially effective and herbs can be used in home-made cosmetics for those who want an alternative to commercial preparations.

Herbs are also credited with all sorts of medicinal qualities. In the past it was an essential part of a doctor's education to learn to distinguish beneficial herbs from useless and harmful ones, and these studies laid the foundation of the modern science of botany. Some of the old prescriptions have been verified by science and many modern drugs are still extracted from plants, although other old remedies were apparently based on nothing more than wishful thinking and superstition. (Sometimes the patient may have been merely suffering from a shortage of vitamins which a salad of green herbs made good.) The folklore attached to herbs is part of their charm, but don't dabble in herbal cures without seeking advice from your doctor or a reputable herbalist first.

HARVESTING HERBS

The traditional way to gather herbs is to pick them just as they are coming into flower (when the flavor is strongest) and use them immediately. This way you use them at their best and most attractive.

Many herbs can also be used after they have been dried. You can spread them out on a table to dry in the shade for a couple of days or, these days, the microwave oven provides a more than acceptable alternative. Gather the herbs, spread them on a paper towel, cover them with another paper towel, and zap them with the full power of the microwave for a minute or two. Check them, and if they aren't quite dry, give them some more time with the top towel off. The precise timing depends on what sort of herb it is and how dry the leaves were to start with.

Alternatively, you can freeze the fresh herbs. Just put them in a freezer bag, pop them in the freezer and take what you want when you need them.

CHOOSING HERBS TO GROW

Whether you plan to plant an extensive collection of herbs or just a few, your first choices will obviously include the ones you like best, those that feature in your favourite recipes or craft activities. (Chances are you'll probably already have them, dried, in your kitchen.) It is probably a good idea to grow several plants of these herbs to avoid harvesting them to death. However, don't let unfamiliarity stop you from trying out a plant or two of a herb with looks or fragrance that appeal to you.

PLANTING HERBS

It is a time-honoured tradition to grow herbs in gardens of their own, and if you have the enthusiasm and the space, a small formal herb garden with its beds divided by paths arranged around a central feature such as a statue or a sundial can be very pretty. Most herbs are low growing, and few are all that distinguished in appearance—indeed, some are rather nondescript. Marshalling them into formal beds flatters them, and you can play their subtle foliage colors and textures off against one another. You might, for instance, contrast the gray leaves of sage with the lush green ones of parsley, or the featheriness of dill with the solidity of rosemary; and the variegated and fancy-leaved versions of such herbs as sage, balm or mint will enrich your palette.

If a formal garden is not for you, don't despair. There will be a place for herbs in any garden, for they really are very adaptable. Try one of the following ideas.
• Plant herbs in your flower beds. Being mostly low growing, they are best planted at the front, where their subtle greens and grays will set off the bright flowers behind.
• Plant them along the edges of your paths, where they will release their scent on the air as you brush past.
• They can look especially good in front of roses—and they will hide the rose bushes' thorny legs—but be careful if you have to spray the roses. You won't want the spray drifting onto the herbs and rendering them dangerous to eat.
• Be strictly utilitarian and plant them to edge the beds in the vegetable garden. Here they will give you something to look at when the beds are bare between crops.
• Most varieties grow very well in pots, which means that even if all the garden you have is an apartment balcony you can still have the pleasure of fresh herbs.
• Give your herbs a windowbox on the kitchen windowsill so that you can just reach out and harvest as you need them—but only if the window gets the sun, and make sure they are outside in the fresh air. Magazines are full of pictures of pots of herbs growing in the kitchen itself, but herbs are not indoor plants. They survive inside for a few weeks, but they get straggly and leggy and you won't get much of a harvest.
• However you choose to grow herbs in your garden, don't plant them too far from the kitchen door. Nothing is more frustrating than to find you need a sprig or two for some dish and have to make an expedition to the bottom of the garden while a pot boils over.

PROPAGATION

Most herbs can be grown from seed, but it can be a slow process and most gardeners start with purchased seedlings or by taking cuttings or dividing plants. The appropriate method for each plant is discussed under its entry.

MAINTENANCE

Growing herbs is easy. As a general rule, they love sunshine and don't need much watering: indeed the flavour is richest if they aren't encouraged to grow too lush. They don't, however, appreciate being starved so give them good, well-drained soil and some fertilizer occasionally. The main exceptions to the rule are basil and chives, which do best with generous feeding and regular watering, and bergamot and the various mints, which are lovers of damp soil. Most herbs have few specific pest or disease problems. You'll find more detail about requirements and problems in the description of each species.

STRIKING A CUTTING

If you are going to strike a herb from a cutting, take the cutting from a strong, healthy plant early in the morning. The cutting should be 2–4in long. If you are not able to plant it at once, stand it in water so that it does not wilt.

Remove the lower leaves and prepare a small pot with a mix of two-thirds coarse sand and one-third potting compost. Make a hole with your finger or a pencil where the cutting is to go, insert the cutting to about one-third of its length and firm the mix around it. Water well and then cover the pot with a plastic bag to create a mini-greenhouse.

Keep the mix damp but not wet. Once roots have formed, the plant can be planted out in the garden.

1. TO TAKE A STEM CUTTING, cut just below a leaf (node or joint). Do not bruise the stem, and trim the end of the cutting with a razor blade if need be. Prepare a pot, filling it with compost then tapping it to settle the compost.

2. INSERT ALL THE CUTTINGS into a pot (or several pots), first making a hole in the compost with your finger for each cutting and then firming the compost gently around the cuttings. Space the cuttings around the edge of the pot.

3. THEN WATER THE CUTTINGS in well but gently, taking care not to dislodge them. Make sure the container has adequate drainage holes so that the excess water will drain away. If the soil remains too wet, the cuttings will rot.

4. MAKE A WIRE OR BAMBOO FRAME that fits around the pot and is tall enough to clear the cuttings. Place a polythene bag over the frame and pot: the bag will keep the air and soil moist. Place the pot in a position that is out of direct sunlight.

ALCHEMILLA
Alchemilla vulgaris

FEATURES

Alchemilla vulgaris (A. *xanthochlora*), the wild lady's mantle, is a hardy perennial native to the mountains of Europe, Asia, and America. It grows to 9–18in and has rounded pale green leaves, with lobed and toothed edges that collect the dew or raindrops. The water thus collected once was reputed to have healing and magical powers. Feathery heads of yellow-green flowers are produced in early summer and can continue into fall. More popular, and very widely grown as a garden plant, is *Alchemilla mollis* which is very similar in both appearance and properties. The alpine lady's mantle, *Alchemilla alpina*, a smaller plant growing to 6in, is also said to have similar, but more effective, properties.

CONDITIONS

Aspect   Lady's mantle will grow in sun or moderate shade.

Site   It is tolerant of most soils except waterlogged conditions.

GROWING METHOD

Sowing and planting   Lady's mantle self-seeds freely and removing and replanting self-sown seedlings is an easy way to get new plants. Seed can be sown in early spring or fall. Germination takes about two or three weeks but can be erratic. Fall-sown seedlings will need to be overwintered under glass. Plant them out in spring 18in apart. Established plants can be propagated by division either in spring or fall.

Feeding   The lady's mantles are tolerant plants, but be careful to avoid overwatering. Mulch alchemillas lightly in the spring and the fall and apply a balanced general fertilizer in spring.

Problems   None.

THE "LADY" to whom the name lady's mantle refers, was the Virgin Mary, to whom the herb was dedicated during medieval times.

Pruning   Cut back flowerheads as they start to fade to prevent self-seeding. Cut back dead foliage in late fall.

HARVESTING

Picking   Young leaves can be picked as required throughout the summer, after the morning dew has dried.

Storage   Leaves can be dried and stored in airtight dark glass jars.

Freezing   Not suitable for freezing.

USES

Culinary   Young leaves can be added to salads in small amounts. They have a mild, but somewhat bitter taste.

Medicinal   In medieval times the lady's mantle was dedicated to the Virgin Mary, and was considered to be particularly a woman's herb, as it was used to treat a wide range of womens' problems, including menstrual problems, menopause, breastfeeding, and inflammations. It was also used as a wound healer for external use, and to make a mouth rinse for use after tooth extraction.

Cosmetic   Lady's mantle can be used to make a soothing and healing rinse that is good for skin complaints.

Gardening   Alchemilla is widely used as an edging plant as well as being grown in flower borders, and the attractive feathery heads of yellow-green flowers are particularly popular with flower arrangers.

ALCHEMILLA AT A GLANCE

A pretty perennial with rounded leaves and feathery flowerheads, it was traditionally a woman's herb. Hardy to 4°F (zone 7).

JAN	/		
FEB	/		*PARTS USED*
MAR	plant 🌱		Leaves
APR	plant 🌱		Flowers
MAY	plant 🌱	harvest 🍃	*USES*
JUN		harvest 🍃	Culinary
JULY		harvest 🍃	Medicinal
AUG		harvest 🍃	Cosmetic
SEPT	plant 🌱	harvest 🍃	Gardening
OCT	/		
NOV	/		
DEC	/		

ANISE HYSSOP
Agastache foeniculum

FEATURES

Anise hyssop, or agastache, is a perennial herb, similar to mint in appearance, but with a somewhat neater, clump-forming habit, and growing to about 2–3ft. The mid-green, nettle-shaped leaves have an aniseed scent. Long spikes of purple flowers, attractive to bees and butterflies, are produced from mid summer onwards. A native of North America, it is not quite as hardy as the better known European members of the mint family. Although perennial, it tends to be short-lived and is best propagated every year, or at least every three years.

CONDITIONS

Aspect Anise hyssop needs full sun (although it may tolerate a little light shade in mild areas) and shelter from cold winds. It may need winter protection if the temperature drops below about 23°F.

Site It grows best in a rich, moisture-retentive soil although it will grow in most garden soils if given a sunny position.

GROWING METHOD

Sowing and planting Anise hyssop can easily be propagated by division in spring and by seed and cuttings. The seeds need warmth to germinate and are best sown under glass in spring. Germination takes 10–20 days. Prick out the seedlings when they are large enough to handle and plant out in mid spring at about 18in apart. Seed can also be sown outdoors in fall when the soil is warm, but the young plants will need winter protection. Cuttings can be taken in mid to late summer, and the rooted cuttings can be overwintered in a greenhouse or cold frame then planted out in spring.

BEES AND BUTTERFLIES are attracted to the tall purple-blue flower spikes of anise hyssop, borne from mid summer onwards.

Feeding Do not allow to dry out. Keep well watered in summer. Mulch lightly in spring and fall and apply a balanced general fertilizer in spring.

Problems Anise hyssop rarely suffers from pests or disease, except that seedlings may damp off and the plants may suffer from mildew in hot summers.

Pruning Cut back old flowerheads and woody growth in fall to keep plants compact and to prevent them becoming straggly.

HARVESTING

Picking Pick the young leaves just before the plant flowers. Cut flowers just as they are beginning to open.

Storage Dry leaves in a cool, airy space and store in dark, airtight, glass jars.

Freezing Put leaves in a freezer bag; freeze for up to 6 months.

USES

Culinary The leaves can be used to make a refreshing aniseed-flavored tea. They can also be used, like borage, in summer fruit cups, and can be added to salads and used as a seasoning, particularly in savory pork and rice dishes. The flowers will add color to salads and fruit cups.

Craft The scented leaves of anise hyssop can be used in pot-pourri.

Gardening Anise hyssop is an excellent bee herb. Attractive white-flowered varieties, "Alabaster" and "Alba", are also available.

AGASTACHE AT A GLANCE

A perennial herb, very similar to mint in appearance, and with a refreshing aniseed flavor. Hardy to 14°F (zones 8-9).

JAN	/		PARTS USED	
FEB	/		Leaves	
MAR	plant		Flowers	
APR	plant			
MAY	plant	harvest	USES	
JUN		harvest	Culinary	
JULY	plant	harvest	Craft	
AUG	plant	harvest	Gardening	
SEPT	plant			
OCT	/			
NOV	/			
DEC	/			

BERGAMOT
Monarda didyma

FEATURES

A member of the mint family with a pungent citrus-like flavour, bergamot can reach 2–3ft in height. The wild bergamot, *Monarda didyma*, also known as bee balm, is a hardy herbaceous perennial, but there are annual, biennial, and perennial varieties with brilliant scarlet red, purple, pink, or white flowers in summer. Bergamot is semi-dormant during winter, sending up squarish stems in spring bearing dark green, ovate leaves with toothed margins. The flowers attract bees.

CONDITIONS

Aspect   Prefers a sunny location; tolerates partial shade.

Site   An excellent border plant for moist soil. Grow in a humus-rich soil containing a lot of organic matter. Mulch well with leaves, straw, or compost to retain moisture and keep down weeds around this shallow-rooting herb.

GROWING METHOD

Sowing and planting   Can be grown from seed, but seeds are very fine and often unreliable—this herb is easily cross-pollinated and plants may not be true to the parent in color or form. Sow seeds in spring in trays of seed compost, covering the tray with glass. Seeds germinate within 2 weeks. Transplant seedlings to the garden when they are 3in high. More reliable is root division in spring: take sections of runners or sucker shoots from the outside of the clump, which will have roots throughout the bed. Discard the center of the clump and pot the other sections. Plant out when they are growing strongly, 32in apart.

Feeding   Water well—like all members of the mint family, bergamot requires water at all times. Add general fertilizer to the backfill when planting. Give another application of fertilizer each spring.

Problems   Powdery mildew and rust can affect bergamot. Cut back and remove diseased parts.

Pruning   In late fall prune the plant back close to ground level. It will regenerate in spring. To increase the strength of the plant, cut flowerheads before they bloom in the first year. After flowering, the plant may be cut back to within 1¼in of the soil surface as this can promote a second flowering in fall.

HARVESTING

Picking   Leaves for making tea are stripped from stems both just before and just after flowering. The colorful flower petals can also be harvested.

Storage   Leaves can be part dried in a shady place for 2 or 3 days and then drying can be completed in a very low oven. Flowers do not store well and so should only be picked as required.

MOST COLORFUL OF HERBS, bergamot is indigenous to the Americas. Native Americans brewed Oswego tea from its leaves.

Freezing   Put sprigs in a freezer bag. They can be frozen for up to 6 months.

USES

Culinary   Fresh leaves can be used in summer fruit drinks or punches, and fresh flower petals are good for decorating salads. Leaves are also used for making tea.

Medicinal   The herb tea can be used to relieve nausea, flatulence, vomiting, colds, etc.

Craft   Dried leaves can be used in pot-pourris. The oil is used in perfumery, to scent candles etc.

Garden   The colorful flowers attract bees and this herb is therefore a good companion for plants that need insect pollination.

BERGAMOT AT A GLANCE

Attractive perennial border plant, with aromatic leaves that can be used to make a refreshing tea. Hardy to 4°F (zone 6).

Month	Activity		Parts used / Uses
JAN	/		**PARTS USED**
FEB	/		Leaves
MAR	plant		Flowers
APR	plant		
MAY	plant	harvest	**USES**
JUN	plant	harvest	Culinary
JULY		harvest	Medicinal
AUG		harvest	Craft
SEPT	plant	harvest	Gardening
OCT	plant		
NOV	/		
DEC	/		

BORAGE
Borago officinalis

FEATURES

A fast-growing annual or biennial growing 2–3ft tall, borage bears star-shaped flowers with protruding black anthers in summer. They are usually bright sky-blue, although they can sometimes be pink or white. The bush bears many sprawling, leafy branches with hollow stems, which can be quite fragile. The stems are covered with stiff white hairs and the grayish-green leaves are also hairy.

CONDITIONS

Aspect Prefers sunny locations but grows in most positions, including partial shade. It needs plenty of space. The brittle stems may need staking to prevent wind damage.

Site Grows well in most soils that are aerated, moist and mulched to keep weeds down.

GROWING METHOD

Sowing and planting Sow seed directly into the garden and thin out the seedlings later, leaving 24in between plants. Seedlings do not transplant well once established. Successive sowings every 3 to 4 weeks will extend the harvesting period. It self-sows readily and its spread may need to be controlled.

Feeding During spells of hot, dry weather borage plants should be kept well watered. Apply a balanced general fertilizer once each spring or use controlled-release granules.

Problems Blackfly can be a problem. Treat with liquid horticultural soap. Mildew may also be a problem late in the year. If so, plants are best dug up and removed.

HARVESTING

Picking Pick the leaves as required while they are fresh and young. *Caution:* handling fresh leaves may cause contact dermatitis. Use gloves. Harvest the open flowers during the summer months.

Storage The leaves must be used fresh; they cannot be dried and stored. The flowers can be crystallized and then stored in airtight jars.

Freezing The leaves cannot be frozen. The flowers may be frozen in ice cubes.

USES

Culinary Borage has a faintly cucumberish taste and leaves can be added to salads, and drinks such as Pimms. Flowers may be frozen in ice cubes for cold drinks, used raw on salads, or to decorate cakes and desserts if crystallized. *Caution:* it may be a danger to health. It is now under study because of the presence of alkaloids.

IN THIS GARDEN blue borage and white garlic grow side by side. In the old days, soldiers ate the flowers of borage to give them courage.

Medicinal Borage tea was used for colds and flu. The leaves and flowers are rich in potassium and calcium. Borage has been found to contain gamma linoleic acid (GLA) and is now being more widely grown as a commercial crop.

Cosmetic The leaves can be used to make a cleansing facial steam.

Craft The flowers can be added to pot-pourri.

Gardening Borage is regarded as an excellent companion plant in the garden, especially when it is planted near strawberries.

BORAGE AT A GLANCE

A tall, fast-growing annual with bristly leaves and small bright blue star-shaped flowers. Hardy to 4°F (zone 6).

Jan	/		
Feb	/	**Parts used**	
Mar	plant	Flowers	
Apr	plant	Leaves	
May	plant	harvest	
Jun	plant	harvest	
July		harvest	**Uses**
Aug		harvest	Culinary
Sept		harvest	Medicinal
Oct	/		Cosmetic
Nov	/		Craft
Dec	/		Gardening

Cats Meow

CATMINT
Nepeta cataria

FEATURES

Nepeta cataria, catmint or catnip, is a perennial, native to Europe and Asia. There are several varieties of catmint grown in gardens, all with slightly different growing habits, including *N. mussinii* and *N. x faassenii*, which have similar properties. In general they are low-growing perennials reaching 1–3ft in height. Fine white hairs cover both the stem, which is square as in all members of the mint family, and the gray-green leaves. These are coarse-toothed and ovate, although the base leaves are heart-shaped. The tubular summer flowers are massed in spikes or whorls. White, pale pink, or purplish blue in color, they produce very fine seeds. Cats find some catmints very attractive.

CONDITIONS

Aspect   Prefers an open, sunny position but tolerates partial shade. Most fragrant in good sunlight.
Site   Catmint does best in fertile sandy loams.

GROWING METHOD

Sowing and planting   Catmint self-sows readily by seeding, once it is established, and can also be grown from cuttings taken in spring. To do this, cut a 4in piece from the parent plant, remove the tip and lower leaves, and place the cutting in a moist soil medium. Cuttings take root in 2 to 3 weeks. Divide mature plants into three or four clumps in spring or fall.

Feeding   As members of the mint family have a high water requirement, keep this plant moist at all times. Do not stand pots in water, however, as this can drown the plant. Mulch lightly in spring and fall, and give a balanced general fertilizer in spring. Feed with nitrogen-rich fertilizer such as poultry manure in spring for more leaf growth.

Problems   Catmint is basically pest free.
Pruning   Prune back each year to keep bushes in shape.

HARVESTING

Picking   Pick fresh leaves as required. Cut leafy stems in late summer when the plant is in bloom. Hang them to dry in a cool, shady place.
Storage   Strip leaves and flowers from dried stems and store in airtight jars.
Freezing   Leaves can be put in a freezer bag and frozen for up to 6 months.

USES

Culinary   Fresh young leaves were once a popular salad ingredient and were used for herbal teas, although they are less popular now.

THE POWDER BLUE FLOWERS and softly aromatic leaves of Nepeta x faassenii are most attractive to human eyes and noses.

Medicinal   Catmint was once used as a cold remedy. (The leaves have a high vitamin C content.)
Craft   Dried flowers and leaves are used in pot-pourri mixtures, and in toys for cats.
Gardening   Plant it near vegetables to deter flea beetles. The scent is also said to deter rats.

CATMINT AT A GLANCE

A spreading perennial with aromatic gray-green leaves, it is particularly attractive to cats. Hardy to 4°F (zone 6).

Month			Parts used
JAN	/		Leaves
FEB	/		Flowers
MAR	plant		
APR	plant		
MAY	plant	harvest	USES
JUN	plant	harvest	Culinary
JULY		harvest	Medicinal
AUG		harvest	Craft
SEPT	plant	harvest	Gardening
OCT	plant		
NOV	/		
DEC	/		

CHICORY
Cichorium intybus

FEATURES

This is a large perennial plant, often grown as an annual. It reaches 3–5ft or more in height. The intense sky-blue, fine-petalled flowers, borne in summer, open in the morning but close up in the hot midday sun. The broad, oblong leaves with ragged edges, reminiscent of dandelions, form a rosette around the bottom of the tall, straggly stems. The upper leaves are much smaller, giving a bare look to the top of the plant. Some varieties can be cultivated by forcing and blanching, when the lettuce-like heart of the chicory plant turns into chicons.

CONDITIONS

Aspect   Prefers full sun. May need support.
Site   These plants require deep, rich, friable soil for best growth.

GROWING METHOD

Sowing and planting   Sow seeds in spring, into drills or trenches 1.25in deep, and thin the seedlings to 12in apart when they are established. Seeds may also be germinated in seed trays and seedlings transplanted into the garden during the months of spring.

Feeding   Keep chicory well watered during spells of hot weather. Add compost to the garden bed in mid summer, but do not provide too much nitrogen or the leaves will grow rapidly at the expense of root growth.

Problems   No particular pests or diseases affect this plant.

HARVESTING

Picking   Pick young green leaves of chicory when they are required. Pick newly opened flowers in summer. Dig up roots in fall.

Storage   The leaves cannot be stored either fresh or dried. The root can be dried and then rendered into a powder.

Freezing   Not suitable for freezing.

Forcing   Lift roots in fall or winter, trim off the leaves to about 1inch from the root, and keep in the dark in a bucket of dry sand to force sweet, new growth which can be harvested in a few weeks.

USES

Culinary   Use young leaves as soon as they are picked, either in salads or in cooking, and forced leaves as winter salad. The strong, bitterish flavour is similar to dandelion. Flowers can be crystallized and used to decorate cakes and puddings. Roasted chicory root is widely used as a coffee substitute.

CHICORY is thought to have been one of the "bitter herbs" the Israelites ate with the Passover lamb. Christians thought it was an aphrodisiac.

Medicinal   A bitter tonic and digestive can be made from the leaves, and a laxative from the roots.
Caution: Excessive continued use may cause eye problems.

CHICORY AT A GLANCE

A tall, straggly perennial with intense bright blue flowers, often grown as annual for forcing. Hardy to 4ºF (zone 6).

JAN	/		**PARTS USED**
FEB	/		Leaves
MAR	plant		Flowers
APR	plant		Roots
MAY	plant	harvest	Shoots
JUN	plant	harvest	
JULY	plant	harvest	
AUG		harvest	**USES**
SEPT		harvest	Culinary
OCT	force		Medicinal
NOV	force		
DEC	force		

CHIVES

Allium schoenoprasum, A. tuberosum

GARLIC CHIVES *are taller than regular chives and have pretty white flowers.*

DAINTY CLUSTERS *of mauve flowers and tubular leaves characterize common chives.*

CHINESE CHIVES *are eaten as a vegetable in China; here we substitute spring onions.*

FEATURES

Chives are perennial herbs that make an attractive edging for a herb garden or bed of mixed annuals and perennials. They grow in clumps from very small bulbs that send up 12in tall grass-like, hollow, tubular, green leaves, tapering to a point at the top. The plants produce flower stems in summer. The flowers of the common chive, *A. schoenoprasum,* take the form of a dense, globular head of pinkish to pale purple blossoms. Chinese or garlic chives (*A. tuberosum*) have a flowerhead composed of star-like, white flowers and flat, narrow, light to dark green leaves. Chives can be grown successfully in small containers and clumps can even be potted up and brought indoors to keep in the kitchen.

CHIVES AT A GLANCE

This hardy perennial herb is highly valued for its tasty green leaves. Ideal for salads. Hardy to 4°F (zone 6).

JAN	/		
FEB	/		PARTS USED
MAR	plant		Leaves
APR	plant	harvest	Flowers
MAY	plant	harvest	Buds
JUN	plant	harvest	
JULY	plant	harvest	USES
AUG		harvest	Culinary
SEPT		harvest	Medicinal
OCT		harvest	Gardening
NOV	/		
DEC	/		

CONDITIONS

Aspect	Chives tolerate a wide range of conditions but grow best in a sunny position.
Site	Chives do best in rich, moist, but well-drained soil, but will tolerate a wide range of conditions.

GROWING METHOD

Sowing and planting	The simplest way to propagate chives is by division. Lift a clump in spring, separate into smaller clumps and replant into fertile ground. Chives can also be grown easily from seed, but need warm conditions to germinate, so are best sown indoors in early spring, with bottom heat. Alternatively, wait until late spring or summer to sow outdoors. Plant clumps 8in apart, in rows 1–2ft apart.
Feeding	Water chives well, especially during hot months. At planting time dig in compost or well-rotted manure and a balanced general fertilizer.
Problems	Chives can suffer from rust. Cut back and burn diseased growth, or, if bad, remove the plant completely. Mildew may also be a problem, and greenfly may attack pot-grown plants.

HARVESTING

Picking	Pick leaves as available. Do not snip off just the tips or the chive will become tough and fibrous. Clip the leaves or blades close to the ground, leaving about 2in still intact. Harvest chives regularly to keep the crop growing. Pick flowers when fully open, but before the color fades.

BORNE IN LATE SPRING, the flowers make chives one of the most decorative of herbs and a first-rate plant for edging a bed, either in a herb garden or in an old-fashioned cottage garden. Choose plants in flower if possible; some strains are much more richly colored than others.

Storage Chives do not store very well.

Freezing Leaves can be frozen for about 6 months. Chop them, put them in a freezer bag, and freeze them for use when needed at a later date.

USES

Culinary Leaves of the chive, *A. schoenoprasum,* have a delicate, mild onion flavour and are added to soups or casseroles during the last moments of cooking. Chopped leaves are also used in salads, in herb butter, as a garnish over other vegetables and in the French *fines herbes*. The flowers can be eaten fresh, tossed in salads, or made into spectacular herb vinegars or butters. All parts of the Chinese chive, *A. tuberosum*, have a mild garlic flavour and the unopened flower bud has a special place in Asian cuisines.

Medicinal The leaves are mildly antiseptic and also promote digestion.

Gardening Chives are recommended companions for roses, carrots, grapes, tomatoes, and fruit trees. They are said to prevent scab on apples and blackspot on roses.

COMFREY
Symphytum officinale

COMFREY LEAVES are handsome but you cannot eat them fresh—they are as rough as sandpaper.

ATTRACTIVE IN GROWTH and in foliage, comfrey makes an unusual tall groundcover. Other species have blue or white flowers.

FEATURES

This large, coarse, hairy perennial grows to 39in or more high. It has dark green, lanceolate leaves, which reach 10–12in long, and clusters of bell-shaped flowers in pink-purple or white in summer. The sticky qualities of its rhizome, which is black outside and has juicy white flesh within, gave rise to its nickname of slippery root; its other name, knit-bone, comes from its use in healing. The plant dies down over winter but makes a strong recovery in spring and can be quite invasive in the garden. Confine it to distant parts of the garden where it forms a backdrop.

CONDITIONS

Aspect   Prefers sun or semi-shade, but tolerates most conditions.

Site   Prefers moist, rich soils. Prepare beds with plenty of compost and farmyard manures.

GROWING METHOD

Sowing and planting   Comfrey can be propagated from spring plantings of seed, by root cuttings at any stage of its life cycle or by root division in fall.

Feeding   Comfrey requires a great deal of water. For best growth mulch in spring and fall and apply a balanced general fertilizer in spring.

Problems   May suffer from rust or powdery mildew from late summer. Destroy affected parts.

Pruning   Cutting flowers encourages more leaf growth.

HARVESTING

Picking   Leaves can be picked from early summer to the fall. Up to 4 cuttings a year can be taken. Dig up roots in fall.

Storage   The leaves can be dried and then stored in airtight containers.

Freezing   Can be frozen for 6 months.

USES

Culinary   Not recommended as controversy surrounds the use of young leaves in salads. Dried leaves are sometimes used to make a herbal tea.

Medicinal   The plant contains high concentrations of vitamin B_{12} but a great deal would need to be eaten daily to have any beneficial effect, and some studies suggest that certain alkaloids in the plant can cause chronic liver problems. Roots and leaves are used as a poultice for inflammations, bruises, etc.

Cosmetic   An infusion of leaves makes a cosmetic wash.

Gardening   Comfrey is best used as a liquid manure: steep fresh leaves in water for several weeks. Leaves can also be used to promote decomposition in the compost heap, and so plant it close by.

COMFREY AT A GLANCE

A coarse, hairy, spreading perennial, which can be used to make an excellent organic fertilizer. Hardy to 4°F (zone 6).

JAN	/		**PARTS USED**	
FEB	/		Leaves	
MAR	plant		Roots	
APR	plant			
MAY	plant	harvest	**USES**	
JUN	plant	harvest	(Culinary)	
JULY	plant	harvest	Medicinal	
AUG	plant	harvest	Cosmetic	
SEPT	plant	harvest	Gardening	
OCT	plant	harvest		
NOV	/			
DEC	/			

DANDELION
Taraxacum officinale

FEATURES

A perennial flower often seen as a weed in lawns or neglected places, dandelion produces a flat rosette of deeply lobed, bright green leaves from a big, fleshy taproot. Bright yellow flowers are produced in spring and summer on hollow, leafless stems and develop into puffy, spherical seedheads—dandelion clocks—the individual seeds of which float away on the breeze when ripe. Dandelion has a milky sap and its hollow flower stems differentiate it from other similar weeds, such as hieraciums.

CONDITIONS

Aspect   Grows best in full sun.
Site   Not fussy as to soil but you will get the biggest and best roots and less bitter leaves by growing it in good quality, friable soil.

GROWING METHOD

Sowing and planting   Considered a weed in most yards, the problem is usually restricting or removing it rather than growing it. Remove flowerheads before it sets seed. It is difficult to dig out as any bit of root left will regrow. It is best grown in a bottomless container to confine the roots. Although it is perennial, for the best crops dig out the mature plants each spring or two and replant from small pieces of root.

Feeding   Keep the soil evenly moist. Avoid excessive fertilizing. If the bed had well-rotted manure dug into it, no further fertilizing is required. For container growth, incorporate controlled-release fertilizer into the potting mix at planting time and feed the growing plants monthly with liquid fertilizer.

Problems   No particular problems.
Pruning   Remove flower stems as they rise or, if the pretty flowers are wanted, deadhead as they

DANDELIONS are often considered a weed, but the yellow flowers are very pretty and the leaves are full of vitamins.

fade to stop unwanted seed formation. If seedheads are allowed to ripen, dandelion becomes an invasive weed.

HARVESTING

Picking   Fresh spring leaves can be picked while small and sweet. Bigger, older leaves are very bitter. Bitterness can be reduced by blanching, that is, excluding light. Do this by covering the plant with an upturned tin or flower pot, being sure that all holes are covered. The leaves are ready for picking when they have lost all or most of their green color. Harvest roots only in late fall or winter or they will lack flavor and body. Pick flowers as they open for use fresh.

Storage   Leaves and flowers must be used fresh but roots are stored by first roasting and grinding them and storing in an airtight jar.

Freezing   Roasted, ground roots will stay fresher and more flavorsome if stored in the freezer.

USES

Culinary   Young, sweet leaves are highly nutritious and can be used in salads, stir frys, or to make teas. The ground roots are used as a coffee substitute. The flowers are used to make wine.

Medicinal   The sticky, white sap of the dandelion is used to treat warts and verrucas. Dandelion coffee is sleep inducing and a detoxicant said to be good for the kidneys and liver. The leaves are a powerful diuretic.

Cosmetic   Eating the leaves is said to be good for the skin.

Craft   A yellow-brown dye is made from the roots.

DANDELION AT A GLANCE

This familiar "weed" with its yellow flowers and "dandelion clock" seedheads has many herbal uses. Hardy to 4°F (zone 6).

JAN	/		PARTS USED
FEB	/		Leaves
MAR	plant		Flowers
APR	plant	harvest	Roots
MAY	plant	harvest	
JUN		harvest	
JULY		harvest	USES
AUG		harvest	Culinary
SEPT	plant	harvest	Medicinal
OCT		harvest	Cosmetic
NOV	/		Craft
DEC	/		

DILL
Anethum graveolens

FEATURES

A hardy annual herb growing to 2–3ft, dill looks very like fennel, with its threadlike, feathery, aromatic, blue-green leaves. It has a single, thin taproot rising above the ground to form a long, hollow stalk. This stalk branches at the top to support a 6in wide mass of small, yellow flowers, appearing in clusters, in summer. Flat, oval seeds, brown in color, are produced quickly and in great quantities.

CONDITIONS

Aspect   Prefers full sun. May need support and protection from strong winds.

Site   Light, free-draining but fertile soils. Will not do well in cold, wet conditions.

GROWING METHOD

Sowing and planting   Sow seed from spring to fall. Successive planting every fortnight is recommended to ensure that there is continuous cropping. Sow the seeds in shallow furrows, with at least 2ft between the rows, and then thin the seedlings out to 1ft apart when they have reached approximately 2in in height. Dill will quite often self-sow, so choose a permanent position for the initial plantings.

Feeding   Keep well watered, especially in hot weather. Mulch well throughout spring and summer with well-rotted organic matter such as compost or farmyard manure.

Problems   No particular problems.

HARVESTING

Picking   Dill leaves can be picked within 2 months of planting. Clip close to the stem in the cooler parts of the day. Several weeks after the plant

THE FEATHERY LEAVES and greenish-yellow flowers of dill make a graceful summer picture. The flowers are used in making spiced olives.

blossoms, pick the flowerheads and place them in a paper bag—store in a cool, dry place until seeds ripen—or stems can be cut and hung upside down until seeds ripen and fall.

Storage   Leaves and stems do not keep for more than a couple of days in the refrigerator before drooping and losing flavor. Dry leaves by spreading them thinly over a firm, non-metallic surface in a warm, dark place. After drying, place them in an airtight container. Seeds are dried in a similar manner.

Freezing   Leaves and stems can be frozen for up to six months, and pieces broken off as required.

USES

Culinary   Dill has a pronounced tang which is stronger in seed than leaf. Fresh leaves are used in many dishes, and as a garnish. The seeds are used ground or whole in cooked dishes, as well as in the making of vinegars, pickles, and herb butters. Dried leaves are often added to soups or sauces. Dill is a great favorite in fish dishes. Tea can be made from the seeds.

Medicinal   Dill was traditionally an important medicinal herb for coughs, headaches, digestive problems etc, and dill water or "gripe water" is still used.

Gardening   Dill is considered an ideal companion plant for lettuce, cabbage, and onions.

DILL AT A GLANCE

A hardy annual with feathery blue-green leaves. Leaves and seeds are popular in cooking. Fairly hardy to about 14°F (zone 8).

JAN	/	**PARTS USED**	
FEB	/	Leaves	
MAR	plant 🌱	Seeds	
APR	plant 🌱	Stems	
MAY	plant 🌱 harvest 🌿		
JUN	plant 🌱 harvest 🌿	**USES**	
JULY	plant 🌱 harvest 🌿	Culinary	
AUG	plant 🌱 harvest 🌿	Medicinal	
SEPT	plant 🌱 harvest 🌿	Gardening	
OCT	harvest 🌿		
NOV	/		
DEC	/		

ELDER
Sambucus nigra

FEATURES

A deciduous shrub or small tree, elder or elderberry grows up to 20–28ft tall and has rough, corky bark and compound leaves composed of five or so toothed, dark green leaflets. Heads of creamy white, scented flowers appear in summer leading to shiny, blue-black berries in fall. The flowers attract bees while the berries are eaten by birds.

CONDITIONS

Aspect   A sunny position is best although the plant will tolerate bright, dappled shade or a few hours of full shade each day.

Site   Friable, fertile soil that drains well yet stays moist is best, but elder accepts a wide range of soil types. Grows well on chalky soils.

GROWING METHOD

Sowing and planting   Plants can be grown from seed sown in spring, or suckers, with their own roots, can be dug and detached from the parent plant. This can be done at any time but spring is best. Elders can also be propagated by cuttings. Take hardwood cuttings in late summer or tip cuttings in spring. Root in containers of very sandy potting mix. Pot up and overwinter under glass before planting out into their permanent position. If you are planting a group or row, leave at least 10ft between plants to allow room for the suckers to develop.

Feeding   Elders like moisture at their roots at all times, especially in hot, dry weather. If rainfall is regular, mature plants need little extra water. In average garden soils no special fertilizing is required, especially if you mulch beneath the plants with well-rotted organic matter. If soil is not very fertile, a ration of a complete plant food once in early spring is sufficient.

THE CREAMY-WHITE FLOWERS of the elder are strongly scented. They appear in clusters during early summer.

Problems   No particular problems.

Pruning   Elder grows rapidly and in smaller gardens may need to be cut hard back in late fall or early spring to prevent it growing too large.

HARVESTING

Picking   Flowerheads are picked in the morning but only when all the flowers on each head have bloomed. Dry spread out on a fine net in a cool, dark, airy place. Berries are picked when ripe.

Storage   Dried flowers can be removed from their stems and stored in airtight containers. Ripe berries can also be dried and similarly stored.

Freezing   Berries that have been cooked for a few minutes may be frozen for later use.

USES

Culinary   Fresh flowers are made into elderflower wine and cordials, and jams and jellies. The berries can also be made into jams or jellies and the juice can be fermented into elderberry wine. Berries should not be eaten raw.

Cosmetic   Cold elderflower tea splashed onto the face daily tones and soothes the skin and is good for the complexion generally. Leaves can also be used to make a soothing, healing wash.

Medicinal   An infusion of flowers is a remedy for respiratory problems, fevers, colds, and sore throats and has a mild laxative effect. Berries are a mild laxative and are also used to treat coughs, colds, bronchitis, etc.

Gardening   Elderberries, with their dense growth and suckering habit, make a good privacy screen and reasonable windbreak.

ELDER AT A GLANCE

Deciduous tree with aromatic white flowers and purple berries, with many different uses. Hardy to 4°F (zone 6).

JAN	/		
FEB	/		
MAR	/	PARTS USED	
APR	plant 🌱	Flowers	
MAY	plant 🌱 harvest 🍃	Berries	
JUN	harvest 🍃	Leaves	
JULY	/		
AUG	/	USES	
SEPT	plant 🌱 harvest 🍃	Culinary	
OCT	plant 🌱 harvest 🍃	Medicinal	
NOV	/	Cosmetic	
DEC	/	Gardening	

FEVERFEW

Tanacetum parthenium, syn. Chrysanthemum parthenium

FEATURES

A perennial flower, feverfew has aromatic, finely cut leaves and clusters of long-lasting small, white daisy-like flowers in summer. The plant is densely foliaged and grows about 2ft tall. Leaves are usually a fresh, light green but a golden foliaged form, "Aureum", is also sold. Pretty double-flowered forms are also available.

CONDITIONS

Aspect Prefers full sun or light shade. Plants may grow lax and flower poorly in areas that are too shady. The golden form may scorch in full sun.

Site Average, well-drained garden soil is all that is needed. In over-rich soils plants produce too much soft, leafy growth.

GROWING METHOD

Sowing and planting Easily grown from seed sown in early spring. Press seeds just beneath the surface where the plants are to grow. Established plants can be dug up in fall and divided into several new plants. Each division should have its own roots and the divisions should be replanted immediately. Soft-tip cuttings taken in early summer will also root easily. Make cuttings about 3in long and insert them into small pots of very sandy potting mix. Place in a warm but shady and sheltered spot and keep them moist. Roots should form in about 3 weeks.

Feeding Do not overwater. Feverfew does not thrive on neglect but does not need frequent watering. Overwet conditions will cause the plant to rot.
Mulch lightly in spring and fall and apply a balanced general fertilizer in spring.

Problems No major problems.

Pruning Can be cut back after flowering to keep a compact shape and to minimize self-seeding.

HARVESTING

Picking All the upper parts of the plant are useful medicinally and whole plants may be harvested any time they are in full bloom. Fresh, young leaves can be harvested any time, but are best before the plant flowers. Do remember that plants need their leaves to live and you should grow enough plants so that picking is not concentrated on just one or two. Pick flowers just as they open.

Storage Dry upper parts, including leaves, stems, and flowers, in a cool, dark, airy place. (Hang flowers upside down to dry.) When dry, coarsely chop and store in an airtight jar.

Freezing Freshly picked leaves can be wrapped in foil and frozen, for up to 6 months, for later use.

FOR THE HERB GARDEN, most people prefer this single, daisy-like feverfew but there is also a very pretty double white one.

USES

Medicinal Tea made from the dried upper parts is drunk to relieve indigestion and period pain. It has gained a reputation for the treatment of migraines. Eating one or two fresh leaves every day may help prevent the onset of migraines in sufferers but in some people this causes mouth ulcers.

Cosmetic Feverfew makes a useful moisturizer.

Craft Flower stems placed in linen closets will discourage moths. An infusion of the leaves makes a mild disinfectant.

Gardening Feverfew is attractive and gives a good display when plants are massed together or used to border paths. It is attractive to bees and is often planted near fruit trees to assist pollination.

FEVERFEW AT A GLANCE

Perennial herb with aromatic leaves and daisy-like flowers that has a reputation for treating migraines. Hardy to 4°F (zone 6).

JAN	/		PARTS USED
FEB	/		Flowers
MAR	plant		Leaves
APR	plant		Stems
MAY	plant	harvest	
JUN	plant	harvest	USES
JULY		harvest	
AUG		harvest	Medicinal
SEPT	plant	harvest	Cosmetic
OCT	/		Craft
NOV	/		Gardening
DEC	/		

HERB ROBERT
Geranium robertianum

FEATURES

A biennial herb, often grown as an annual, herb Robert may reach a height of 12–18in. It has deeply lobed, toothed leaves which sometimes develop a reddish cast. Pinkish flowers appear in spring in airy clusters. In the wild, the plant is widely distributed in temperate parts of the northern hemisphere. Explosive seed capsules make the plant potentially invasive where the conditions suit it.

CONDITIONS

Aspect Full sun or part shade are equally suitable.
Site Not particularly fussy about soil types as long as they drain freely. Average garden soil is quite satisfactory.

GROWING METHOD

Sowing and planting Herb Robert can be grown from seed saved from last year and sown shallowly in spring or from cuttings of basal shoots taken in middle to late spring. Make cuttings about 3in long and insert them into small pots of very sandy potting mix. Keep lightly moist in a warm, bright, but shaded place. Roots should form within a month and the new plants can either be placed in the garden or potted up to grow bigger. Herb Robert will self seed freely and is considered to be a weed by many gardeners.

Feeding Herb Robert does not need a lot of water and in places where summers are mild regular rainfall can be sufficient. If watering is necessary, water deeply once a week rather than giving more frequent light sprinklings. In garden beds that are mulched regularly with well-rotted organic matter, no further fertilizer is needed.

Problems The fungus disease rust, which attacks all

HERB ROBERT has one of those scents you either like or loathe. It is said to be named after St Robert who discovered its medicinal qualities.

plants of the *Geranium* and *Pelargonium* genera, can disfigure the foliage and weaken the plant. It appears as yellow spots on the upper surface of the leaf with raised lumps of "rust" underneath. Rust occurs mainly during warm, humid weather. To control it, either pick off affected leaves at the first sign of infection or spray the plant with a fungicide suitable for the condition (the label will tell you). Don't drop or compost any of the affected leaves. They should be burnt or placed into the rubbish bin.

HARVESTING

Picking Leaves are used fresh and may be picked at any time as required.
Storage Not usually stored.
Freezing Not suitable for freezing.

USES

Medicinal Traditionally, herb Robert has been used to treat a range of complaints as varied as toothache and conjunctivitis. *Caution:* do not use without expert supervision.
Gardening Herb Robert plant is pretty enough in its own right and makes a good addition to a wild garden.

HERB ROBERT AT A GLANCE

Traditionally used as a medicinal herb, herb Robert is now often considered a weed. Hardy to 4°F (zone 6).

JAN	/	
FEB	plant 🌿	
MAR	plant 🌿	**PARTS USED**
APR	plant 🌿	Leaves
MAY	plant 🌿 harvest 🍃	
JUN	harvest 🍃	**USES**
JULY	harvest 🍃	Medicinal
AUG	harvest 🍃	Gardening
SEPT	harvest 🍃	
OCT	/	
NOV	/	
DEC	/	

HYSSOP
Hyssopus officinalis

FEATURES

A semi-evergreen sub-shrub growing 24–32in tall, hyssop has many erect stems clothed in narrow, lanceolate, sage green leaves. Spikes of small flowers appear on top of each stem in summer. Usually these flowers are blue-violet but they may also be pink or white. The whole plant exudes a pungent aroma and the leaves have a bitter taste.

CONDITIONS

Aspect   Full sun produces compact growth and the strongest flavour but hyssop tolerates shade for part of the day.

Site   Likes light, fertile, well-drained soils but will grow in any reasonably fertile soil as long as it drains freely.

GROWING METHOD

Sowing and planting   Hyssop can be grown from seed, softwood cuttings or division of the roots. Sow seeds in spring in trays of seed compost. Cover lightly, keep moist, and when seedlings are big enough to handle, prick out into small, individual pots to grow on. Plant out about 12in apart when plants are about 8in tall. Take 3in cuttings in early summer and insert into pots of sandy potting mix. Keep moist and in bright, sheltered shade and roots will form within a month. To divide, lift an established plant in late fall or early spring. Cut the root mass into several smaller sections, each with its own roots. Replant immediately.

Feeding   Keep soil moist, especially during the warmer months but do not overwater. Hyssop is a resilient plant that can often get by on rain. A ration of balanced general fertilizer in spring when new growth appears is enough.

Problems   No particular problems.

Pruning   When new growth begins in spring, pinching

THE RICH BLUE FLOWERS of hyssop adorn the garden in spring, and they are much loved by bees who make superb honey from them.

out the tips of young stems will encourage the plant to become more bushy and thus produce more flowers. Trim after flowering to maintain shape.

HARVESTING

Picking   Flowers for using fresh or for drying are picked when in full bloom and individual stems can be harvested as needed.

Storage   Cut bunches of flowering stems, tie them together and hang them upside down in a dim, airy place. When they are dry, crumble them into airtight jars.

Freezing   Not suitable for freezing.

USES

Culinary   One or two fresh leaves, finely chopped and added late, give an appealing piquancy to soups and casseroles while fresh flowers can be used to add flavor and color to salads.

Medicinal   Tea, made by infusing the dried stems, leaves, and flowers in boiling water, is taken to relieve the symptoms of colds; hyssop leaves are often a component in mixed herbal tonics and teas. *Caution:* do not use during pregnancy or for nervous people. Avoid strong doses and do not use continuously for long periods.

Cosmetic   Oil distilled from hyssop is used in perfumes and other commercial cosmetics. At home, it may be added to bath water, and cooled hyssop leaf tea is a cleansing, refreshing facial rinse.

Gardening   Hyssop is a decorative plant and very attractive to bees and butterflies. Use it in a border of mixed flowers or grow it as an edging to paths.

HYSSOP AT A GLANCE

A decorative semi-evergreen shrub with narrow green leaves and spikes of blue flowers. Hardy to 4°F (zone 6).

JAN	/	PARTS USED	
FEB	/	Leaves	
MAR	plant	Stems	
APR	plant	Flowers	
MAY	plant	harvest	
JUN	plant	harvest	
JULY		harvest	USES
AUG		harvest	Culinary
SEPT	plant	harvest	Medicinal
OCT	plant		Cosmetic
NOV	/		Gardening
DEC	/		

LAVENDER
Lavandula

FEATURES

Lavender is a traditional herb and cottage garden plant. An evergreen, bushy shrub with aromatic, narrow, gray-green leaves, it bears spikes of blue-mauve (and in some varieties pink or white) fragrant flowers in summer. There are many species and varieties to choose from, most hardy but some only half hardy, and the fragrance and herbal properties will vary with the different types. Heights vary from 12in to 32in or more. "Common" or "English" lavender is *Lavandula angustifolia* (favourite varieties include "Alba", "Hidcote", and "Munstead"). Popular half hardy lavenders include *L. dentata* and *L. stoechas*.

CONDITIONS

Aspect   Best grown in an open, sunny position, but will tolerate some shade. Lavender will not do well in cold, wet conditions.

Site   Prefers well-drained soil, but it need not be rich. If it is acid, add lime.

GROWING METHOD

Sowing and planting   Some lavenders will flower the first year from an early sowing, but taking cuttings is the easiest way to get the lavender you want. Take 2in cuttings with a heel or base of old wood in summer. Trim off lower leaves and insert into pots of a sandy potting mix. Keep on the dry side until the cutting has taken root and new leaf shoots appear. Pot on into a good quality potting mix. Plant in the garden in spring 18–24in apart. Layering is easily done in the fall with most hardy lavenders.

Feeding   Water only in dry weather as lavenders do not require a great deal of water. Applications of a balanced general fertilizer will improve fragrance. Less cold-resistant varieties may need winter mulching.

Problems   In wet conditions lavender may suffer from gray mould or botrytis. Remove and burn affected parts.

Pruning   Trim in spring and again after flowering to keep a compact shape and prevent the bush from becoming straggly. The final trim of the year should be well before the last frosts as frost will damage soft new growth. Do not cut back into old wood as this is unlikely to re-shoot.

HARVESTING

Picking   Flowers can be cut just as they open. Leaves can be picked at any time.

Storage   Dry by hanging in bunches in a dry, airy, hot place. Store dried leaves and flowers in airtight jars.

Freezing   Not suitable for freezing.

ENGLISH LAVENDER is distinguished from the dumpier French, Italian and Spanish types by its slender flower spikes.

USES

Culinary   Fresh or dried flowers and leaves are used to flavour sugars, jellies, ice creams, and cheeses. Flowers can also be crystallized and used as decoration on cakes.

Medicinal   Lavender has traditionally had many medicinal uses, including soothing and sedating and healing burns, cuts, and stings. The oil has a strong anti-bacterial action. It is also used to treat headaches.

Cosmetic   Lavender is used to make skin and hair washes.

Craft   Dried lavender spikes are used in pot-pourris, perfumed sachets, and dried arrangements. Lavender is used to make essential oil and floral waters. It is also an insect repellent.

Gardening   Popular, widely grown cottage garden plants.

LAVENDER AT A GLANCE

Popular fragrant garden plants with narrow silvery leaves and strongly scented flowers. Hardiness varies: 4 to 23°F (zones 7-9).

JAN	/		PARTS USED
FEB	/		Flowers
MAR	plant		Leaves
APR	plant		
MAY	plant	harvest	
JUN	plant	harvest	USES
JULY	plant	harvest	Culinary
AUG	plant	harvest	Medicinal
SEPT	plant	harvest	Cosmetic
OCT	/		Craft
NOV	/		Gardening
DEC	/		

LEMON VERBENA
Aloysia triphylla, syn. Lippia citriodora

FEATURES

A large, bushy, deciduous shrub that grows 3–10ft in height, lemon verbena has long, lemony-scented, narrow leaves. Spikes or sprays of small white to mauve flowers appear in the axils of the leaves in summer. The leaves give this plant its herby quality, and their fragrance can be released simply by brushing against them in the garden. It can be grown in containers and in cooler areas brought indoors over winter, although container plants do not reach the same height as garden plants.

CONDITIONS

Aspect   Requires a sheltered, sunny position with winter protection. Against a sunny wall is ideal.

Site   Likes rich soils. Needs mulching against frosts.

GROWING METHOD

Sowing and planting   Grow from softwood cuttings in late spring or hardwood cuttings in the fall. Trim a 5in piece from the parent bush, removing a third of the upper leaves and a few of the lower leaves. Place in a sandy potting mix. Moisten the mix and cover the pot with a plastic bag to create a mini-greenhouse. Pot on into good quality potting compost when the cutting has taken root and shows renewed leaf growth. Plant in the garden when the plant is growing strongly.

Feeding   The plant is tolerant of dry conditions and will rarely require watering except when grown in a pot. Mulch with straw in the fall to protect from frost. Give an application of a balanced general fertilizer in spring.

Problems   Spider mite and whitefly can be a problem. Hose leaves frequently to remove the pests or use organic soap and pyrethrum or recommended chemicals.

Pruning   Prune each season to contain its straggly

THIS HERB was introduced to European gardens from Chile in 1746. The name Aloysia honours Queen Maria Louisa of Spain.

growth habit, and cut out frost-damaged shoots in spring. It can be trained into a formal standard.

HARVESTING

Picking   Sprigs of leaves can be harvested at any time.

Storage   Hang the branches in a cool, airy place and strip off the leaves when they are dry. Store dried leaves in airtight jars. Fragrance remains for some years.

Freezing   Put in a freezer bag and freeze for up to 6 months.

USES

Culinary   Fresh or dried leaves can be used for herbal tea or in cooking where a lemony flavour is required, as with fish, poultry, marinades, salad dressings, and puddings, and to flavour oils and vinegars.

Medicinal   Lemon verbena tea has a mild sedative effect and is good for nasal congestion and indigestion. *Caution:* long-term use may cause stomach irritation.

Cosmetic   The leaves can be used in skin creams and the essential oil is used in perfumery.

Craft   The strong long-lasting fragrance makes dried leaves a popular component of pot-pourris and sachet fillings.

Gardening   Lemon verbena is an attractive border and container plant.

LEMON VERBENA AT A GLANCE

A deciduous shrub with lemon-scented leaves which are popular ingredients in pot-pourris and sachets. Hardy to 23°F (zone 9).

JAN	/	
FEB	/	**PARTS USED**
MAR	/	Leaves
APR	/	
MAY	plant ✤ harvest ✤	**USES**
JUN	harvest ✤	Culinary
JULY	harvest ✤	Medicinal
AUG	plant ✤ harvest ✤	Cosmetic
SEPT	plant ✤ harvest ✤	Craft
OCT	/	Gardening
NOV	/	
DEC	/	

NASTURTIUM
Tropaeolum majus

FEATURES

A popular trailing garden plant. Compact varieties grow to about 24in while large varieties can spread up to 10ft. The wide leaves are roundish and dark green to variegated in color and have a peppery taste. The funnel-shaped, five-petalled, and spurred flowers appear in late spring and summer and range from creamy white through yellow to salmon, brilliant orange, and red. Some varieties have double flowers and all have a slight perfume. Each bud produces a cluster of seeds. (Double forms do not produce seed.) This plant grows well in containers.

CONDITIONS

Aspect Prefers full sun although it will grow in semi-shade. Leaf growth is more pronounced in shady situations and may hide the blooms.

Site Nasturtiums do not like an over-rich soil but good drainage is necessary. Too rich a soil will encourage leaves at the expense of flowers.

GROWING METHOD

Sowing and planting For early flowers sow the large seeds under glass in spring. Plugs or small pots are ideal. Plant out 8in apart when all danger of frost has passed. Seeds can be sown outdoors in May directly where they are to grow, but the plants will not flower until a few weeks later than the early sowings.

Feeding Do not water excessively, especially when plants are well established. Nitrogen encourages the growth of leaves. More flowers and seeds will be produced if you hold back on the fertilizer and compost.

Problems Sap-sucking blackfly (aphids) love nasturtiums. Vigorously hose the pest off or treat the plant with an appropriate spray.

TROPAEOLUM means "a little trophy", so named because the shield-shaped leaves and golden, helmet-like flowers suggested piles of armour.

Caterpillars, particularly those of the cabbage white butterfly, can also be a problem.

HARVESTING

Picking Pick fresh leaves, buds, and flowers as required. Harvest seeds just before they lose their green color.

Storage Leaves and flowers do not store well and should be used immediately. Buds and seeds can be pickled in vinegar, stored in airtight jars and used at a later date.

Freezing Put in a freezer bag; freeze for up to 6 months.

USES

Culinary All parts of this herb are edible and have a spicy, peppery flavour. Fresh leaves and flowers are used in salads or the flowers can be used alone as a garnish. Buds and seeds are used as a substitute for capers. *Caution:* do not eat large quantities at one time.

Gardening Because they are so attractive to aphids, nasturtiums are excellent companion plants for vegetables such as cabbages, broccoli, and other brassicas. The aphids will flock to the nasturtiums and leave the vegetables alone.

NASTURTIUM AT A GLANCE

Attractive trailing annuals with brightly colored flowers, grown for decoration and for the kitchen. Hardy to 23°F (zone 9).

JAN	/		
FEB	/		**PARTS USED**
MAR	plant 🖐		Leaves
APR	plant 🖐		Flowers
MAY	plant 🖐	harvest 🌿	Buds
JUN	plant 🖐	harvest 🌿	Seeds
JULY		harvest 🌿	
AUG		harvest 🌿	**USES**
SEPT		harvest 🌿	Culinary
OCT		harvest 🌿	Gardening
NOV	/		
DEC	/		

OENOTHERA
Oenothera biennis

FEATURES

Oenothera, the evening primrose, is a hardy biennial with many upright, leafy stems. In summer each of these stems is topped with a cluster of golden yellow, sweetly fragrant flowers which open towards the end of the day. The scent is strongest in the evening. The foliage, which is bright green, forms a rosette around the base of the plant. Evening primrose should be planted with caution as it self-seeds prolifically and spreads fast in favoured locations.

CONDITIONS

Aspect Full sun is preferred.
Site Not very fussy about soil and grows in most places so long as the drainage is good. This plant thrives in average garden soils.

GROWING METHOD

Sowing and planting Grows from seed sown in fall or early spring directly where it is to grow. Thin seedlings out so that there is at least 1ft between them.

Feeding Do not overwater. Once established, plants are fairly drought tolerant. Feeding is not necessary. Rich soils can lead to excessive foliage growth and weak or deformed stems.

Problems No particular problems.

Pruning Pruning is not necessary. Snap off flower stems after the blooms have faded but before seeds ripen. This plant self-seeds freely and can create a major weed problem. Allow one plant to seed in order to regenerate the plants but collect the seed before it falls.

HARVESTING

Picking Leaves may be picked at any time, while seeds

EVENING PRIMROSE earns its name by blooming at dusk. There are perennial species that keep their blooms open all day.

are harvested when ripe in fall. Pick flowers in bud or when just open. The small roots may also be dug in spring or fall.

Storage Seeds are stored in airtight containers. Other parts of the plant are used fresh.

Freezing Not suitable for freezing.

USES

Culinary All parts of the plant are edible. Fresh leaves are used in salads or can be lightly steamed or stir fried. Seeds can be eaten raw or used in cooking.

Medicinal Tea made from the leaves is good for coughs and colds and is a tonic for the liver, kidneys, and intestines. An oil (GLA, gamma linoleic acid) contained in the seeds has been credited with amazing therapeutic powers, and evening primrose is now being grown commercially on a large scale.

Gardening Evening primrose is a pretty plant and a good partner for other meadow flowers such as Californian poppies.

OENOTHERA AT A GLANCE

The evening primrose is a pretty, fragrant, yellow-flowered biennial, now much grown commercially. Hardy to 4°F (zone 7).

Month	Activity		Parts used / Uses
JAN	/		**PARTS USED**
FEB	/		Leaves
MAR	plant		Stems
APR	plant		Flowers
MAY	plant	harvest	Buds
JUN	plant	harvest	Seeds
JULY		harvest	Roots
AUG		harvest	
SEPT	plant	harvest	**USES**
OCT		harvest	Culinary
NOV	/		Medicinal
DEC	/		Gardening

PARSLEY

Petroselinum

HERE GROWING with lettuces, sage, and nasturtiums, curly parsley makes a very attractive addition to any bed of herbs and vegetables.

NO NEED TO DESPAIR when parsley flowers as the flowers are edible too. This Italian parsley can also be used in flower arrangements.

CURLY PARSLEY is the prettiest of garnishes and the essential ingredient in a bouquet garni. Here it grows with white alyssum.

FEATURES

Parsley grows from a strong tap root with erect, 12in tall stems bearing divided, feather-like, small leaves which may be flattish or curly depending on variety. Tiny, yellowish-green flower clusters are borne on tall stalks in summer, and produce small, brown, oval and ribbed seeds. Common varieties of this biennial or short-lived perennial plant include curly parsley, *P. crispum*, plain-leaved or Italian parsley, *P. crispum* var. *neapolitanum*, and Hamburg or turnip-rooted parsley, *P. crispum* var. *tuberosum*.

CONDITIONS

Aspect Grow in full sun or light shade.
Site Parsley plants like a rich, deep, well-drained soil.

GROWING METHOD

Sowing and planting Sow seed under cover in spring in pots or plug trays rather than seed trays as parsley dislikes being transplanted. The seed can be difficult to germinate so help to create optimum conditions by soaking the seeds in warm water for 24 hours and then pouring boiling water over the soil to raise the temperature. Plant the young seedlings out, 6in apart, after they have grown several true leaves. If parsley is grown in containers, the pots should be at least 8in deep, and the longer tap root of Hamburg parsley will require a pot that is even deeper. Once parsley plants are established in the garden, the mature plants can be left to self-sow when they go to seed during the summer months in their second year of growth.

Feeding Keep the soil moist and do not let it dry out in dry weather. Occasional feeds of a nitrogen-rich liquid fertilizer will promote more leaf growth.

Problems Carrot fly and root aphids can be particular problems. Destroy affected plants. Slugs also love young plants.

Pruning Parsley can be kept productive by frequent pruning and by nipping out the flower stalks whenever they appear.

ITS FINE TEXTURE AND RICH GREEN COLOR makes parsley an ideal edging plant. Here it is used to set off the varied tones and textures of a formal vegetable garden, but it would look equally fine as a foil for brightly colored flowers.

HARVESTING

Picking   New growth comes from the centre of the stem, and so always pick parsley from the outside of the plant. Pick this vitamin-rich, nutritious herb as needed. Dig up young roots of Hamburg parsley in fall.

Storage   Broad-leaved Italian parsley, with its stronger taste, gives a better result when dried than the other varieties.

Freezing   Curly parsley freezes well. Put sprigs in freezer bags and freeze for up to 6 months.

USES

Culinary   Parsley is used in salads, as a garnish, and in cooking. Hamburg parsley is used as a root vegetable.

Cosmetic   An infusion can be used as a hair rinse. Chew raw parsley to promote a healthy skin.

Medicinal   Parsley is very nutritious and it is a strong diuretic. Fresh parsley is a breath freshener, and is recommended for taking away the smell of garlic on the breath. It has been used in poultices and to make an antiseptic dressing for wounds and bites. *Caution:* Do not use medicinally during pregnancy.

Gardening   Parsley makes an attractive edging plant.

PARSLEY AT A GLANCE

Parsley, with its tasty green leaves, is one of the best known of all the culinary herbs. Frost hardy to 4°F or below (zone 7).

JAN	/		PARTS USED
FEB	/		Leaves
MAR	plant 🌱		Flowers
APR	plant 🌱	harvest 🌿	Roots
MAY	plant 🌱	harvest 🌿	
JUN	plant 🌱	harvest 🌿	USES
JULY		harvest 🌿	Culinary
AUG		harvest 🌿	Medicinal
SEPT		harvest 🌿	Cosmetic
OCT	/		Gardening
NOV	/		
DEC	/		

PINKS
Dianthus

FEATURES

Popular garden plants, pinks are very pretty, short-lived, hardy perennials. A wide range of species and varieties is available, which vary in height from about 6in to 24in or more. One of those with the longest herbal tradition is *Dianthus caryophyllus*, the clove carnation. The rich, sweet, clove scent of the flowers has made it popular in perfumery for more than 2000 years. Generally pinks have narrow, gray-green, lance-shaped leaves. The flowers appear in spring or summer, in shades of pink or white, and are usually highly fragrant. Plants can become straggly after a few years, and are best discarded and replaced with young plants that have been grown from cuttings.

CONDITIONS

Aspect	Pinks prefer a sunny, sheltered site.
Site	Grow them in a very well-drained soil that is not too rich, and preferably alkaline.

GROWING METHOD

Sowing and Planting	Pinks can be grown from seed, but the resulting plants can be very variable. Sow the seed under glass in trays of gritty seed compost in spring or fall. Take care not to overwater and be sure to ventilate well. Plant out in spring, after hardening off, at about 1ft apart. Named forms can be propagated by cuttings, division, or layering. Take cuttings in late summer. Plants can also be layered at this time of year. The plants can also be dug up after they have finished flowering, and any rooted stems can be severed and replanted.
Feeding	Pinks tolerate relatively dry conditions. Be careful not to overwater. Pinks need little feeding. A light dressing of a balanced general fertilizer may be given in early spring. Do not

DIVINE FLOWERS. The name Dianthus comes from the words "dios", meaning divine, and "anthos", meaning flower.

	mulch as this can cause the stems to rot.
Problems	The main pest is red spider mite. Also virus, leaf spots, and leaf-attacking insects may cause problems.
Pruning	Remove dead flowerheads to prolong flowering.

HARVESTING

Picking	Pick flowers when newly open. If the petals are to be used in cooking, remove the white heel from each of the petals as this has a very bitter flavour.
Storage	Dry on racks in a cool, airy place. Petals can also be crystallized.
Freezing	Not suitable for freezing.

USES

Culinary	Fresh petals can be used in salads, and also puddings and savory dishes. They can also be used to flavour oils, vinegar, syrup, or white wine. Crystallized petals can be used to decorate cakes and puddings.
Medicinal	The petals can be used to make a tonic cordial, or can be infused in white wine to make a nerve tonic.
Craft	Dried petals can be used to add color and scent to pot-pourri mixes, and used to make scented sachets etc.
Cosmetic	Fresh petals can be used to scent a variety of cosmetic products.
Gardening	Pinks are amongst the most decorative of all the garden herbs.

PINKS AT A GLANCE

Attractive perennials with highly fragrant flowers, which have a long tradition of use in perfumery. Hardy to 4°F (zone 7).

Month	Activity		PARTS USED
JAN	/		Petals
FEB	/		
MAR	plant		
APR	plant		USES
MAY	plant	harvest	Culinary
JUN	plant	harvest	Medicinal
JULY	plant	harvest	Craft
AUG	plant		Cosmetic
SEPT	plant		Gardening
OCT	/		
NOV	/		
DEC	/		

POT MARIGOLD
Calendula officinalis

FEATURES

A bushy hardy annual with light green leaves and brightly colored flowers in shades of orange from spring to fall. The traditional cottage garden pot marigolds have single, bright orange flowers, but many more decorative double and semi-double varieties are readily available. However, if these are allowed to self-seed, which they will do freely, the single form will eventually come to dominate again.

CONDITIONS

Aspect
Pot marigolds grow best in full sun or light shade. They can become leggy if grown in deeper shade.

Site
Pot marigolds are very tolerant plants, growing in most soils that do not get waterlogged, but they do best in well-drained, not too rich soils.

GROWING METHOD

Sowing and planting
Propagate from seed sown in spring or fall.
Plant out 12–18in apart. Pot marigolds will self-sow freely.

Feeding
Do not allow the soil to become waterlogged. No special feeding required.

Problems
Slugs may eat the young leaves. Blackfly may be a problem late in the season. Cut out infested areas and spray with horticultural soap. Mildew may also be a problem, but generally this does not occur until flowering is over. Remove and burn affected parts to prevent it from spreading.

Pruning
No special requirements. Pinch out growing tips to prevent the plant becoming leggy. Deadhead regularly to encourage continuous flowering.

POT MARIGOLD AT A GLANCE

A popular annual herb with brightly coloured flowers that have a wide range of herbal uses. Hardy to 5°F or below (zone 7).

JAN	/	*Parts used*	
FEB	/	Flowers	
MAR	plant ✎	Leaves	
APR	plant ✎		
MAY	plant ✎	harvest ❀	
JUN	harvest ❀	*Uses*	
JULY	harvest ❀	Culinary	
AUG	harvest ❀	Medicinal	
SEPT	plant ✎	Cosmetic	
OCT	/	Craft	
NOV	/	Gardening	
DEC	/		

IN THE AMERICAN CIVIL WAR doctors on the battlefield used marigold flowers to treat the soldiers' wounds.

HARVESTING

Picking
Pick the flowers just as they open for use fresh or dry. Pick leaves when they are young for fresh use.

Storage
Dry pot marigold flowers slowly at low temperatures, on a non-metal rack in a cool airy place.

Freezing
The petals can be frozen in ice cubes and used as required to decorate drinks.

USES

Culinary
Petals can be used fresh in salads, butters, and cheeses, and also in cooked dishes including omelettes, soups, etc. They can also be used to add color to rice dishes. Young leaves can also be added to salads.

Medicinal
Pot marigold flowers have antiseptic, anti-fungal, and anti-bacterial properties and have traditionally been used medicinally for a wide range of conditions, including the treatment of wounds, burns, stings and bites, chilblains, and varicose veins. An infusion was also used as an eyewash. The sap from the stem is said to remove warts.

Cosmetic
Pot marigold can be used to make a range of cosmetic preparations. For example, infused flowers can be used to make skin and hair care preparations. Used in a skin lotion, they are said to help clear up spots.

Craft
The dried petals can be used to add color to pot-pourri. The fresh petals produce a yellow dye.

Gardening
A traditional and popular cottage garden flower. Being sensitive to temperature, they give an indication of the weather. Open flowers are said to forecast a fine day.

ROSA GALLICA
Rosa gallica var. officinalis

FEATURES

A prickly shrub that can reach a height of 4ft, the apothecary's rose, *Rosa gallica*, is a dense bush that spreads by suckers, often forming impenetrable thickets. The fragrant, semi-double, deep pink-red flowers appear in summer, followed in fall by dull red hips. Leaves are elliptical in shape and leathery.

CONDITIONS

Aspect From south-east Europe and western Asia, apothecary's rose is best grown in full sun. An open site with good air movement helps reduce fungal diseases.

Site Grows in a wide range of soil types but drainage must be good, especially in areas of high summer rainfall. Deep, friable clay-loam with plenty of well-rotted organic matter is best.

GROWING METHOD

Sowing and planting Can be grown from seed collected from ripe hips in fall but sown in spring, or from suckers detached from the parent plant in late winter. Each sucker must have its own roots; replant at once. Take hardwood cuttings about 8in long in late fall; insert them into potting compost or vacant garden beds and keep moist. Rooted cuttings can be potted up or planted into the garden a year later.

Feeding Established plants can survive on rain alone in areas of regular rainfall but the plant will look and flower better if given an occasional deep soaking during dry spells in summer. Give a balanced general rose fertilizer in spring. Mulch in spring with well-rotted organic matter to improve the soil, feed the plant and conserve moisture.

Problems Suffers from the usual rose problems: aphids, caterpillars, scale insects, and fungus diseases,

THE "RED ROSES" in old recipes always meant the apothecary's rose, but you can substitute any sweetly scented red rose from your garden.

especially in humid conditions. Combined insecticide/fungicide, usually sold as "rose spray", controls aphids, caterpillars, and fungus diseases, and may also include a foliar feed.

Pruning Does not need annual pruning and can be left alone for years. To rejuvenate an old bush, cut stems to the ground in winter.

HARVESTING

Picking Hips are harvested in fall when fully ripe; flowers can be picked for immediate use as they appear.

Storage Both hips and flowers may be stored for a few days in sealed containers in the refrigerator. The petals can be dried for use in pot-pourris, herbal sachets, etc.

Freezing Rose hips and flowers are best used fresh.

USES

Culinary Rosehips are made into jellies, syrups, and liqueurs (all have a very high proportion of vitamin C). Petals are used to flavour vinegar or are crystallized and eaten as a sweet.

Medicinal Infusions made from the hips and/or petals are said to be good for headaches and a range of other common complaints such as diarrhoea, fever, mouth ulcers, and toothache.

Craft Hips and petals are used in crafts. Dried petals are added to pot-pourris. Attar of roses, an essence extracted from the flowers, is a perfuming agent.

Cosmetic Petals can be used to perfume creams, etc.

Gardening This makes a good large-scale groundcover, barrier planting or hedge.

ROSA GALLICA AT A GLANCE

The apothecary's rose is a prickly shrub, grown for its vivid, highly perfumed flowers and its hips. Hardy to 4°F (zone 7).

JAN	/	PARTS USED	
FEB	plant	Flowers	
MAR	plant	Hips	
APR	/		
MAY	/	USES	
JUN		harvest	Culinary
JULY		harvest	Medicinal
AUG	/		Craft
SEPT		harvest	Cosmetic
OCT	plant	harvest	Gardening
NOV	plant		
DEC	/		

ROSEMARY
Rosmarinus officinalis

THIS STANDARD ROSEMARY grows in a pot with Mexican daisies providing a dash of color around its base.

TRADITIONALLY a bringer of good fortune, rosemary is often grown by a path or steps, where its fragrance can also be enjoyed as you pass.

FEATURES

A perennial, evergreen, woody shrub, rosemary has thin, needle-like leaves, which are glossy green above and are whitish to gray-green and hairy below. They have a fragrance reminiscent of pine needles. In spring, small-lobed flowers appear among the leaves. They are pale blue to pinkish or white, depending on the variety. There are several varieties of rosemary, ranging in habit from the upright (*R. officinalis*) to the dwarf (*R. officinalis* "Nana") and the prostrate (*R. officinalis* "Prostratus"). Among the many very popular varieties are "Miss Jessop's Upright" (which is very good for hedges) and pink rosemary (*R. officinalis* "Roseus"). Rosemary bushes can be between 20in and 6ft 6in in height, depending on variety. This is a good herb to grow in containers, and it also grows well in seaside positions where not much else will grow, as it will withstand salt.

CONDITIONS

Aspect   Rosemary likes a sunny, sheltered and reasonably dry position. Although hardy in most areas, protection is advised in severe weather and in colder areas, particularly for young plants.

Site   Rosemary needs to be grown in a well-drained soil in order to lessen the risk of root rot, and the plant is more fragrant when it is grown in alkaline soils.

GROWING METHOD

Sowing and planting   Propagate mainly from cuttings and layering. Seeds are not often used because they have long germination times and tend not to come true to type. Take 4in long cuttings in late spring or early fall, trim off the upper and lower leaves and place the cuttings in small pots containing a moist mixture of two-thirds coarse sand and one-third compost. Cover with a plastic dome and set aside in a semi-shaded position until roots and new leaves form. Or layer by scarifying the underside of a lower branch and firmly securing it to the soil with a wire peg. Cover with sand and keep moist until roots form. Cut off and replant.

Feeding   Prefers soil to be on the drier side; give average garden watering. Mulch in spring and also give an application of a balanced general fertilizer at this time.

Problems   No particular problems.

Pruning   Prune if compact bushes are desired. Trim after flowering to prevent plants becoming straggly. Do not cut back in the fall or when there is a danger of frosts as the plants could be damaged.

HARVESTING

Picking   Fresh leaves or sprigs 2–4in long can be picked as required. Pick flowers in spring.

Storage   Dry sprigs in a cool, dry place, strip leaves from the stems and store in airtight jars.

Freezing   Store sprigs in plastic bags and freeze for up to 6 months. To use, crumble before they thaw.

ROSEMARY BUSHES *will take hard pruning but don't cut into leafless wood, which will not sprout. That's what has happened here.*

ROSEMARY FLOWERS *have a subtle scent, sweeter than the leaves. They are usually blue, but can be pink or white.*

USES

Culinary Fresh, dried, or frozen leaves are used in cooking, marinades, and salad dressings. Fresh leaves are used in vinegars, oils, teas, and butters. Fresh flowers are good in salads or as decorations for puddings and desserts.

Medicinal Rosemary has many uses, including treatment for headaches, digestive problems, and poor circulation. It has anti-bacterial and anti-fungal properties, and can also be used as an insect repellant. *Caution:* do not use in large doses.

Craft It is used in pot-pourris and herb wreaths.

Cosmetic Rosemary hair rinses help control greasy hair.

ROSEMARY AT A GLANCE

Evergreen shrub with fragrant leaves and flowers, much used in cooking and crafts. Hardiness varies: 4 to 23°F (zones 7-9).

JAN		harvest	
FEB		harvest	
MAR	plant	harvest	PARTS USED
APR	plant	harvest	Leaves
MAY	plant	harvest	Flowers
JUN	plant	harvest	
JULY	plant	harvest	USES
AUG	plant	harvest	Culinary
SEPT		harvest	Medicinal
OCT		harvest	Craft
NOV		harvest	Cosmetic
DEC		harvest	Gardening

"SEVEN SEAS" has the richest blue flowers of any rosemary cultivar. Its growth is upright, but less dense and compact than most rosemaries.

SAGE
Salvia

PURPLE SAGE grows here in this wonderfully exuberant herb and vegetable garden, contributing to the subtle harmony of colors. It has cotton lavender growing on its left and a fancy-leaved lettuce on its right.

FEATURES

Sage is an evergreen sub-shrub growing to about 30in. The long, oval, gray-green leaves, velvety in texture, have a slightly bitter, camphor-like taste, while the flowers, borne on spikes in spring, are colored from pink to red, purple, blue, or white, depending on variety. There are many varieties of this beautiful herb. The most common hardy edible types are common or garden sage (*S. officinalis*), purple sage (*S. o.* "Purpurascens"), and golden or variegated sage (*S. officinalis* "Icterina"); and the more tender tricolor sage (*S. o.* "Tricolor"), and pineapple sage (*S. elegans*, syn. *S. rutilans*) are also popular. Sage needs to be replaced every four years or so as the plant becomes woody. Many ornamental sages are also grown in gardens.

CONDITIONS

Aspect Most varieties prefer a sunny, sheltered, well-drained position.

Site Garden beds in which sage is to be grown should have a rich, non-clayish soil. Add lime to acid soils, followed by plenty of organic matter. Good drainage is absolutely essential for sage plants, and so you may find it necessary to raise the beds to at least 8in above the surrounding level.

GROWING METHOD

Sowing and planting Common sage can be grown from seed. Germination takes 2–3 weeks. Plant out when

SAGE AT A GLANCE

Evergreen shrub with silver-gray leaves used in the kitchen for stuffing, herb teas, etc. Hardiness varies: 4 to 23ºF (zones 7-9).

JAN	/	**PARTS USED**	
FEB	/	Leaves	
MAR	plant harvest	Flowers	
APR	plant harvest		
MAY	plant harvest		
JUN	plant harvest	**USES**	
JULY	harvest	Culinary	
AUG	harvest	Medicinal	
SEPT	plant harvest	Cosmetic	
OCT	harvest	Craft	
NOV	/	Gardening	
DEC	/		

SALVIA GRAHAMII, very strong in flavor, is a metre-tall shrub from Mexico, usually grown for its long display of bright flowers.

THE PURPLE-BLUE FLOWERS of common sage go very well with its gray leaves. Trim them off when they fade to keep the garden neat.

THE LEAVES of purple sage fade as they mature, but new shoots continue to add touches of color all summer. Flowers are purple-blue.

all danger of frost is passed, spacing plants 18–24in apart. Cuttings 4in long can be taken in spring or fall. Remove the upper and lower leaves and plant the cuttings in small pots containing a mix of two-thirds coarse sand to one-third compost. Water, then cover plants with a plastic bag to create a mini-greenhouse. Plant out when the cutting has developed roots and new leaves. Sage may also be layered; scarify the lower side of a branch and peg it into the soil to take root.

Feeding	Give a deep soaking once a week in dry spells. Apply a balanced general fertilizer in spring.
Problems	Spider mites can be a problem and will need to be sprayed with an insecticide. If the plant suddenly flops over for no apparent reason this is probably due to bacterial wilt affecting the vascular system. Remove affected plants. Root rot can be avoided by providing good drainage.
Pruning	Prune in spring to keep a compact, bushy shape. Cut off flowerheads as the flowers fade to stop plants from setting seed.

HARVESTING

Picking	Leaves or flowers can be picked at any time as required. For drying purposes, harvest leaves before flowering begins.
Storage	Dry leaves on racks in a cool, airy place and then store them in airtight jars.
Freezing	Leaves can be chopped, packed in freezer bags and then frozen for up to 6 months.

USES

Culinary	Fresh or dried leaves are used extensively as a flavouring in stuffings, marinades, and cooking. The individual fruity flavour of pineapple sage complements citrus fruits and the edible flowers look decorative in salads or as a garnish. Sage leaves of many varieties can be used in herbal teas, vinegars, and herb butters.
Medicinal	Sage has long been highly regarded for its healing properties. Uses include treating colds, sore throats, and mouth ulcers. *Caution:* do not take in large quantities or for extended periods.
Cosmetic	Sage hair rinses, used regularly, will darken gray hair.
Craft	Dried leaves, especially those of purple sage can be added to pot-pourri.
Gardening	It is said that sage can be planted with cabbages to deter cabbage white butterflies.

SAVORY
Satureja

BOTH SAVORIES, winter and summer, are alike in their four-petalled, white flowers. This is the perennial winter savory.

SUMMER SAVORY, being an annual, has to be sown afresh each spring. Many cooks consider it superior in flavour to winter savory.

FEATURES

Summer savory (*S. hortensis*) is an annual plant growing to about 1ft and with small, narrow, grayish leaves that turn slightly purple during summer and early fall. The leaves are attached directly to a pinkish stem, and small white flowers appear on the plant in summer. The winter savories, both the upright (*S. montana*) and the prostrate (*S. montana* "Repens") varieties, are perennial forms and have low-growing (they may reach 1ft) or sprawling habits. Glossy, dark green, lanceolate leaves grow from woody stems in summer and white to lilac flowers are grouped in terminal spikes.

CONDITIONS

Aspect
Both varieties of savory prefer to be grown in full sun. They do not like very cold, wet conditions, and winter savory may require some winter protection.

Site
Savories like well-drained, alkaline soils. Use a soil testing kit to see how much lime to add to an acid soil. Summer savory prefers a richer soil and is ideal for container growing; winter savory favours a less rich, rather sandy soil.

GROWING METHOD

Sowing and planting
Sow seeds of summer savory directly into their final garden position in spring, after the weather has warmed up. Lightly cover them with soil and keep the soil around them damp. When the seedlings are established, thin them out to 6in apart and give the plants support by mounding soil round the base. Although it can be grown from seed, winter savory is best propagated by cuttings and root division done during either the spring or the fall. Remove the upper and lower leaves of 4–5in long cuttings and insert the trimmed stems into a mixture of two-thirds coarse sand and one-third compost. Water the container and cover it with plastic supported on a wire or bamboo frame to make a mini-greenhouse effect. Plant the seedlings out when new leaves appear and a root structure has developed. Pieces of the divided root of the parent plant can be potted up and grown on and later these can be transplanted into the open garden.

Feeding
Water these plants regularly although both summer and winter savories are able to tolerate dry conditions. Mulch winter savory in winter and spring and give a dressing of a balanced general fertilizer in spring.

Problems
Savories are not worried by pests or diseases to

THE ANCIENT ROMANS considered savory to be the most delightfully fragrant of all herbs: the poet Virgil sang its praises.

WINTER SAVORY is so called because it is available in winter when summer savory dies off—but you can, of course, eat it in summer too.

any great extent with the exception of root rot, which sometimes can affect the winter varieties. Good drainage is essential for these plants.

Pruning Winter savory can be pruned in fall after it has finished flowering, but leaving it unpruned will leave top growth to protect the shoots below. It can be pruned in early spring—this will also provide cuttings from which you can grow new plants.

HARVESTING

Picking Fresh leaves of both summer and winter varieties can be picked at any time for immediate use or for drying.

Storage Dry leaves in a cool, airy space and then store them in airtight jars.

Freezing Pack sprigs in freezer bags and freeze for up to 6 months.

USES

Culinary Summer savory has a peppery flavour and is called the "bean herb" as it complements beans and other vegetables. It is also used in herb vinegars and butters. Winter savory is

stronger and coarser and has a more piney taste: use it with game meats and terrines. Either summer or winter savory can be used to make savory tea.

Medicinal Summer savory is said to be good for the digestion, for the treatment of stings, and as a stimulant.

SAVORY AT A GLANCE

Both summer and winter savory have strong flavours and are used in cooking. Hardy to 4 to 14°F (zones 7-8).

JAN		harvest	PARTS USED
FEB		harvest	Leaves
MAR	plant	harvest	
APR	plant	harvest	
MAY	plant	harvest	USES
JUN		harvest	Culinary
JULY		harvest	Medicinal
AUG		harvest	
SEPT	plant	harvest	
OCT		harvest	
NOV		harvest	
DEC		harvest	

THYME
Thymus

A GARDEN SEAT surrounded by a collection of thymes makes a fragrant resting place. Position the creeping thyme (Thymus serpyllum) in front of the seat as it can be trodden on. Thyme has several cultivars, with white, pink, or magenta flowers in spring.

FEATURES

Thyme is one of the most common of garden herbs, and very many varieties are grown. Most thymes are low, creeping plants although some will grow to 10–12in. The shape of the bush and the color and aroma of the leaves depends on the variety. The leaves are evergreen in shades of green, silver, and gold, and small pink or sometimes white flowers are produced in early summer. Not all thymes are used in cooking, the most commonly used varieties including lemon-scented thyme (*T. x citriodorus*), caraway thyme (*T. herba-barona*), common garden thyme (*T. vulgaris*), orange thyme (*T. vulgaris* "Fragrantissimus"), and silver posie thyme (*T. vulgaris* "Silver Posie"). Thyme plants are perennials but usually need replacing every two or three years.

CONDITIONS

Aspect   Prefers full sun or partial shade.
Site   Prefers a light, well-drained, not too rich soil, ideally neutral or slightly alkaline, and kept on the dry side. Adding compost will help keep the soil friable. The soil should not be too acid, if necessary add lime.

THYME AT A GLANCE

Common garden herbs, thymes are popular not only for cooking but also as garden plants. Hardy to 4°F or below (zone 7).

JAN		harvest	PARTS USED
FEB		harvest	Leaves
MAR	plant	harvest	Flowers
APR	plant	harvest	Sprigs
MAY	plant	harvest	
JUN	plant	harvest	
JULY		harvest	USES
AUG		harvest	Culinary
SEPT	plant	harvest	Medicinal
OCT		harvest	Craft
NOV		harvest	Gardening
DEC		harvest	

GROWING METHOD

Sowing and planting Thymes can be propagated from seed, but this tends to give inferior plants, and named varieties should be propagated by cuttings, division, or layering. If seed is used, sow in spring and take care not to overwater as the seedlings are prone to damping off. Dividing mature plants is the most successful method of propagation. During spring or summer, gently lift the parent plant, cut it into two or three sections, each with good roots, and replant elsewhere in the garden. Cuttings taken in spring or summer and layering are also satisfactory methods of propagation.

Feeding Do not overwater. Thymes prefer a dryish soil. Water adequately in dry spells. No fertilizer needed.

Problems Spider mites or aphids can affect this herb. Treat with a recommended insecticidal spray. Root rot will set in if the soil is waterlogged.

Pruning Prune or clip to prevent woodiness. Trim after flowering to prevent plants becoming straggly.

HARVESTING

Picking Fresh leaves and flowers can be picked as required or the whole plant can be cut back to within 2in of the ground in summer.

Storage Leaves are dried on the stem by hanging branches in a warm, airy place. Branches are then stripped and stored in airtight jars.

Freezing Pack in small airtight containers or freezer bags; can be frozen for up to 6 months.

USES

Culinary Thyme is a classic component of the French bouquet garni. Varieties of thyme add special, individual flavours to many dishes. Both leaves and flowers can be eaten fresh in salads or used as garnishes or as a flavouring to honey, vinegars, stuffings, butters, or teas.

Medicinal Thyme has strong antiseptic properties and is used to treat sore throats and as a mouthwash. *Caution:* avoid during pregnancy.

Craft Can be added to pot-pourris and herb sachets.

Gardening Thymes can be grown for their decorative effect as their low, matting habit makes them excellent edging or rockery plants.

"SILVER POSIE", a small, sprawling shrub with white variegated leaves and abundant pale flowers in spring, here offers scent to the passer-by.

ANCIENT GREEKS AND ROMANS considered thyme honey the finest of all, and many modern connoisseurs of honey agree with them.

COMMON THYME, Thymus vulgaris, here sprawls over a carpet of creeping thyme, sometimes called "Shakespeare's thyme".

WOOLLY THYME is almost prostrate in habit, its leaves covered in gray fur. The flowers are pale pink but not very abundant.

VALERIAN
Valeriana officinalis

FEATURES

Valerian is a tall, spreading hardy perennial, growing to about 3–5ft in height. It is native to Europe and Asia where it is found in grassland and damp meadows, close to streams. It has finely divided mid-green leaves and heads of small white or pale pink flowers that are produced in early summer. Both cats and rats are said to find the smell of valerian attractive, and it is said that the Pied Piper of Hamelin carried the root in order to charm the rats away!

CONDITIONS

Aspect Valerian will grow in full sun or deep shade, as long as the roots are cool. The plants may need to be staked if they are grown in exposed positions.

Site Valerian is tolerant of most soils, but prefers moist conditions.

GROWING METHOD

Sowing and planting Valerian can be propagated by division in spring or fall, replanting the divisions immediately into well prepared ground. The seed can be sown in spring, directly where it is to grow. But for more reliable results sow the seed under glass in trays of seed compost. Do not cover the seeds as this will delay germination. When the young plants are large enough to handle they should be planted out in the garden approximately 2–3ft apart. When grown in good conditions, valerian will self-seed.

Feeding Keep well watered as valerian prefers moist conditions. Mulch lightly in spring and also apply a dressing of a balanced general fertilizer in spring.

VALERIAN AT A GLANCE

A tall but undistinguished, strong-smelling herb, with powerful healing properties. Fully hardy to 4°F or below (zone 7).

JAN	/	
FEB	/	
MAR	plant 🖐	
APR	plant 🖐	
MAY	plant 🖐	
JUN	/	
JULY	/	
AUG	/	
SEPT	plant 🖐	harvest 🌾
OCT	plant 🖐	harvest 🌾
NOV	/	
DEC	/	

PARTS USED
Roots

USES
Medicinal
Cosmetic
Gardening

IN THE TWO WORLD WARS an infusion made from valerian was used to treat shell-shock and nervous disorders.

Problems Generally free from pests and diseases.

Pruning Cut valerian back after flowering to prevent self-seeding. The top growth can be cut down in fall.

HARVESTING

Picking Dig up the roots in late fall, when the plants are in their second or third year of growth.

Storage To dry, cut the roots into thin slices and dry in an oven at 120–40°F, turning frequently.

Freezing Not suitable for freezing

USES

Medicinal Valerian has been used for many centuries for its healing properties. Traditionally, the root has been used for its sedative and anti-spasmodic effects, and for the treatment of a wide range of conditions, including nervous conditions, insomnia, headaches, and exhaustion. *Caution:* Do not take valerian in large doses or for extended periods of time. This herb is best taken only under expert supervision.

Cosmetic Despite its rather unpleasant aroma, valerian has been used in perfumery.

Gardening Nowadays, valerian is used more in the garden than for its medicinal properties. Although not the most decorative of herbs, it is useful to add height at the back of the border. It is also said to be a good companion plant, encouraging the growth of nearby vegetables and other plants by stimulating earthworm activity and increasing phosphorus availability.

VIOLET
Viola odorata

FEATURES

Viola odorata, the sweet violet, is a low-growing perennial just 6in tall with a wider spread. The dark green leaves are roundish or kidney-shaped with scalloped edges. Small, very sweetly fragrant flowers appear on short stalks in late winter and early spring. They are usually violet in color but there are also mauve, blue, and white forms. Violets spread rapidly by creeping roots.

CONDITIONS

Aspect
Sun in winter and bright dappled shade in summer are ideal. Flowering is disappointing in too much shade.

Site
Violets tolerate most soils but do best in deep soil rich in well-rotted organic matter, preferably from composted fallen leaves. Soil must drain freely but it must also remain moist between showers or watering.

GROWING METHOD

Sowing and planting
Violets are easily established by division. Lift immediately after flowering and separate the cylindrical runners. Each division should have its own roots but roots usually form later if they are absent. Plant so that the runners are firmly in contact with the soil but not buried. Scatter seed, collected from ripe but unopened seed pods, where it is to grow or, for better germination, onto trays of seed compost. Cover lightly, keep moist, and place trays in a bright but shady and cool place. The seedlings can be transplanted when they are big enough to handle.

Feeding
Once established, violets can usually get by on rain where it falls regularly, as long as the soil conditions suit them. If they never go dry for long periods, violets will flourish. Place a mulch of well-rotted manure around plants, but not over the root crown, each spring (this can be hard to do in a densely planted area), or sprinkle a ration of a balanced general fertilizer over the plants in spring. Once or twice during summer, water over the plants with a liquid, organic fertilizer or seaweed-based soil conditioner.

Problems
Lay bait for slugs and snails, which chew holes in the leaves and destroy flowers. Spider mites and aphids can also damage plants by sucking sap. Spider mites should be treated with an insecticide as soon as they are seen. Aphids are easily controlled with low toxicity pyrethrum, garlic, or fatty acid sprays. If the plants fail to flower, the cause may be too much or too heavy shade or too much high nitrogen fertilizer.

Pruning
No pruning is necessary, but if flowers fail to form cut all the leaves off in early winter to encourage spring bloom.

VIOLETS are notoriously shy: if your flowers hide, cut plants back in winter so the flowers are displayed against fresh, not-too-tall growth.

HARVESTING

Picking
Pick flowers as they open and leaves as needed.

Storage
Flowers may be crystallized for later use.

Freezing
Not suitable for freezing.

USES

Culinary
Crystallized flowers are used to decorate cakes or eaten as a sweet treat. A sweet syrup and a honey can be made with fresh flowers.

Medicinal
An infusion of the leaves and flowers can be taken to relieve the symptoms of colds, etc.

Craft
Flowers are used in pot-pourris, floral waters.

Gardening
Violets are a very desirable groundcover in partly shaded areas. Posies of cut flowers will fill a room with fragrance.

VIOLET AT A GLANCE

Pretty, low-growing perennial with very sweetly fragrant flowers in late winter. Hardy to 4°F or below (zone 7).

JAN	/		PARTS USED
FEB		harvest	Flowers
MAR		harvest	Leaves
APR	plant	harvest	
MAY	plant	harvest	
JUN		harvest	USES
JULY		harvest	Culinary
AUG		harvest	Medicinal
SEPT	plant		Craft
OCT	/		Gardening
NOV	/		
DEC	/		

WORMWOOD
Artemisia

FEATURES

There are many species of artemisia, all with aromatic foliage and pleasant, but not particularly showy, yellow flowers. Wormwood, *A. absinthium*, is an extremely bitter plant with finely divided leaves. The related *A. abrotanum*, is also known as southernwood, or lad's love. There are many ornamental garden artemisias. Sizes and habits, however, vary enormously between species, some being ground-huggers, others being medium-sized, upright shrubs. Leaf shape and color varies, too, and combinations of different artemisias can make very attractive plantings with a silver and gray theme.

CONDITIONS

Aspect   Full sun is essential, as is an open position to ensure good air movement around the plant.

Site   Grows best in moderately fertile, very well-drained soil that contains a small proportion of well-rotted organic matter.

GROWING METHOD

Sowing and planting   Wormwood can be started from cuttings taken in late spring and rooted in small pots of moist, sandy potting mix kept in a bright but not fully sunny spot. It may also be grown from seed sown in spring just beneath the surface, either where plants are to grow or in pots or trays of seed compost.

Feeding   Very little water is needed except in very dry summers. A mulch of well-rotted manure or compost laid under and beyond the plant's foliage canopy (but not right up against the trunk) is usually all the feeding required. Otherwise, sprinkle a handful of general fertilizer under the outer edge of the foliage canopy in early spring.

DESPITE ITS BITTERNESS, some artemisias were thought be be a potent aphrodisiac—hence the other name of "lad's love"

Problems   Artemisias may sometimes suffer from blackfly. This can be treated with a liquid horticultural soap.

Pruning   Cut herbaceous species of artemisia back to ground level in middle to late fall or after frosts have started. Shrubby types may be sheared all over in early spring to make them more compact. Cut back hard in spring if the shrub has become too big and/or untidy.

HARVESTING

Picking   Leaves are harvested by picking whole stems on a hot, dry morning in summer.

Storage   Tie stems together and hang them upside down in a dim, airy place to dry. Dried leaves may be stored in airtight jars.

Freezing   Not suitable for freezing.

USES

Culinary   Although it is extremely bitter, wormwood was traditionally used to flavour wines and aperitifs such as absinthe and vermouth.

Medicinal   *Caution:* different parts of different types of artemisia have various medicinal uses but do not take any of these herbs without the supervision of a trained herbalist.

Craft   Wormwood has insect repellent properties and it can be used to make "moth-repellent" sachets.

Gardening   Wormwood, as all artemisias, has beautiful foliage and a pleasant aroma. A strong infusion of the leaves sprayed onto vegetables or ornamental plants repels caterpillars and snails; just having the plants nearby will drive some pests away.

WORMWOOD AT A GLANCE

Perennial herb with decorative, finely divided silvery foliage, traditionally used to flavour absinthe. Hardy to 4°F (zone 7).

			PARTS USED
JAN	/		Leaves
FEB	/		
MAR	/		
APR	plant ✣		
MAY	plant ✣		USES
JUN	plant ✣	harvest ✤	(Culinary)
JULY		harvest ✤	(Medicinal)
AUG	plant ✣	harvest ✤	Craft
SEPT	plant ✣		Gardening
OCT	/		
NOV	/		
DEC	/		

YARROW
Achillea millefolium

FEATURES

Yarrow is a low, mat-forming perennial that has dense, dark green, fern-like foliage. Flat heads of small flowers appear on top of tall, mostly leafless stems during the later summer months and in fall. They may be white, pink, or yellow. This vigorous grower is well suited to growing in rockeries or on banks. Depending on the soil and situation in which it grows it can vary in height from 2in to 24in.

CONDITIONS

Aspect   Grow in full sun or light shade.

Site   Well-drained, not-too-rich soil is ideal. Plants grow lax, flower poorly and die young in over-rich soil. They will rot if soil stays wet for long periods after rain or watering.

GROWING METHOD

Sowing and planting   Establish yarrow in new areas by dividing the roots of mature plants in early spring or fall. It may also be started from seed sown in spring in trays of moist seed compost. Just cover the seed and place the containers in a warm, bright but shaded spot until germination is complete. Gradually expose containers to more and more sun, and then transplant seedlings into their final site when they are big enough.

Feeding   Water deeply but only occasionally. Yarrow does not require constant moisture as it has deep roots that will find water at lower levels in the soil. No feeding is necessary.

Problems   No particular problems.

Pruning   Cut plants to the ground in middle to late fall or after frosts have started. New growth will appear in spring.

YARROW used to be grown in English churchyards to mock the dead, who supposedly were there because they hadn't eaten their yarrow broth.

HARVESTING

Picking   Harvest leafy stems and flowers on a dry morning when plants are in the early stages of full bloom. Tie them together and hang them upside down in a dry, dim, airy place. If they are to be used to make dried arrangements, hang each flower stem separately.

Storage   When the stems are dry, remove the flowers and leaves and break the leaves and stems into small pieces. Store these in airtight jars.

Freezing   Not suitable for freezing.

USES

Culinary   Young, small leaves have a slightly bitter flavour. Add a few chopped young leaves to salads or sandwiches for a piquant taste.

Medicinal   Herbal tea made from the dried stems, leaves, and flowers is a good general pick-me-up, blood cleanser, tonic for the kidneys, fever treatment and, reputedly, a slimming aid. Also used externally as wound healer.

Cosmetic   An infusion can be used as a herbal skin cleanser.

Craft   Flowers can be used in dried floral arrangements.

Gardening   Although considered a weed in lawns, yarrow is an excellent companion plant, increasing the disease resistance of nearby plants and increasing their flavour and fragrance. It has been called the "plant doctor". Add it to the compost heap to speed rotting.

YARROW AT A GLANCE

Although considered a weed by many, yarrow is an excellent companion plant and herbal tonic. Hardy to 4°F or below (zone 7).

JAN	/	
FEB	/	
MAR	plant	
APR	plant	
MAY	plant	harvest
JUN	harvest	
JULY	harvest	
AUG	harvest	
SEPT	plant	
OCT	/	
NOV	/	
DEC	/	

PARTS USED
Leaves
Stems
Flowers

USES
Culinary
Medicinal
Cosmetic
Craft
Gardening

GROWING CACTI

Although they are part of the large family of succulents, cacti are unlike any other group of plants. With distinguishing features such as ribbed surfaces, waxy coating and, of course, their spines, cacti deserve a special place in any creative display, invariably being grown in pots and used as focal points that are easily admired.

Cacti are magnificent plants giving architectural shapes of all kinds from tiny round balls to enormous tree-like growths, the kind of thing you see in cowboy films, and often superb flowers. In many cases the flowers only open at night, and can be wonderfully scented. Cacti need to be grown in pots, at least in winter, when the amount of drinking water they are given is strictly controlled. Too much is inevitably fatal. If they are not too heavy, pot-grown plants can be moved outside in summer, making the focal point in a bed of architectural plants. They can even be taken out of their pots, and placed in, for example, a special gravel bed, where there is excellent drainage. Alternatively, they can be grown in a special display bed in a large conservatory or greenhouse. Take care though not to confuse epiphytic cacti with the desert kind. The former tend to grow high up in trees, under the leafy canopy, in shady conditions. The latter demand day-long bright light.

KEY TO AT A GLANCE TABLES

PLANTING

FLOWERING

At a glance charts are your quick guide.
For full information, consult the accompanying text.

LEFT: A fine collection of well-grown cactus shows some of the extensive range of these fascinating plants. Variations in shapes and heights of the rounded barrel types with the vertical column cactus adds interest to the display.

GROWING CACTI

What is a cactus? What is a succulent?

A cactus is a succulent plant—but not all succulent plants are cacti. Succulent plants are xerophytes, plants able to escape or endure prolonged drought conditions. Succulents have the capacity to store water in swollen stems and roots, while some withdraw into the soil or shed their foliage in times of stress. Although succulent plants and cacti do share some characteristics, cacti have certain features that distinguish them from other plant families, including other forms of succulent plants.

FEATURES OF CACTI

Plant structure

Cacti are mainly round or cylindrical in shape, with a ribbed surface that allows for shrinkage as water is lost from the plant. The ribbed edges of cactus plants expose less surface area to the sun, which helps to reduce moisture loss. Waxy coatings on their outer surfaces also cut down moisture loss in extreme heat. Cacti have sharp, sometimes horny spines that deter animals from grazing and also provide some shade for the body of the plant. Cactus spines are in fact modified

GOLDEN BARREL CACTI dominate this carefully planned landscape of cactuses and succulents. These plants are growing in raised beds to ensure that they have perfect drainage.

leaves that have evolved to cut down moisture loss in the usually dry conditions of their native environment. There is a considerable range of spine types and sizes.

In cacti the breathing pores (stomates) enabling gas exchange between the plant and the atmosphere are located deep inside the plant walls and tend to be less numerous than those of many other plants. These stomates generally open only at night, avoiding water evaporation in the heat of the day. All cacti possess areoles, which are small woolly cushions from which emerge the spines and flower buds. These are found on top of warty protrusions known as tubercles. Many cacti have jointed parts that can be shed from the plant; these strike roots as they touch the ground and so aid in the distribution and continuity of the species.

Flowers

Cactus flowers are like jewels, glorious and showy, but they are also very short lived. Many last only one or two days while others are nocturnal, opening in the middle of the night and fading before dawn. The flowers have a silky or satiny texture and come in all colours except a true blue, although violet and purple are well represented. Many cacti have flowers in shades of pink, red, or yellow. After the flowers have been pollinated, brightly colored fruits form—these are usually red and very long lasting. In their native habitats, many cacti are pollinated by birds, especially humming-birds, while the night-flowering types are pollinated by moths, bats, or other nocturnal creatures.

Types of cacti

Cacti are roughly grouped into three types: round or barrel cacti such as the golden barrel (*Echinocactus* species) and *Mammillaria* species; elongated cacti such as column cactus (*Cereus* species) and silver torch (*Cleistocactus* species); and jointed cacti such as *Opuntia* species and crab cactus (*Schlumbergera* species).

The cristate or crested cacti are the result of mutations that cause the growing tip of a shoot to broaden out into a band, forming strange, tortuous shapes. These mutations may be due to genetic changes or they may be due to the plant suffering unusual stress.

Native habitat

True cacti, almost without exception, are native to the Americas. Although not all cacti have their origins in real deserts, the greatest number of species occur in the low rainfall areas of the south-western United States and Mexico.

Cacti in these regions of desert plains endure scorching heat by day and often freezing nights. Sporadic rainfall of generally less than 10in per annum allows the plants to store just enough water to survive. Heavy dews and the occasional snowfall augment the water supply. Snow insulates plants against cold and, when it melts, the water is directed to the plant roots.

The next largest group of species originates in the dry areas of central and eastern Brazil. Some cacti come from quite high elevations where conditions are still very harsh, but where the daytime temperatures do not reach the extremes of the true deserts.

On rocky slopes of mountains and high plateaux, the soil is often poor and the water drains away rapidly. Plants are exposed to intense sunlight and freezing night temperatures, high wind and often snow. Small cacti find a foothold among rocks and crevices that hold just enough water for survival while affording some shelter from wind. Many cacti from these habitats have dense woolly spines that provide protection from both searing sun and intense cold. Lower down the slope, large column cacti branching from heavy bases start to be seen. These and the large barrel types are able to withstand exposure to very strong winds.

A few species of cactus such as *Epiphyllum* and *Schlumbergera* are native to humid jungle environments where they grow as epiphytes on trees and sometimes on rocks. Although adapted to low light, they can also tolerate dry seasons. Some remain high in the tree canopy where there is more light while others start lower down, scrambling up as they grow towards the light.

Human use

A number of cacti have long been used by humans as food and in medicines. The fruit of some species is eaten fresh, cooked, or dried. Indian fig (*Opuntia ficus-indica*) is probably the best known of these edible cacti, but the fruits of some of the hedgehog cacti (*Echinocereus* species) and the tiny fruits of some *Mammillaria* species are also considered delicacies. In Mexico, the aromatic fruits of *Ferocactus wislizenii* are stewed, candied, and made into sweets, giving this species the common name of candy cactus. However, it is not recommended that you taste any part of a cactus unless you are certain that it is an Indian fig or another known edible variety. Many cacti contain alkaloids, which can be extremely damaging to health. On the other hand, heart-stimulant drugs are made from species of the cactus *Selenicereus*, which is widely cultivated both in the United States and Europe for this purpose.

Growing cacti under glass

It is very hard trying to group cacti with other plants; somehow they never look right. They are generally best arranged together, possibly with some excellent succulents. Fortunately, cacti come in such a wide range of shapes, from tiny quirky balls to grand theatrical vertical pillars, that you can always create a lively, contrasting mix.

The best displays of cacti are invariably in a large glasshouse where you can create a small scene from say South America. This gives you the space to plant the cacti reasonably well apart so that they can be seen from all angles, and with space to the front so that you are not endangered when they have got sharp, vicious spines. The cactus' shape is often so striking that its poor flowers seem unimportant.

Generally speaking, a dry environment must be provided, especially in winter, with bright light and excellent drainage. But when buying a cactus do try and find out where it comes from, so that you can provide the correct growing conditions. Unless you are very lucky, that almost certainly means growing them under glass, indoors or in a conservatory, where you can manufacture their special needs. And these needs mean either replicating desert or jungle conditions.

Established desert cacti grown in pots need three parts John Innes No. 2 with one part grit, well mixed together giving an open, free-draining soil. In summer they need watering (letting them dry out between each drink) and feeding as much as any thriving plant. Use special cactus feed or tomato fertilizer to encourage flowering. Over winter keep the plants dormant at about 45°F, only occasionally watering to prevent them from completely drying out and shrivelling. In fact over-watering is the commonest cause of death. When in doubt, do not water. Good light does though remain essential.

Strangely enough, some cacti prefer steamy, jungle-like conditions, which are harder to provide. Such cacti tend to be epiphytes which grow high in the branches of trees, not exposed in the open ground. You can still grow them in pots but you must provide a winter temperature nearly 50°F higher than that for the desert kind, with year-round

A PROFUSION of clear yellow flowers conceals the whole top of this Trichocereus huascha (*previously called* Echinopsis).

TERRACOTTA POTS make ideal containers for growing cacti and succulents. Displayed at different levels, all plants can be easily seen.

humidity. The key to success remains open, free-draining compost, and in summer constant shade from strong sunlight (in the wild they would grow well protected by the tree canopy). A summer feed will boost the show of flowers.

Growing high up, these cacti tend to send out tumbling, trailing stems and they make good ingredients for a hanging basket. The Christmas cactus (see page 224) is an astonishing sight in full flower, especially when it is a flashy scarlet. Most people grow it as a pot plant on a table, and though fine, it is never as good a spectacle as when seen from below.

GROWING CACTI IN CONTAINERS

Cacti are easy-care potted plants and can be grown as single specimens or combined in shallow bowls to make a miniature cactus garden. Miniature cactus gardens can be of great interest. You could feature a mixture of several small-growing species or you may want to display a single fine, clustering plant that has been increasing over the years. Cacti are ideal for growing on balconies or patios as they do not mind drying out and appreciate shelter from the rain.

Cactus plants definitely look most attractive when grown in terracotta pots or glazed ceramic pots; in the glazed pot range, the ones decorated in blues and greens seem to suit the cactus best. When you are choosing a pot for an individual specimen, try to find one that is not much larger than the plant's rootball.

HANDLING A CACTUS USING FOLDED PAPER

WHEN HANDLING CACTI, use a band of cardboard or folded paper held firmly around the cactus to avoid the spines.

Cacti grown in containers must be potted into a very sharp-draining mix. For a small number of pots, it may be best to purchase a cactus mix from your local nursery. If you are potting a large number of plants or filling large pots, it will probably be more economical to buy the mix in bulk (if possible), or to buy the ingredients for making your own mix: this should include bags of special horticultural sand or grit (avoid builder's sand) and John Innes No. 2. Though you may think that desert cacti in particular grow in sand alone, that is not true. They need rather more soil than added drainage material. A ratio of three parts of soil to one of grit is fine.

Pots can be displayed on purpose-built stands, on pedestals, or on the ground. Pots to be put on the ground should not be in direct contact with the soil and must be elevated very slightly to allow air to circulate under the pot base. You can purchase "pot feet" or simply use pieces of broken terracotta or stone to elevate your pot.

Potted cacti team well with Mexican and Mediterranean style decor, for example, black wrought-iron furniture or rustic unpainted timber pieces. You could extend this decorating idea by adding some feature wall tiles.

Growing cacti outdoors in summer
Like most pot plants, cacti like to stand outside during the summer. Alternatively, they can be tapped out of the pot and planted in a special bed which is very free draining. This guarantees them excellent light levels while they are in full growth and ensures that they have plenty of fresh air. It also avoids the danger of baking in an inadequately ventilated or poorly shaded glasshouse. The chances of being attacked by greenhouse pests is also reduced. Overall, a spell outside gives healthier, sturdier plants.

What is more, creating a special group of cacti in a gravel garden which sets off their shapes, or on a rockery, adds style and interest to your garden. If you are growing the taller, column cacti try moving them outside before they become too big and then experiment with uplighting them at night. In a bare, minimalist garden they make quite an impact. It is absolutely essential to keep all spiny cacti well away from sites where children play.

HANDLING CACTI

To avoid injury from the spines when handling a cactus, use a band made of cardboard or folded newspaper. Place the band around the plant to steady it and hold firmly where the two pieces come together. This should prevent your hands from coming into contact with the spines and should not damage the cactus. You should, of course, also wear sturdy gloves. When handling larger specimens of cactus plants, you may need another person to help you. In this case, you should each use a paper band, or wooden or plastic tongs such as kitchen tongs, to lift and move the cactus. It is a difficult, heavy job to move large cactus plants but careful planning before planting—deciding on the new, permanent location of your cactus and preparing the planting hole—should help you to avoid problems in the future.

WATERING

It is important to remember that at any time of the year, cacti should only be watered when the soil or potting mix has dried out completely. Withholding water from plants may result in slower growth, but this is better than killing the plants through

RICHLY COLOURED SILKY FLOWERS on a cactus can look greatly at odds with the spines. In fact the flowers are often short-lived, though flowering reliably occurs each year. Two of the most reliable flowering kind are Rebutia and Mammillaria species.

watering too much or too often. Plants watered too often while they are dormant and unable to use or store water will rot and die. Large plants, because of their greater ability to store water, will need watering much less often than smaller plants. Potted plants will need watering more often than plants in the ground, especially during warmer weather, and the larger the container the less often it will need watering.

Until you feel confident about the frequency of watering needed, it is a good idea to dig into the soil or growing mix with a stick, a pencil or a thin bamboo stake to check the degree of dryness. In small pots, up to 4in diameter, the top 1–2in must be dry before more water is applied. In a 8in pot, the soil should be dry at a depth of 3in or more. Plants that have just been repotted should not be watered for at least a week afterwards. With any cactus, enough water should be applied at any one watering to thoroughly saturate the soil or mix. The frequency of watering will, of course, depend on the weather. If it is very hot and windy, plants will dry out much faster than they would in either warm, calm weather or cold conditions. In cold weather, plants may need watering only every 4–6 weeks or even less often, while in very hot weather they may need watering every few days.

Overhead watering will not hurt the cacti as it also washes dust off their surfaces, but do not do this late in the day, especially in humid districts, as water remaining on the plant overnight may predispose it to rotting. (You should note that some succulents should not be watered this way because of the waxy bloom on their foliage.) Alternatively, you should simply water the soil surface using a watering can or sit the whole pot in a container of water and allow the moisture to be drawn up from below. If available, rainwater is ideal for cacti. Cacti do not like alkaline water, so if your water supply is known to be alkaline, it may be worth collecting rainwater.

FERTILIZING

The most convenient method of fertilizing cacti is to use granular, slow-release fertilizers. A formulation containing trace elements, but low in nitrogen, is ideal. These fertilizers should be applied in spring to feed the plants slowly throughout their growing season. Follow the label directions and do not exceed the recommended amount. Feeding when plants are dormant may damage them and is a waste of fertilizer, which only starts to be released once soil temperatures rise. In the garden, you can use pelleted poultry manure as an alternative, but do not be too heavy handed.

PROPAGATION

Growing from seed

Seed is best sown in spring. Cactus seed should be sprinkled or placed on the surface of a seed-raising mix and lightly covered with the mix. You can mix very small seeds with fine sand for a more even sowing or put the seeds in a cone of paper from which you can gently shake them. Seed may germinate in a few days or a few weeks depending on the species. Keep the growing mix damp, but not soggy, by standing the pot in a container of water to draw up moisture, and then drain off any excess water from the seed-raising pot. Overhead watering will dislodge the seed. Once the seed has germinated, it may be several months before the seedlings are large enough to handle and pot up individually.

Although many home-grown cactus will not set viable seed because of the lack of suitable pollinators, it is possible to hand pollinate sometimes with good results. Use a small paintbrush to collect the pollen from one flower then gently

PROPAGATING BY CUTTINGS

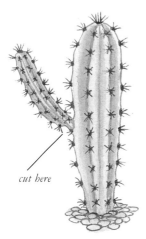

1. TAKE CACTUS cuttings by cleanly removing an offshoot from the parent plant.

cut here

2. THE BASE of the cutting should be slanted towards the central core of the stem. Dry the cutting for a few days before planting.

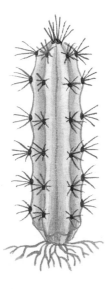

3. ROOTS are formed at the centre stem core. The amount of time taken to form roots varies with the species of cactus and the season of the year.

dust this into the centre of another flower. Pollen should go on to the stigma which is the organ in the centre of the flower surrounded by numerous pollen-bearing stamens.

It is fairly easy to collect seed from cacti with fleshy fruits. Once the fruit is fully coloured and ripe, pick off the fruit, slit open and squeeze out the seeds which should be cleaned and dried before sowing. It is more difficult to obtain the seed of cacti which normally shed their seed as the fruits dry and split. As the fruit is nearing maturity, a paper or mesh bag can be tied around the fruit to catch the seeds as they are dispersed from the maturing fruit.

Growing from cuttings

Some cacti form numerous offsets, which you can remove and pot up separately to start a new plant. Cut away any offsets from the parent plant by pushing a sharp knife down into the soil to sever any underground joints.

Some cacti can be propagated from cuttings of the plant, which must be taken with a very sharp, clean knife or pruning shears. You should take cactus cuttings in spring, as the new growth begins. The cuttings or offsets with wounds must be allowed to dry for a few days, or a few weeks if necessary, until the cut area is completely dry and callused over. Cuttings can be taken from side shoots or even the head of the main stem. Slant the cut towards the core of the stem and allow the cutting to dry; this should encourage roots to develop from the stem core. When the cuttings have dried, insert them into very coarse sand. Plants should not be watered until roots start to form. The time that it takes for this to happen varies from one to six months.

Propagating by grafting

Grafting of cacti is usually done simply to produce unusual effects. Different coloured cacti may be joined together, or a barrel-shaped cactus may be grafted on the top of a column type. A flat graft is the easiest technique to use. Simply cut both the understock and the scion (the piece to be grafted on to the top of the understock) straight across, join the two sections neatly, and hold them in place with rubber bands or fine, strong cactus spines. At the optimum time of year— mid-spring to early fall—the graft may "take" within two weeks. Cleft and side grafts are also used, but these are not so easy for beginners.

BUYING A CACTUS

Many of the larger garden centers and nurseries will sell good-quality cactus plants that have been obtained from specialist growers. These are often small, reasonably priced plants, which will introduce you to the amazing range of cactus forms and become the beginning of a collection. Some specialist cactus nurseries sell direct to the public or by mail order. Garden centers and specialist growers are generally able to give you the right advice about the care and culture of your new plants. Novelty cactus are also on sale from florists or department stores, but the sales staff in these places are not, as a rule, qualified to give correct advice on cultivation.

Any cactus you buy must look clean and firm, and there must be no soft or decaying areas anywhere on the plant. It should not look pale or elongated, which would indicate that the cactus may have been kept for too long in poor light. The cactus must also be free of insect pests such as mealybugs, which resemble small, white, sticky patches of cotton wool and are often found between the spines.

WHAT CAN GO WRONG?

Cacti can be attacked by a range of sap-sucking insects such as aphids, mealybugs, scale insects, thrips, and two-spotted mites. Healthy, vigorous plants grown in good conditions are much less likely to succumb to an attack of these pests.

If your plants are attacked—and if you cannot manually remove the pests—you may need to spray with a registered insecticide. You will sometimes be able to dislodge mealybugs and scale insects with a cotton bud dipped in methylated spirit. Overhead watering will often discourage mites and aphids.

Soft rots and root decay are almost impossible to treat if they have become well established. If this is the case, cut away the rotted section with a sharp, clean knife to expose any healthy tissue, remove a healthy section of the plant, and then dry it and treat it as a cutting. Dusting the exposed clean tissue of the cactus with sulfur is sometimes also helpful. Most rots are caused by overwatering, especially when plants are not in active growth. If you are unsure whether or not to water, do not! When you do water, soak the cactus thoroughly and then allow the soil to dry out before you water again.

GLASSHOUSE COLLECTIONS offer a variety of shapes, like this magnificent vertical Euphorbia and Pandanus with pendulous leaves.

PROPAGATING BY GRAFTING

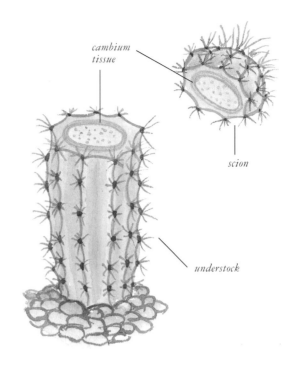

cambium tissue

scion

understock

1. WHEN GRAFTING, is most important to line up the cambium tissue of both the understock and scion to ensure a good graft union.

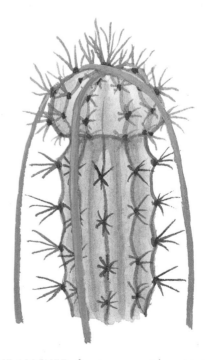

2. ONCE ALIGNED, firm pressure must be maintained. Rubber bands can be used to go right around the graft and the pot, or use fine pins, cactus spines, or toothpicks to hold the graft in place.

APOROCACTUS
Rat's Tail Cactus

APOROCACTUS FLAGELLI *IS ONE of the most common types to be found and is quite easy to grow, it's colorful purple-red blooms adding a touch of vibrant color to the garden in summer.*

FEATURES

Partial Shade

A good group of cacti with its botanical name in dispute; this is now classified as *Aporocactus*. These lovely, epiphytic plants are native to rainforests or damp mountainous areas of tropical and subtropical regions of the Americas where they grow from the branches of trees. Their stems are mainly jointed and flattened, tending to be long and narrow with few if any spines. They are pendulous and branching, bearing scarlet or pink flowers on the tips of the branches in late spring or early summer. These plants are delightful when grown in pots or hanging baskets which can be used for indoor decoration while the cactus is in flower. Where temperatures fall below 50°F they should be grown in a glasshouse.

Varieties: The two most commonly found plants are *Aporocactus flagelliformis* and *A. martianus*. The latter has larger flowers than the former. Appearing in early summer, they are vivid red on gray-green stems. The plant only grows to 5in high, but can spread up to 3ft. *A. flagelliformis* is easier to grow. Its hanging growth may reach 5ft. Its purple-red blooms appear in spring when it makes a terrific sight with its snake-like stems topped by the colorful flowers.

CONDITIONS

Aspect: Being epiphytic, the plants need to be grown with some degree of shade during the day. It is particularly important during the hottest, brightest part of the day. A morning of sun, and afternoon of shade is fine.

Site: Grow in special epiphytic compost. Make sure that it is extremely free-draining.

GROWING METHOD

Propagation: Plants can be grown from seed sown in spring, but are easier to grow from stem cuttings taken in spring or summer.

Feeding: From late spring until late summer, provide a high potash or tomato feed once a month. Exceeding this dose is counter productive.

Problems: Will not thrive in full sun or if overwatered.

FLOWERING

Season: Rat's tail cactuses will flower either in late spring or early summer.

Fruits: Flowers are followed by papery fruits.

APOROCACTUS AT A GLANCE

Dramatic cactuses for a hanging basket, with long trailing stems and bright showy flowers. 43°F min (zone 11).

JAN	/	
FEB	/	
MAR	transplant	☝
APR	repotting	☝
MAY	flowering	✽
JUN	flowering	✽
JULY	/	
AUG	/	
SEPT	/	
OCT	/	
NOV	sow	☝
DEC	/	

RECOMMENDED VARIETIES
Aporocactus flagelliformis
A. martianus

COMPANION PLANTS
Epiphyllum
Hatiora
Schlumbergera
Selenicereus

ASTROPHYTUM
Bishop's Cap

FASTEST GROWING of all species of bishop's cap, Astrophytum ornatum *bears many yellow flowers annually after about five years.*

DEEPLY DEFINED RIBS and white scales around the upper body characterize Astrophytum ornatum, *also known as star cactus.*

FEATURES

Sun

This very small genus originates in Texas and Mexico. The two most sought-after species are virtually spineless and covered in white scales instead. The bishop's cap or bishop's mitre, *Astrophytum myriostigma*, has an unusual dull purple, bluish, or green body that is speckled all over with white scales. In the wild it may be 2ft high and 8in across, but in cultivation it is unlikely to reach melon size—and then only after many years. Its flowers are bright yellow, with the outer petals black tipped. *A. asterias*, known as the sea urchin or sand dollar cactus, is grey-green, slow growing and rarely more than 2–3in high, eventually growing to a width of about 4in. It has spectacular bright yellow flowers with deep red centres.

Varieties   *A. ornatum* has pronounced spines on its very well-defined ribs. It is a cylindrical shape and it grows to about 1ft. During the summer it produces yellow flower. There are many different varieties and hybrids of these popular and attractive species. If you are just starting a collection of astrophytum, it is well worth growing *A. capricorne*, known as the goat's horn cactus. It is quite a small cactus, reaching a height of only about 8in. Its common name was inspired by the bizarre form of its twisted spines which wrap themselves around the cactus instead of sticking up vertically in the usual way. This makes handling the plant quite a problem as its spines tend to get snapped off very easily.

CONDITIONS

Aspect   Plants grow best in full sun, but may need a little shading if grown under glass.
Site   Soil must be very free draining and should contain very little organic matter.

GROWING METHOD

Propagation   Easy to raise from seed sown in spring.
Feeding   Give low-nitrogen liquid plant food in spring and mid-summer or use slow-release granules.
Problems   Overwatering causes them to rot and die.

FLOWERING

Season   Warm spring or summer flowering.
Fruits   Flowers followed by fleshy, ovoid green or red berries with long seeds within.

ASTROPHYTUM AT A GLANCE

There are four species of these slow growing, attractive roundish cactuses that like arid conditions. 50°F min (zone 11).

JAN	/	RECOMMENDED VARIETIES
FEB	/	*Astrophytum asterias*
MAR	/	*A. capricorne*
APR	sow	*A. myriostigma*
MAY	transplant	*A. ornatum*
JUN	flowering	
JULY	flowering	COMPANION PLANTS
AUG	flowering	Echinocactus
SEPT	/	Epostoa
OCT	/	Gymnocalycium
NOV	/	Mammillaria
DEC	/	Rebutia

CEREUS
Column Cactus

THE LARGE AND VERY BEAUTIFUL *flowers of* Cereus uruguayanus *appear after dark and are worth waiting up for.*

THE BLUE-GREEN STEMS *of* Cereus *species are distinctly notched where the areoles and spines emerge.*

FEATURES

Sun

With a diverse range of origins from the West Indies to eastern South America, many of these cactuses are almost tree-like, while most form upright sturdy columns. The best-known species, *Cereus uruguayanus* (syn. *C. peruvianus*), is tree-like and can grow to 10ft or more with a stout, blue-green body notched where spines emerge. The "Monstrose" form makes a jumble of oddly shaped, blue-gray stems. Another tree-like species, *C. validus*, can also reach about 10ft high. Once established, it has pink-tinged white flowers in summer.

C. chalybaeus is a column cactus, often tinged blue or purple, with well-defined ribs bearing spines that mature to black. Its flowers are also white with the outer petals magenta or red.

CEREUS AT A GLANCE

An excellent choice if you like tall, quick growing vertical cactuses, many with beautiful, night-opening flowers. 45°F min (zone 11).

JAN	/	
FEB	/	
MAR	sow	
APR	transplant ❁	
MAY	repotting	
JUN	flowering ❁	
JULY	flowering ❁	
AUG	/	
SEPT	flowering ❁	
OCT	/	
NOV	/	
DEC	/	

RECOMMENDED VARIETIES
Cereus aethiops
C. chalybaeus
C. hildmannianus
C. uruguayanus
C. validus

COMPANION PLANTS
Astrophytum
Echinocactus
Gymnocalycium
Mammillaria

CONDITIONS

Aspect These cactuses prefer to be grown in an open situation in full sun. Keep them well away from even the lightest shade.

Site The soil must be free draining, but need not be rich. Column cactuses come from areas with poor rocky soil. Although the size and proportion of these plants make them easiest to accommodate in a desert garden, column cactuses can also be grown in containers, which may need some extra weight such as stones or gravel in the base to stop them tipping over. Note however that some, such as the columnar *C. validus* and *C. hildmannianus monstrose*, have the potential to reach 20ft and 15ft. Of the two, the latter makes the most interesting shape with a contorted vertical stem.

GROWING METHOD

Propagation Grow plants from seed sown in spring or from cuttings of side branches.

Feeding Feed container-grown plants low-nitrogen liquid fertilizer monthly in summer. Ground-grown plants do not need feeding.

Problems No pest or disease problems are known.

FLOWERING

Season The large and lovely nocturnal flowers appear during spring and summer. The flowers usually appear after dark and fade before dawn.

Fruits Flowers are followed by round or oval fleshy fruits that ripen to yellow or red or purple.

CLEISTOCACTUS
Cleistocactus

TUBULAR FLOWERS *grow directly from the stem of the silver torch cactus. A single flower near the crown creates a bird-like appearance.*

BACK-LIT BY LOW SUN*, the fine silvery spines of this cactus become a real feature as the silhouette of the narrow column is defined.*

FEATURES

Sun

Although there are 45 species of *Cleistocactus*, all native to South America, very few are in general cultivation. Mostly branching from the base, these are upright column cactuses densely covered with fine spines that give them a silvery, woolly look. Although they look interesting as single stems, these cactuses are most spectacular when they are mass-planted. Their heights vary from 3–10ft but they are all fairly slender. The flowers, which emerge almost at right angles from the sides of the column, are mostly in shades of red and are pollinated by humming-birds in their natural habitats. The flowers never open very wide. These cactuses are fairly slow growing, making them ideal for pot culture, but they also can be grown in the open ground in conservatories. For plants in containers, regular potting on seems to produce the best growth.

CLEISTOCACTUS AT A GLANCE

These are generally quick-growing, spreading plants requiring plenty of space. Dramatic at full size. 45°F min (zone 11).

JAN	/	RECOMMENDED VARIETIES
FEB	/	*Cleistocactus brookei*
MAR	sow	*C. hyalacanthus*
APR	/	*C. jujuyensis*
MAY	transplant	*C. strausii*
JUN	flowering	*C. winteri*
JULY	flowering	
AUG	flowering	COMPANION PLANTS
SEPT	/	Aeonium
OCT	/	Espostoa
NOV	/	*Kalanchoe tomentosa*
DEC	/	Ferocactus
		Sansevieria trifasciata
		Yucca

Varieties The most commonly cultivated species is *C. straussii*. It grows about 6½ft high and forms clumps almost as wide. It is the species most often known by the name silver torch, and has cerise-red flowers in summer. *C. hyalacanthus* (syn. *C. jujuyensis*) is usually less than 3ft high, with columns covered in hairy, brownish to cream spines and flowers that may be bright scarlet to orange-red. *C. brookei* has one of the biggest growth potentials. Its height and spread are indefinite. In the wild it forms a superb show of red or orange flowers.

CONDITIONS

Aspect The plants need a position with continuous bright light and frequent watering during the growing season when the summer is hot. Over winter they must be kept bone dry, with a severe reduction in water from late fall.

Site Must have free-draining soil or cactus mix.

GROWING METHOD

Propagation Can be grown from seed or from stem cuttings or offsets during the warmer months.

Feeding Apply granular slow-release fertilizer in spring or feed the plants with weak solutions of liquid plant food through the growing season.

Problems Very susceptible to overwatering. If plants are indoors, mealybugs may be a problem.

FLOWERING

Season Flowers are red or pink, but also yellow, orange, or green. Most flower in summer.

Fruits Small, rounded, yellow, green, or red.

ECHINOCEREUS
Hedgehog Cactus

CYCLAMEN-PINK flowers stand like coronets to envelop the entire crown of this hedgehog cactus.

PRETTY LAVENDER-PINK flowers on Echinocereus pectinatus may be followed by edible fruits in ideal growing conditions.

FEATURES

Sun

Hailing from the south-west of North America, all 47 species in this group are in cultivation. It is a very variable genus: some types are globular, while others form short columns, some of which are pencil thin. The group is also split when it comes to their spines. Some species are heavily spined, while others are relatively smooth. Most are clump-forming or clustering, and in ideal conditions clumps of up to 3ft wide are found. Some species have edible fruits reputed to taste like strawberries. The best known of these are *Echinocereus pectinatus, E. engelmannii, E.reichenbachii,* and *E. subinermis.* The range of flower color in this group extends from white to yellow, orange, bright red, pale pink, magenta, and violet.

ECHINOCEREUS AT A GLANCE

Dramatic small cactuses, with flowers bursting through the skin. Many attractive species. 50°F min (zone 11).

			RECOMMENDED VARIETIES
JAN	/		*Echinocereus chloranthus*
FEB	/		*E. cinerascens*
MAR	sow		*E. engelmannii*
APR	transplant		*E. knippelianus*
MAY	flowering	❀	*E. pectinatus*
JUN	flowering	❀	*E. reichenbachii*
JULY	/		*E. scheeri*
AUG	/		*E. subinermis*
SEPT	/		*E. triglochidiatus*
OCT	/		
NOV	/		
DEC	/		

Varieties *E. knippelianus* is a striking cactus, with a dark green, almost smooth body, few spines, and pink to purple spring flowers. *E. subinermis* is one of the few yellow-flowered species, while *E. triglochidiatus* has brilliant scarlet flowers and a great range of forms. The "must have" hedgehog cactus for any collector is *E. reichenbachii* with purple-pink flowers; it makes a tidy smallish shape being 1ft high and 8in wide.

CONDITIONS

Aspect Prefers full sun with good air circulation.

Site Use a well-drained standard cactus mix. If being planted outside over summer, dig plenty of grit into the soil.

GROWING METHOD

Propagation Can be grown from seed sown in spring or from offsets taken in spring or summer.

Feeding Apply slow-release granules in spring or use weak liquid plant food in the growing season.

Problems Outdoors, few problems are encountered. If plants are grown under glasss, mealybugs or scales may be troublesome.

FLOWERING

Season Flowers appear some time during spring or summer. The flower buds form inside the plant body and then burst through the skin near the stem tips, often leaving scars.

Fruits Flowers are followed by fleshy fruits, most of which ripen to red although some fruits are green or purple.

EPIPHYLLUM
Orchid Cactus

THE CENTRE *of a lovely orchid cactus is dominated by a branched, star-like stigma surrounded by pollen-bearing stems.*

EMERGING FROM *the edge of the flattened stems, the rich red flowers of a hybrid orchid cactus cascade down from a basket.*

FEATURES

Shade

Partial Shade

This group of epiphytic tropical American cactuses is known as orchid cactus because of the gorgeous, large flowers. Few of the true species are available, but the many spectacular named varieties have huge flowers 4–8in across, in shades of cream, yellow, salmon, various pinks, and reds. Some of these cultivars have a tendency to change color according to light levels and temperatures. Stems of the orchid cactus are almost spineless, broad, flattened, and leaf-like with flowers emerging from buds that are formed on the edges of these stems. These cactuses are natural epiphytes growing in tree canopies in tropical forests. As a result, they do well growing in hanging baskets or against a wall or tree that they can use for support as they scramble up.

EPIPHYLLUM AT A GLANCE

Stunning, beautiful often scented flowers on cactuses that look highly impressive in hanging baskets. 50°F min (zone 11).

		RECOMMENDED VARIETIES
JAN	/	*Epiphyllum crenatum*
FEB	/	"Fantasy"
MAR	sow	"Hollywood"
APR	transplant	"Jennifer Anne"
MAY	flowering	*E. oxypetalum*
JUN	flowering	*E. pumilum*
JULY	flowering	"Reward"
AUG	/	
SEPT	/	
OCT	/	
NOV	/	
DEC	/	

Varieties Some of the large-flowered types are slow to produce their first blooms and must be very mature before they flower regularly. However, the lovely species *Epiphyllum oxypetalum*, known as "Belle de Nuit", is nocturnal with huge white, scented flowers unfolding on warm nights to close again by daybreak. If you only have room for one small orchid, *E. laui* is an excellent choice. It grows 1ft high by 1½ft wide, and produces scented white flowers about 6in long.

CONDITIONS

Aspect Unlike many cactuses, they prefer dappled, filtered shade out of direct sunlight.

Site The soil mix must be relatively fertile, but above all open and free draining.

GROWING METHOD

Propagation Can be grown from seed sown in spring, but hybrids must be increased from stem cuttings taken during summer to early fall.

Feeding Apply granular slow-release fertilizer in spring or regular liquid feeds in the growing season.

Problems Usually trouble free in the right conditions.

FLOWERING

Season Flowers are produced on mature plants from late spring through summer. Some flowers are quite long lasting. The original species are mostly night blooming, but the majority of those available today are day flowering.

Fruits Red fruits may form on some plants.

HATIORA SALICORNIOIDES
Drunkard's dream

UNOPENED BUDS FORMING on the tips of each slender segment of this plant are like small, glowing torches.

A LOVELY MATURE specimen of drunkard's dream in a hanging basket allows its fine shape to be appreciated in or out of flower.

FEATURES

Partial Shade

These plants bear no apparent likeness to the spiny plants so readily recognized as cactuses. They tend to be upright in early stages, but become pendulous under their own weight and so are ideal for hanging baskets. A large potted plant may need heavy stones in the container base to counterbalance the cactus's weight. The stem segments are mid-green to bronze and are topped by small, yellow to orange tubular, or funnel-shaped flowers in spring. This Brazilian group of plants includes ground growers and epiphytes and it is easy to imagine them growing from the fork or branch of a tree. *Hatiora salicornioides* is called drunkard's dream because the dense growth of tiny jointed stems resembles hundreds of tiny bottles. In Australia it is also called dancing bones.

HATIORA AT A GLANCE

Genus with many excellent species, well worth including in any collection of first-rate cactuses. 50°F min (zone 11).

		RECOMMENDED VARIETIES
JAN	/	*Hatiora ephiphylloides*
FEB	/	*H. gaertneri*
MAR	sow	*H. rosea*
APR	transplant	*H. salicornioides*
MAY	flowering	
JUN	flowering	
JULY	/	COMPANION PLANTS
AUG	/	Astrophyllum
SEPT	/	Epiphyllum
OCT	/	Rebutia
NOV	/	Schlumbergera
DEC	/	Selenicereus

CONDITIONS

Aspect Drunkard's dream grows best in filtered sunlight or in a position that has morning sun and afternoon shade.

Site The epiphytic kind need some shade to replicate their natural growing conditions, just under the tree canopy. Either provide filtered sunlight, or a position with morning sun and reasonable afternoon shade. Spray regularly to provide high levels of humidity, especially on hot days, when in full growth from spring to fall.

GROWING METHOD

Propagation These plants can be grown from seed sown in spring, but it is much easier to strike cuttings from the jointed stems in spring through to early fall.

Feeding Apply a low-level nitrogen liquid feed once a month during the growing season.

Problems This is generally a very easy plant to grow and it has no specific pest or disease problems.

FLOWERING

Season Small, orange to yellow tubular flowers appear from the lower half of the plant in spring. Although the flowers are not spectacular, they give the impression of tiny lights on the ends of the stems. The most impressive thing about most of these plants, is their distinctive, unusual, non-cactus like dangling growth. From a distance *H. salicornioides* looks a bit like the jangled stems of a mistletoe.

Fruits The flowers of drunkard's dream are followed by tiny white fruits.

MAMMILLARIA
Mammillaria

THE MATURING RED FRUITS of Mammillaria prolifera *surround each rounded stem. This species readily forms large colonies which makes it a satisfying plant to cultivate, both for the novice and more experienced growers.*

FEATURES

Sun

This is probably the most popular group of cactus among growers and collectors and there are about 150 species in the genus. The largest number of these cactuses are native to Mexico, but their habitat also extends through the south-western United States south to Colombia and Venezuela. Instead of ribs, these cactuses all have tubercles which vary greatly in shape. These plants are sometimes also known as pincushion cactuses.

MAMMILLARIA AT A GLANCE

Some Mammillaria should be in every collection, for their flowers and shape, especially the terrific white snowballs. 45°F min (zone 11).

		RECOMMENDED VARIETIES
JAN	/	*Mammillaria baumii*
FEB	/	M. bocasana
MAR	sow	M. bombycina
APR	transplant	M. candida
MAY	flowering	M. carmenae
JUN	flowering	M. elongata
JULY	flowering	M. geminispina
AUG	flowering	M. hahniana
SEPT	flowering	M. plumosa
OCT	/	M. zeilmanniana
NOV	/	
DEC	/	

Varieties

While it is impossible to cater for all tastes, the following few species indicate the variety within the group. *Mammillaria carmenae* has feathery, white or cream spines fanning out from the woolly body, and rich creamy flowers. It rarely grows more than 4in high, forming pretty clusters. *M. bombycina* has red, brown, or yellow spines pushing through the woolly surface of the plant. This species is quick to make offsets to form a good-looking specimen, especially when topped with a ring of pretty cerise-pink flowers. *M. longimamma,* called the finger mound cactus, has fat, stubby tubercles like smooth, dark green fingers with tufts of yellow spines on each tip. Flowers borne in late spring are quite large and rich yellow, while fruits that follow are fleshy and green, not unlike the cactus itself. *M. geminispina* is another excellent cactus with small rounded shapes, and is distinguished by a covering of white spines, white areoles, and white flowers. Even better, after a few years it will start to produce plenty of young plants, eventually creating an eye-catching mound. Old lady or birthday cake cactus, *M. hahniana,* is named for the almost perfect ring of cerise flowers on the crown of the plant, which is followed by another ring of red candle-like fruits.

Snowballs

M. plumosa, M. bocasana, and *M. sempervivi* are so densely covered in white wool below the spines that they resemble snowballs or powder puffs—they are sometimes referred to by these common names.

THE SMALL CERISE FLOWERS of Mammillaria hahniana *encircle the crown of the plant when fully developed.*

THIS COLUMNAR SPECIES of Mammillaria *has its crown covered with buds and flowers in spring. It is very rewarding to grow.*

Growth habit Most of these cactuses are small and rounded and thickly covered with spines, but some have finger-like stems. Most produce offsets freely, making a good show in pots or in a bed, but a few, however, are solitary growers. These cactuses are popular and satisfying to grow not only because of their easy cultivation, but because they produce rings of beautiful flowers around the crown of the plant in spring to early summer even when quite young. Spines vary from straight to curved, soft and feathery to almost rigid, and come in variable colors.

Size There is a great variation in height and size, and although a few of these cactuses may reach 12–16in in height, by far the greatest number will never exceed 6in. The ultimate spread of these species is harder to determine, but where there is space and where growing conditions are suitable, some may keep on spreading indefinitely. However, as it is easy to remove the offsets, their vigor need never be a problem.

CONDITIONS

Aspect Grow plants outdoors in full sun, but if they are under glass provide shading at the hottest time of day.

Site These cactuses are easy to grow. In pots, provide the standard cactus compost which will be free draining. When growing them in outdoor beds over summer, or in conservatory beds, make sure that the soil is on the poor side.

GROWING METHOD

Propagation These plants can be grown from seed sown in spring or by division of offsets in spring and summer. When the cactuses become quite prolific, as in the case of *M. geminispina*, it is worth removing smaller plantlets as they appear, not so much to create new plants as to maintain an aesthetically pleasing shape. It is also worth ensuring that one particularly good plant is always kept alone, without offspring, so its shape can be fully appreciated.

Feeding Apply small quantities of granular slow-release fertilizer in spring. You can also use low-nitrogen soluble liquid fertilizer at weak concentrations every month through the growing season.

Problems Some species form a thick tuberous root and these will rot if overwatered. *M. longimamma* is one of these, but all species must be considered vulnerable to overwatering.

FLOWERING

Season This cactus group produces its flowers during spring or summer, sometimes giving a second flush later in the season. They also tend to flower reliably year after year. The range of flower colors includes white, yellow, and orange with a wide range of shades of pink, red, and purple.

Fruits The berry-like fruits that follow the flowers are often bright red, but may also be green.

OPUNTIA
Opuntia

AN IMPENETRABLE BARRIER *has been formed where two species of* Opuntia *have become intermingled.*

FLAT, PADDLE-SHAPED *segments and the sizeable growth of the edible* Opuntia ficus-indica *make an impact in the landscape.*

FEATURES

Sun

Variously known as prickly pear, Indian fig, and cholla, with many more local common names, this is a very large genus of cactus with a vast geographical range. Opuntia are jointed or segmented cactuses with mainly padded and flattened joints, although sometimes these are cylindrical or rounded. Species occur naturally from southern Canada and throughout the Americas, continuing to Patagonia on the tip of South America. Long grown as living fences in their native areas, many prickly pears were introduced to other countries for this purpose, with disastrous results.

OPUNTIA AT A GLANCE

The largest group of cactus with some outstanding plants; excellent shapes, flowers and dangerous spines. 41°F min (zone 11).

JAN	/	RECOMMENDED VARIETIES
FEB	/	*Opuntia basiliaris*
MAR	sow	*O. clavarioides*
APR	transplant	*O. ficus-indica*
MAY	flowering	*O. microdasys*
JUN	flowering	*O. imbricata*
JULY	flowering	*O. tunicata*
AUG	flowering	*O. verschaffeltii*
SEPT	flowering	*O. vestica*
OCT	/	
NOV	/	
DEC	/	

Prickly pear *O. aurantiaca, O. stricta,* and *O. vulgaris* and a number of other species have become quite appalling weeds in Australia, Africa, and India. By 1925, there was estimated to be above 10 million acres (25 million hectares) of land infested by prickly pear in Australia. A huge programme of biological control was initiated, involving the introduction of the *Cactoblastis* moth and cochineal insects.

Indian fig The Indian fig, *O. ficus-indica,* is widely grown in many parts of the world for its fruit. It is a tree-like cactus up to 17ft high and wide.

Other types Although many species of opuntia are too large to place anywhere except in a large desert garden, there are numerous other shapes and sizes, with some that are suitable for pot culture. Bunny ears, *O. microdasys,* has dark green pads dotted with white areoles, and white, yellow, or brown bristles. The brown-bristled form is known as teddy bear ears. These plants rarely grow more than 16–24in high and wide, and suit both containers or the yard. *O. tunicata* is a small, spreading bush about 24in high and up to 3ft wide. Its thick, creamy spines take on a satin sheen in sunlight. Beaver tail, *O. basilaris,* has purple-gray flat pads with few spines and spreads by branching from the base, so is rarely more than 16in high. *O. erinacea* is clump-forming with flattened blue-green pads, but it is the variety *ursina* with masses of fine hair-like spines—known as grizzly bear cactus—that attracts many growers. In the wild it grows in California and Arizona, has 4in long pinky orange flowers, and grows about 18in high.

THE VIVID RED FLOWERS are tightly ridged across the top of the young leaves of this Opuntia. The flowers of most species are usually produced in spring or summer, and are followed by succulent fruits later in the season.

Chollas It is well worth knowing something about this rare group, which are rarely seen outside specialist botanical collections. The chollas (pronounced "choyas") are enormously variable in their habit of growth. They include the very spiny, almost furry-looking *O. bigelovii*, which grows to about 3–6½ft high, and the more open, tree-like *O. versicolor*, which may reach almost 13ft in height. Most of this group have easily detached segments, in particular the jumping cholla, *O. fulgida*, which hooks on to anything that passes, usually taking root and growing where it falls.

CONDITIONS

Aspect Best grown in an open, sunny situation.
Site Provide container-grown plants with sharply drained, standard cactus mix. In the garden, they tolerate a wide range of soils as long as they drain well. All opuntias dislike having their roots cramped in a small space. The larger plants should eventually be moved to a border in the glasshouse. If you opt for a regime of constant potting up, note that the spines are vicious.

GROWING METHOD

Propagation Easily grown from stem segments which should be separated from the parent plant from spring to fall. They can also be grown successfully from seed sown in spring.
Feeding In spring and mid-summer, plants in the ground can be given pelleted poultry manure or granular slow-release fertilizer. Potted plants should have a dose of slow-release fertilizer in the spring or an occasional liquid feed during the growing season.

Problems Few problems are encountered if growing conditions are suitable. The two worst offenders to look out for are scale insects and mealybugs. You will invariably need to spray to remove them, since the dangerous spines prevent you from getting in close to carry out treatment with a swab.

FLOWERING

Season The flowers of opuntia are produced sometime during spring or summer, depending on species. The majority of species has yellow flowers, but these may also be orange, purple, or white. For example, the bright yellow flowers of *O. tunicata* appear from spring to summer, while *O. basilaris* bears its bright rose-pink flowers in summer.
Fruits Berry-like fruits form after the flowers fade, and in some species these are edible. The Indian fig has bright yellow flowers that are followed by deep red to purple fruit. It is widely cultivated around the world for its fruit. Prepare the fruit for eating by washing and using a brush to remove the spines. Slice off the top and bottom, slit the skin, and peel. Serve in slices with a squeeze of lemon or lime juice. You can also use the pulp to make jam. *O. cochenillifera* is a source of cochineal - although today this dye is mainly synthesized.

PARODIA
Ball Cactus

DENSELY COVERED with fine yellow spines, the species Parodia claviceps *can be slow to form colonies.*

BRIGHT YELLOW FLOWERS are a feature of Parodia magnifica, *a deeply furrowed species which is not heavily spined.*

FEATURES

Sun

Partial
Shade

While the species is now known as parodia, you will find that many ball cactuses are still under the old name of notocactus. These superb cactuses are native to Brazil, Paraguay, Uruguay, and Argentina. Mostly rounded in form, although a few are column shaped, they are easy to grow and flower profusely. Many ball cactuses have deeply furrowed surfaces, but the coverage of spines varies greatly; some forms are thickly covered and others have quite sparse spines. *P. concinnus* is a small tubby shape with primrose-yellow flowers, while *P. leninghausii* can form a thick column up to 3ft high and has large yellow flowers. *P. herteri*, prized for its hot pink-purple flowers, is squat-shaped and blooms when it reaches tennis-ball size. *N. uebelmannianus* is another squat grower, with large purple or yellow flowers.

CONDITIONS

Aspect	Ball cactuses will grow in full sun or in very light shade. When standing pots outdoors in summer, make sure that the plants receive some shade around midday.
Site	When growing in pots, use a standard well-drained compost. In the ground, ball cactuses like equally well-drained soil with some well-rotted compost that slightly increases fertility.

GROWING METHOD

Propagation	Grow from seed in spring or from offsets taken in summer. None of the species will produce offsets until quite mature. Increase watering in the spring and allow the soil to dry out between waterings during the summer.
Feeding	Apply slow-release fertilizer in spring, or feed the plants with some low-nitrogen liquid fertilizer every 6–8 weeks throughout the growing season.
Problems	This is generally a trouble-free type of cactus that is easy to grow.

FLOWERING

Season	The flowers appear on the crown of ball cactuses during the spring or summer months. The central stigma of the flower is nearly always a deep reddish-purple to pink color. While the majority of the ball cactuses have yellow flowers, it is possible to obtain other species that have attractive flowers in red, pink, purple, or even orange colors. Contact a cactus nursery which specializes in parodia.
Fruits	In ideal growing conditions, as in the wild, you may find that after the flowers fade fleshy fruits ripen to red.

PARODIA AT A GLANCE

Parodia are generally globular or spherical, ribbed spiny cactuses from South America. Funnel-shaped blooms. 45°F min (zone 11).

JAN	/	RECOMMENDED VARIETIES
FEB	/	*Parodia chrysacanthion*
MAR	transplant	*P. concinna*
APR	flowering	*P. herteri*
MAY	flowering	*P. horstii*
JUN	flowering	*P. leninghausii*
JULY	flowering	*P. magnifica*
AUG	sow	*P. mammulosa*
SEPT	/	*P. nivosa*
OCT	/	*P. rutilans*
NOV	/	*P. schwebsiana*
DEC	/	

SCHLUMBERGERA
Christmas Cactus

A VIVID SCARLET HYBRID of Schlumbergera truncata *makes a desirable potted plant to brighten winter days.*

FLOURISHING IN LIGHT SHADE, this Christmas cactus is the cerise-pink color that most people associate with the species.

FEATURES

Partial Shade

This group of easily grown cacti originated from only about six species, and now features almost 200 cultivars of popular flowering pot plants which are more familiar to some as *Zygocactus*. *Schlumbergera* species, or Christmas cacti, are epiphytic and grow on trees or sometimes rocks in their native Brazilian habitat where their flowers are pollinated by humming-birds. Their popularity as pot plants is assured because most of them flower in fall or winter, hence their common name. They have flat, jointed stems arching into small bushes, making them ideal for hanging baskets as well as pots. They come into vigorous growth in summer, and start flowering once the day length is less than 12 hours. Christmas cacti make excellent gifts.

SCHLUMBERGERA AT A GLANCE		
High performance pot plants which give a big show of bright color around Christmas. Easily grown. 45°F min (zone 11).		
JAN	flowering ❀	RECOMMENDED VARIETIES
FEB	flowering ❀	*Schlumbergera "Bristol Beauty"*
MAR	/	*S.* x *buckleyi*
APR	sow ✍	"Gold Charm"
MAY	flowering ❀	"Joanne"
JUN	transplant ✍	"Lilac Beauty"
JULY	/	*S. opuntioides*
AUG	/	*S. truncata*
SEPT	/	
OCT	/	
NOV	flowering ❀	
DEC	flowering ❀	

Varieties The silky, irregularly-shaped flowers are mainly in shades of pink or red, but hybrids can be almost pure white to cream, salmon, apricot, cerise, violet, and scarlet. Some display yellow tones that revert to pink as temperatures fall. *S. truncata*, the crab cactus, and *S.* x *buckleyi*, the Christmas cactus, provide the origins of many of the modern hybrids.

CONDITIONS

Aspect Best in partial shade or with morning sun and afternoon shade in a sheltered situation.

Site For an established pot plant, John Innes No. 2 with added grit for good drainage is ideal. Repot every three years in the spring. It is too tender to be grown outdoors.

GROWING METHOD

Propagation These plants are easy to grow from cuttings of stem sections taken in spring or summer.

Feeding A light, regular summer feed will promote plenty of new growth and guarantee an excellent display of flowers.

Problems Generally easy to grow, these plants will suffer if grown in full sun and may not flower. Overwatering causes root rot and subsequent collapse of stems.

FLOWERING

Season Masses of flowers appear in fall or winter. Once flower buds have formed, do not move the plants until buds begin to open. Flowers in spring if kept at 36–39°F over winter. Gradually increase the temperature in spring.

SELENICEREUS
Selenicereus

THESE PLANTS ARE CULTIVATED for their beautiful white, cream, or pale pink fragrant flowers, which open at night. It is amazing to see such a glorious flower emerge at dusk from a fairly ugly-looking stem but, of course, it will have faded by the following morning.

FEATURES

Partial Shade

There are about 20 species in this group of very long-stemmed climbing epiphytic cactuses. They are native to the forests of the south-western United States, central America, the West Indies, and Colombia, where they live on trees or rocks. *Selenicereus* species have long been cultivated in Mexico for a drug used in the treatment of rheumatism and in Costa Rica for a heart-stimulant drug. They are now being cultivated in Germany and elsewhere for use in medicine, especially in the treatment of heart disorders. These plants have long, angled, or tubular stems bearing small spines on the ribs, but it is their aerial roots that enable them to climb and cling on to their host plants. They will continue to grow upwards and spread as long as they find support.

SELENICEREUS AT A GLANCE

Strange, thin climbing stems with outstandingly beautiful, scented flowers, from South American forests. 59°F min (zone 11).

		RECOMMENDED VARIETIES
JAN	/	*Selenicereus grandiflorus*
FEB	/	*S. hamatus*
MAR	sow 🖐	*S. innesii*
APR	/	*S. pteranthus*
MAY	transplant 🖐	*S. spinulosus*
JUN	flowering ❀	
JULY	flowering ❀	
AUG	flowering ❀	COMPANION PLANTS
SEPT	/	Epiphyllum
OCT	sow 🖐	Hatiora
NOV	/	Schlumbergera
DEC	/	Selenicereus

Varieties *S. grandiflorus* is the species most often grown. Its flowers have outer petals that are yellow to brown, but the inner flower is pure white. Two other species found in cultivation are *S. pteranthus* and *S. spinulosus*. Both have cream, white, or pale pink flowers. These plants can be grown in the ground, or rooted in large pots set against some strong support.

CONDITIONS

Aspect Being epiphytic, these extraordinary cactuses need to be kept out of direct sunlight. They like filtered, dappled light, or as second best, light for half the day, shade for the rest.

Site Plants need well-drained compost with added decayed organic matter. An orchid mix would suit them.

GROWING METHOD

Propagation Plants are easily grown from stem segments taken from spring to early fall. They can also be grown from seed sown in spring.

Feeding Apply slow-release fertilizer in spring, or liquid feed occasionally in the growing season.

Problems No specific pests or diseases are known, but keep an eye out in the summer for scale insects and mealybugs.

FLOWERING

Season The spectacular, scented flowers do not appear until the plants have become quite mature. They open on summer evenings.

Fruits The fleshy fruits are hairy or spiny.

GROWING SUCCULENT PLANTS

These unique plants vary greatly in size, shape, and leaf color, and they originate from a wide variety of habitats. One thing all succulents have in common, they are show-stoppers in the garden. They look striking against other plants, as contrasts or accents in the landscape, or when grown as individual eye-catchers.

A collection of succulents of different sizes and colors can make an attractive garden display without the need to add any other type of plant. They can also be used to vary and complement a display of cactuses to great effect. The other great advantage of succulents is that many of them can be teamed with a wide range of non-succulents without looking out of place. They can be used as feature plants, as groundcovers, in mixed borders, or as container specimens.

KEY TO AT A GLANCE TABLES

PLANTING

FLOWERING

At a glance charts are your quick guide.
For full information, consult the accompanying text.

LEFT: A perfect specimen of Agave *species dominates the planting in this well-planned succulent garden. The distinctive foliage of* Kalanchoe beharensis *fills the foreground while* K. fedtschenkoi *blooms in the background.*

FEATURES OF SUCCULENTS

Succulents are xerophytes, plants that store water in their stems, leaves, or roots to withstand harsh, dry conditions. Their thick, fleshy leaves are often covered with a waxy coating or fine hairs to reduce loss of moisture through transpiration. Although some succulents have spines on their stems or foliage, these are carried singly and do not arise from areoles, the little "cushions" that bear cactus spines. Succulents originate from a wide range of climatic regions.

Succulents come from a variety of habitats and while many are sensitive to cold, there are others that tolerate temperatures well below freezing. While all cactuses are in the one botanical family *Cactaceae*, succulents belong to a wide range of families that includes both the daisy family *Asteraceae* and the lily family *Liliaceae*.

SUCCULENTS IN THE GARDEN

Succulents are easy to incorporate into the garden as they mix very well with both cactuses and non-succulents, and they are particularly useful in the garden when planted to provide foliage contrast. Here, their distinctive forms and colors can be shown to great advantage. All that they require is to be associated with plants that enjoy the same aspect and have similar soil and water requirements.

The vast majority of succulents like to be grown in an open, sunny situation. The soil must drain well and if there is any chance of waterlogging, garden beds should be raised above the existing soil level as described in the introduction to cactus growing. The addition of some well-decayed compost or manure will improve soil aeration and drainage, as well as giving the plants a good start in life.

A SURVIVOR of harsh conditions, this tender carpobrutus produces flowers on and off throughout the year in the wild.

GRADED SIZES of terracotta bowls are used to display succulents. The top bowl contains Haworthia *species, the centre bowl has sedums and the lowest bowl is planted with echeverias.*

GROWING SUCCULENTS IN CONTAINERS

Succulents can be grown in almost any type of container as long as there is adequate drainage. They can be grown in standard pots or hanging baskets, troughs, and window boxes, or turned into amusing novelties by planting them in old teapots or kettles, hiking boots, pottery ornaments, or anything else that takes your fancy—as long as the container allows excess water to drain away.

Some succulents have enormous appeal for children, the most popular being *Kalanchoe tomentosa* and sedums. As long as the children do not kill these plants with kindness—usually by overwatering—succulents will survive with the minimum degree of attention.

The great range of color in leaves alone can make for interesting groupings of pots of either single or mixed succulent species. A few succulents are also ideal for growing in hanging baskets. These include lampranthus and *Kalanchoe brossfeldiana*, while burro's tail must be grown this way. Mother-in-law's tongue, too, is most often grown as a container plant able to survive most conditions, both indoors and out. Large specimens of succulents can be used as feature or specimen plants in the garden or on a terrace. These include the Madagascar palm, silver jade plant, agaves, and aloes. Those succulents that have sharp spines are best positioned away from regularly used paths and entrances. Succulents that rely on finely detailed foliage patterns to make their mark, such as *Agave victoriae-reginae*, make lovely potted plants positioned where their form and markings can be seen to best advantage. Slow growers such as this agave can remain happily in the one pot for many years.

WATERING AND FERTILIZING

Most succulent plants prefer to be watered fairly regularly during the growing season, being kept drier during their dormant phase. Living in a very mild area with high winter rainfall need not rule you out of growing succulents, as long as the soil drainage is rapid. If your soil is sandy and quick draining, it will, of course, need watering much more frequently than a heavier and more moisture-retentive soil. As with all plants, you will need to become familiar with your own soil to gauge the frequency of watering required by succulents. However, succulents will generally not die rapidly if they run out of water, and it is better to water them too little than too much.

Most succulents can be grown without supplementary fertilizer unless the soil is extremely poor. Organic matter added to the soil before planting will often supply all the necessary nutrients, but low-nitrogen fertilizers can also be used during the growing season. Excess fertilizer, and especially excess nitrogen, will result in soft growth that may not stand up to tough growing conditions. If you feel that feeding is necessary, use granular slow-release fertilizers or half-strength soluble liquid plant foods. Small amounts of low-nitrogen fertilizers formulated to encourage flowering and fruiting, such as some tomato or rose foods, may also be suitable for some succulents.

PROPAGATION

Propagation from cuttings

Most succulents are very easy to grow from stem cuttings. If the stems are fairly slim, you can pot cuttings into coarse sand with a little added coir peat. Thick fleshy stems are best cut from the plant, dusted with sulfur and then allowed to dry for a few days before potting up. You can take cuttings from tips or from further down the stem—it does not seem to matter where the cutting comes from. The cuttings are best taken in the spring or mid-summer, when new roots will quickly appear. Most succulents will also grow readily from leaf cuttings. Simply break off a firm mature leaf cleanly, leave it

---

PROPAGATING BY LEAF CUTTINGS

1. CLEANLY snap off a healthy, mature leaf from the stock plant and put it aside to dry.

2. INSERT only the leaf base into a mix of equal parts coarse sand and perlite, or coarse sand with a little coir peat.

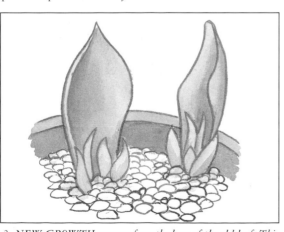

3. NEW GROWTH emerges from the base of the old leaf. This may take a few weeks depending on the species and time of year.

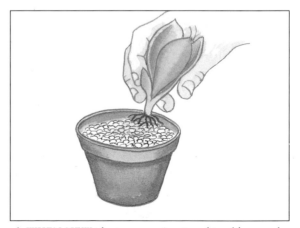

4. WHEN NEW plants are growing strongly and have good root systems, pot them on individually.

THE YELLOW-GREEN FOLIAGE of stonecrop Sedum nussbaumeranum *flushes pink in the sun. This is one of the 280 species of plants in the genus* Sedum, *many of which are good ornamentals. Their wide range of habitats varies from the tropics to cold regions.*

to dry for a few days and then insert just the base of the leaf into the growing mix. One species which will root easily this way but never make a plant is senecio. The single leaves of this plant readily form roots, but never develop further. Some species will strike even if cuttings are left sitting on top of the mix, producing roots and tiny new leaves from the base of the old leaf. A few species develop bulbils on their flowering stems and can be detached and treated like cuttings to form separate plants.

Propagation by division

Some succulents form clumps in which individual plants have their own roots. In this case, simply dig up the whole clump and pull it apart, making sure each division has some roots and shoots. If, however, you have broken off a piece without roots, you should simply treat it as a cutting. Sometimes you will need to cut through the clump with a knife, which may result in the severing of sections of the plant. If you have cut through the entire plant, or even cut through half the plant, either discard that piece or dust it with sulfur before replanting it.

Clump-forming plants like echeverias or houseleeks are best propagated by division, but sometimes you may want to remove single rosettes to give to friends or, with the latter, grow them elsewhere in the garden. If you use a narrow-bladed knife or spatula, you can usually insert this carefully between rosettes to lever out individual plants.

Layering

Many succulents will produce roots wherever they come into contact with the soil. Once you know that a section has its own roots, it can be dug up and replanted. You can encourage this layering by pegging down a section of stem with a small stone, a hairpin, or an opened paper clip. Good examples of these self-layering plants are lampranthus and London pride, or *Crassula*.

Growing from seed

Although seedling plants may be slow growing and take a number of years to flower, many growers prefer this method of propagation as they find it very satisfying. If you want to try growing from seed, use a ready-made seed-raising mix or make your own from three parts of horticultural sand and one part of coir peat. Firm the mix into a container and water well. Sow fine seed on top of the mix and leave the container uncovered. Larger seeds can be covered to a depth of between equal to and twice the seed diameter. Use a spray mister to lightly water the seeds, cover the container with a sheet of glass or plastic and keep in a bright warm place, protecting it from direct sunlight. Check every few days to see whether the seed mix needs watering; if it does, use a spray mister or set the container in a larger one of water and allow the mix to slowly draw up the water from below. Do not water heavily from above as the water may dislodge the seeds that you have sown.

The time taken for seeds to germinate will vary enormously, ranging from a few days to several weeks. Once seed has germinated, leave the cover partially off the pot to reduce humidity without sending the tiny plants into shock. Increase this exposure to the atmosphere gradually until the seedlings are looking strong and the cover is entirely off. Once they are large enough to handle, they can be potted up into small, individual pots.

Unfortunately it is all too easy for seedlings to fail because of excess moisture in the potting mix and the atmosphere. Despite the high failure rate, it can be fun to grow succulents from seed. As the majority of succulents grow so easily from cuttings or division, not many growers bother to raise seeds. There are some species, however, that can only be propagated from seed. As with any other group of plants, there is always the chance that a seedling plant will exhibit some interesting variation in color or form. These chance seedlings often give rise to new cultivars.

WHAT CAN GO WRONG?

Soil and watering
• Succulents are generally a very trouble-free group of plants. Their greatest enemy is heavy, poorly drained soil and an excess of water especially during the cooler months of the year. Most will take plenty of water during the growing season as long as the soil or potting mix drains well, but while the plants are dormant in cold weather, they will rot if the soil is kept wet all the time. A monthly watering would be adequate in a dry winter.

Pests
• Snails will sometimes eat some types of succulents leaving ugly scars that can ruin the appearance of the plant. Search for snails and destroy them or use a proprietary snail bait, taking care not to put pets or children at risk.
• Mealybugs can be a problem with any type of plant grown under shelter where conditions are dry and warm. These sap suckers, which resemble little sticky patches of cotton wool, can be wiped off with a cotton bud dipped in methylated spirits; if the infestation is severe, the plant may need spraying.

Weeds
• Weeds can spoil the appearance of a lovely patch of succulents but as many of these plants grow into clumps of rosettes or as low groundcovers, weeding can be difficult. It is hard to extract weeds without breaking these often brittle plants. Before you set your plants in the garden, turn the soil over well, water it and wait for weeds to appear. Remove the weeds by hand or spray with glyphosate. It is worth repeating the process if you have weed problems elsewhere in the garden. Make sure you dig out the bulbs of persistent perennial weeds, such as oxalis, prior to planting succulents. These stubborn weeds are almost impossible to remove completely if they appear amid a dense-growing cluster of succulents. Act before it is too late.

CLEAR YELLOW is one of the newer but quite stable colors among the hybrids of flaming Katy.

A STURDY COLUMN of fleshy leaves supports the pink flowers of this houseleek. This stem will slowly die off after the flowers fall.

CRASSULA
London Pride

PRETTY, STARRY FLOWERS lift the leathery looking foliage. Tiny plantlets often develop after the flowers have fallen.

ADAPTABLE AND TROUBLE-FREE, London pride can survive among rocks in tiny amounts of soil.

FEATURES

Sun

Partial Shade

In warm climates, this semi-prostrate plant is a very vigorous grower, but it can be useful and decorative as a groundcover or as a filler plant in a rockery. In any event, crassula is very easy to control if it ever exceeds its allotted space. It can be upright or somewhat sprawling in habit, and when sprawling it roots itself into the ground as it spreads. It can alternatively be grown in pots or hanging baskets. Plants grow about 6–10in high, but can be taller. In warm, humid areas, one plant may spread 20in or more in a season. The fleshy leaves may be rounded, oblong, or spoon shaped, and the small pink and white starry flowers are carried on slender stems high above the foliage.

CRASSULA AT A GLANCE

Superb succulents with fleshy leaves ranging from the tiny to 15ft high in the wild. (41°F min (zone 11).

		RECOMMENDED VARIETIES
JAN	flowering ✽	*Crassula falcata*
FEB	/	*C. galanthea*
MAR	sow ☜	*C. helmsii*
APR	transplant ☜	*C. milfordiae*
MAY	flowering ✽	*C. ovata*
JUN	flowering ✽	*C. rupestris*
JULY	flowering ✽	*C. sarcocaulis*
AUG	/	*C. schmidtii*
SEPT	flowering ✽	
OCT	/	
NOV	/	
DEC	flowering ✽	

CONDITIONS

Aspect   Crassula is suited to growing in sun or partial shade. Growth is more compact when the plant is situated in full sun. It benefits from being stood outside over summer, or it could be planted out in a special raised bed with excellent drainage.

Site   Almost any kind of well-drained soil will suit this plant. Plants in containers prefer a mix that drains well, but also contains plenty of organic matter.

GROWING METHOD

Propagation   This plant is very easily grown from stem cuttings taken any time during the warmer seasons. Tiny plantlets emerging from bulbils may sometimes form on the tips of flowered stems. These plantlets may be pegged down on a pot of coarse sandy mix to grow on and form roots.

Feeding   Potted plants may need some slow-release fertilizer applied in spring. Plants grown in beds rarely need supplementary feeding.

Problems   Crassula is generally an easily-grown, tough, trouble-free plant. The only problems occur in the glasshouse over summer, when you should keep an eye out for mealybugs and aphids and spray accordingly.

FLOWERING

Season   Small pink and white starry flowers appear in spring. These are sometimes followed by bulbils, which grow into new plants.

CRASSULA ARBORESCENS
Silver Jade Plant

ROUNDED SILVERY LEAVES edged in red make this shrubby succulent an asset in the mild garden, in or out of flower.

RUSTY RED-BROWN CALYCES remain on the bush long after the pale starry flowers have fallen.

FEATURES

Sun

Partial Shade

Growing to over 8½ft in its native South Africa, this plant is more often seen at about 5ft when container-grown, or somewhat taller in the ground. It blends well with a range of plant types, including evergreens that enjoy the same conditions, and can be used most successfully to add height to a desert garden or a succulent display. It develops a sturdy trunk and numerous branches which carry leathery, gray-green oblong leaves with a fine red margin, sometimes dotted with tiny red spots. Plants sold as *Crassula ovata* are probably the same as or very similar to this species.

CRASSULA AT A GLANCE

C. arborescens is a highly attractive South African succulent with pink fall flowers and thick waxy leaves. 41°F min (zone 11).

JAN	/	RECOMMENDED VARIETIES
FEB	/	*Crassula arborescens*
MAR	/	*C. falcata*
APR	sow	*C. galanthea*
MAY	/	*C. helmsii*
JUN	transplant	*C. milfordiae*
JULY	/	*C. ovata*
AUG	/	*C. rupestris*
SEPT	/	*C. sarcocaulis*
OCT	flowering	*C. schmidtii*
NOV	flowering	
DEC	flowering	

CONDITIONS

Aspect Full sun is preferred, but this plant will tolerate shade for part of the day if necessary. However, the more light it receives the better it does.

Site This plant can be grown in any type of well-drained soil. Container-grown plants will benefit from annual repotting, or from having the top third of the compost replaced.

GROWING METHOD

Propagation This plant is most easily grown from leaf cuttings, which must be removed with the stem attached. It can also be grown from stem cuttings or seed. All methods of propagation are best carried out in warm weather.

Feeding Fertilizing is generally unnecessary, but a small amount of slow-release fertilizer can be given to container-grown plants in spring.

Problems This is a tough, trouble-free plant that is quite easily grown. The only possible irritation is that the plant may repeatedly get too big for its container. Eventually, the best solution is to replace the oversize plant with a vigorous cutting. This will mean that you can start all over again with a small pot.

FLOWERING

Season Flowering is profuse. Masses of small, pink, starry flowers adorn the shrub in late fall to winter.

EUPHORBIA CAPUT-MEDUSAE
Medusa's Head

CORONETS OF SMALL FLOWERS *on the mature stems of Medusa's head lighten the appearance of the heavy stems.*

MEDUSA'S HEAD CAN BE PLANTED OUT *over summer in a gap between paving, producing a dramatic eye-catching effect.*

FEATURES

Sun

Although growing only 1ft high, this multi-branched succulent makes an impact. The rounded, thickened stem may grow partly underground, but from this stout stem a mass of gray-green knobbly branches emerge. A well-grown plant may have a diameter of up to 3ft. Small green leaves sprout from the tips of the warty branches. Ideal as a feature for a desert or succulent garden, this plant can also be container grown. Like all the plants in this group, the milky latex in the stems is caustic and may cause severe skin problems; wear gloves and protect eyes when handling it.

EUPHORBIA AT A GLANCE

E. caput-medusae is a fine architectural South African plant with branching stems and whitish flowers. 55°F min (zone 11).

JAN	/	
FEB	/	
MAR	sow 👆	
APR	transplant ✏️	
MAY	flowering ✿	
JUN	flowering ✿	
JULY	flowering ✿	
AUG	/	
SEPT	/	
OCT	/	
NOV	/	
DEC	/	

RECOMMENDED VARIETIES
Euphorbia amygdaloides var. *robbiae*
E. characias subsp. *characias*
E. c. subsp. *wulfenii*
E. griffithii "Dixter"
E. x *martinii*
E. myrsinites
E. palustris
E. polychroma
E. schillingii

CONDITIONS

Aspect   These plants should be grown in full sun with good air circulation around them.

Site   The soil must be well drained, but does not need to be rich. Whether growing in pots, or in the open ground over summer, make sure that plenty of grit is added to the compost or soil.

GROWING METHOD

Propagation   Medusa's head can be grown from stem cuttings taken during the warmer months, or from seed sown in spring.

Feeding   Plants grown in containers can be given a small amount of slow-release fertilizer in spring. Plants grown in the garden should not need supplementary feeding. If the soil is particularly poor though, a regular liquid feed will give the plant a decent boost.

Problems   Medusa's head is generally not prone to problems unless overwatered.

FLOWERING

Season   The cream or green flowers of this plant appear in spring or summer. The true flower is small, but it is fringed with attractive creamy white, bract-like surrounds. In a poor summer it may be best to move it back under glass where it will flower better in the higher temperatures.

EUPHORBIA MILII
Crown of Thorns

THE FLORAL DISPLAY of crown of thorns lasts many months but is more prolific in spring and summer.

THE WHITE-BRACTED FORM of crown of thorns is less vigorous than the species. It can be shaped into a neat and pretty pot plant.

FEATURES

Sun

This extremely spiny, semi-succulent plant sprawls over the ground. In warm-climate gardens it provides groundcover for places where people or animals are to be excluded, over walls or under windows, and is virtually maintenance-free. Heights vary from 3 –4½ft the latter in ideal conditions. It is valued for its almost year-round display of bright red bracts which surround the insignificant flowers. In a big pot it makes a very striking feature. The leaves are a soft mid-green and can be plentiful or sparse depending on conditions, warm and wet is best.

EUPHORBIA AT A GLANCE

An excellent if spiny plant, with good bright colors, demanding a warm, humid conservatory. 54°F min (zone 11).

		RECOMMENDED VARIETIES
JAN	/	*Euophorbia characias* subsp.
FEB	/	*wulfenii*
MAR	repotting 🌱	*E. dulcis* "Chameleon"
APR	sow 🌱	*E. griffithii* "Dixter"
MAY	flowering ❀	*E. g.* "Fireglow"
JUN	transplant 🌱	*E.* x *martinii*
JULY	flowering ❀	*E. myrsinites*
AUG	/	*E. polychroma*
SEPT	/	*E. schillingii*
OCT	/	
NOV	/	
DEC	/	

CONDITIONS

Aspect   This has to be grown in a pot or border in the conservatory. Sun or light shade is fine. Note that the more you adhere to its ideal conditions, also keeping it warm and wet, the taller and bushier it grows, and the more frequently the flowers appear on new growth. In its native Madagascar it makes a highly effective hedging plant which keeps out all intruders. With limited room it may be best to keep it healthy without encouraging too much spiny growth.

Site   Grow in any type of soil that is free draining.

GROWING METHOD

Propagation   Propagate from stem cuttings taken in late spring or early summer. This is also a good time to prune the plant if you need to control its spread, and the prunings can be then used as a batch of cuttings.

Feeding   Slow-release fertilizer can be applied in spring, but this is unnecessary unless the soil is extremely poor.

Problems   This plant is generally quite trouble-free.

FLOWERING

Season   The long flowering period of this plant is technically from spring through to late summer. However, there are likely to be some flowers on it at almost any time of year in very warm conditions.

KALANCHOE BLOSSFELDIANA
Flaming Katy

A MOUND OF BRIGHT RED FLOWERS all but obscures the foliage on this well-grown specimen of flaming Katy.

THREE VARIETIES of flaming Katy, bright pink, yellow, and red, are used here as bedding plants with white alyssum.

FEATURES

Partial Shade

This is familiar to most people as a potted flowering plant. It has scalloped, fleshy dark green leaves, often edged with red, and the original species has bright scarlet flowers. It has been extensively hybridized and there are now forms with flowers in white, yellow, and various shades of pink. There may be some color change or variation depending on aspect and climatic conditions, especially as flowers start to fade. Some of the bright pinks tend to revert to the species scarlet. A very easy-care pot plant for use indoors or out, this is also a fine summer plant for the garden. In ideal warm conditions in the glasshouse border where there is plenty of space, the stems will sprawl and take root, creating new plants.

KALANCHOE AT A GLANCE

K. blossfeldiana is a superb, reliable pot plant with heads of bright flowers to brighten up the glasshouse. 50°F min (zone 11).

		RECOMMENDED VARIETIES
JAN	/	
FEB	flowering 🌸	*K. beharensis*
MAR	flowering 🌸	*K. eriophylla*
APR	flowering 🌸	*K. grandiflora*
MAY	sow ✍	*K. marmorata*
JUN	/	*K. pubescens*
JULY	transplant ✍	*K. pumila*
AUG	/	"Tessa"
SEPT	/	*K. tomentosa*
OCT	/	"Wendy"
NOV	/	
DEC	/	

CONDITIONS

Aspect   In the garden, flaming Katy prefers morning sun and afternoon shade or light shade all day. Indoors, these plants should be given plenty of bright light.

Site   Flaming Katy grows best in a well-drained soil that also contains plenty of decayed organic matter. In the open garden make sure that the soil has plenty of added drainage material so that the roots are not kept too wet for too long.

GROWING METHOD

Propagation   Very easily grown from either leaf or stem cuttings, taken during the warmer months. The cuttings should be dried out for a few days before planting.

Feeding   In spring, apply slow-release fertilizer or a small amount of pelletted poultry manure in the open garden. It does not respond well to soil that is too fertile.

Problems   Flaming Katy is generally free of pests and disease.

FLOWERING

Season   The true flowering time is late winter to spring, but commercial growers now force plants so that they are available in flower almost all year round. In the home yard, in the ground or in pots, they should bloom at the proper time. Flowers will generally give several weeks of bright color. After flowering, trim off spent flower heads.

LAMPRANTHUS
Lampranthus

THE PROLIFIC FLOWERING lampranthus makes great seasonal impact. It is ideal as groundcover or for a border planting in dry areas.

A BRILLIANT TAPESTRY of color is created in this mixed planting which highlights the use of lampranthus.

FEATURES

Sun

This group of plants is native to South Africa and is ideal for low-maintenance gardens in areas with low rainfall. Lampranthus is best known as a creeping or trailing plant used as a groundcover, but some species are bushier and more like shrubs. Stems of many species root as they spread, making them ideal for soil binding on banks or simply for stopping blowing sand or soil. The fleshy gray-green leaves are angled or cylindrical, and growing stems may reach 20in or so, but are more often around 12in. Individual plants may spread 12in or more in a growing season. The daisy-like flowers, which only open in sun, are shiny, brilliantly colored, and borne in such profusion that the foliage and stems are all but obscured.

LAMPRANTHUS AT A GLANCE

Prime ingredients for a dry seaside summer garden, offering big bright clusters of flowers. 5°F min (zone 7).

		RECOMMENDED VARIETIES
JAN	/	*Lampranthus aurantiacus*
FEB	flowering ✽	*L. auratus*
MAR	sow	*L. brownii*
APR	/	*L. haworthii*
MAY	/	*L. spectabilis*
JUN	transplant	*L. s.* "Tresco Brilliant"
JULY	flowering ✽	
AUG	flowering ✽	
SEPT	flowering ✽	
OCT	/	
NOV	/	
DEC	/	

Varieties   Species commonly grown include *Lampranthus aurantiacus*, with orange flowers; *L. roseus*, with pink flowers; and *L. spectabilis*, with purple to magenta flowers. Many lampranthus sold in nurseries are cultivars or hybrids bred for garden use.

CONDITIONS

Aspect   These plants must be grown in full sun or flowers will not open.

Site   Can be grown in almost any type of soil as long as it is well drained. Try to replicate its natural habitat which is mainly coastal South African near-desert conditions; dry and arid.

GROWING METHOD

Propagation   Lampranthus are easily grown from stem cuttings taken from spring to fall. Species can be grown from seed sown in spring.

Feeding   Fertilizing is generally unnecessary as plants grown "hard" usually flower better.

Problems   Snails sometimes graze on foliage causing damage. Plants will not survive in heavy, poorly drained soil.

FLOWERING

Season   Flowers appear through late winter and spring or during summer depending on the conditions and the species grown. Flowers may be orange, red, yellow, purple, cream, and many shades in between. In good conditions they will provide excellent, striking colors, especially the bright orange *L. aurantiacus*.

LEWESIA
Lewisia

FEATURES

Sun

The genus has 19 or 20 hardy species, and is exclusively American. The best place to grow them is on a well-drained south-facing slope, in a rock garden or even on a wall. They are low growing, often with bright flowers which are funnel shaped. The color range is mainly on the pink-magenta side, with some that are yellow and white. There are many excellent kinds to chose from, the best being *L. bracyhcalyx* which flowers in late spring and early summer, *L. cotyledon* which flowers from spring to summer in purple-pink, and *L. tweedyi* which flowers at the same time in a peachy-pink color. The best thing about lewesias is that they hybridize easily, and a collection of different plants should soon yield interesting offspring. The excellent Cotyledon Hybrids come in all colors from yellow-orange to magenta.

LEWESIAS AT A GLANCE

Marvellous small early season flowers in a wide range of colors. Excellent in small pots. Hardy to 5°F (zone 7).

JAN	/	RECOMMENDED VARIETIES
FEB	/	*Lewesia brachycalyx*
MAR	repotting	*L. cotyledon*
APR	/	*L. c. Sunset Group*
MAY	flowering	*L. Cotyledon Hybrids*
JUN	flowering	"De Pauley"
JULY	/	"George Henley"
AUG	/	"Guido"
SEPT	sow	*L. pygmaea*
OCT	/	*L. tweedyi*
NOV	transplant	
DEC	/	

CONDITIONS

Aspect These plants need full sun to thrive and if their position, the base of a wall perhaps, also reduces winter wet, all the better.

Site The soil must be fast draining, and to that end you must dig in plenty of horticultural sand or grit to provide the kind of conditions that the plant receives in its native California. Lewesias also enjoy reasonable fertility, with some added compost.

GROWING METHOD

Propagation Since lewesias freely hybridize, you do not have to do too much propagating. But you can propagate favourite colors by seed (except for the Cotyledon Hybrids) in the fall, or pot up offsets in the summer.

Feeding Plants grown outside in the border might benefit from an early-spring application of a standard plant feed. Pot-grown lewesias, perhaps on a show bench in an alpine house, benefit from a mild liquid feed in the early spring.

Problems A fatal problem for lewesias is excessive moisture during the winter, otherwise watch out for slugs and snails. Remove them by hand each night to prevent the plants from becoming an instant salad.

FLOWERING

Season Lewesias are highly valued for their smallish tubular flowers, generally about 1in across. They are most highly visible when the plant is growing in a crack in a wall. In the garden they would be rather lost.

LITHOPS
Living Stones

THIS CLUSTER of intricately patterned Lithops turbiniformis *is livened by a bright yellow flower.*

LOOKING JUST LIKE A MOUND OF PEBBLES, a large number of living stones fills this shallow bowl.

FEATURES

Sun

Living stones, stone plants, pebble plants and flowering stone are just a few of the common names assigned to these curious succulents. They are so completely camouflaged that it would be very easy to miss them entirely unless they were in flower. In their native south-west and South Africa, they generally grow buried in sand with only the tips of their leaves exposed. Their bodies are composed of a pair of very swollen, fleshy leaves on top of a fused double column with a gap or fissure along their length. The upper surfaces of the leaves are variously patterned and textured according to species and conditions. These plants are best grown in small pots where their curious shapes and markings can be observed. They make an excellent display.

LITHOPS AT A GLANCE

Astonishing tiny succulents in a wide range of colors and patterns. Highly collectible. 41°F min (zone 11).

JAN	/	RECOMMENDED VARIETIES
FEB	/	*Lithops aucampiae*
MAR	sow 🖐	*L. dorothea*
APR	transplant 🖐	*L. julii*
MAY	flowering ❀	*L. mormorata*
JUN	flowering ❀	*L. karasmontana*
JULY	flowering ❀	*L. salicola*
AUG	flowering ❀	*L. schwantesii*
SEPT	flowering ❀	*L. turbiniformis*
OCT	/	
NOV	/	
DEC	/	

CONDITIONS

Aspect   These plants should be grown in a position where there is full sun all day. They are best grown in pots on show benches in a glasshouse. They can cope with extreme heat, and attempts to shade them during the hottest part of the day are quite unnecessary.

Site   The soil provided for living stones should drain very rapidly and small gravel or pebbles should be used as a mulch. Only use very fine pieces of gravel to set off the plants, though with some varieties it is tempting to camouflage them. It is amusing to let visitors see if they can distinguish between the real stones and the plants.

GROWING METHOD

Propagation   These plants can be grown from divisions of offsets or from seed in spring to early summer. As living stones are not rapid growers, the clumps are best left undivided until they are about 4in across.

Feeding   Half-strength soluble liquid plant food can be given every 4–6 weeks through the active growth period

Problems   Most problems arise from overwatering or a poorly drained growing medium. Look out for ahpids when in flower.

FLOWERING

Season   Flowers that emerge from the fissure of the living stone are daisy-like and yellow or white.

PELARGONIUM OBLONGATUM
Pelargonium

A SURPRISE ADDITION to a collection of succulents is Pelargonium obligatum. *It is a marvellous plant with a good display of flowers in late spring and early summer. It is also an excellent plant for maintaining a continuous show of flowers in a collection of succulents.*

FEATURES

Sun

It might sound odd to include a pelargonium in a group of succulents, but about 220 of the 280-odd species are just that. (Do not confuse them with the hardy outdoor geraniums.) *Pelargonium oblongatum* comes from South Africa, in particular the northern region of Namaqualand. It was not actually collected until the early 19th century, making it quite a recent pelargonium since most of the others were collected well before this. It has a 6in long oblong tuber (hence the Latin name), leaves with coarse hairs, and pale yellow flowers delicately feathered with maroon markings. It is definitely a collector's item, and could be the start of a collection with the orange-red *P. boranense* discovered in 1972 in Ethiopia, and *P. carnosum*, also from Namaqualand.

PELARGONIUM AT A GLANCE

P. oblongatum is a pelargonium with a difference. Try this species succulent with delicate pale yellow flowers. 36°F min (zone 10).

		RECOMMENDED VARIETIES
JAN	/	*Pelargonium abrotanifolium*
FEB	/	*P. cucullatum*
MAR	/	*P. fruticosum*
APR	repotting	*P. graveolens*
MAY	flowering	*P. papilionaceum*
JUN	flowering	*P. peltatum*
JULY	/	*P. radens*
AUG	/	*P. tomentosum*
SEPT	sow	
OCT	/	
NOV	transplant	
DEC	/	

CONDITIONS

Aspect   The key requirement is bright sun; the more heat the better. In its native landscape it completely avoids any shade.

Site   It needs to be grown in a pot where it can be properly cared for. Provide an open, free-draining compost. It is surprisingly easy to keep provided it is kept on the dry side while dormant in the summer. Active growth is, as in the southern hemisphere, from fall onwards. Leaf drop is in the spring.

GROWING METHOD

Propagation   While it can be raised from seed, as with all pelargoniums stem cuttings give an extremely high success rate. Take them in mid-fall, as new growth begins, and keep warm over winter avoiding a chilly windowsill. When mature, water well in the winter-spring period, with a reduction over summer.

Feeding   Provide a mild fortnightly liquid feed when in full growth to boost the flowering show in the spring.

Problems   Keep a check for aphids. They form tight packed clusters on the tasty young stems; spray accordingly. Once they take hold they can become quite a nuisance.

FLOWERING

Season   There is a show of star-shaped flowers in the spring. After the bright blowsy colors with sharp reds and lipstick pinks of the more traditional pelargoniums like "Happy Thought" they come as a quieter, interesting surprise.

SEDUM
Stonecrop

A POPULAR CONTAINER or rockery plant, the rarely seen stonecrop Sedum adolphii *takes on pink to red colors in cold weather.*

STARRY FLOWERS with intricate centres are a feature of stonecrop species. Colors include white, pink, red, and yellow.

FEATURES

Sun

Partial Shade

Most plants in this large and diverse group of succulents are ideal for growing in pots, as well as in the garden where they can be used as edging, in rockeries, or tucked into walls. *Sedum spectabile* is often planted in perennial borders where other succulents may look out of place. *S. sieboldii* has spreading stems and rarely exceeds 6in in height. It has very attractive, almost round, blue-green leaves arranged in threes. It has a variegated green and gold form. *S. spathulifolium* forms a dense, low mat of small rosettes. Its variety "Cape Blanco" has a white bloom on gray-green or purplish rosettes. *S. adolphii* has yellowish green, star-like rosettes with reddish hues at times. Although capable of growing to 1ft, it is more usually 8in in height.

SEDUM AT A GLANCE

About 400 species, from annuals to shrubs, with a terrific range of shapes and strong colors. Most hardy to 5°F (zone 7).

		RECOMMENDED VARIETIES
JAN	/	*Sedum cauticola*
FEB	/	"Herbstfreude"
MAR	/	*S. kamtschaticum*
APR	transplant	*S. morganianum*
MAY	/	"Ruby Glow"
JUN	/	*S. rubrotinctum*
JULY	flowering	*S. spectabile*
AUG	flowering	*S. s.* "Brilliant"
SEPT	flowering	*S. spurium* "Schorbuser Blut"
OCT	sow	"Vera Jameson"
NOV	/	
DEC	/	

CONDITIONS

Aspect Full sun is best for most species, but some will tolerate light shade.

Site The soil or potting mix must be very well drained for these plants, and the addition of organic matter for garden plants will give them a decent boost, but only moderate levels are required.

GROWING METHOD

Propagation Division of plants is best done in the early spring. Cuttings can be taken at any time during the warm summer months.

Feeding Slow-release fertilizer or a little pelleted poultry manure given in the spring. In the main, they are best left alone with only a little cutting away of dead stems. Keep a watch at night for attacks by slugs and snails, especially when new spring growth is appearing.

Problems These plants are usually trouble-free.

FLOWERING

Season Flowering time depends on species, but many flower in summer to fall. Flowers of several species are attractive to butterflies and bees, such as *S. spectabile* which has large flower heads of mauve-pink, rosy red, or brick red on stems 16–24in high in fall. *S. sieboldii* has starry pink flowers that appear in masses in late summer or fall. *S. adolphii* has starry flowers that are white. "Ruby Glow" is a low-spreader with dark ruby red flowers appearing from mid-summer into the fall, and "Herbstfreude" produces marvellous pink fall flowers that eventually turn copper-red.

GROWING ORCHIDS

Orchids make up one of the largest families of all the world's flowering plants. They occur on every continent except Antarctica and have a most remarkable diversity of habitat, form, and color. While the greatest number of orchids is found in tropical and subtropical regions, they can also be found in near-desert conditions, tundra, and in mountain country.

Orchid flowers vary in size from large, showy blooms the size of saucers to tiny treasures a couple of millimetres across. Some types of orchid are truly breathtaking in their beauty while others may be quite strange and almost ugly to some eyes, but all are simply fascinating. All orchids should have the spent flowers cut off once they are past their best. Due to the vast diversity of the orchid family, there can be orchids flowering in any season of the year. Some will adhere strictly to their season whereas others may bloom intermittently throughout the year.

LEFT: The fantastically flamboyant flowers of this Laeliocattleya Quo Vadis *"Floralia" are sure to brighten up any display.*

TYPES OF ORCHIDS

The vast majority of orchids in cultivation are epiphytes that grow on trees, but they use the tree as support only—they are not parasites. Other orchids are lithophytes that grow on rocks, or terrestrial types that grow in the ground. Orchids are further distinguished by the way they grow: monopodial orchids, mainly epiphytes, grow with a single stem and produce aerial roots, while sympodial orchids have a rhizome (running root) that produces a pseudobulb from which growth emerges. Many sympodial orchids are terrestrial. Orchids from cooler and more temperate regions are terrestrials but they can occur in warm regions too. Epiphytic orchids are found only in warmer areas.

HYBRIDS

Orchids in the wild hybridize occasionally, and so natural hybrids arise. In their natural situations orchids are pollinated by a range of creatures, including bees, wasps, birds, bats, and beetles. Today, commercial growers and enthusiasts making deliberate cross-pollinations are responsible for introducing many new orchid cultivars and varieties each year. There are now at least 100,000 registered orchid hybrids. Since the 1890s all orchid hybrids have been registered in what is now called the Orchid Hybrid Register run by the Royal Horticultural Society in London. This was previously known as Sanders' Orchid Hybrid Lists, named after the orchid enthusiast who began the daunting task of documenting the whole range of orchids and their parentage.

ORCHID CULTURE

For many years orchid culture was strictly the province of the rich and powerful, not only because of the cost of actually acquiring the plants but also because of the cost of building and heating structures for their successful cultivation. Nowadays special prize-winning plants are still expensive but the advent of plant tissue culture, which allows large numbers of plants to be propagated from very little material, has meant that plants are generally more affordable. There is now a huge number of enthusiasts growing orchids all over the world.

Today many orchids are cultivated commercially for the cut-flower trade. Apart from that, only the vanilla orchid, *Vanilla planifolia*, has commercial value. Its flowers grow on a vine and it is cultivated in tropical regions for its aromatic bean, used widely to flavour food.

BUYING ORCHIDS

For a long time the main source of orchids was plants collected in the wild. Now, with loss of habitat and deforestation of many of the world's tropical forests, it is important to conserve and protect what remains. Plants have been collected to the point of extinction in many regions and trade in endangered species is monitored by an international body, CITES or the Convention on International Trade in Endangered Species.

Orchids for sale in specialist or other nurseries are largely cultivars that have been multiplied and grown by commercial growers. If you are starting an orchid collection, you would be better off keeping to the hybrids. These are more plentiful, usually with bigger blooms, and are replaceable if accidentally killed. The species should only be grown by the skilled specialist.

Specialist nurseries have staff who are generally very knowledgeable and eager to help beginner growers, as well as catalogues to help with your choice of plants. Buy your plants while in bloom or choose ones you have seen in other people's collections or in catalogues. Choose the orchid that will give you the greatest pleasure.

Some orchid groups come in a wide range of colors and have an extended flowering season, and you may want to stay with certain color tones or concentrate on plants that flower at different times of the year. Do not let other people influence your choice.

Once you are "hooked" on orchids consider joining an orchid society as you will learn a large amount about the plants from other members. You will also have the chance to buy or exchange plants at the society's meetings.

GROWING CONDITIONS

Shade and ventilation

Orchids are not necessarily more difficult to grow than other plants if you give them the right climatic and cultural conditions. Many cool-growing orchids come from high mountain regions with frequent cloud and mist and they will not thrive in the tropics. Likewise, tropical

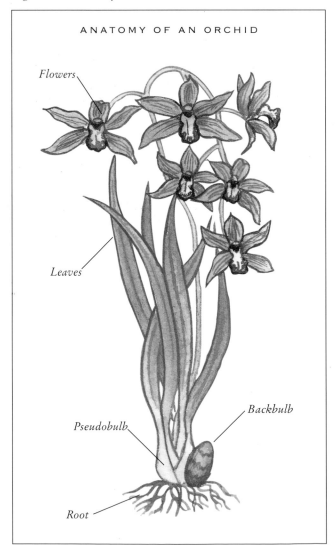

ANATOMY OF AN ORCHID

Flowers

Leaves

Pseudobulb

Backbulb

Root

orchids will die quite quickly if not given adequate heat and humidity. Some varieties can be grown in the open in summer. Often the dappled shade from taller trees is enough to provide good growing conditions, or you can build a shadehouse for protection from sun and wind.

Keeping orchids indoors

Orchids are becoming increasingly popular as houseplants, partly due to their high profile but also as modern hybrids, with greater tolerance and color ranges, are developed.

Modern homes often have a dry atmosphere, but as orchids prefer a humid environment, some moisture should be provided for them. By grouping orchids together or by growing them with other plants that like the same conditions, such as bromeliads and ferns, you can create a suitable microclimate for the plants. You can also stand your plants on humidity trays containing gravel or porous clay pellets. These retain moisture when plants are watered and gradually release it through evaporation, increasing the humidity. However, you should not just rely on the humidity trays to water your orchids—if roots take up too much water through the bottom of the pot they can rot. Instead, take the plants to a sink and water there, letting it flow through the pot and then leave to stand until fully drained before returning to the trays. Another way of creating the right atmosphere is to mist the foliage of the plants regularly with water, especially in warm conditions; this also helps to keep leaves dust-free.

Although orchids do not enjoy direct summer sunshine, good light must be provided if growing indoors. Place the plants near a window where they will get good light but not bright sun, which could scorch their leaves. If the plants are not getting enough light the leaves may become elongated and dark green in color, and they may even grow towards the light, becoming top heavy. Provide shade on a south-facing windowsill with a net curtain or a piece of greenhouse shade cloth to protect the plants.

Orchids enjoy a variety of room temperatures—some cool, some warm, some in between—so the correct room should be chosen for your plants. If the room is heated most of the time, the temperature not dropping below 60°F, then this is a warm climate. Although warm loving orchids will like this, do not place the plants too close to the heat source or else there is a danger of them overheating. Cooler growing orchids would prefer an unheated room indoors where the temperature drops to 50°F—if kept too warm flowering can be restricted.

Conservatories

A conservatory can make a good environment in which to keep orchids. Grow them together with other plants to create the right humid, shaded conditions.

Spraying water and misting is easier in a conservatory than indoors, providing a higher level of humidity and a better environment to grow the more challenging types. If possible, spray the floor with water daily, especially in warm weather. This will evaporate throughout the day, saturating the air. You could also make a water feature, such as a pool or waterfall, around which you can grow orchids and other moisture-loving plants.

Some heat may be required in the conservatory during the winter, as well as extra shading and ventilation in the summer. The same rules apply as with growing indoors regarding the temperature ranges; cool 50–68°F, intermediate 52–77°F, warm 60–77°F. Try not to mix orchids that need different temperatures.

The blooms of this Vanda x Ascocentrum *hybrid are perfectly shaped and finely speckled in red with rose pink margins.*

Shadehouses

If you have more than a few pots of cool orchids you may decide to house them in a shadehouse for the summer. You can make a simple structure of treated timber or galvanized piping covered with wooden or metal laths. Synthetic shadecloth providing 50 per cent shade is good, although a higher degree of shading may be required for some orchids. Laths or shadecloth will cut down the force of strong winds without making the atmosphere stagnant.

Greenhouses

Greenhouses should have roof vents that can be opened to allow hot air to escape and side vents to draw in cooler air. In very warm conditions wall or ceiling fans can keep the air moving if the humidity and heat become too high. In summer you will also need to provide shading.

Bringing orchids indoors

Many orchids can be brought into the house when in flower. For those with a short flowering period this is fine, but if the flowers last six to eight weeks it is best to cut off the flowers and enjoy them in a vase after about four weeks indoors, to avoid a setback in the plant's growth.

GROWING METHOD

Containers

Orchids can be grown in most types of containers, including terracotta and plastic pots, and baskets of wooden slats or wire. Most like to be grown in pots just

PROPAGATING A CYMBIDIUM ORCHID

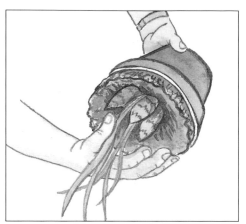

1. Gently ease the plant out of its pot. Run a knife blade around the inside rim if necessary.

2. Use a sharp knife or secateurs to sever the old leafless backbulbs from the younger growths.

3. Remove the old roots and leaf bases from the backbulb and pot it up. Label it clearly.

4. After several weeks or months a leaf shoot appears. It should flower in three years.

large enough to contain their roots. Many epiphytes will have aerial roots that will grow outside the container.
• Plastic pots are the most commonly used because of their relatively low cost, light weight, and ease of cleaning.
• Terracotta pots look attractive and have the advantage of "breathing", that is, allowing better aeration of the mix inside the pot. They are, however, more expensive, are heavy even before planting, dry out more quickly, and their porous surface can allow the growth of algae and slimes and the build-up of fertilizer salts.
• Hanging baskets are essential for some orchids, such as stanhopeas, as their flower spikes grow downwards. The baskets must be lined with soft material, such as coconut fibre, so that the flower spikes can penetrate it.

It is a good idea to have all your orchids in the same type of container, either plastic or terracotta. This will help you to settle on a watering programme and looks more professional.

Mounting an orchid on bark
Some orchids are happiest attached to slabs of cork or tree fern fibre. To grow on bark, either choose an orchid already established on a piece of cork, or transfer one from a pot, picking a plant that has a suitable habit. If the plant has a long, creeping rhizome between the pseudobulbs and is already climbing out of its pot then it is ideal. Plants with tightly packed pseudobulbs do not grow easily on bark.

Potting mixes
There are many types of mix for the cultivation of orchids, but they all have one thing in common: they are fast draining and provide good aeration for plant roots. Bark is the basis of most orchid composts, usually pine bark in various sizes and grades. It is used alone for some orchids or it may be mixed with charcoal, gravel, perlite, peanut shells, spent mushroom compost, coarse river sand, coir peat, and sometimes blood-and-bone or slow release fertilizer. Sometimes a mix of only two items, such as pine bark and charcoal, is used. In most cases the potting mix or growing medium is simply there to anchor the roots of the plant. Nutrients and water have to be applied regularly throughout the plant's growing season.

Watering
The amount of watering needed depends on the time of year, the weather, the growing mix and the type of orchid.

Watering

The amount of watering needed depends on the time of year, the weather, the growing mix and the type of orchid.

In hot weather, while plants are in active growth, most need daily watering or at least spray misting to maintain moisture around their roots. In conditions where humidity is low and the temperature high, plants may need spraying with water three or four times a day rather than watering around the roots. Damping down the floor of a glasshouse can lower the temperature and increase the humidity when needed.

In cool weather and when plants are completely or fairly dormant, some types are seldom watered. Many originate from regions with well-defined wet and dry seasons. In the wet season they make new leaves and pseudobulbs, in the dry season they rest from growth but produce flowers just before their new growing season begins. In most cases allow them to dry out between waterings. Other types may need watering about once a week during their rest period. Plants constantly watered while they are dormant are likely to collapse and die from root rots. No one can tell you exactly when to water: you have to learn by observation and experience. More orchids are killed through overwatering than anything else. Just remember orchids have growth periods and rest periods.

Feeding

As with water, apply fertilizer only to orchids in active growth. Plants can absorb nutrients only in solution and so regular watering helps orchids absorb the fertilizer. Never apply fertilizer to plants that are bone dry. Always water them first, apply the fertilizer, then water again. It is better to underfeed rather than overfeed: too much can burn and cause problems while giving less simply means that plants grow more slowly.

Garden centres stock fertilizers specially formulated for orchids, some to promote vegetative growth and others to promote flowering, the idea being that you switch from one to the other at a certain stage in the growing season. Other fertilizers are sold as complete plant foods. Soluble plant foods can be applied through the growing season or slow release granular fertilizers applied as new growth begins and again after three or four months. Fertilizers high in nitrogen are best used to promote growth while those high in potassium and phosphorus will help promote flowering. Details of fertilizer ratios are listed on the sides of packets or bottles.

Orchids growing on slabs should be fertilized by spraying with dilute soluble fertilizer. Spray when damp and the weather overcast so that no burning occurs.

PROPAGATION

Many orchids are propagated in nurseries by tissue culture, allowing a huge number of plants to be grown from a small amount of the parent plant. Plants grown from seed are also cultured in flasks. This is useful for sending plants to other countries as the plants have been grown in sterile conditions and will therefore pass quarantine regulations. They are transferred from flasks to individual pots when large enough to survive.

At home, most orchids are propagated by division of existing plants, by removing offsets that have some developed roots or by growing new plants from dormant pseudobulbs. Methods vary and the technique best suited to each group is outlined in the plant entries. Division is best done straight after flowering, as new growth appears.

WHAT CAN GO WRONG?

Orchids are remarkably trouble free. Adequate spacing of plants, good ventilation, and good cultural practice should minimize problems. Remove dead or decaying material to keep plants clean and looking good. Isolate any sick plants from the rest and wash your hands and disinfect any tools before handling healthy plants. If you have to use chemicals for pest or disease control, do not spray buds or flowers as they may be distorted. It is usually the newest, most tender parts that are affected.

Pests

• Snails can chew holes in buds and flowers. Remove them by hand or place a few pellets on top of the pots to catch them before they reach the flowers.
• Vine weevils also chew holes in buds and flowers. They are hard to control but some insecticidal dusts may be able to help.
• Several types of scale insect may attack a range of orchids. Small infestations can be gently washed or wiped off with a damp cloth. For heavy infestations spray with an insecticide.
• Red spider mites may be prevalent in warm, dry weather. They can make the foliage mottled and dull looking. Overhead watering and misting the undersides of the leaves helps to discourage them. However, you may actually need to dust or spray the plant with a registered miticide.

Diseases

• Fungal leaf disease. There is a large range of fungal leaf diseases that may attack various orchids, especially in overcrowded or very humid conditions. It may be quite difficult to control them without resorting to a fungicide. Improving ventilation and spacing out the pots should help. Avoid overhead watering and try not to water late in the day if you are plagued with fungal problems.
• Virus disease. There are a number of virus diseases that may attack orchids and there is no cure. Symptoms are variable and may include pale greenish-yellow spots, streaks or patterns of brown, black concentric rings, or other patterns along the leaf blade. Serious orchid growers will generally destroy plants affected by virus disease. If you do not want to do this you must isolate the affected plant. Virus diseases may be transmitted through sap-sucking insects such as aphids, which must be controlled, and you must wash your hands and disinfect tools after working on a plant suspected of being diseased.
• Bulb or root rots are caused by organisms found in the potting medium. The organisms flourish when conditions are overwet. Rotted pseudobulbs or roots must be cut away cleanly from the healthy ones and all the old mix washed off. Scrub and disinfect the pot before refilling it with fresh potting mix and replacing the plants. Make sure the mix is very well drained; do not overwater. Some fungicides, used as drenches, can help control the problem.

MOUNTING ORCHIDS ON BARK

WHY GROW ON BARK?

Many of the orchids grown in cultivation are in nature tree-dwelling, or epiphytic. They use the trees in the rainforests as a perch on which to grow, enabling them to grow nearer to the light. Orchids that grow in this way often have a creeping habit and produce a lot of aerial roots. These are two characteristics that make them difficult to grow in a pot. They are better mounted on a piece of cork bark and allowed to grow across its surface.

PREPARING YOUR PLANT

First you will need to select the plant that you are going to mount. It must have quite a creeping habit of growth with an elongated rhizome between the pseudobulbs. A plant that has a tight cluster of pseudobulbs will not fit well and will have to be regularly remounted. The advantage of growing orchids on bark is that they can remain there for many years without having to be disturbed. If the plant outgrows the first piece, it can be trained on to another piece attached to the original.

The plant should have a healthy active root system to make it easier for it to quickly establish itself in its new position. When moving any plant, wait until it is just starting its new growth as this is when new roots are formed and the plant will suffer the least disturbance.

Choose a piece of cork bark or even a tree branch on which to mount your orchid that will give it enough room to grow for at least a few years. You may even want to mount several plants on the same large piece of wood, to make an interesting feature in your greenhouse.

Other equipment that you will need includes some sphagnum moss and coconut fiber, which will combine to form a moist area around the roots. If you cannot find these particular items then a mixture of similar moist but fibrous substances will do. Some plastic coated wire or fishing line should be used to attach the plant to the bark. After a period of time, once the plant has become established and rooted itself on to the bark, the wire will become obsolete and can be removed if wanted.

MOUNTING THE ORCHID

Take the plant out of its pot, clean away the old compost and trim any dead roots—it will produce new ones once established. Carefully wrap the moss and fibre mixture around the base of the plant, where the roots will weave their way into it, and position the plant on the bark. Secure it with some wire and, while holding it in place, tighten the wire or fasten the fishing line. Take care not to let the wire cut into any part of the plant. It is best to pass the wire in between the pseudobulbs, across the rhizome and away from the new shoots to avoid damage. Attach a wire hook to the top of the bark so you can hang it up in your greenhouse. Make sure it is sprayed or dunked in water daily to prevent drying out.

Remove the orchid from its pot, clean the compost from the roots and trim back a little. Mix moss and fibre together to form a pad on which to place the plant to provide a moist surface for the roots.

It is important to choose a type of plant, preferably with a healthy root system, that will lend itself to being mounted on bark. You will also need plastic-coated wire, pliers, a piece of cork bark and some sphagnum moss or coconut fibre.

Wrap the base of the plant with the moss mixture and position on the bark. Tie a piece of plastic-coated wire around the base of the plant, avoiding shoots or roots, and tighten just enough to keep the plant in place. Attach a hook and hang where it can be regularly sprayed.

CONVERTING A FISH TANK

AN INDOOR GROWING ENVIRONMENT

A house can be too dry an atmosphere to keep orchids successfully. This is especially true for the small growing ones that tend to dry out more quickly than the plants in larger pots. An interesting and fun way of growing them in the home is to convert an old, disused aquarium into a miniature orchid house. A humid atmosphere will be created inside the glass tank, preventing the plants from becoming too dry. The orchids can be mixed with companion plants that enjoy the same conditions as long as they stay small so the tank is not outgrown quickly.

TOP RIGHT An old, disused fish tank makes an ideal growing environment for miniature orchids. Choose some plants which will stay small and not quickly outgrow the space. Companion plants that will also remain small are helpful to the overall environment.

MIDDLE Making sure that the tank will not leak, fill the base with a layer of expanded clay pellets. These absorb the moisture sprayed on them which then gradually evaporates around the plants creating a humid atmosphere. Add some decorative pieces of wood, bark, or rock to create an interesting feature of your indoor garden.

BELOW Lastly, include the finishing touches of the plants including maybe some miniature ferns and foliage plants to complement the orchids. Regularly spray the plants and pellets in the tank to create humidity and remove the plants when you are actually watering them to prevent a build up of too much water in the base. Place near a window and use some shade cloth to cover the tank if too much bright sun is available. A lid is not essential but can be used.

GREENHOUSE CULTIVATION

WHY USE A GREENHOUSE?

To get the best out of your orchids it is advisable to set up a greenhouse especially for them. This means that you can get the growing conditions exactly right. Within this greenhouse you can regulate the temperature and humidity of the air throughout the year and determine how much light, water, and ventilation the plants receive. A better environment can be created and so a wider range of orchids can be grown in a greenhouse than in the home.

POINTS TO CONSIDER

You may wish to convert an existing greenhouse or start afresh with a newly built structure. Whatever you decide, it is important that the greenhouse is positioned in the right place. As orchids prefer a shady environment, it is best to position your greenhouse in a shaded part of the garden, near to deciduous trees as these will provide shade in the summer and let in the light in winter when they have lost their leaves. Some extra shade may be needed during summer though, when the sun is at its brightest, as orchid leaves can be easily scorched. Use paint shading on the glass or netting, which can be removed for the winter, or a combination of the two depending on your own greenhouse's situation. The orchids should be kept in dappled sunlight to gain the right amount of light; if too dark then their growth and flowering will be inhibited.

Most traditional greenhouses have glass in their roofs but there are more modern materials available now that need less maintenance, including twin or triple thickness polycarbonate sheeting. This is a rigid plastic sheeting that is very strong and acts as an extremely good insulator, cutting down on the heating requirements for the winter months. It does not matter what type of roofing material you decide to use, but it is important that you make sure that the greenhouse is well ventilated. On hot days, the temperature can rise dramatically and will quickly suffocate the plants inside if there is not enough ventilation available in the greenhouse. Side panels that open in the walls and roof ventilators should be incorporated into your greenhouse so that they can be opened on hot days to give plenty of air movement.

PREPARING YOUR GREENHOUSE

Heating is very important for orchids during the colder months of the year. Cooler growing orchids enjoy a drop in temperature but even they will not tolerate temperatures much below 50°F. Warmer varieties need a few more degrees, a minimum of 60°F, so need an extra heat supply. This can be supplied by an electric, gas, or oil fuelled greenhouse heater. Take the advice of a good supplier to choose the right equipment for your particular set up. A maximum/minimum thermometer is also a very useful piece of equipment as it allows you to keep a check on what the temperature is dropping to at night.

Benches and shelving are ideal ways to arrange your plants at the height that is comfortable for you and your plants. Large plants can be stood lower down, or even on the floor, while smaller pots can be placed on the benches or shelves. If space is at a premium then use the area above the shelves to hang plants up too. This is ideal for orchids that like a bit of extra light and they, in turn, will give a little extra shade to the plants growing below them. If your orchid collection is just beginning then they may have to share their space with other plants already living in your greenhouse. This is fine as long as they all need the same conditions. If the orchids are not compatible with your other plants then it may be necessary to partition the greenhouse with transparent, UV-treated polythene to form two or more separate growing environments. This is also a good idea if you plant to grow a mixed collection of some warm and some cool growing orchids.

CREATING THE RIGHT ATMOSPHERE

One of the best things about growing orchids in a greenhouse is that you can create a humid atmosphere in there for them. Spray the floor of the greenhouse regularly with water, especially in warm weather to keep the temperature down and the air moist. Another way of creating humidity is by growing other types of shade loving plants underneath the benches, such as ferns. This all adds to the overall atmosphere and the orchids will grow better because of it.

Spraying and watering can be done with a watering can, but as your orchid collection grows it may take many trips to fill up the can. A more convenient alternative is to install a hose pipe system that can then reach all parts of the greenhouse, maybe even with a watering lance attached to the end of it. This will allow you to regulate the amount of water that you give to each individual plant; as well as giving the choice of a variety of spraying and misting head attachments.

Brighten up an ordinary conservatory with a few orchids. They will enjoy the light, airy environment as well as added moisture from daily misting. Some winter insulation may be necessary as seen here with the bubble polythene covering the door.

ABOVE *If you have the space then why not create your very own walk-through tropical paradise with impressive foliage plants accompanying the orchids which can live happily in this habitat. Climbing plants can create shade but be careful that they do not harbour pests.*

RIGHT *Make the best use of your greenhouse by creating maximum bench space and also using the space above the plants to hang some orchids in baskets and hanging pots. Foliage plants placed underneath the benching help with the humidity as well as the use of a humidifier, seen here on the floor.*

ANGULOA
Tulip orchid

The Anguloa clowesii *is known as the "Tulip Orchid" because of its amazing cup-shaped flower which has a rocking lip inside it.*

A strong scent and incredibly waxy blooms are typical of this family as is seen in this Anguloa virginalis.

FEATURES

Terrestrial

This fascinating orchid—known as the tulip orchid due to its tulip-shaped flower—has another common name, cradle orchid. This names describes the lip inside the cup-shaped flower which rocks back and forth when the bloom is tipped. The genus *Anguloa* is closely related to the lycastes with which they can interbreed, making an *Angulocaste*. The species originate from Colombia, Venezuela, and Peru and are mainly terrestrial plants. Large, broad leaves are produced in the summer months from the new growth, but in the fall these die off as the plant goes into its deciduous rest for winter. Its dark green pseudobulbs will then lie dormant until the following spring.

ANGULOA AT A GLANCE

Better for the experienced grower. The flowers last a long time and are hightly scented. Will reach 24in.

JAN	rest	
FEB	rest	
MAR	water and feed	
APR	water and feed	
MAY	flowering, water and feed	
JUN	flowering, water and feed	
JULY	water and feed	
AUG	water and feed	
SEPT	water and feed	
OCT	rest	
NOV	rest	
DEC	rest	

RECOMMENDED VARIETIES
A. cliftonii (yellow with red markings)
A. clowesii
A. uniflora (white)
A. virginalis

Another feature of this genus is that the long-lasting flowers are strongly scented, often similar to a liniment fragrance.

CONDITIONS

Climate The anguloas need cool conditions with a winter minimum of 50°F, and summer maximum of 86°F.

Aspect Due to the soft, annual leaves, shade is required in the summer.

Potting Mix A medium grade bark is ideal with some finer grade bark or peat mixed in.

GROWING METHOD

Propagation It is quite a slow growing orchid, often making just one pseudobulb a year, so will not increase in size enough to divide easily. Back bulbs will sometimes re-grow if removed and potted up separately.

Watering While the plant is in its winter rest, and is leafless, the compost should be kept dry. Watering can be resumed at the start of the new growth in spring. While it has leaves the plant should not dry out. In the fall the new pseudobulb will have been completed and the leaves will turn brown and drop off. Stop watering the plant at this point.

Feeding Plants will benefit from regular feeding while in growth so that the new pseudobulb can develop in the short growing season.

Problems As long as the compost is kept dry during winter then no problems should occur. Avoid water collecting inside new growth.

FLOWERING SEASON

Late spring to early summer.

ASPASIA
Aspasia species

This charming, compact plant is easy to grow and will re-bloom very easily, even as a houseplant in a room with a little warmth.

The pretty, star-shaped flowers of Aspasia lunata *nestle around the base of the attractive, leafy plant. Several single flowers are produced.*

FEATURES

Epiphytic

This is a compact and flowering orchid perfect for the beginner. *Aspasias* are a small group of orchids, the genus containing only about ten different species. These originate from the tropical Americas, and are found growing from Nicaragua to Brazil over quite a widespread area. Although not a common orchid, it is actually quite easy to grow, increasing freely in size and producing flowers regularly and easily. Its habit is fairly compact, the height of the soft-leafed pseudobulbs reaching only around 6in, making it ideal for a small collection. Due to its naturally epiphytic nature, the plant has a creeping habit with an elongated rhizome connecting the pseudobulbs. This means that it quickly outgrows pots and is in need of annual re-potting. However, with orchids that have a tendency to do this, the plant is often happier out of the pot than in it.

CONDITIONS

Climate Slightly cold sensitive so prefers a minimum temperature of 54°F in winter, up to 86°F in summer.
Aspect Has pale, soft leaves so a little shade in summer will prevent paling or scorching.
Potting Mix A medium grade general bark potting mix.

GROWING METHOD

Propagation This orchid readily produces new growths and so multiplies quite quickly. Therefore, the plant can be divided every few years if required but will do well to be left alone to grow into a specimen plant, which will produce many flowers at once.
Watering The plant does not always follow a strict seasonal pattern so keep it simple by watering more frequently only when in active growth and reducing this to a minimum when not.
Feeding Use a higher nitrogen feed when applying in the growing season, a weak solution every two to three waterings.
Problems If cultural conditions are suitable then it should have no specific problems.

FLOWERING SEASON

Varies but mostly spring and summer. Flower buds emerge from the base of the new growth and stay around plant's base.

ASPASIA AT A GLANCE

Easy to grow. Compact, attractive plant up to 5in high.
Flowers, often in succession, 1¼in across.

JAN	rest	SEPT	water and feed
FEB	rest	OCT	rest
MAR	flowering, water and feed	NOV	rest
		DEC	rest
APR	flowering, water and feed		
MAY	flowering, water and feed	**RECOMMENDED VARIETIES**	
JUN	flowering, water and feed	*A. epidendroides* (brown petals with a purple and white lip)	
JULY	flowering, water and feed	*A. lunata*	
AUG	flowering, water and feed		

BIFRENARIA
Bifrenaria species

Bifrenaria tyrianthina *is an unusual species to grow and is stunning with its large pink blooms on upright stems.*

The more commonly seen B. harrisoniae *has a curiously furry texture and a contrasting purple lip. It is a popular and easy orchid to grow.*

FEATURES

Epiphytic

The charming and popular bifrenarias were once classified as cymbidiums, and show a resemblance to them in their flower shape. These orchids, however, mostly come from Brazil but can also be found widely distributed throughout Panama, Trinidad, northern South America, and Peru. *Bifrenaria* has always been a popular orchid for beginners and proves easy to grow and flower in the amateur's cool mixed collection. It is a compact growing plant with long-lasting, heavily textured flowers sitting around the base of the plant. As a bonus the flowers are sweetly scented. They are epiphytic orchids in nature, growing on the higher branches of trees in the South American rain forests. It is possible to grow these orchids quite successfully in a cool to intermediate greenhouse, conservatory, or even on a windowsill with other companion plants. If in a greenhouse, the plants could be grown in a hanging basket near the light coming through the roof.

CONDITIONS

Climate	A temperature range of 50–77°F, with ventilation in the summer months.
Aspect	Good light all the year round but provide some shade in the hottest months.
Potting Mix	A general medium grade bark compost is ideal with good drainage qualities.

GROWING METHOD

Propagation	This orchid is a fairly slow grower so it could be a few years before it is ready to be divided. Best to leave as a specimen plant for as long as possible. May propagate from back bulbs that are removed and are potted up separately at potting time.
Watering	Keep compost on the dry side during the winter months when the plant is not growing. With the onset of the new growth in the spring resume watering to get the new pseudobulb plumped up by the fall.
Feeding	The plant responds to a light feeding during the growing season. Use a higher nitrogen plant food every two or three waterings.
Problems	No specific problems known if the cultural conditions are suitable.

FLOWERING SEASON

Long-lasting through spring and summer.

BIFRENARIA AT A GLANCE

Dark green broad foliage reaches 8in from pseudobulb. Single flowers with bearded lip low at base.

JAN	rest		NOV	rest
FEB	rest		DEC	rest
MAR	flowering			
APR	flowering, water and feed		RECOMMENDED VARIETIES	
MAY	flowering, water and feed		*B. atropurpurea* (dark purple-brown)	
JUN	water and feed		*B. harrisoniae*	
JULY	water and feed		*B. tyrianthina*	
AUG	water and feed			
SEPT	rest			
OCT	rest			

BLETILLA
Chinese ground orchid

The slightly ridged pattern on the lip of this Chinese ground orchid is very pretty when viewed at close quarters.

Reliable and easy-care, clumps of Bletilla striata *multiply readily. They enjoy filtered sun in most conditions.*

FEATURES

Terrestrial

Bletilla is one of a small group of terrestrial orchids from China, Japan, and Taiwan. This is a very easy orchid to cultivate. It is deciduous, dying back to ground level in the fall or early winter. It grows from a pseudobulb that looks like a corm, each producing about three bright green pleated or folded leaves up to 16in long. Flowers are slightly bell shaped, cerise-purple to magenta, and carried on one slender stem—there may be 10–12 blooms on a stem. The lip of the flower is beautifully patterned in white and cerise. There is a white form, "Alba", but it is not as vigorous. The blooms usually last a few weeks if conditions are good.

BLETILLA AT A GLANCE

Easy to grow for cool conditions similar to an alpine house. Bright purple flowers give a good winter show.

JAN	flowering, rest	OCT	rest
FEB	flowering, rest, re-pot	NOV	rest
		DEC	rest
MAR	flowering, water and feed, re-pot		
APR	flowering, water and feed, re-pot	RECOMMENDED VARIETIES
MAY	water and feed	*B. striata*
JUN	water and feed	
JULY	water and feed	
AUG	water and feed	
SEPT	water and feed	

CONDITIONS

Climate This is a very cool growing orchid and will thrive in a greenhouse if it is kept frost-free, at a minimum temperature of 41°F. Can be placed outside in summer and even planted in the ground in frost-free areas.

Aspect This orchid needs to be planted in a sheltered spot with dappled shade. It must have protection from hot sun in the middle of the day.

Potting mix Needs well-drained mix or soil with plenty of humus so that it can retain moisture during dry periods.

GROWING METHOD

Propagation Congested clumps of plants can be divided in late winter to early spring. Replant the pseudobulbs at the same depth as they were previously and remove dead leaves.

Watering Needs plenty of regular watering during hot weather through spring and summer. When the leaves begin to yellow off, decrease watering and then stop as the plant dies down.

Feeding Apply slow release fertilizer in spring or give liquid plant food at half strength every two or three weeks during the growing season to help increase growth.

Problems No specific problems are known. Foliage burns if exposed to too much hot sun in summer and plants will rot in a poorly drained medium. Keep the plant dry when not in leaf.

FLOWERING SEASON

Flowers between late winter and spring.

BRASSIA
Spider orchid

The spider orchids are fascinating with their long, thin petals and unusual green coloring, seen in this species, Brassia verrucosa.

This larger flowered hybrid, Brassia *Rex* has the characteristic sweet fragrance that these orchids are known for.

FEATURES

Epiphytic

This group of epiphytic orchids are extremely popular. The attractive leafy plants are easy to keep and flower well when given plenty of light. They are known for their spidery flowers, which give them their common name. The blooms are long lasting, staying on the plant for many weeks and giving off a very pleasant fragrance. There have been many hybrids developed between the species, giving extra size and quality to the flowers, for example *B*. Edvah Loo. Brassias have also been used to make hybrids with other genera such as miltonias and odontoglossums, to produce miltassias and odontobrassias, which inherit the star-shaped flowers and showy appearance of the parent. Grow the brassias in hanging baskets near the light to achieve maximum flowering potential. In this environment they also produce prolific aerial root growth.

CONDITIONS

Climate	They thrive in a cool or intermediate temperature; 50–54°F at night in winter to 68–77°F in summer.
Aspect	Brassias need light to encourage flowering, so place in a south facing aspect with a little shade from the brightest sun.
Potting Mix	Medium or coarse mixture of bark chippings.

GROWING METHOD

Propagation	The plant should produce several growths from one pseudobulb when it reaches a mature size, which will increase the size of the plant quickly. It can then be divided. Make sure divisions are not too small otherwise they will not flower well. Keep a minimum of four to six pseudobulbs.
Watering	Keep the compost moist all the year round. Watering can be reduced in winter months to prevent compost waterlogging. Regular watering while in growth and spraying of leaves and aerial roots will benefit the plant.
Feeding	Only apply fertilizer when the plant is in growth. Use a water-soluble feed and pour through the compost as well as adding it to the water used for misting leaves and roots.
Problems	Brassias may not flower well if not enough light is provided, especially in winter.

FLOWERING SEASON

Generally late spring and summer.

BRASSIA AT A GLANCE

Easy to grow. Fragant flowers on long spike, up to 20in. Compact plant, 6–8in high.

JAN	rest	OCT	rest
FEB	rest	NOV	rest
MAR	rest	DEC	rest
APR	rest		
MAY	flowering, water and feed	RECOMMENDED VARIETIES	
JUN	flowering, water and feed	*B*. giroudiana	
JULY	flowering, water and feed	*B*. maculata	
		B. verrucosa	
AUG	flowering, water and feed	*B*. Edvah Loo	
		B. New Start	
SEPT	rest	*B*. Rex	
		(all green/yellow)	

BULBOPHYLLUM
Bulbophyllum species and hybrids

Bulbophyllum *Jersey has a wonderful rich red coloring and an unusual shaped flower inherited from its parents.*

This is B. lobbii, *an orchid that is well known for its lip that rocks back and forth when the flower is moved.*

FEATURES

Epiphytic

The genus *Bulbophyllum* is one of the largest in the orchid family and includes some of the most extraordinary looking flowers in the orchid kingdom. It is closely related to, and often classified with, the genus *Cirrhopetalum*. They are extremely widespread, being found in South East Asia, Africa, Australia, and the tropical Americas. The habit and appearance of the plants and flowers are as variable as their place of origin. Some have tiny flowers that you need a magnifying glass to see; others have large, unusually shaped, showy blooms. A characteristic of many of these orchids is a curiously rocking lip, which attracts certain pollinating insects to the flowers. Some are also fragrant, however this is not always pleasant. The orchids try to attract carrion flies, so they send out the scent of rotting meat. They make good specimen plants, growing well in, and over the edge of, hanging baskets, in which they can stay for years.

CONDITIONS

Climate	Due to the widespread nature of these orchids, there are both cool and warm growing species available, so check with your supplier when making a purchase. Most of the Asian types are cool, whereas the African species tend to be warmer.
Aspect	They can take a lot of light so grow well in a hanging basket near the greenhouse roof.
Potting Mix	Need an open medium or coarse grade bark with even some perlite or larger perlag mixed in to make it free draining.

GROWING METHOD

Propagation	Most will grow quickly into large clumps with multiple growths so can be divided after only a few years. Alternatively leave growing in a basket for many years until the orchid completely envelops the basket.
Watering	Let bulbophyllums dry out in between waterings and take care not to overwater them when in growth. If the pseudobulbs start to shrivel then they are too dry. By growing them in a coarse bark in open baskets they should not stay too wet.
Feeding	Give feed only when in growth, and apply this as a foliar feed by spraying it on the leaves as well as pouring through the compost. A weak dilution every two or three waterings is ideal.
Problems	No specific problems are known if the cultural conditions are suitable.

FLOWERING SEASON

Depends on the species or hybrid grown.

BULBOPHYLLUM AT A GLANCE

Strange appearance, with a variety of shapes and sizes, from 1¼–12in high. Flowers ⅛–3in across.

JAN	rest	RECOMMENDED VARIETIES
FEB	rest	*B. careyanum* "Fir Cone Orchid"
MAR	rest, re-pot	
APR	rest, re-pot	*B. graveolans* (cluster of green and red flowers at the base)
MAY	water and feed, re-pot	
JUN	water and feed	*B. lobbii*
JULY	water and feed	*B. macranthum* (purple)
AUG	water and feed	*B. purpureorachis* (brown flowers creeping up a spiral stem)
SEPT	water and feed	
OCT	rest	
NOV	rest	*B. vitiense* (small pink)
DEC	rest	

CYMBIDIUM
Cymbidium species and hybrids

Masses of small blooms clustered on a flower stem are a feature of many of the miniature cymbidium hybrids.

Potted cymbidiums are at home outdoors in the summer. Plants in flower should be displayed indoors in a cool position.

FEATURES

Terrestrial

Epiphytic

Cymbidiums are probably the most widely cultivated of all orchids. They originate in temperate or tropical parts of north-western India, China, Japan, through south-east Asia, and Australia. There are now thousands of cultivated varieties. These hybrids have flowers classed as standard size (4–6in across), miniature (about 2in across) or intermediate. The leaves are strap-like, upright, or pendulous, and 20in or more in length in standard growers. The foliage of the miniature plants is narrower and shorter, in keeping with the overall dimensions of the plant. Cymbidiums have a wide appeal as the flowers are decorative and long lasting.

CYMBIDIUM AT A GLANCE

Popular and widely grown. Flowers vary from 1½–4in. Easy to grow in light, cool conditions.

JAN	rest, flowering	NOV	rest, flowering
FEB	rest, flowering, repot	DEC	rest, flowering
MAR	flowering, water and feed, re-pot	RECOMMENDED VARIETIES	
APR	flowering, water and feed, re-pot	*C. erythrostylum* (white)	
MAY	water and feed	*C. lowianum* (green)	
JUN	water and feed	*C. traceyanum* (brown)	
JULY	water and feed	*C.* Amesbury (green)	
AUG	water and feed	*C.* Bouley Bay (yellow)	
SEPT	rest, flowering, water and feed	*C.* Gymer (yellow/red)	
OCT	rest, flowering	*C.* Ivy Fung (red)	
		C. Pontac (burgundy)	

Flowers
The range of flower colors covers every shade and tone of white and cream, yellow and orange, pink and red, brown and green, all with patterned or contrasting colors on the lip. Flowers are carried on quite sturdy stems standing well clear of the foliage. As many are in bloom in winter they can give a special lift to the season. Many have flowers that will last six to eight weeks.

Choosing
Choose plants both by flower color and time of blooming. With careful selection you can have a *Cymbidium* in bloom every month from early fall through to late spring. Selecting plants in flower will tell you exactly what you are getting. Some orchid nurseries sell tissue cultured mericlones of these orchids as young plants: these are much cheaper but you will have to wait three to four years for them to reach flowering size. Backbulbs, if available, are also an option although these too take up to four years to flower. Buying seedlings is also cheaper and you will have the thrill of their first flowering, not knowing in advance what the flowers will be like. The parent plants may be displayed or the nursery should be able to give you an idea of the likely color range, which extends through the spectrum.

CONDITIONS

Climate
Ideal conditions are humid year round, with winter temperatures not reaching much below 46–50°F and summer temperatures that are generally below 86°F. It is advisable to place the plants outside in summer. To initiate flowering many, but not all, require a distinct drop between their day and night temperatures.

Pink-flushed white flowers are popular with many Cymbidium *growers. Note the lovely spotting on the lip.*

GROWING METHOD

Propagation   Grow new plants from backbulbs (older, leafless bulbs). These may look dead but will regrow if they are detached from the younger growths when you are dividing plants after flowering. Clean old leaf bases and trim off any old roots. Plant the bulbs into small individual or large communal pots, about one-third of their depth into a mixture of coir peat and bark. Keep damp but not wet. Once good leaf and root growth are evident, pot up into normal mix. Plants grown this way generally flower after about three years.

Watering   Frequency of watering is determined by the time of year. The mix should be moist but not wet. Always give enough at one watering for water to pour through the mix. Plants may need watering daily in summer or only every few days if conditions are wet. Water about once every one to two weeks in winter.

Feeding   Feeding can be as easy or as complicated as you like. You can simply give slow release granular fertilizers during the growing season. Or, alternatively, you can use soluble liquid feeds regularly through spring and summer. Some growers like to use high nitrogen fertilizers during spring, switching to special orchid foods or complete fertilizers that are high in phosphorus and potassium in summer. Some of these are applied monthly, others in half strength more often. It is important to follow label recommendations and not to overdo it.

Problems   Unfortunately cymbidiums are prone to some diseases, quite apart from the normal range of pests. Virus disease can be a problem and so maintain strict hygiene by disinfecting hands and tools to avoid it spreading. Bulb rots can also be a problem if potting mixes contain too much fine material, which impedes drainage. Fungal leaf spots can occur in crowded or very wet conditions. Keep an eye out for snails, slugs and aphids as your plants come into bud because they can quickly ruin your long-awaited flowers. They will attack both buds and long spikes.

Support   Light cane or metal stakes should be used to support the flower spikes as they develop. Carefully insert the support beside the developing spike and use plastic coated tie-wire or string to tie the spike as often as needed to train it into position.

FLOWERING SEASON

In bloom through fall, winter and spring with just a few summer varieties. Plants in flower can be brought into the house for decoration. Moving a plant in bud from a cool greenhouse to a warm room can make the buds drop so wait until the flowers are open and set until you move it. The cooler the plant is kept, the longer the flowers last, which is on average six to eight weeks.

Cut flowers   Professional growers cut the flower spikes a week after all flowers on the spike are open to prevent any check in the plant's growth.

Aspect   These plants will not flower if they do not get sufficient light. They will grow in the open with dappled shade from trees or with only morning sun in summer, but they can actually take full sun almost all day during the winter. A shadehouse with 50 per cent shade is suitable in summer. If you can see that your plants have very dark green leaves then they aren't getting enough light and are very unlikely to flower. These plants need good ventilation and protection from strong winds and rain when placed outside. In winter, place them in the lightest position available within a cool greenhouse, conservatory, or in an unheated, light room.

Potting mix   Mix or soil must be very free draining. Many species in their habitat grow in hollow branches of trees, in decayed bark and leaf litter. Hybrids can be grown in aged, medium-grade pine bark, or in pine bark plus coir peat, bracken fibre, charcoal, or even pieces of foam. Plants need to be anchored and supported but must have free drainage and good aeration around the roots. Prepared, special orchid composts are satisfactory, especially if you only have a few plants. Cymbidiums must always be potted with the base of the pseudobulb either at, or preferably just above, the level of the compost.

Containers   Make sure that there are enough drain holes in the container and, if not, punch in more. Cymbidiums are quite vigorous growers and if placed in 8in pots they will probably need potting and maybe dividing every two or three years. It is best to pot plants into containers that will just comfortably accommodate their roots. They can then be potted on into the next size when necessary. Plants that have filled their containers and need dividing are best left until spring, and then divided into sections with no fewer than three pseudobulbs per division. If divided soon after flowering in spring the plants will then have a full six months growing season ahead of them to settle into their new pot.

3.

CYMBIDIUMS

1 Cymbidium *Red Beauty* x *Gorey* is a standard variety of the Cymbidium, *which can reach 3¼ft in height, with tall sprays of rich pinkish-red flowers.*

2 A compact type of Cymbidium, *this beautifully colored* C. *Mini Dream "Gold Sovereign", has an unusual shade of butter yellow with yellow markings on the lip too, making a striking combination.*

3 Large flowered standard variety Cymbidium *Sleeping Nymph "Perfection" is sought after for its striking combination of apple-green petals and sepals and yellow marked lip, which is lacking the usual red pigment.*

4 These orchids can reach a fair size if they are left undivided and are of the larger growing type, as this C. *Havre des Pas shows. They will produce a better show if they are allowed to grow into a larger specimen.*

5 For the more modest space available, a compact variety such as C. *Red Valley "Brilliant" will give a marvellous show, while taking up less space.*

2.

DENDROBIUM
Dendrobium species and hybrids (Asian)

A dark blotch of color in the throat is a feature of many types of dendrobium, including this Dendrobium nobile.

One of the finest yellow orchids is Dendrobium fimbriatum. *The beautiful, finely fringed lip is greatly admired.*

FEATURES

Epiphytic

By far the largest number of *Dendrobium* species come from sub-tropical and warm regions of Burma, the Himalayas, Thailand, China, and Malaysia. Some of the most commonly cultivated are the varieties of species such as *D. nobile*. These are known as soft-cane dendrobiums. Many Asian species have long, cane-like growth which can grow up to 3¼ft tall, although many others are within the 12–18in range. Some are very upright while others have pendulous growth so they must be grown in hanging baskets. The species described here can be grown in a cool glasshouse where night temperatures do not fall much below 50°F.

DENDROBIUM AT A GLANCE

Popular as houseplants and flowers as cut blooms. Hybrid varieties good for beginners. Various sizes and types.

JAN	rest	
FEB	rest, flowering	
MAR	water and feed, flowering	
APR	water and feed, flowering	
MAY	water and feed	
JUN	water and feed	
JULY	water and feed	
SEPT	water and feed	
OCT	rest	
NOV	rest	
DEC	rest	

RECOMMENDED VARIETIES

D. aphyllum (pink/cream)
D. chrysanthum (yellow)
D. densiflorum (golden)
D. fimbriatum (yellow, dark centre)
D. nobile (dark pink)
D. Christmas Chimes (white, dark centre)
D. Red Comet (dark pink)
D. Stardust (pink/white)

Types
Some species of *Dendrobium* are evergreen while others are deciduous. The latter lose their leaves during their dormant period, which coincides with their dry season. Both types are epiphytic and are found growing on branches of trees or sometimes on mossy rocks in their habitat. The plants will easily grow into large clumps over years, producing a very spectacular show.

Flowers
A few dendrobium varieties produce single flowers but most produce large, showy sprays containing numerous flowers. The color range is vast. White, cream, yellow, pale green, pink, red, maroon, purple, and magenta are all represented in this colorful group. Some have flowers of one single tone while many have contrasting blotches of color in the throat or on the lip of the flower. Many are strongly fragrant.

D. nobile
D. nobile is a soft-cane stemmed type that can grow from 12–30in high. The species is pink with deeper cerise tips on the petals and a dark maroon blotch on the lip. The numerous cultivars of this species include many with similar tonings of lavender, purple, and red, but some have pure white petals with yellow or dark red markings on the lip.

D. chrysanthum This is an evergreen orchid with canes that often grow over 3¼ft long. It has a pendulous habit and so is best grown where its stems can hang naturally. Simulating its natural growth this way seems to promote more consistent flowering. Flowers are deep golden yellow with deep red blotches in the lip on a graceful, arching stem.

D. aphyllum
D. aphyllum (syn. *D. pierardii*) is a deciduous species that prefers to grow in a hanging basket. Its canes can grow to over

The deep gold throat of this softly colored pink and white hybrid of Dendrobium nobile *provides an exciting contrast.*

In cool, humid conditions Dendrobium nobile *and its cultivars will produce a profusion of flowers.*

3¼ft and its delicate, pale flowers can best be enjoyed at eye height. The flowers are pale mauve to pink with the palest creamy yellow lip.

D. fimbriatum Another yellow-flowered species of *Dendrobium* that grows with tall, upright canes sometimes reaching over 3¼ft. It is evergreen and the flowers are produced on the tops of canes one year or more old. Flowers may appear even on older canes that no longer bear leaves. This flower is golden yellow and the lip is delicately fringed. The variety *oculatum* is a richer, deeper gold with a deep maroon blotch in the centre of the lip. These dendrobiums can be grown either in heavy pots that have pebbles added in the base to balance the top weight of the canes, or in a hanging basket.

CONDITIONS

Climate The preferred conditions depend on the species. Cool types grow in glasshouses or conservatories, whereas warm types will live on a windowsill indoors.

Aspect These dendrobiums tolerate partial shade to full sun depending on the species. Those with red, bright pink, and yellow flowers tolerate much more sun than those with white or pale green flowers.

Potting mix Free-draining mixes must always be used. These may contain coarse bark, tree-fern fibre, sphagnum moss, perlite, and even pebbles if extra weight is needed to stabilize the containers. These plants should never be overpotted. Use a container that will comfortably hold the plant roots with a little room to spare.

GROWING METHOD

Propagation All grow from divisions of the existing plants once they have filled their pots. Divide after flowering. Some species produce offsets or aerial growths which can be removed from the parent plant once roots are well developed. Older stems of deciduous species containing dormant buds can be laid on damp sphagnum moss and kept moist until roots develop. This may take several months.

Watering During active growth in warm weather mist or water regularly, two or three times a week. Give only occasional watering in winter; keep those from monsoonal areas dry at this time.

Feeding Feed only during the growing season and not during fall or winter. Use regular applications of soluble orchid fertilizer.

Pruning Restrict pruning to removal of spent flowering stems. Do not cut out old canes of species such as *D. fimbriatum* which flower on older stems unless they have shrivelled, turned brown or died off.

Problems Chewing and grazing insects, such as snails, slugs, caterpillars, and weevils, can all damage these plants but they are a particular nuisance on the flowers. Plants grown in glasshouses may be troubled by mealybugs and mites, as well as fungal diseases if there is poor ventilation.

FLOWERING SEASON

Most flower in spring but the range may be from late winter to early summer depending on growing conditions and the species.

DENDROBIUM
Dendrobium species and hybrids (Australian)

This pretty cultivar of Dendrobium speciosum *has been given the name "Aussie Sunshine". Individual flowers are finely shaped.*

Lighting up this garden in late winter to spring are the long cream to yellow trusses of Dendrobium speciosum.

FEATURES

Epiphytic

There are about seventy Australian species of *Dendrobium* but only a few are cultivated outside Australasia. These epiphytic and lithophytic orchids can have cane-like or thick swollen pseudobulbs, but sometimes the pseudobulbs are not visible at all, as in *D. linguiforme*, which creeps over rocks producing small, fleshy, ribbed foliage. Most of these orchids have rather leathery, sometimes very rigid, leaves, and plants not in flower excite little interest. These dendrobiums are extensively grown by amateurs and professionals alike and most people recognize the "rock lily", *D. speciosum*.

Flowers	The majority of the Australian *Dendrobium* species have small individual flowers, although these may be clustered on long sprays. An exception to this is the Cooktown orchid, *D. bigibbum*, floral emblem of the state of Queensland, which has larger flowers in rosy pink to purple.
Cut flowers	Most Australian species do not make good cut flowers and blooms may last only three weeks or so on the plant. The flowers of *D. bigibbum*, however, are long lasting and cut well. They are often included in mixed bunches sold as Singapore orchids.
D. speciosum	The rock lily or king orchid, *D. speciosum*, is possibly the species most often grown. It has very thick, fairly long, slightly curved pseudobulbs and large, stiff, dark green leaves. It grows on rocks, logs or in hanging baskets, and clumps may spread in time to over 3¼ft across. In its habitat it sometimes forms large clumps high up in trees. It is very easy to grow and its long, arching sprays of cream to yellow flowers have a light honey scent. Flowering, which usually occurs from late winter through to early spring, can vary from year to year.
D. kingianum	The pink rock orchid, *D. kingianum*, is the species of *Dendrobium* most extensively hybridized. Numerous named cultivars are available from specialist growers and some amazing colors are being produced. The true species has short, thickish pseudobulbs topped with leathery leaves and produces little rounded, pink, or mauve flowers. There are also forms that have white or almost purple flowers. This is another easy-care orchid which is very appealing.

DENDROBIUM AT A GLANCE

Normally three years old before flowering. Flowers last up to six weeks. Strap-like leaves vary from green to silver.

JAN	grow on, reduce watering	SEPT	reduce watering
FEB	grow on, reduce watering	OCT	flowering; keep frost free
MAR	re-pot, feed	NOV	flowering, reduce watering
APR	remove and pot on offsets	DEC	flowering, reduce watering
MAY	remove offsets, mist foliage		
JUN	flowering, mist and water	RECOMMENDED VARIETIES	
JULY	flowering, mist and water	*D. kingianum* (pink)	
AUG	reduce watering	*D. speciosum* (yellow)	
		D. Delicatum (white)	

The Cooktown orchid, Dendrobium bigibbum, *is at home in the tropics, thriving in constant warmth and humidity.*

Image right:
Rosy purple is one of the naturally occurring color variations in the species Dendrobium bigibbum.

D. Delicatum Probably one of the most attractive of all these orchids is the hybrid *D. Delicatum* which is a cross between *D. kingianum* and *D. speciosum*. It has long, slender pseudobulbs and produces an abundant display of upright flower spikes that may be white or palest pink, sometimes with a darker lip.

D. gracilicaule A vigorous grower often found naturally on trees that don't shed their bark. It has long, narrow, cane-like pseudobulbs and produces cream to golden yellow flowers in early spring. This is a good orchid to establish in a basket. A natural hybrid of this species and *D. speciosum* is D. *x gracillimum*, which is among the most prolific and free flowering of all these orchids, producing masses of creamy flowers each year.

D. falcorostrum Not so easy to cultivate but well worth the effort is the beech orchid, *D. falcorostrum*, which is becoming very scarce in the wild. Its preferred natural host is the Antarctic beech, *Nothofagus moorei*, which has been overcleared. This beautiful orchid has creamy white, scented flowers in short sprays that develop on top of thickish pseudobulbs that may be 6–10in long.

D. linguiforme The pseudobulbs are not visible in the tongue orchid, *D. linguiforme*, which creeps over rocks. It produces small, fleshy, ribbed foliage and abundant sprays of feathery, cream flowers appear in spring.

CONDITIONS

Climate Preferred climate depends on the species. Some grow best in the warm, others prefer cool to intermediate conditions.

Aspect Most prefer dappled sunlight, although some tolerate full sun.

Potting mix Many dendrobiums are best grown on slabs, logs, old stumps, or rocks. In containers the mix should be very coarse bark, crushed rock and tree-fern fibre.

GROWING METHOD

Propagation Most are best propagated by dividing clumps straight after flowering. Those that produce offsets from the tops of canes can have the offsets gently detached and replanted once they have developed a good root system of their own.

Watering Most of these dendrobiums prefer regular, abundant watering during spring and summer. In the cooler months water very occasionally. Dendrobiums from tropical areas with defined wet and dry seasons should be kept quite dry in their dormant stage to prevent early growth starting.

Feeding Feed with complete soluble fertilizers during spring to early summer or with slow release granules or water-soluble feed. Do not feed at all during fall or winter.

Pruning Restrict pruning to the removal of spent flower stems.

Problems Most of these plants are fairly trouble-free, although damage can be caused by slugs, snails, caterpillars, and weevils chewing flowers and new leaves. Fungal leaf diseases may attack plants that are grown in conditions where humidity is high. This is a real problem in glasshouses, especially if the ventilation is poor.

FLOWERING SEASON

Flowering time depends on species and regional growing conditions. Most flower in late winter to spring.

DISA
Disa species and hybrids

The pale flower of this lovely Disa *cultivar clearly shows the nectar-bearing spur. Red-flowered cultivars dominate most collections.*

Buds and flowers at various stages of development ensure a long flowering season for this Disa *hybrid.*

FEATURES

Terrestrial

Only one species of *Disa* is common in cultivation: *D. uniflora*, which has generally bright scarlet flowers. Flowers are mainly scarlet with red and gold venation but some golden yellow ones are found in their natural habitat. This terrestrial genus can be difficult to cultivate successfully as many species come from habitats that have soil that is permanently damp but never waterlogged. These conditions are not very easy for the orchid grower to duplicate. Disas produce a rosette of basal leaves from which a flowering stem over 24in high will emerge. Flowers are large, 3–5in across and borne in groups of mostly three or more blooms.

DISA AT A GLANCE

Unusual and challenging orchid preferring moist conditions. Bright flowers are 2–3in across.

JAN	water	OCT	water
FEB	water	NOV	water
MAR	water	DEC	water
APR	flowering, water		
MAY	flowering, water	**RECOMMENDED VARIETIES**	
JUN	flowering, water and feed	*D. uniflora*	
JULY	flowering, water and feed	*D.* Inca Princess	
AUG	flowering, water and feed		
SEPT	water		

CONDITIONS

Origin This group of orchids is mainly native to tropical and southern Africa and is also found in Madagascar.

CONDITIONS

Climate *Disa* needs a frost-free climate. Most are cool growers and tolerate temperatures down to about 41°F; 77°F is the preferred upper limit.

Aspect Grows best in partial shade with some sun early in the morning. In total shade plants will grow but not flower.

Potting mix The mix or soil should be moisture retentive but never soggy. A suitable mix might contain perlite, coconut fibre peat, chopped sphagnum moss, and medium-fine bark.

GROWING METHOD

Propagation Divide plants when re-potting. This should be about every two years after flowering, never more than three years apart.

Watering Avoid watering the foliage if possible. Allow water to soak up from below by standing pots in a container of water. Never allow the pots to dry out but greatly decrease water in cool weather.

Feeding Apply soluble liquid fertilizer, at a quarter to half the recommended dilution rate, while plants are actively growing.

Problems No specific problems are known if cultural conditions are met.

FLOWERING SEASON

Generally from early summer to fall, but this can vary.

ENCYCLIA
Encyclia species

Commonly known as the cockleshell orchid, the shape of the lip that gives Encyclia cochleata *its name can be seen clearly here.*

The scarlet encyclia is E. vitellina, *well known and sought after for its vibrant orange coloring.*

FEATURES

Epiphytic

Another very easy and popular group of orchids. The genus of *Encyclia* was originally classified with the epidendrums so are closely related and require very similar growing conditions. Most of the encyclias are found in Central and South America, but some inhabit Florida and the West Indies, as in the case of *E. cochleata*. This orchid was the first tropical epiphytic orchid to flower in the United Kingdom. Originally discovered in the Americas, it was brought back by the plant hunters to the Royal Botanic Gardens at Kew in London. It has the common name of cockleshell orchid, due to the shape of its upturned, almost black, lip, and is the national flower of the Central American country of Belize. The orchid will flower for months on large specimen plants. Most of the *Encyclia* species are green in color but *E. vitellina* is bright orange. Many of the green-flowered species are also sweetly scented.

CONDITIONS

Climate	The most popular are cool growing needing a temperature range of 50–77°F.
Aspect	A light position is required, out of direct sunshine in summer to avoid scorching. Grow well in hanging baskets in a shaded greenhouse, or as windowsill plants.
Potting Mix	An open and free-draining bark mix is good; aerial roots are often made outside the pot.

GROWING METHOD

Propagation	Can be divided and propagated after growing into a large plant over a number of years. To ensure flowering the next year, do not make individual plants too small.
Watering	Frequently water during summer—its main growing season. When not in growth it should be partially rested; just a little water is required to keep the pseudobulbs plump.
Feeding	Feed only when the plant is in active growth when it can gain full benefit from the added nutrients. Apply both in the water poured into the pot and also in the spray given to the leaves and aerial roots.
Problems	No specific problems are known if cultural conditions are suitable.

FLOWERING SEASON

Can vary but mainly the summer months.

ENCYCLIA AT A GLANCE

Very easy to grow; ideal in most situations. Compact plant, 8–10in high, flowers 1¼–2¼in across.

JAN	rest		OCT	rest
FEB	rest		NOV	rest
MAR	rest		DEC	rest
APR	flowering, water and feed			
MAY	flowering, water and feed		RECOMMENDED VARIETIES	
JUN	flowering, water and feed		*E. cochleata*	
JULY	flowering, water and feed		*E. lancifolia* (cream)	
AUG	flowering, water and feed		*E. mariae* (green/white)	
SEPT	water and feed		*E. pentotis* (cream/green)	
			E. radiata (pale green)	
			E. vitellina (orange)	

EPIDENDRUM
Crucifix orchid

A bright pink cultivar of Epidendrum ibaguense *flowers well each year but is not as prolific as the orange-flowered species.*

Tough, reliable and flowering over many months, the crucifix orchid makes a fine garden plant in tropical countries.

FEATURES

Epiphytic

Terrestrial

This genus and its species is a large and varied group that originated in tropical America. Growth can be rampant and needs thinning out every couple of years. Plants in pots may need support. This orchid will grow without almost any attention but rewards good culture. The species *E. ibaguense* flower is orange and yellow but there are many cultivars with flowers in shades of red, pink, mauve, yellow, or white. Individual flowers are fairly small but they are carried in groups on top of reedy canes that can be 6½ft or more tall. The fleshy leaves are leathery in texture and yellowish green, especially in full sun.

E. ibaguense is one of the most familiar of the *Epidendrum* species, also known as *E. radicans* or its common name of crucifix orchid, so called because of the cross shape of the lip, when turned upside down.

Habit The crucifix orchid has a tall, reed-like habit of growth so requires some space to grow to its full potential.

CONDITIONS

Climate Grows best in an intermediate greenhouse, with a minimum of 54°F in winter.

Aspect Tolerates full sun to dappled shade. Where this orchid is grown in more tropical climates, as a bedding plant in garden borders, it is very tolerant of changing conditions and rough treatment.

Potting mix The mix or soil must be able to drain rapidly but any mixture of coarse bark, crushed rock, gravel, compost, or commercial potting mix is suitable.

GROWING METHOD

Propagation Is very easy to propagate as it produces plantlets with aerial roots on the older canes. Detach them and pot up when they are sufficiently developed during the warmer months. Large clumps can also be divided.

Watering Thrives if given regular watering during the warm months of the year and less frequent waterings in winter.

Feeding Give soluble liquid fertilizer every three or four weeks during warm weather or dress the roots with aged cow manure. In warm conditions feed year round.

Problems Trouble-free but fungal leaf diseases can occur if the weather is too cool and wet. Succulent new leaves are often eaten by slugs.

EPIDENDRUM AT A GLANCE

Easy to grow. Repeat flowers all year round. Can reach 5ft in height but flowers are only 1¼ in across.

JAN	rest, little water	
FEB	rest, little water	
MAR	increase water, re-pot	
APR	water and feed	
MAY	water and feed	
JUN	water and feed	
JULY	water and feed	
AUG	water and feed	
SEPT	water and feed	
OCT	reduce water	
NOV	reduce water	
DEC	rest, little water	

RECOMMENDED VARIETIES

E. cristatum (brown spotted)
E. ibaguense (red/yellow)
E. ilense (pale cream)
E. pseudepidendrum (green/orange)
E. wallissii (lilac/brown)
E. Pink Cascade (pink)
E. Plastic Doll (green/yellow)

The hybrid E. Plastic Doll *flowers easily on a very young plant and continues to bloom prolifically over the years.*

Epidendrum Pink Cascade *is almost never out of flower; don't cut off the old flower stem as this will produce buds over and over again.*

FLOWERING SEASON

Can flower almost all the year round.

OTHER EPIDENDRUMS TO GROW

This is a very large group of orchids with many varied species and hybrids available. They are easy to keep and are very rewarding. The plants have long flowering seasons, and some are sequential flowerers, producing more and more buds time after time throughout the year. All need similar cultural requirements to those of the crucifix orchid.

E. ilense
This is a very tall growing species from the Tropical Americas, reaching up to 6½ft in height. The leafy cane-like pseudobulbs are semi-deciduous, losing their leaves after a year or so. The curious flowers come in bunches from the top of the newest and oldest pseudobulb, the old ones reflower-ing for many years. The blooms are creamy yellow and around ¾in across; the lip, which hangs down, is strangely frilled into lots of tiny threads giving a bearded effect. Flowers can appear on very young plants only 6in high.

E. pseudepidendrum
Perhaps a confusing name but this is yet another different *Epidendrum*. This species will grow with a similar habit to the *E. ilense* and they grow well when positioned together. This one has a very hard, waxy flower with bright green petals and sepals, swept back from the brilliant orange lip, making a striking combination.

E. Plastic Doll
This is a primary hybrid between the two species mentioned previously and it inherits qualities from both. It flowers on very young plants, and has a waxy yellow flower with a frilled lip. When larger, the plant should re-flower continually to give a perpetual show. The plant can grow tall in time as well but generally it is a very easy and rewarding orchid to keep.

E. Pink Cascade
Another primary hybrid of *E. ilense* but this time it has been crossed with another species, *E. revolutum*. The Pink Cascade orchid tends to hold more flowers on the stem at one time. As the name suggests, its flowers are bright pink in color. Do not cut the flower stems on this orchid, as they will flower again and again from the top of the leafy cane.

Epidendrum cristatum *grows very tall and in a large clump. Each stem produces a head of highly patterned flowers.*

ERIA
Eria species

A larger growing member of the Eria *family is* E. sessiflora *with its tall spike of dainty cream flowers that are sweetly scented.*

For more of a challenge try growing erias in a cool to intermediate greenhouse or conservatory, among other similar orchids.

FEATURES

Epiphytic

This is quite a large genus, containing about 500 species, but not many species are grown in cultivation or in amateur collections. They are quite variable in their plant size and habit, but the flowers tend to be of a similar size and shape. *E. sessiflora* is quite a large growing species with a very tall spike of many creamy white flowers; *E. coronaria* in contrast has a short habit with a short swollen stem in place of a pseudobulb but has very similar cream blooms. Many of the erias are scented as well. The family of erias are originally found growing as epiphytes on the trees in the rain forests of the Malaysian Peninsula, the islands of New Guinea and Polynesia as well as some parts of Australia. The plants often have to undergo a wet and dry season in the high altitude monsoon areas so their regime of watering and resting follows this pattern.

CONDITIONS

Climate	These plants enjoy a cool to intermediate temperature range of 54–83°F from winter to summer.
Aspect	Protect the plants from the bright sun with some shading during summer to prevent the foliage from getting too red or even burnt.
Potting Mix	A medium grade of bark will be adequate and you may want to mix in some general potting compost to help keep them moist during the main growing season.

GROWING METHOD

Propagation	These orchids are not easily propagated by division as they grow and multiply slowly.
Watering	Take care not to over water during the winter when the plant is at rest. Give water once a week during the growing season, keeping the compost moist at all times.
Feeding	The plant will respond to added fertilizer during the growing season. Use a soluble fertilizer every two weeks, spraying on the leaves and pouring into the pot.
Problems	No specific problems are known if cultural conditions are suitable.

FLOWERING SEASON

Quite short-lived. Blooms for three to four weeks in mainly winter and spring seasons.

ERIA AT A GLANCE

An unusual genus and mostly for the more experienced grower. Charming, small flowers and variable plant size.

JAN	flowering, rest
FEB	flowering, rest
MAR	flowering, rest
APR	flowering, rest
MAY	flowering, water and feed
JUN	water and feed
JULY	water and feed
AUG	water and feed
SEPT	water and feed
OCT	rest
NOV	flowering, rest
DEC	flowering, rest

RECOMMENDED VARIETIES

E. coronaria (cream)
E. javanica (yellow)
E. pubescens (yellow with hairy stems)
E. rosea (pink flush)
E. sessiflora (white)

GONGORA
Gongora species

The Gongora's *pendant spikes of curious shaped flowers are a constant source of amazement, as seen in this* G. bufonia.

These are easy orchids to grow and are an ideal addition to any cool collection. This G. truncata *is a fragranced example.*

FEATURES

Epiphytic

This fascinating and simple to grow group of orchids originate from the American tropics. They are epiphytic, growing into large clumps over the years. The distinctive ridged pseudobulbs produce pendant flower spikes of varying lengths. The flowers that are held along the length of the thin stem are curiously shaped; the column is elongated and the sepals swept back from it almost like the wings of an insect. This is designed to attract a particular flying insect for pollination. Gongoras are relatively easy to grow in the mixed collection as well as being free flowering and usually scented.

Although flowers only last a few weeks, a mature plant will often produce many flower spikes in succession over the summer months. These orchids are best grown in a basket or net pot.

CONDITIONS

Climate	The gongoras are cool growing, needing a drop to 50°F in winter. Around 60°F in summer is acceptable.
Aspect	These orchids have broad, soft green leaves so can easily burn in the sun. Good light in winter and dappled shade in summer.
Potting Mix	Needs an open free-draining potting material such as plain bark chippings.

GROWING METHOD

Propagation	Once grown into a substantial specimen can be divided up into smaller plants. Only three pseudobulbs are needed for re-flowering.
Watering	As the plants grow in open baskets, they will dry out quickly so regular watering is necessary. Immerse the whole plant in water if need be, particularly in summer.
Feeding	Only feed when the plant is in active growth, during spring or summer. You can put fertilizer into the water that the plant is being dunked into and leave it for several minutes to let the plant benefit.
Problems	No specific problems are known if cultural conditions are suitable.

FLOWERING SEASON

Usually summertime—very free flowering.

GONGORA AT A GLANCE

Ideal for beginners and growing indoors. Plants are 4–8in in height and flower spikes reach 1ft 4in.

JAN	rest
FEB	rest
MAR	water and feed
APR	water and feed
MAY	flowering, water and feed
JUN	flowering, water and feed
JULY	flowering, water and feed
AUG	water and feed
SEPT	water and feed
OCT	rest
NOV	rest
DEC	rest

RECOMMENDED VARIETIES

G. bufonia (cream/red)

G. galeata (orange/brown)

G.maculata (yellow/red)

G. quinquinervis (brown/cream)

G. truncata (pink/cream)

LAELIA
Laelia species

The queen of laelias is Laelia purpurata *and this variety,* carnea, *is especially beautiful with its subtle salmon-colored lip.*

A cooler growing species is L. gouldiana, *which has long-lasting large pinkish purple flowers on a long, upright stem.*

FEATURES

Epiphytic

There are many different *Laelia* species, coming mostly from Central and the more northern parts of South America. The showy blooms and relative ease of culture make it popular with beginners. It is a varied genus; the size of the plant can vary from 2in high, up to 28in high, and the flower sizes for these species are similarly different. Colors range from pure white, yellow, lavenders, and pinks to deep purples. They are very closely related to the *Cattleya* family and have been extensively interbred to produce the beautiful *Laeliocattleyas*. *L. purpurata* is perhaps the most well known, being called the queen of laelias. It is the national flower of Brazil and has more

cultivated varieties than any other orchid. The laelias have thick, leathery leaves on the top of usually elongated pseudobulbs. Flowers come from inside a sheath at the apex of the newest pseudobulb.

CONDITIONS

Climate	There are both cool and intermediate growing laelias so check the label. The cooler ones need to drop to 50°F in winter, while others need a slightly warmer temperature of 54°F minimum.
Aspect	Give good light all year round, this is important to encourage flowering. Avoid direct summer sun, which can scorch leaves.
Potting Mix	Use a very open, coarse bark mix to make sure the roots are never too wet.

GROWING METHOD

Propagation	Although a little slow growing, some laelias will readily propagate after a few years of growing into a larger sized mature plant. Some will shoot from old back bulbs that can be removed at potting time and grown on in a warm, humid place.
Watering	Make sure the compost dries out in between waterings. In winter keep dry unless the pseudobulbs start to shrivel.
Feeding	Only apply a liquid feed and mist foliage when the plant is actually in growth.
Problems	No specific problems are known if cultural conditions are suitable.

FLOWERING SEASON

Most of the laelias are summer flowering, or produce from new pseudobulb in fall.

LAELIA AT A GLANCE

Long-lasting, bright flowers, some fragranced. Plants come in a variety of sizes, from 2–18in.

JAN	rest
FEB	rest
MAR	rest
APR	rest, re-pot
MAY	flowering, water and feed
JUN	flowering, water and feed
JULY	flowering, water and feed
AUG	flowering, water and feed
SEPT	water and feed

OCT	rest
NOV	rest
DEC	rest

RECOMMENDED VARIETIES

L. anceps (lavender)
L. fallalis (lavender)
L. briegeri (yellow)
L. harpophylla (orange)
L. pumila (purple)
L. purpurata (various: white to purple)

LEPANTHOPSIS
Lepanthopsis species

A truly miniature orchid, Lepanthopsis astrophorea "Stalky", has flowers only a few millimetres across but is seldom out of bloom.

Although small in stature, a mature specimen will grow into a larger plant measuring 3–4in across if left undivided for years.

FEATURES

Epiphytic

This is one of several orchid genera, including *Pleurothallis* and *Dryadella*, that is truly miniature. The plant size reaches only 1¼in at the most and the flower stem is about the same again. The plant produces a tiny spray of these exquisite little flowers, which measure only ⅛in across. The flowers are a vivid deep purple and star-shaped, which makes them a little easier to pick out, however you may still need a magnifying glass. The unusual orchid, *L. astrophorea* "Stalky", is just one of a genus of around 25 different species widely found in Central America. This genus was originally classified with the *Pleurothallis* until it was proclaimed to be different enough to be given its own name. It grows well with other members of the "Pleurothallid Alliance" including masdevallias. It can be grown for many years in the same small pot, as it will not outgrow it very easily and will stay almost perpetually in flower.

CONDITIONS

Climate This orchid is mostly cool growing but will tolerate slightly warmer intermediate conditions if necessary.

Aspect Provide good shade for this little plant so it does not dehydrate too much.

Potting Mix As it is growing in a tiny pot and has a very fine root system, use a fine grade of bark with a little perlite and sphagnum moss.

GROWING METHOD

Propagation Will propagate quite easily once you have let the plant grow on for several years to fill the pot. For best results, though, keep as one plant; it won't take up that much room.

Watering Small pots tend to dry out more quickly than large ones so water regularly to keep from drying out. Mist the foliage also.

Feeding Give the plant a little weak orchid feed during the summer when it is in its more active growth.

Problems No specific problems are known if cultural conditions are suitable.

FLOWERING SEASON

Can be all the year round on a mature plant; generally does not have a strict flowering season. Long lasting for such tiny flowers.

LEPANTHOPSIS AT A GLANCE

Miniature, only 1¼in high but small flowers bloom continually. Best in sheltered, controlled environment.

		RECOMMENDED VARIETIES
JAN	water	*L. astrophorea* "Stalky"
FEB	water	
MAR	water, re-pot	
APR	water, re-pot	
MAY	water	
JUN	water and feed	
JULY	water and feed	
AUG	water and feed	
SEPT	water	
OCT	water	
NOV	water	
DEC	water	

LYCASTE
Lycaste species and hybrids

This orchid, with its delicate pink and white flowers, is derived from Lycaste skinneri, known to some as the queen of lycastes.

Large leaves and flowers on single stems are features of the Lycaste *species. This orchid shades prettily from dusky rose to white.*

FEATURES

Epiphytic

Terrestrial

This group of mostly epiphytic orchids originate in cloud forests in Central America and northern parts of South America. Most are found in the forks of trees but some grow in pockets of leaf litter on rocks. Lycastes can grow into clumps with large leaves and they need space to show to advantage. They produce robust pseudobulbs from which the leaves emerge in the spring. In fall the leaves will die off. Flowers are borne singly on leafless stems but each pseudobulb may produce several stems. In the most commonly grown species *Lycaste skinneri* (syn. *L. virginalis*) the flowers may vary from pure white to rose pink. There are other species and numerous hybrids with green, yellow, or even deep red flowers. Some beautifully shaded or mottled.

For beginners A good species to try is *L. deppei* from Mexico and Guatemala. This is a green flower flecked with red and with a red-spotted yellow lip. It is also fragrant.

CONDITIONS

Climate All are frost sensitive and not ideal for the tropics. Many are happy in a 50–86°F range. Some species may drop lower during their dry rest.

Aspect Plants require good shade in summer. Early morning sun with shade for the rest of the day is suitable. Ensure good air circulation.

Potting mix Use a mix of crushed fine to medium bark. Do not overpot. Select a pot large enough to take the root ball with a little extra space.

GROWING METHOD

Propagation Divide plants after flowering if they are very crowded. Leafless pseudobulbs can be detached from the clump and potted up.

Watering Give ample water during hot weather and when in active growth but avoid overhead watering. Keep compost dry when dormant.

Feeding Plants respond well to regular fertilizing during the growing season. Use soluble liquids or granular fertilizers. Those formulated for cymbidiums are suitable.

Problems No specific problems are known if cultural conditions are suitable.

FLOWERING SEASON

Mainly winter to early spring.

LYCASTE AT A GLANCE

Relatively easy to grow but best in greenhouse. Deciduous, with flowers in spring with the new growth.

JAN	rest	OCT	rest
FEB	rest	NOV	rest
MAR	flowering, water and feed	DEC	rest
APR	flowering, water and feed		
MAY	flowering, water and feed	RECOMMENDED VARIETIES	
JUN	flowering, water and feed	*L. aromatica* (yellow)	
JULY	flowering, water and feed, re-pot	*L. crunenta* (yellow)	
		L. deppei (green/red)	
		L. skinneri (white/pink)	
AUG	water and feed	*L. Auburn* (pink)	
SEPT	water and feed	*L. Always* (pink/red)	

MASDEVALLIA
Kite orchid

This spotted hybrid Masdevallia *has a pattern of deep magenta markings on a white ground.*

Emerging from a base of heavy leaves, this clear yellow Masdevallia *hybrid has long, very fine tails on its flower.*

FEATURES

Epiphytic

Terrestrial

These unusual flowers are not obviously divided into petals and sepals but appear as solid, sometimes triangular shapes, often with long tails. Flowers may come singly or in small sprays above or within the foliage. The color range includes white, pink, red, yellow, orange, and greenish brown. Some flowers have contrasting venation that looks like stripes. Masdevallias are native to tropical America where they occur from warm lowlands to high altitudes. Plants may be epiphytes, lithophytes, or terrestrial and most are found in high elevations in cloud forests. They lack pseudobulbs, growing from a root system that produces short, upright stems, each with a single fleshy leaf.

MASDEVALLIA AT A GLANCE

Miniature orchids, 1¼– 6in high. Best in cool greenhouse. Flowers ¼–1¼ in across with long tails.

JAN	rest	NOV	rest
FEB	rest	DEC	rest
MAR	water and feed,		
APR	water and feed, re-pot	RECOMMENDED VARIETIES	
		M. barlaeana (red)	
MAY	water and feed, re-pot	*M. coccinea* (varies)	
		M. tovarensis (white)	
JUN	water and feed, re-pot	*M.* Angel Frost (yellow)	
		M. Marguerite (orange)	
JULY	water and feed	*M.* Whiskers (orange/ purple)	
AUG	water and feed		
SEPT	water and feed		
OCT	water and feed, rest		

CONDITIONS

Climate This orchid is frost sensitive but classed as cool growing; it prefers a range of about 50–75°F.

Aspect Needs about 70 per cent shade in the summer months; less in winter. Maintain high humidity but keep air moving with fans as good ventilation is needed to grow these little plants well.

Potting mix Use a small pot just large enough for the roots. Use a compost of fine-grade bark mixed with charcoal, perlite, and pea gravel.

GROWING METHOD

Propagation This is not easy. Large clumps may be divided after some years. Each division should be made up of at least four stems to make sure they continue to grow well.

Watering Keep the compost moist at all times, especially in warm weather. Growing in small pots, with fine compost, they tend to dry out easily.

Feeding Use soluble liquid plant foods, which can be applied during normal watering in the growing season diluted to half strength.

Problems No specific pest or disease problems are known if the exacting growing conditions are met. If the long flower tails shrivel in warm weather the humidity is too low or the temperature is too high.

FLOWERING SEASON

Flowering depends on species but most flower through spring or summer. When grown to a large plant, masdevallias will provide a lovely show of dainty blooms.

ODONTOGLOSSUM
Tiger orchid

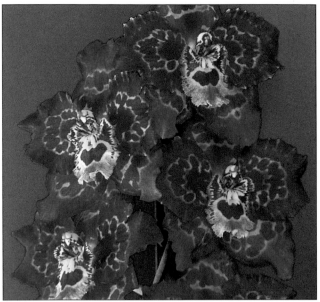

Brilliant colors and intricate patterns are now appearing in many of the newer Odontoglossum hybrids.

The darker pattern cleverly mimics the flower shape on this pretty tiger orchid, which makes a good houseplant for a cool room.

FEATURES

Epiphytic

This large group of evergreen orchids comes from Central and South America. They are epiphytes or lithophytes and most occur at high altitudes. They grow from pseudobulbs from which one or two leaves emerge. The flower spikes are very variable and may be short or tall, upright or arching in habit, but all originate from the base of the pseudobulb. Some species are grown but it is the hybrids that are widely cultivated. Hybrids occur in almost every color of the rainbow and are marked in an extraordinary range of patterns. The odontoglossums will readily breed with other closely related genera to give an ever increasing range of flower types. This interbreeding can also often make the plants much more tolerant to warmer or cooler conditions. Some examples are crossed with *Oncidium* to make *Odontocidium*, with *Miltonia* to create *Odontonia* and with *Cochlioda* to make *Odontioda*. When a third genus is involved then the names change again—for example *Odontoglossum* x *Oncidium* x *Cochlioda* makes a *Wilsonara*.

CONDITIONS

Climate Needs a frost-free, but generally not hot, climate and prefers a temperature range from 50–77°F. High humidity is essential for this orchid.

Aspect Needs shade, especially in summer when shadecloth of about 70 per cent should be used. Reduce in winter to provide maximum light to encourage flowering.

Potting mix Needs very open and free-draining soil. A suitable mix would contain medium grade bark, charcoal, pea gravel, or very coarse, washed sand. A little chopped sphagnum moss can be added. Do not overpot. Use pots just large enough to confine the roots.

GROWING METHOD

Propagation Divide plants after flowering but only when the container is overflowing. Plants resent frequent disturbance.

Watering Never allow plants to become bone dry but roots should never be sodden. Frequency of watering depends on the mix used and the weather. Mist plants in hot, dry weather.

Feeding Use soluble liquid plant foods at half the recommended strength every couple of weeks through the warmer months.

ODONTOGLOSSUM AT A GLANCE

Popular and easy to grow houseplants. Different varieties with attractive dark green foliage and sprays of flowers.

		RECOMMENDED VARIETIES
JAN	less water	
FEB	less water	*O. crispum* (white)
MAR	water and feed	*O. cordatum*
APR	water and feed	(yellow/brown)
MAY	water and feed	*O. hallii* (yellow)
JUN	water and feed	*O. laeve* (brown/white)
JULY	water and feed	*Odontocidium* Purbeck
AUG	water and feed	Gold (yellow/brown)
SEPT	water and feed	*Odontonia* Boussole
OCT	less water	"Blanche" (white)
NOV	less water	*Vuylstekeara* Cambria
DEC	less water	"Plush" (red/white)

This beautiful Odontoglossum *hybrid has been bred from the white species* O. crispum *giving it its clear color and arching spray.*

Bright, golden yellow is a very popular color in this easy to grow group of orchids which are often chosen as ideal beginner's plants.

Problems   No specific pest or disease problems are known for this orchid.

FLOWERING SEASON

The flowering season is very variable, depending on the species or hybrid.

OTHER ODONTOGLOSSUMS TO GROW

O. crispum   This species, with pure white flowers, was imported into Britain in large quantities at the beginning of the 20th century, when it commanded enormous prices. Still sought after, it is not found in such abundance as it used to be. Hybrids that have been made with it still retain the beautiful white coloring but tend to be easier to grow, making them good for beginners.

O. cordatum   A more compact species which is relatively easy to grow and flower for the amateur enthusiast. Star-shaped golden yellow and chestnut brown flowers are approximately 2½in across and between three and six are held on a short arching spray.

O. hallii   Larger growing, the plant height being around 12in with a spray of large yellow flowers, spotted in brown which have the added bonus of being scented and usually summer flowering.

O. laeve   Although this species has small flowers, colored in dark green and brown with a contrasting white and magenta lip, there are a lot of them held on a very tall, branching flower spike which can be up to 3¼ft high.

The flowers have a strong, sweet fragrance, which will fill your greenhouse. The plant is strong and vigorous growing which makes it good for ease of culture. There are literally thousands of *Odontoglossum* hybrids available with new ones being produced all the time; here are some examples to choose from.

Vuylstekeara Cambria "Plush"   This is a complex hybrid between three different genera, which make up part of the "*Odontoglossum* Alliance" of related genera. It is one of the all time classic hybrids and has been around since the 1930s and is still very popular today. Its ease of culture and free-flowering habit make it an ideal beginners' orchid as well as being very showy with its large bright red flowers, the lip white with red spotting.

Odontocidium Purbeck Gold   This is another classic variety, this time in a brilliant golden yellow, the petals and sepals with just a touch of chocolate brown. Flowers are 3in across on a spray reaching 12–20in, depending on the maturity of the plant. These orchids are very easy to grow and flower.

Beallara Tahama Glacier "Green"   The addition of *Brassia* into the breeding of this hybrid gives the flower a stunning, star-shaped appearance. The large blooms can measure up to 2½in across. The translucent green of the flower is contrasted with the dark red in its centre. Produces tall sprays with between six and a dozen of these showy, long-lasting flowers. Tolerant of varying temperatures, this orchid will flower well in cool or warm environments. A vigorous grower, it makes an excellent specimen plant in just a few years.

1.

3.

5.

ODONTOGLOSSUM

1 Sanderara *Rippon Tor "Burnham"* is a very reliable bloomer, always in the late spring and rewards the grower with an attractive arching spray of patterned flowers.

2 Odontioda *Grenadier is just one of the many red hybrids that include the bright red species* Cochlioda noetzliana *in its family tree giving the striking color that we see here and in many other red hybrids.*

3 Odontocidium *Purbeck Gold shows the introduction of the genus* Oncidium *into the breeding so giving us the bright yellow influence which also makes the plants very tolerant and easy to grow as houseplants.*

4 A more unusual type is this Colmanara *Wild Cat, which is certainly wild with its leopard spotting and readily branching spikes giving lots of long-lasting flowers. Also cool growing.*

5 Most colors are represented in this widely hybridized family and purple is no exception as seen here in the beautiful Vuylstekeara *Monica "Burnham".*

6 The Brassia *influence is clear here with the large star-shaped flowers of the* Beallara *Tahoma Glacier "Green" which is a robust and free-flowering ideal pot-plant.*

7 Odontioda *Moliere "Polka" has amazing, frilled edges to the flowers and an extremely intricate patterning in pinks and purples covering the whole flower.*

8 Odontioda *Marie Noel "Burgogne" is another highly frilled flower which makes a particularly attractive arching flower spike on a mature plant.*

PLEIONE
Pleione species and hybrids

The small treasures that make up the Pleione species are often best grown as container plants where they can be enjoyed at close range. Among the features to watch out for is the contrasting lip of the flower, which is delicately fringed.

FEATURES

Epiphytic

Terrestrial

Extremely cold tolerant, these orchids are native to cool areas of northern India, and to southern China and Taiwan where they are usually found in damp woodland. They are deciduous and may be terrestrial, epiphytic, or lithophytic. They die down completely in winter and renew the small pseudobulbs in spring. Plants are rarely more than 6in high and may spread to about 12in. They grow in very shallow pots. Flowers appear before the leaves and are most often white, pink, mauve, purple, or even yellow. The lip may be fringed and spotted. Individual blooms are not long lasting but make a fine display when planted en masse. Each small pseudobulb flowers only once and then produces a folded, elliptical leaf. Pleiones make very easy orchids for beginners and especially for enthusiast children. Their compact habit and ease of culture make them ideal house plants for a very cool windowsill or greenhouse. Some alpine growers even include them in their collections. The pots can be placed out of doors for the summer months.

CONDITIONS

Climate   Some are frost hardy, others frost tender but all prefer cool to cold conditions. A minimum temperature in winter of 10°F is acceptable to these plants as long as they are in their leafless, dormant phase.

Aspect   Needs a sheltered spot in filtered sunlight with shade during the hottest part of the day. Glasshouse-grown plants will need heavy shading and cooling in summer.

Potting mix   The mix of bark, pea gravel, small pebbles, and chopped sphagnum moss or fibre peat must be perfectly drained.

GROWING METHOD

Propagation   Plants need re-potting annually at the end of winter when old pseudobulbs can be discarded. It is then, in the early spring, that the new shoots are just starting to grow, with the flower buds inside. As well as removing last year's dead pseudobulb, trim back the dead roots when re-potting. Some varieties are likely to break double each year so the number of pseudobulbs multiply easily over the years. Occasionally, small extra pseudobulbs can be formed at the top of the old, shrivelled bulb. These can be

PLEIONE AT A GLANCE

Very easy to grow and ideal for greenhouse. Can reach 6in high and flowers average 2in across.

JAN	rest	
FEB	repot, flowering	
MAR	flowering, water and feed	
APR	flowering, water and feed	
MAY	water and feed	
JUN	water and feed	
JULY	water and feed	
AUG	water and feed	
SEPT	flowering, rest	
OCT	flowering, rest	
NOV	rest	
DEC	rest	

RECOMMENDED VARIETIES

P. formosana (lilac pink)
P. formosana var. *alba* (white)
P. maculata (white/red)
P. praecox (pink)
P. speciosa (cerise)
P. Eiger (lavender)
P. Piton (lilac)
P. Shantung (yellow)
P. Stromboli (pink)
P. Versailles (pink)

There are many hybrid pleiones which add to the range of shades of pink, white, and yellow including this striking Pleione Soufriere.

Hybrid Pleione Shantung *is just one of the easy growing orchids that are ideal beginner's plants for the cool greenhouse or conservatory.*

Watering removed at potting time and planted in with the larger main bulb. In a few years time, these will be large enough to flower. Keep soil moist once growth has started in spring. Water regularly during flowering and the development of the pseudobulbs. These orchids make fine root systems which can dry out easily if not regularly watered. When pseudobulbs are fully matured, reduce the frequency of watering. Keep plants dry in winter while dormant and leafless. To avoid resting pseudobulbs from becoming too wet during winter remove from their pots after their leaves have fallen and leave to dry out in an empty tray or pot. You can also see clearly when the new growth starts and can then pot them up again.

Feeding Give regular, weak liquid fertilizer once growth commences and continue until pseudobulbs are well matured.

Problems Slugs and snails are a constant problem but there are no other specific pest problems. Plants can die from root rot if they are constantly wet while dormant or if they dry out completely during the growing season when they can dehydrate.

FLOWERING SEASON

Most species flower in spring but some flower in the fall.

OTHER PLEIONES TO GROW

P. formosana Probably the most popular *Pleione* species to grow, the number of bulbs multiplies up quickly over the years so a superb show can be achieved in quite a short time. Soft lavender pink petals and sepals with dark pink and brown spotting on the white lip.

P. formosana var. alba A pure white, albino form of the above species which has only a touch of yellow in the centre of the lip. The pseudobulbs are also devoid of any purple coloring and are a clear apple green. Grows slightly smaller than the pink variety.

P. speciosa Known for its very vibrant cerise colored flowers which will brighten up the early spring months when it is in flower.

P. maculata An unusual species as this one flowers in the fall, one of only two species that does. White blooms, with dark red patterning in the lip, are also unusual in a mostly pink dominated genus.

P. praecox The second fall flowering species, this time in traditional pink. These two grow in just the same conditions as the spring flowering types but are perhaps a little more of a challenge.

A few hybrid pleiones have been bred between the species; the following are a few examples which are easy to grow:

P. Eiger One of the first to flower in the spring season, short stem with a pale lavender flower, very pretty and easy to keep.

P. Piton A very large sized flower in comparison to the others, 2½in across, on a taller stem, 4in high, a lovely subtle purple shade with bold spotting on the lip.

P. Shantung One of the most well known of the hybrid pleiones due to it being a yellow hybrid, the darkest form being *P.* Shantung "Ducat". Grows well but may not multiply as quickly as some of the others. The most commonly seen variety is P. Shantung "Ridgeway" AM/RHS, a soft yellow with a pink blush.

ROSSIOGLOSSUM
Clown orchid

This bright yellow and red flower is nicknamed the clown orchid after the distinctive character of the bloom.

The flowers of the Rossioglossum are showy and lasting, especially this easy-to-grow hybrid R. Rawdon Jester.

FEATURES

Epiphytic

This incredibly showy and fascinating orchid was originally part of the *Odontoglossum* family. Probably the best known of the species is *R. grande*, commonly known as the clown orchid. A little man in a colorful yellow and red outfit can be seen at the top of the lip. A few hybrids have been made between some of the species such as R. Jakob Jenny (*grande* x *insleayi*) and R. Rawdon Jester (*grande* x *williamsianum*). The pseudobulbs are oval-shaped and a handsome green with a pair of large, broad leaves in the same color. The flowers tend to be very long lasting with quite a waxy texture and reaching an amazing 6in across from petal tip to petal tip.

ROSSIOGLOSSUM AT A GLANCE

Good for beginners in the home or conservatory. Flowers reach 6in across and spike 12in above foliage.

JAN	rest	OCT	flowering, rest
FEB	rest	NOV	rest
MAR	rest	DEC	rest
APR	rest		
MAY	flowering, water and feed	RECOMMENDED VARIETIES	
JUN	flowering, water and feed	*R. grande*	
JULY	water and feed	*R. insleayi*	
AUG	water and feed	*R. williamsianum*	
SEPT	flowering, water and feed	*R.* Jakob Jenny	
		R. Rawdon Jester	
		(all yellow/brown)	

CONDITIONS

Climate   Traditionally a popular orchid to grow in a cool greenhouse or conservatory, with a minimum temperature of 50°F throughout the year.

Aspect   The leaves prefer a shady position so protect from bright sun. Dappled shade is preferred; a north facing aspect in summer is ideal and south facing in winter.

Potting Mix   A fairly open mix is ideal, bark based with some peat or similar mixed in.

GROWING METHOD

Propagation   Rossioglossums are quite slow to grow and take many years to reach an easily dividable plant. Therefore, leave the plant until the pot is full before moving to a larger size and only split when necessary and possible.

Watering   Likes a well-defined resting period in winter, which goes on well into spring. Water regularly from the point when the new growth starts increasing over the growing season and decrease to a stop in the fall. Allow compost to dry out a little in winter.

Feeding   Use a half strength general plant food every two or three waterings in the growing season.

Problems   If a dry rest period is not observed then the plant can suffer from over-watering in the winter which can lead to root rot. Avoid spraying the foliage in winter as this can lead to spotting which can cause fungal infection.

FLOWERING SEASON

R. grande traditionally flowers in fall but some hybrids, such as *R.* Rawdon Jester will bloom easily in late spring and summer.

STANHOPEA
Stanhopea species and hybrids

Native to Nicaragua, Colombia, and Venezuela, Stanhopea wardii *has a more pleasant smell than some species of this genus.*

The weird and sinister-looking flowers of Stanhopea tigrina *are a botanical curiosity enjoyed by many growers.*

FEATURES

Epiphytic

Sometimes known as upside-down orchids, stanhopeas must be grown in hanging containers as the flowers emerge from the base of the pseudobulbs and will otherwise be squashed. They push straight through the bottom of the basket and hang down below the foliage. Stanhopeas are evergreen epiphytes from Central and South America. They grow from a fairly large, ribbed pseudobulb and produce large, solitary, dark green leaves. The strange-looking flowers are large, heavy and strongly perfumed. Not everyone finds the perfume pleasant. Flowers are not long lasting but appear in succession. Plants grow rapidly and are very easy to grow into large specimens.

STANHOPEA AT A GLANCE

Easy to grow but can reach 16in high. Flowers are large and strongly scented but short lived.

JAN	occasional water	SEPT	water and feed
FEB	water and feed	OCT	water and feed
MAR	flowering, water and feed	NOV	occasional water
		DEC	occasional water
APR	flowering, water and feed		
MAY	flowering, water and feed	RECOMMENDED VARIETIES
JUN	flowering, water and feed	*S. graveolans* (yellow)
		S. oculata (cream)
JULY	flowering, water and feed	*S. tigrina*
		S. wardii
AUG	flowering, water and feed	*S.* Assidensis (yellow and red)

Species   *Stanhopea tigrina*, with its fleshy yellow flowers blotched dark maroon-red, is the species most often cultivated, although *S. wardii* is also seen. It also has yellow flowers but with plum to purple spots.

CONDITIONS

Climate   Prefers a cool, humid climate with a minimum of 50°F and tolerates warmer temperatures in summer with shade and high humidity.

Aspect   Grows in dappled sunlight in a well-ventilated glasshouse.

Potting mix   Line the container with soft coconut fibre or other material so that the stems can push through easily. The mix of coarse bark, alone or with charcoal, must be free draining.

GROWING METHOD

Propagation   Divide the pseudobulbs after flowering, but not until the container is full to overflowing. Large specimens are the most rewarding, producing many spikes.

Watering   Water freely during warm weather and mist plants if humidity drops. Water only occasionally in winter.

Feeding   During the growing season apply weak liquid fertilizer every two weeks.

Problems   Can be prone to red-spider-mite or scale insect if not enough humidity is provided. Mist foliage regularly to prevent this.

FLOWERING SEASON

Summer or fall, depending on species. Remove spent flowers once they have faded.

GROWING BROMELIADS

Bromeliads are attractive plants that are easy to cultivate, both in the greenhouse, as conservatory specimens or as lush, exotic house plants. Their showy but unusual blooms are quite unlike any other flowers, while their foliage, colors, and shape hint at their tropical native habitats.

Today many species of bromeliad are threatened in the wild because the forests and woodlands of their natural habitats are rapidly vanishing. There has also been over-collection, and as many species grow very slowly from seed they are not regenerating fast enough to keep up with demand. However, many species are now being cultivated and preserved in botanic gardens and in the collections of both amateur and professional growers, so that home gardeners can continue to grow these interesting plants. Many exciting plants are sold through garden centres, nurseries, and supermarkets—all are well worth buying for the enjoyment they will provide.

LEFT: Exotic foliage and an epiphytic habit make bromeliads rewarding and sometimes challenging to grow. Larger displays for the conservatory or greenhouse can be created by attaching individual plants to old tree branches.

ORIGINAL HABITAT

Most of this large, very diverse group of plants originated in tropical America, with a few species from subtropical America and one species of *Pitcairnia* native to West Africa. Probably the best known of all bromeliads is the pineapple. Its distribution extends from the state of Virginia in the United States south to Chile and Argentina. Bromeliads are most common in rainforests but a few occur naturally in deserts, often dropping their leaves during the driest seasons.

INTRODUCTION TO HORTICULTURE

The first bromeliad introduced to horticulture outside its native habitat was the pineapple, brought to Spain from Guadaloupe in the West Indies by Christopher Columbus on his second voyage to the New World at the end of the fifteenth century. Although it had long been cultivated in the West Indies it caused quite a sensation in Europe.

By the seventeenth century a number of wealthy people were building heated glasshouses in order to be able to cultivate exotic tropical plants such as pineapples, although it was not until the late eighteenth and early nineteenth centuries that heated glasshouse culture became more commonplace. Glasshouses were still, however, the province of the wealthy.

During this period large numbers of bromeliads were introduced into Europe. In the early nineteenth century most went to France and Belgium, where there were the greatest number of enthusiasts and authorities on the subject. By the end of the century, however, collectors from many other European countries were growing and writing about this fascinating group of plants.

This century, with a few notable exceptions, collecting and interest has been most common in the United States, where the Bromeliad Society was established in Florida in the 1950s. Today, however, the cultivation of bromeliads is popular worldwide.

WHERE TO GROW BROMELIADS

In their native habitats, bromeliads thrive in tropical and sub-tropical environments, favored with heavy rainfall, filtered sunlight, and mild or warmish temperatures.

There are a few species that will tolerate cooler conditions although frost, wind, and rain during the winter months has an adverse effect on plants—damaging leaves and disfiguring growth. Other desert species will tolerate extreme heat and full sunshine, but generally bromeliads prefer warmth, filtered sunlight and shelter from strong winds. Occasionally plants may be stood outdoors during the summer months in a partially shaded position, but in general they should be confined to the

Vibrant red bracts remain even after the flowering of Guzmania *"Luna" has finished, thus extending the period when this plant is of particular interest.*

"Blue-flowered torch" is the name sometimes applied to Tillandsia lindenii. *It does, in fact, bear deep purple flowers that appear from the pink-flushed floral bracts.*

greenhouse or conservatory and for indoor culture. The occasional trip outside for a shower to remove dust and grime will pay dividends. The wide leaves accumulate dust even in the cleanest of homes, which reduces their ability to absorb sunlight and inhibits healthy growth.

Light is important if you are to enjoy a good show of bracts and flower spikes, and indoors specimen plants can be reluctant to flower. However, the lack of a flower is a small price to pay as the foliage shapes and colors of most bromeliads more than compensate.

Potted plants can be moved around at will, brought into the house or conservatory when they are looking their best, and returned to the greenhouse when they need additional care and attention. In a mixed grouping it is also possible to bring those plants that have flower spikes or are looking particularly attractive to the front of a display, moving less spectacular specimens back for a rest.

One method of display is to make a bromeliad "tree" so that the plants are seen as epiphytes, looking as they would in their natural environment (see page 288).

FEATURES

In their native habitats some bromeliads are ground dwellers while others grow on rocks or cliff faces, but many are epiphytes using other plants, especially trees, for support although they are not parasites. Most have spirally arranged leaves that channel water into the center of a rosette, which acts as a water storage tank. In their habitats these "tanks" provide a home for insects with aquatic larval stages and a breeding place for many species of tree frogs. The leaves also have fine water-absorbing scales although these are rarely obvious.

Leaves may be in various shades of plain green but many have foliage that is attractively patterned in stripes, transverse bands, or spots. Silvery gray, deep maroon, and bright crimson leaves are also found, along with a range of two-toned or multi-colored leaves. Some have leaves with smooth edges while others are very spiny or serrated.

One group that displays a vast range of foliage types is *Tillandsia*, which includes many species with a recognizable rosette of leaves as well as the fine, gray, web-like Spanish moss (*T. usneoides*) which grows in long swags draped from tree branches. The leaves are thread-like on stems covered with silver scales.

Bromeliad flowers may be spectacular and showy, held on upright or arching stems, or they may be short, blooming low down in the centre of the rosettes. Some flowers last only a few days while others can remain fresh and attractive over several weeks. The color range is as extensive as the range of forms. Although some cut well and last a week or two in a vase, they are generally unsuitable as cut flowers. Whole plants in flower are often used instead to create unusual floral arrangements.

CONDITIONS

Containers
When growing bromeliads in pots, it is often necessary to crock the base of the pot with stones or terracotta chips. This provides weight in the base so that the often top-heavy plants do not constantly tip over. Terracotta pots are useful in this regard, as they are heavy enough to provide stability. Many plants are themselves so decorative with their patterned leaves and bright flowers that a simple plain container is the best choice.

Sharing a need for warmth and humidity, greenhouse displays of several different species create an exotic, almost tropical feel. Plants will appreciate shading from strong summer sun and regular misting with rainwater to maintain humid conditions.

Compost
For plants that are happiest clinging to the cleft in a tree or nestled in the leaf litter on a tropical forest floor, the compost used will dictate whether the plants are going to survive or die. The compost must imitate the natural tendency for free drainage coupled with good moisture retention. Nutrients in the wild would come from rotting leaves and dead insects that become trapped in the watery reservoir of the plants. However it is not advisable to feed your plants this way. A compost that contains a controlled release fertilizer can be used, but so long as it is coarse and free draining they will be happy.

Orchid and African violet composts are sold in garden centers and these are ideal—combining the water holding properties of peat or composted bark chips, with the free draining properties of grit or sharp sand. Leafmold would be equally suitable if you can get hold of it.

Planting
Bromeliads are very prone to rotting off if the base of the plant is kept consistently moist. A free draining compost will help, as will plenty of crocks in the bottom of the pot.

When potting it is also important to not plant too deep. The base of the plant should be level with the surface of the compost. Too deep and excess water will not be able to drain away from the central reservoir.

House plants

Light is important for good flowering and foliage color but even some of the most decorative bromeliads, like the urn plant (*Aechmea fasciata*), will thrive in the home. Bromeliads can be rather large for the average home, although a good range of smaller species and varieties are available. They look particularly striking in simple surroundings, more like a piece of art or sculpture than the traditional potted house plant.

Greenhouse growing

Those with greenhouses have the perfect environment to experiment with a wide range of bromeliads. The warm conditions and bright light will also encourage flowering. Shading in full summer is advisable, as is damping the floor to maintain high levels of humidity. Epiphytic species can be grown on pads of sphagnum moss or old logs and hung from the greenhouse glazing bars for a decorative display. Regular misting will be essential.

Conservatory culture

For the conservatory that is used for plants rather than soft furnishings, bromeliads offer a wide range of colors and forms to play with. They are quite unlike any other house plants but are easy and rewarding to grow. Larger specimens will relish the space a conservatory has to offer, and hanging specimens like Spanish moss (*Tillandsia usneoides*) will add a decorative, almost magical touch. For the more adventurous, a way of displaying a wide range of bromeliad habits is to plant up a "tree".

Many bromeliads do well in conditions that suit cymbidium orchids and growers enjoy cultivating these contrasting plant groups together. Both enjoy a free flow of air around them and a degree of humidity at all times.

A bromeliad tree

Tree stumps, especially old tree-fern stumps, make ideal hosts for bromeliads, as do pieces of weathered driftwood. Pieces of driftwood of various sizes make more or less portable "trees", which can be moved around to suit seasonal conditions or to provide striking decorative effects in different places around the house, greenhouse or conservatory, perhaps for a special event.

To attach plants to the tree, wrap the roots in sphagnum moss or peat and fix them on firmly with upholstery webbing, nylon fishing line, or old stockings. Small specimens may be attached using a little PVA glue, although you should not let the glue smother the roots.

The roots of small plants may be passed through the holes in rounds or squares of ½–1in plastic mesh and a pad of sphagnum moss placed underneath them before the mesh is stapled or tied to the tree. The type of plastic mesh sold to keep leaves out of guttering is ideal. An artificial log can also be made from this mesh by forming a cylinder and packing it with chopped bark and moss. Push the plant roots through into the growing medium and tie them on with plastic-coated wire or fishing line. Once plants are established the ties can be removed. These cylinders are light and can be suspended from greenhouse staging, glazing bars, conservatory support bars or hung in partially-shaded windows.

To grow bromeliads successfully indoors there must be plenty of light or the rich color of the foliage will not be maintained. Plants should be positioned near a sunny window but not close to the glass where the leaves may be scorched. If there is not enough light it will be obvious after a time that leaves are becoming pale and drawn. Extra light may need to be provided artificially.

Plants also need a fairly humid atmosphere, so if you have central heating or the room gets warm, sit plant pots on a bed of pebbles or gravel in a saucer of water. The pot base must be above the water level so that the potting mix is not constantly sodden. Spray-misting the plants with water is also beneficial. This can be done daily in summer but much less often in winter. Foliage should be wiped down with a damp cloth from time to time to remove dust or taken into a gently running shower for a good rinse. If possible take plants outside and gently hose them down.

GROWING METHOD

Watering

Bromeliads growing on logs or moss pads are best watered by spray misting. If you only have a few plants this can be done with a hand sprayer but larger collections will need hosing with a fine spray. Those with a vase form are best

BROMELIAD TREE

Bromeliad plant attached to plant

Tree stump

watered from above, allowing the water to fill the central cup or reservoir. As this overflows it will give roots the moisture they need. In the warmer months when plants are in active growth they may need watering two or three times a week, with misting on the other days. In winter watering once a week should be enough. If the water in your area is "hard" (has a high mineral concentration) you should collect rain water to use on your bromeliads.

Feeding

Opinions vary on the value of feeding these plants. In nature leaves and other debris fall into the vases of plants, slowly decaying and providing nutrients to the plant. If you do fertilize, make sure that it is in very weak concentrations, not too often and never in winter. Some professional growers prefer to use a little slow release fertilizer around the root zone of the plant while others use well-diluted water soluble fertilizers as a spray. If using a spray, use only a quarter to half the recommended dilution rate given for other foliage or indoor plants, and apply it only after the plant has been watered and when it is not in the sun or on very hot days. It is best not to pour even dilute fertilizer into the vase of the plant as this may scorch the foliage.

PROPAGATION

Plants that have bloomed will slowly die off over the next year or two. However, they will replace themselves by producing offsets, often called "pups", generally from the side of the base of the plant. It is best to wait until the offset has a firm base and is at least one-third the size of the parent plant before removing it. Cut off the offset as close as possible to the mother plant using a sharp knife or secateurs. This is best done some time between spring and mid-fall. A few plants produce pups higher up on the plant and these are easily detached by hand.

Any discolored or brown leaves should be removed before potting up, and long, woody running stems (stolons) should be shortened. Offsets should be potted up into small pots containing a coarse seed and cutting compost or two parts sharp sand to one part peat or

The striking cream and green striped foliage of this Guzmania *cultivar makes this bromeliad showy and decorative all year round. The red floral display is an added bonus.*

composted bark. Some growers like to dust the base of the offset with a fungicide as a disease preventive. Don't push the offsets in too deep or they may rot. Spray mist daily, unless there is a cold spell, and roots should form on the offset in a matter of weeks. The best time to propagate by division of offsets is during the growing season, which is from spring through to mid-fall.

WHAT CAN GO WRONG?

Adequate spacing of plants, good ventilation and good cultural practice should minimize problems. Remove any dead or decaying material to keep plants clean and looking good. If you have a sick plant, isolate it from the rest of the collection and wash your hands and disinfect any tools used before handling healthy plants. If you have to use chemicals for pest or disease control, do not spray the buds or flowers as they may become distorted. Fungicidal powders may also be used.

Pests

• Scale insects. These small sap suckers appear as soft brown spots that can be easily pushed off with a finger nail. Wipe off scales with a damp cloth or spray with a suitable insecticide at half the recommended strength. Never use oil-based formulations on bromeliads as this smothers the natural breathing pores and the plant will die of suffocation.
• Mealybugs. These soft white insects resemble small

sticky pieces of cotton wool. They are usually found clustered in the leaf axils and so may be difficult to reach. Wipe them off if possible or use a suitable insecticide. They are usually only a problem if the bromeliads are grown in crowded or badly ventilated conditions.

General disorders

• Lowest leaves brown at the base. This may be caused by heavy, poorly drained mix, overwatering or deep planting.
• Inner leaves rolled or stuck together. The air may be too dry, the plant may need misting or the central vase may have completely dried out.
• Brown leaf tips. These may result from poor drainage or from overwatering, or indicate that the atmosphere is dry.
• Brown patches on leaves. These may be caused by strong sun or very high light intensity, overwatering or poor drainage.
• Bottom leaves straw to light brown in color. This is usually a sign of natural ageing as the older leaves die off.

AECHMEA
Aechmea species and cultivars

The floral bracts of "Ensign", a cultiver of Aechmea orlandia, *are made up of tightly overlapping, scarlet segments.*

Long flowering and adaptable, Aechmea weilbachii *makes a good choice of plant for fairly warm conditions.*

FEATURES

Epiphytic

These are possibly the most widely grown and best known of all the bromeliads. Generally very easy to cultivate, they can be container grown or attached to a log "tree". Although aechmeas originate from Central and South America, most tolerate temperatures down to about 41°F making them suitable for cooler conservatories. Species vary in size from a petite 6in to over 24in, although this size would be rare in cultivation. Larger plants can become top heavy so a terracotta or earthenware pot is

AECHMEA AT A GLANCE

A tolerant plant. Leaves are strap-like and vary in color. Plants produce floral bracts after three years.

JAN	grow on, reduce watering	SEPT	/
FEB	grow on, reduce watering	OCT	flowers, fruit; keep frost free
MAR	re-pot, feed	NOV	flowers, reduce watering
APR	remove and pot on offsets	DEC	flowers, reduce watering
MAY	remove offsets, mist foliage		
JUN	bracts, flowers, mist and water		
JULY	flowers, mist and water		
AUG	/		

RECOMMENDED VARIETIES

A. chantinii
A. fasciata
A. fulgens discolor

Foliage

advisable for extra stability.
There is an amazing diversity of form and foliage color in these bromeliads. Leaves are in a rosette, forming a vase shape with an open cup in the centre. They may be completely shiny green, or green above and burgundy beneath, deep burgundy on both sides or streaked, banded, or spotted with silver, or entirely silvery black. There are also variegated forms with either yellow-gold or pink variegations on a green background. Many are sharply spined along the leaf margins (needing careful handling) while others are almost smooth edged.

Flowers

Many aechmeas have long-lasting flowers that make them popular for indoor decoration. Although the true flowers are often quite small they are enclosed within showy bracts that come in a great range of colors. The inflorescence or flowering spike may be red, blue, yellow, purple, pink, orange, or white and lasts for months.

Fruits

Berry-like fruits follow the flowers and often persist on the plant over a long period.

A. fasciata

One of the most popular species is *Aechmea fasciata* or "Urn" plant, which has gray-silver spined leaves cross-banded in silver. The whole leaf surface is densely covered with silvery scales, giving a powdery effect. The flower spike is a large, showy pyramid of pink bracts enclosing the blue flowers, which age to red.

Foster's Favorite

An attractive dwarf variety is *A.* "Foster's Favorite", which has deep burgundy foliage and a pendulous flowering spike of deep

Aechmea fasciata *is one of the easiest bromeliads to grow and produces a magnificent pink flowerspike that will last for months.*

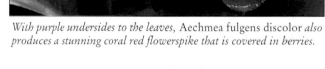

With purple undersides to the leaves, Aechmea fulgens discolor *also produces a stunning coral red flowerspike that is covered in berries.*

blue flowers. These may be followed by red berries. Both these forms are tolerant of a wide range of conditions.

A. chantinii   *A. chantinii* is variable both in size and foliage color. It is sometimes called Amazonian zebra plant because of its green to almost black foliage, which is heavily barred. The long-branched flowering spike is generally red or orange with flowers being red or yellow. Tends to be more cold sensitive than some.

Other species   *A. fulgens discolor* has attractive foliage and is commonly called the "Coral berry" aechmea. This species is hard to beat with its green strap-shaped leaves that are a deep purple beneath. A spike of purple flowers will turn into decorative coral red berries.

CONDITIONS

Position   Needs a frost-free climate. The plants do best in warm to hot, humid conditions with a cooler spell in winter. Morning sun, filtered sunlight or shade seems to suit this plant group. Most aechmeas like sheltered situations, preferably with overhead shading. Although some species have origins in harsh environments it is best to give them all some shelter in non-extreme conditions.

Potting mix   Plants will thrive in a very coarse, open, soilless compost. Water must be able to drain straight through. Take care not to plant too deep to avoid rotting.

GROWING METHOD

Propagation   Start new plants by removing the offsets or pups from the parent plant once the offsets have reached about one-third of the size of the parent. Cut off and pot separately.

Watering   The cup at the centre of the rosette must be kept filled with water. Plants probably need watering twice weekly or more in summer and every week or two in cold weather. Be guided by the weather and feel how moist the compost is. Mounted plants need spray watering daily in summer but much less often in winter.

Feeding   Apply slow release granules to the compost in spring. Mounted specimens may be given a foliar spray of liquid plant food at about one-third the recommended strength. Over feeding will not encourage more vigourous growth—it will scorch the leaves and roots.

Problems   There are no specific problems for this group if given reasonably good cultural and environmental conditions.

FLOWERING SEASON

Flowering times are variable but many bloom in late summer and fall, and many of them continue into winter.

ANANAS
Ananas species

The pineapple with its familiar crown of stiff leaves develops in the centre of the plant. This one is almost mature.

The forms of Ananas *with variegated leaves are very attractive year round, even without the flowers.*

FEATURES

Terrestrial

Pineapple, *Ananas comosus*, is one of several species that make up this terrestrial bromeliad genus. All originate in tropical America. They have a rosette of very stiff, spiny leaves and produce purple-blue flowers with red bracts on a stem rising from the centre of the plant. After the flowers fade the fruit is formed. *A. bracteatus* is grown for its showy flowers, which are followed by bright red mini pineapples. The variety *striatus* has leaves edged and striped cream to white. Unfortunately, to produce pineapples *A. comosus* must be grown in the right conditions. The form with cream striped leaves is the most popular. In bright

light variegations may turn pinkish. Take care when siting these plants as the foliage spines are sharp.

CONDITIONS

Position	Needs a frost-free climate with a winter temperature above 50°F. Needs full sun or very bright light to flower and fruit. Very bright light also brings out the best color of variegated forms.
Potting mix	All growing media must be well drained. Use coarse bark or peat-based mix and a heavy pot for additional stability.

GROWING METHOD

Propagation	Grows from suckers or offsets from the base of the plant or from the tuft of leaves on top of the fruit. Peel off the lower basal leaves to reveal a stub and leave the stub in a dry, airy place to dry before planting it sometime from spring to fall.
Watering	In summer water two or three times a week. In winter check before watering, which may be needed only every week or two.
Feeding	Give slow release fertilizer in spring and early summer if desired.
Problems	No specific problems are known for home growers but base and stem will rot if plants are too wet.

FLOWERING SEASON

	Flowers appear from late spring to summer, depending on the season.
Fruit	Fruit may take two years or more to mature, especially in cooler conditions, but the foliage makes up for this.

ANANAS AT A GLANCE

To produce pineapples grow in a hot conservatory. Flowers are purple-blue with red bracts; fruit forms after flowers.

JAN	reduce water, move to 50°F.	SEPT	water every two weeks
FEB	water every two weeks	OCT	water every two weeks, keep frost free
MAR	remove and pot on offsets	NOV	water every two weeks
APR	remove and pot on offsets	DEC	water every two weeks
MAY	feed and light		
JUN	flowering, water three times weekly	RECOMMENDED VARIETIES	
JULY	flowering	*A. comosus*	
AUG	water three times weekly	*A. comosus striatus*	

BILLBERGIA
Billbergia species

Bright red, overlapping bracts almost conceal the small flowers of this showy Billbergia *hybrid.*

This pendulous inflorescence reveals a mass of small blue-green flowers emerging from pink bracts.

FEATURES

Epiphytic

Terrestrial

One of the most easily grown of all bromeliads, billbergias are widely grown as house plants and are suitable for colder rooms in the house. They adapt to a wide variety of conditions, making them a good choice for the beginner. Leaves are rather stiff and form tall, tubular rosettes. Foliage is spiny and may be mottled, banded or variegated in colors from mid-green to blue-, or gray-green. Flower spikes often arch or droop. Flowers are generally not long lasting but some species flower on and off all year. Bracts are often pink or red with green or blue flower petals. Queen's tears, *Billbergia nutans*, is probably the most common. It has narrow, gray-green

leaves to 12in with blue and green flowers and pink bracts. It has been widely used in hybridizing.

Other species *B. x windii* is a much larger leaved species producing 18in flower spikes over the gray-green leaves. Also, look out for *B. zebrina* and *B. pyramidalis*—both larger, more exotic species.

CONDITIONS

Position Needs frost free conditions with a minimum temperature above 41°F. Most species do best in fully sunny locations but need shade from the hottest summer sun, which tends to scorch leaf tips.

Potting mix Any open, free-draining mix is suitable. Many experienced growers consider this plant does best without enriched soil conditions.

GROWING METHOD

Propagation Grows fairly easily from divisions or offsets of older plants taken during the winter months.

Watering Don't water too frequently but keep the cup filled with water. Spray misting to maintain a humid atmosphere around the plant is an ideal way to maintain good growth.

Feeding Some growers advocate regular liquid feeding through the growing season, others prefer not to give supplementary feeding.

Problems There are generally no problems.

FLOWERING SEASON

Flowering times vary according to species and growing conditions.

BILLBERGIA AT A GLANCE

Suitable for mounting on a log or in a pot. Flowers on and off all year but not long lasting. Pink bracts are spectacular.

JAN	flowering, water	RECOMMENDED VARIETIES
FEB	water	
MAR	/	*B. decora*
APR	feed	*B. nutans*
MAY	flowering, mist, repot	*B. nutans* "Variegata"
JUN	water and mist	*B. pyramidalis*
JULY	water and mist	*B. x windii*
AUG	buy plant	
SEPT	water	
OCT	/	
NOV	remove offsets	
DEC	flowering	

GUZMANIA
Guzmania species

Shining foliage in pink and green forms a most decorative rosette in this variegated Guzmania.

Gorgeous red flower bracts tucked into green leaves make this G. lingulata *"Empire"* look like a decorated Christmas tree.

FEATURES

Epiphytic

This is a large group of mainly epiphytic bromeliads with a few terrestrial species. They are grown for their lovely spreading rosettes of satiny, smooth-edged foliage, as well as for their striking flowering stems. They have been widely hybridized with *vrieseas* to produce stunning cultivars. Mature plants may be from up to 3¼ft wide when fully mature. *Guzmania lingulata* is a handsome species with shiny, mid-green leaves, and a rich, bright red inflorescence. Leaves can be up to 18in long. *G lingulata minor*, the scarlet star, is much smaller with leaves just 5in long. Named varieties include "Exodus", "Empire", "Cherry" and "Gran Prix".

GUZMANIA AT A GLANCE

Ideal for conservatory as pot plant or mounted. Grown for rosettes of spineless foliage and bright red flowering stem.

JAN	water	DEC	keep frost free
FEB	keep warm		
MAR	keep warm	RECOMMENDED VARIETIES
APR	repot		
MAY	remove suckers and offsets	*G. dissitiflora*
		G. lindenii
JUN	flowering, mist, feed	*G. lingulata*
		G. monostachya
JULY	flowering, mist, water	*G. "Amaranth"*
		G. "Cherry"
AUG	mist	*G. lingulata "Empire"*
SEPT	reduce misting	*G. "Exodus"*
OCT	keep frost free	*G. "Gran Prix"*
NOV	keep frost free		

Leaves Leaves may be plain glossy green, cross-banded in contrasting colors or finely patterned with stripes. At flowering time the central leaves may color, adding to the brilliant color display.

CONDITIONS

Position Grows happily in a warm, frost-free greenhouse or conservatory or on a bright windowsill in the home. Prefers bright filtered light away from draughts.

Potting mix Needs a free-draining mix able to retain some moisture or use ready-made orchid compost. Use a pot that is just slightly larger than the root ball. Terracotta pots will give larger plants more stability.

GROWING METHOD

Propagation Grows from offsets or suckers that develop around the stem of the parent plant. Plant out from spring to fall.

Watering Mist daily in summer. Keep water in the cup at all times and water the potting mix twice weekly in summer and just occasionally in winter as necessary.

Feeding Use weak liquid plant foods during periods of rapid growth. Do not feed too early in spring as it can scorch the leaves and roots.

Problems No specific problems provided suitable cultural conditions are given.

FLOWERING SEASON

The showy flowers are long lasting on the plant—perhaps up to two months. Most species and varieties flower during summer and last well into fall.

NEOREGELIA
Neoregelia species

This bromeliad with its fiery red centre is aptly named "Inferno". It is an outstanding example of Neoregelia.

The leaves of this variegated Neoregelia *are outlined in cream, giving it prominence among darker Aechmea hybrids.*

FEATURES

Epiphytic

Terrestrial

Often called heart of flame or blushing bromeliads, neoregelias are very popular for their ease of culture and their dazzling variety. In nature they grow as epiphytes on trees or as terrestrials. Species vary from tiny plants not more than 2in wide to those spreading to over 3¼ft. They can be grown as houseplants or as epiphytes attached to logs in the conservatory (see page 288). However, to enjoy them at their best they should be sited low where their beauty can best be appreciated. The group has been widely hybridized, resulting in some truly outstanding cultivars.

NEOREGELIA AT A GLANCE

Varieties vary in size and flowers do not last long. Similar to guzmanias but broader leaves. Keep frost free.

JAN	water	
FEB	water	
MAR	re-pot if needs it	
APR	remove offset	
MAY	move away from sunlight	
JUN	mist and water	
JULY	flowering, water	
AUG	buy plant	
SEPT	reduce water	
OCT	water crown	
NOV	keep frost free	
DEC	keep frost free	

RECOMMENDED VARIETIES

N. carolinae
N. carolinae marechalii
N. carolinae tricolor
N. spectabilis

Flowering Most varieties produce a startling color change in the centre of the plant at flowering time, the color remaining long after flowering has ceased. This color is mostly red, hence the common name "Blushing Bromeliad". This group lacks the tall, showy flowering spikes of other genera as the flowers—purple, blue, or white—form in the centre of the leaf rosette.

Foliage Leaf rosettes are wide and spreading, the foliage shiny with serrated margins. Leaves may be plain green, red, burgundy, or patterned with stripes, bands, or spots, or even marbled.

N. carolinae *Neoregelia carolinae* is undoubtedly the most commonly grown and numerous lovely hybrids have originated from this species. The straight species forms a compact rosette with leaves about 10in long. The color of the center at flowering varies through shades of crimson to cerise and the flowers are deep violet. *N.c. tricolor* has foliage that is cream and green striped. This takes on a pinky red flush as flowering begins and the centre of the plant turns crimson. Other varieties of this species include those with cream or white margined leaves. *N. carolinae marechalii* is another fine species but without the cream stripes. Leaves are plain olive green but flushed with crimson at the base during flowering.

N. spectabilis The fingernail plant, *N. spectabilis*, has red-tipped olive green leaves banded gray on the undersides. A hardy species, it is best grown in bright light, where the undersides of the leaves take on a rosy pink color. Place high

Small flowers are forming in the vase of leaves on this Neoregelia. *The orange-red shading on the leaves is an added bonus.*

This bromeliad with dark foliage is named "Hot Gossip". Speckled bronze-green leaves are margined in deep pinky red.

up on a shelf so that the gray-barred, pink foliage is seen to advantage.

Other species Another species used in hybridizing is *N. fosteriana* which features burgundy foliage. *N. marmorata* has wide leaves growing about 12in long. They are marbled in red on both sides and have red tips. *N. eleutheropetala* has sharply spined mid-green leaves that turn purple-brown at the centre. The inflorescence mixes white flowers and purple-tipped bracts.

CONDITIONS

Position These plants must be grown in frost-free conditions with a minimum temperature of 50°F. A cool greenhouse, conservatory, or light room are perfect. Most neoregelias grow well in filtered or dappled sunlight. Where summers are very hot with long hours of sunshine, greenhouse shading may be needed. Indoors these plants will thrive in bright light but not direct sun through a window. For shady spots with no direct sun, the plain green leaved varieties will do best.

Potting mix The compost must be free draining and coarse to allow air to the roots. A mix of bark and gravel or coarse sand is suitable, with added charcoal if this is available. Don't overpot as roots may not utilize all the mix and watering becomes a problem. A pot large enough for a year's growth is ideal—stones or large pebbles can be put in the base to prevent the plant toppling over. Keep the leaf bases just above soil level.

GROWING METHOD

Propagation Detach offsets from the parent plant once they are a good size. New roots form more rapidly if the offset is potted into a seed-raising compost mix or a mix of sand and peat or peat substitute, whichever you prefer.

Watering Water should be kept in the cup at all times. Water about twice a week in summer, with daily misting unless the atmosphere is extremely humid. In winter water only occasionally. When watering, flood the central cup so that stagnant water is changed to avoid problems of rot.

Feeding In the house, greenhouse or conservatory, plants can be given slow release fertilizer when active growth resumes in mid-spring and again in early to midsummer. Many growers believe plants grown without fertilizer produce more vibrant colors. Feed once a month in summer or when the plant is actively growing.

Problems There are no specific problems if cultural conditions are suitable. Apart from rots, usually caused by overwatering in cool weather, dying leaf tips are a sign of trouble. This symptom could be caused by cold, by dry, hot conditions, by drought or by frequent overwatering.

FLOWERING SEASON

Flowers are short lived. They do not usually rise above the rim of the cup. Most flower during late spring or summer.

PUYA
Puya species

The gray leaves with their spiny edges and the whole shape of this Puya *species make it look like a giant starfish.*

A heavy pink stem supports the large inflorescence of Puya venusta, *which here is part of a large collection of the species.*

FEATURES

Terrestrial

This group of terrestrial bromeliads contains the largest species known, *Puya raimondii* from Peru and Bolivia, which is capable of growing to 9–12ft high. This very slow-growing plant takes up to 100 years to produce its first flower spike, which contains thousands of individual flowers. Puyas are mostly terrestrial, although some are rock dwellers, and most come from inhospitable habitats in the Andes. In nature most are pollinated by humming birds or starlings. Some come from cold, damp, windswept regions, others from dry grasslands where intense sunlight, heat, and drought are balanced by heavy winter frosts. Many team well with succulents that require similar conditions.

| Appearance | Most are large, from 3¼ft upwards, and grow in clumps so that ample space is needed. The heavily spined leaves may be green or gray and silver and are a decorative feature. They form dense rosettes from which tall spikes of flowers appear. Flowers are green, violet, blue, or white, often with colorful contrasting bracts. |
| Species | *P. venusta* grows to about 4¼ft, producing eye-catching purple flowers on a tall, rose-pink stem and bracts. *P. berteroniana*, over 3¼ft high, has metallic greenish blue flowers. |

CONDITIONS

| Position | Many tolerate cold winters if kept dry. Most endure extremes of climate with very high daytime temperatures and freezing nights. Grows best in the large conservatory or greenhouse border. |
| Potting mix | The growing medium must be coarse and well drained. A mix of coarse sand and crushed rock with added peat or a peat substitute would be suitable. |

GROWING METHOD

Propagation	Remove offsets from spring to fall.
Watering	Water regularly to establish plants but once established they need only occasional deep watering while in active growth.
Feeding	Little or no fertilizer is needed.
Problems	Generally trouble-free and easy to grow.

FLOWERING SEASON

Flowering times vary with species and district. Most have long-lasting blooms.

PUYA AT A GLANCE

Varieties vary in size. Flowers any time of year and last for a long time. Can go outside in summer. Keep frost free.

JAN	keep dry	NOV	keep dry
FEB	keep dry	DEC	keep dry
MAR	water		
APR	remove offsets	**RECOMMENDED VARIETIES**	
MAY	repot	*P. alpestris*	
JUN	water	*P. berteroniana*	
JULY	water, take outside	*P. chilensis*	
AUG	/	*P. coerulea*	
SEPT	bring in	*P. mirabilis*	
OCT	reduce water and remove offsets	*P. venusta*	

TILLANDSIA
Tillandsia species

Fairly common in cultivation, the attractive Tillandsia fasciculata *features an unusual inflorescence of three or four stems.*

Starbursts of silver gray seemingly suspended in mid-air, these tillandsias are growing in baskets along with Spanish moss.

FEATURES

Epiphytic

Tillandsias are mostly epiphytes with very poorly developed root systems, and some absorb water and nutrients through their foliage. Habitats vary from sea level to high altitudes and even the desert. One of the best known is Spanish moss, *Tillandsia usneoides*, with thread-like leaves on long silvery stems. Most species form rosettes of green, gray, or reddish foliage, and those from arid regions have silver scales. Soft green-leaved species are generally native to humid forests and adapt well to pot culture, while many from arid regions are more easily grown on bromeliad "trees" or moss pads. Flowers are tubular and may be violet, white, pink, red, yellow, blue, or green.

TILLANDSIA AT A GLANCE

Easy to look after; grow on a log. Flowers are varied and can appear in almost any month of the year.

JAN	mist twice weekly	DEC	mist twice weekly
FEB	mist twice weekly		
MAR	mist twice weekly, remove offsets	RECOMMENDED VARIETIES	
APR	keep at 61°F; mist twice daily	*T. abdita*	
MAY	flowering, mist	*T. argentea*	
JUN	flowering, mist	*T. bulbosa*	
JULY	flowering, mist	*T. butzii*	
AUG	flowering, mist	*T. cyanea*	
SEPT	mist	*T. usneoides*	
OCT	mist twice weekly, remove offsets		
NOV	mist twice weekly		

CONDITIONS

Position Most species need frost-free conditions—a cool greenhouse or conservatory is ideal. Green-leaved species need filtered sunlight year round while the gray- or silver-leaved varieties can be grown in full or partial sun. With a mixed collection it may be advisable to provide filtered sunlight, especially if the humidity is low.

Potting mix The mix must be very open and well drained. Use fairly coarse composted bark or a special orchid mix, sold at garden centres or nurseries. Driftwood, logs, or cork slabs are ideal for mounting plants.

GROWING METHOD

Propagation Grows from offsets produced sometime during spring to fall. (A few species produce offsets between the leaf axils: these may be difficult to remove without damage.) When they have been cut from the parent plant, allow the bases to dry for a few days before fixing them in their permanent positions with a little PVA glue.

Watering Water or mist plants daily during hot weather. Mounted specimens can suffer if not moistened daily. In cool weather mist several mornings a week.

Feeding Not necessary although a very weak liquid feed during the warmest months of the year may encourage better growth.

Problems No specific problems are known.

FLOWERING SEASON

Flower form and color are variable. Most flower in late spring or summer.

VRIESEA
Vriesea species

The leaves of Vriesea gigantea *are finely checkered or tessellated. This broad, spreading species can grow to 3¼ft across.*

Parrot feather is a name sometimes given to Vriesea psittacina. *This variable species may grow 16–24in wide.*

FEATURES

Epiphytic

Terrestrial

Vrieseas are very adaptable, tolerating conditions in the home, conservatory, or greenhouse. Most are epiphytes growing on trees in forests but some larger species are terrestrials. Some species in the wild are pollinated by nocturnal insects attracted to the scented flowers. Few of these larger terrestrials are grown outside specialist collections. Leaves are spineless and may be plain glossy green or attractively banded, spotted or variegated. They form neat rosettes. Many species have striking bracts. The true flowers are usually yellow, green, or white but the bracts may be red or purple, yellow, or green. Plants may be 6–8in high or reach over 13ft. Some are very wide spreading.

VRIESEA AT A GLANCE

Ideal for mounting or in a pot inside. The scented flowers are long lasting and appear any time of year.

JAN	keep air moist	OCT	remove offsets
FEB	water centre of plant	NOV	keep frost free and water centre of plant
MAR	feed		
APR	remove offsets, repot	DEC	/
MAY	water and mist		
JUN	mist; keep humid	**RECOMMENDED VARIETIES**	
JULY	mist, needs high temperatures	*V. hieroglyphica*	
		V. carinata	
AUG	mist, water centre of plant	*V. x poelmanii*	
		V. x polonia	
SEPT	mist	*V. saundersii*	

CONDITIONS

Climate Copes with very high temperatures if not direct sun; does best in humid conditions. Many species tolerate low, frost-free temperatures. Most prefer bright, filtered light and good air circulation, again similar to the conditions favored by orchids. A group of these plants will create a more humid microclimate.

Potting mix Need good drainage and aeration. Use coarse bark, sand, gravel, and charcoal as the base, with leaf mould, well-decayed compost, or even polystyrene granules added.

GROWING METHOD

Propagation Grow from offsets produced at the base of the plant during spring to fall. In spreading species they will be under the foliage: once they are sufficiently advanced remove them before they distort the foliage.

Watering Keep the cup in the center of the rosette filled. In summer, water two or three times a week, spray misting on the other days or if humidity is low. In the conservatory or greenhouse, damp down the floor on hot days. In winter, water only every couple of weeks but maintain atmospheric humidity.

Feeding Apply slow release granular fertilizer in spring and midsummer, or use soluble liquid foods monthly at half the recommended strength. Ensure fertilizer does not touch foliage. Feed only in the warmer months.

Problem No specific problems are encountered.

FLOWERING SEASON

Species flower at different times of the year. Most have long-lasting flowers.

INDEX

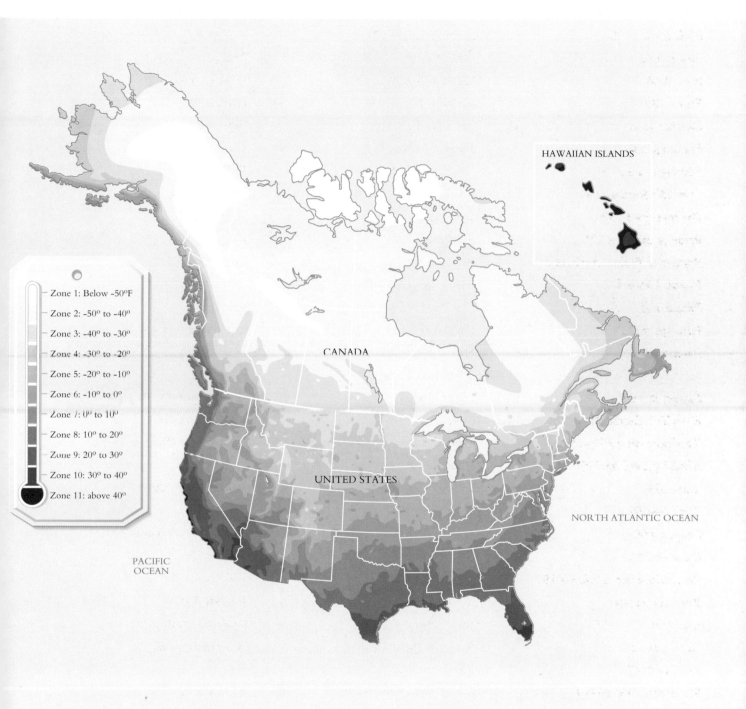

HAWAIIAN ISLANDS

Zone 1: Below –50°F
Zone 2: –50° to –40°
Zone 3: –40° to –30°
Zone 4: –30° to –20°
Zone 5: –20° to –10°
Zone 6: –10° to 0°
Zone 7: 0° to 10°
Zone 8: 10° to 20°
Zone 9: 20° to 30°
Zone 10: 30° to 40°
Zone 11: above 40°

CANADA

UNITED STATES

NORTH ATLANTIC OCEAN

PACIFIC
OCEAN

First published in Canada in 2001 by
Select Editions
8036 Enterprise Street
Burnaby, B.C.
V5A 1V7 Canada
Tel (604) 415-2444

ISBN 1 894426-87-8

Copyright © Text, photography and design Murdoch Books UK Ltd 2001

Senior Project Editor: Anna Osborn
Design and Editorial Assistance: Prima Creative Services

CEO: Robert Oerton
Publisher: Catie Ziller
Publishing Manager: Fia Fornari
Production Manager: Lucy Byrne

Group General Manager: Mark Smith
Group CEO/Publisher: Anne Wilson

Printed in China by Toppan